Harvard Historical Monographs, LXVI

Published under the direction of the
Department of History from the income of the
Robert Louis Stroock Fund

Provincial Magistrates

and Revolutionary Politics

in France, 1789–1795

PHILIP DAWSON

Harvard University Press

Cambridge, Massachusetts

1972

Preface

This book originated at Harvard University as a doctoral dissertation, planned initially in consultation with Alfred Cobban, then a visiting professor, and supervised by Crane Brinton and Franklin L. Ford. A research training fellowship of the Social Science Research Council made possible a year's work in France in 1959–60, where I received much valuable counsel from Marc Bouloiseau and immeasurable benefit from Pierre de Saint Jacob's generous candor and humane knowledge. I am saddened by the fact that since then death has overtaken, successively, Pierre de Saint Jacob, Alfred Cobban, and Crane Brinton.

The dissertation that I completed in 1961 is based essentially on evidence from Burgundy. A grant from the American Philosophical Society made it possible for me to spend two months in France in 1962, principally in Poitou but also in Languedoc and at Angers, La Rochelle, Limoges, Moulins, and Bourges.

My research has been greatly facilitated by archivists, in Paris and in every province and locality where I have worked. It is appropriate to mention especially the late Henri Forestier at Auxerre, Jean Rigaud at Dijon, Arthur Morgand at Mâcon, and François Villard at Poitiers, directors of the respective departmental archives, and Gérard Jarousseau, documentaliste at Poitiers and secretary of the Société des Archives Historiques du Poitou.

For years I have enjoyed an informative and stimulating dialogue on this and related topics with my father, John P. Dawson, and he gave valuable suggestions for the improvement of this book.

During the decade in which I have been attempting, as opportunity offered, to rethink and rewrite, I have learned much from Gilbert Shapiro, George V. Taylor, and Charles Tilly.

A nearly finished version was considerably improved through the thoughtful and helpful criticism of François Furet.

All these men have served the reader well and helped me greatly, and I am most grateful to them.

I should add that translations are mine except as otherwise noted.

Philip Dawson

Peacham, Vermont
August 1971

Contents

Note on References

Excerpts from French documents available in printed versions are usually quoted in English translation. Excerpts from manuscripts are usually given in French, with spelling and punctuation modernized.
The following abbreviations are used in footnotes:

A.N. Archives Nationales
A.D. Archives Départementales de . . .
A.M. Archives Municipales de . . .
B.N. Bibliothèque Nationale
B.M. Bibliothèque Municipale de . . .
AP *Archives Parlementaires de 1787 à 1860, recueil complet des débats législatifs et politiques des chambres françaises, 1ᵉ série (1787 à 1799)*, 82 vols., eds. Jérôme Mavidal and Emile Laurent et al. (Paris, Librairie Paul Dupont, 1867–1913) and 6 vols., eds. Marcel Reinhard and Marc Bouloiseau (Paris, Centre National de la Recherche Scientifique, 1961–1969, in progress).

Tables

Tables

Provincial Magistrates and Revolutionary Politics in France, 1789–1795

I

Bourgeoisie, Royal Offices, and
Revolution in Recent Historical Writing

The history of France at the end of the eighteenth century was influenced powerfully, at times decisively, by collective interests and group actions. Such a statement is a commonplace, useful therefore to describe an area of agreement. Venturing forth from this safe ground, one encounters endless scholarly argument: over the purposes of group actions and their effects on economic, political, and intellectual life, the accuracy of facts reported, the validity of different methods of analysis, and the significance of the whole topic for previous and subsequent human experience. The wide range and the vigor of the debate are signs that it is of greater than parochial interest.

This book is a contribution to the discussion of some of these questions. It is a study of one occupational category: the holders of offices in the royal judiciary at the intermediate level, in the courts generally entitled *bailliages*.[1] They were educated property-owners, prominent in the bourgeoisie in more than three hundred provincial towns. The magistrates in each court acted as a corporate group when occasion arose. In the hierarchy of the kingdom, the magistrates in the bailliages held a distinct position. My study of them is a response to an evolving state of historical scholarship.

Debate over collective interests and group actions originated with the divisive potentialities inherent in the legacy from eighteenth-century France itself. Before 1789, there was keen awareness of the importance of collective prerogatives and obligations, and controversy over their nature and legitimacy.[2] Into this state of affairs, the convocation of the Estates General thrust categories (Clergy, Nobility, Third Estate) which were recognizably antiquated and impractical[3] but could be made to

1. The term *bailliage* had three meanings: the court composed of the judges who acted in the name of the king's *bailli*, the building or room where they held sessions, and the territory under their jurisdiction. The term *sénéchaussée* was a synonym in the sixteenth through eighteenth centuries and was used mainly in the southern and western provinces. The terms are sometimes rendered in English as "bailiwick" and "seneschalcy," but this merely obscures the meaning; these are historical, not current English words, and not equivalents of the French terms in any real sense. Throughout this book, I use "bailliages" as the general plural word (which may include courts that were entitled *sénéchaussées*) and "sénéchaussée" exclusively for particular courts that had that title. Neither term is italicized hereafter.

2. Fundamental issues were set forth, for example, at the *lit de justice* of 12 March 1776, when Turgot presented legislation to abolish the guilds and Séguier defended them: *Recueil général des anciennes lois françaises*, ed. François-André Isambert et al., 29 vols. (Paris, 1821–1833), XXIII, 371–379; *Remonstrances du Parlement de Paris au XVIIIᵉ siècle*, ed. Jules Flammermont, 3 vols. (Paris, 1888–1898), III, 344–354.

3. A month or two before becoming principal minister, the archbishop of Toulouse considered the idea that the new provincial assemblies deliberate as separate orders of clergy, nobility, and third estate and re-

serve definite political interests. Conflict between groups was translated into the retrograde institutional and intellectual frame thus provided. The failure of the royal government to master the conflicting interests was then followed by even more emphatic disagreements, over the form of government appropriate to the collectivity of all Frenchmen, the real nature of social categories and groups, and the rights and duties proper to them. Contrasting perceptions of current facts were matched by opposing ideals. Each set of perceptions and ideals was hardened, through repeated collision with its opposite, into a compact dogma. Only gradually could they be eroded or dissolved.

Historical comprehension of eighteenth-century society having been simplified and, inevitably, distorted, debate among historians necessarily went over much of the same ground. As the eighteenth century has receded into the past, historical curiosity concerning its social divisions and processes has pushed forward, in certain directions, into new territory. More knowledge is presently available about peasants, workingmen, and certain groups of noblemen than could have been possessed by Tocqueville in the middle of the nineteenth century or by Alphonse Aulard at its close. But few historians now would disagree with Albert Soboul when he writes "we do not possess any history of the French bourgeoisie in the Revolution."[4] After this recognition of partial ignorance, divergences begin. They relate to the word and the conception, "bourgeoisie," and to the hypotheses and methods most useful for studying the historical reality.

---

jected it: Etienne-Charles de Loménie de Brienne, *Journal de l'assemblée des notables de 1787*, ed. Pierre Chevallier (Paris, Librairie C. Klincksieck, 1960), pp. 18–19.

4. *Précis d'histoire de la Révolution française* (Paris, Les Editions Sociales, 1962), p. 11. Similarly, Jacques Godechot has remarked that "works on the bourgeoisie in the revolutionary period are still in their infancy": *Revue Historique*, 235 (1966), 207.

The meaning of the word "bourgeois" evolved during some six centuries before the Revolution. Survivals and anticipations multiplied the number of meanings actually employed in any particular period of even a few years. At the end of the eighteenth century, contracts and estate inventories drawn up by notaries in Paris and Chartres applied the word "bourgeois" very restrictively. It referred to those who were well-to-do but had never exercised, or no longer carried on, an economically productive occupation or a liberal profession. In the provincial town, the word very often seems to have been a kind of honorific designation earned together with the wealth acquired during a career. In contrast, the evidence indicates that many a bourgeois of Paris had achieved, more than a stage of life, a social status conferred at birth, transmitted sometimes by marriage and often by inheritance.[5] An inclusive definition was also current and is exemplified in a newspaper article published in 1791. According to this, the word meant anyone whose livelihood depended on property acquired through the work of his ancestors or himself, or on the income from a useful art or commercial activity; in short, everyone who had an income other than from his own manual work, below the noble class, was a bourgeois.[6]

The inclusive definition explicitly refers to lower and upper boundaries of the bourgeoisie. Whether the bourgeoisie is viewed from below or from above continues to affect a historian's conception of it and, accordingly, his initial hypotheses about social stratification. This point is exemplified in the contrasting programs of two eminent scholars recently at work on the subject, Ernest Labrousse and Roland Mousnier.

5. Michel Vovelle and Daniel Roche, "Bourgeois, rentiers, propriétaires," 84e Congrès National des Sociétés Savantes, Dijon, 1959, *Actes,* pp. 419–452, transl. (omitting graphs and tables) in *New Perspectives on the French Revolution,* ed. Jeffry Kaplow (New York, John Wiley & Sons, 1965), pp. 25–46.

6. Georges Pariset, *Etudes d'histoire révolutionnaire et contemporaine* Paris, Les Belles Lettres, 1929), p. 273.

The proposals presented by Labrousse in 1955 looked toward a coordinated, international, statistical history of the bourgeoisie.[7] In every locality studied, the starting point was to be a list of inhabitants, specifying their occupations. The persons engaged in each occupation were to be ranked according to wealth and income. Then occupations were to be ranked according to their practitioners' typical economic position. If the range of economic positions within an occupation was very great, the occupational category would be subdivided into two or more. Essentially, the idea was to reconstruct a census of occupations and to rank these in a single hierarchy for a locality. Provisionally, Labrousse would draw the lower boundary of the bourgeoisie between the merchant-artisan and the worker-artisan. The upper boundary would exclude those who were "established" in the nobility. But initially, doubt was to be resolved in favor of including all persons "suspect of bourgeoisie" by reason of their occupations.

The criticisms of this program advanced by Mousnier originate in a fundamentally opposed view.[8] In his judgment, the most important kind of social group under the ancien régime was not the occupation but the family and, extending outward from it, the group of persons who intermarried. Such a group was composed, according to Mousnier, of men engaged in

7. "Voies nouvelles vers une histoire de la bourgeoisie occidentale aux XVIIIᵉ et XIXᵉ siècles (1700–1850)," *Relazioni del X Congresso Internazionale di Scienze Storiche* (Rome, 1955), IV, 365–396. This report is sometimes described as a continuation of the effort inaugurated by Georges Lefebvre, but in fact no census concept limited the methods or the kinds of evidence Lefebvre suggested: Commission de Recherche et de Publication des Documents Relatifs à la Vie Economique de la Révolution, *Assemblée générale de la Commission centrale et des Comités départementaux, 1939*, 2 vols. (Besançon–Paris, 1942–1945), I, 9–12.

8. "Problèmes de méthode dans l'étude des structures sociales des XVIᵉ, XVIIᵉ, XVIIIᵉ siècles," *Spiegel der Geschichte. Festgabe für Max Braubach*, eds. Konrad Repgen and Stephan Skalweit (Münster, Aschendorff, 1964), pp. 550–564.

5

various occupations, but united by shared ideals, group consciousness, similar kinds (not necessarily equal amounts) of property, typical styles of life; the external mark of these social bonds was marriage between individuals. Mousnier's proposal was to reconstruct not a census of occupations but networks of marriage alliances and kinship from marriage contracts and other documents needed to interpret them. His criticisms of the idea for an occupational census were occasioned in part by the publication of a study, by Adeline Daumard and François Furet, applying Labrousse's idea to Paris in 1749 and analyzing statistically 2,597 marriage contracts, which represent 61 percent of the marriages celebrated in the city in that year.[9] Professorial disagreement echoed in an exchange between research students.[10] The criticisms and countercriticisms rapidly came to require careful study of what each side actually asserted and what was really meant.

The usefulness of a census of occupations, particularly in any study of the bourgeoisie, is undeniable. It is not easy to construct one that is neutral on debatable questions and that leaves the historian uncommitted to some unproven hypothesis or assumption. The program outlined by Labrousse, and carried out in a preliminary way by his students, assumes that socioeconomic classes in eighteenth-century France can be considered a single hierarchy, a pyramid with many individuals in the lowest category and few in the highest.

The image of the pyramid has shaped the views of many writers on social structure. With reference to another historical

9. *Structures et relations sociales à Paris au milieu du XVIIIe siècle* (Paris, Librairie Armand Colin, 1961).
10. Jean-Yves Tirat, "Problèmes de méthode en histoire sociale," *Revue d'Histoire Moderne et Contemporaine*, 10 (1963), 211–218, versus Adeline Daumard and François Furet, " 'Problèmes de méthode en histoire sociale.' Réflexions sur une note critique," *Revue d'Histoire Moderne et Contemporaine*, 11 (1964), 291–298. An informative and just evaluation had been presented by Michel Vovelle in *Annales Historiques de la Révolution Française*, 24 (1962), 99–104.

context, Lawrence Stone has asserted that it is a mirage.[11] He offers two alternative visualizations of early modern English society. Under Henry VII, the uppermost part of the social structure would resemble a skyscraper encircled by exterior ramps: inside the building, there was "a series of floors for status groups based on the ownership of land"; outside, the ramps offered alternative ways from one floor to another through ecclesiastical, legal, commercial, and governmental occupations. Thereafter, according to Stone, the uppermost part of the social structure came to resemble a number of vertical towers, "a series of more or less independent economic and status hierarchies," of which the most conspicuous were land ownership, the church, the law, commerce, and royal office. An architectural scheme of French society in the eighteenth century would have to provide still more possibilities of movement: grand stairways with broad and gradual steps, others narrow and steep, interconnected by passageways and doors with or without locks; ladders and trap-doors; here and there a rope hanging outside from a window and fraying on the sill. The design would incorporate odd visual effects, permitting individuals sometimes to perceive one another without being sure which was on a higher level. After inspecting this structure, a historian might well come to share the impatient desire, actually manifested in the eighteenth century by the architect Claude Nicolas Ledoux, for a radical simplicity. Perhaps a better alternative would be to refrain from trying to visualize the social structure before determining the numbers of individuals and families who moved from each major occupation to another.

The importance of the family in many different social processes has been recognized by social theorists of every persuasion since Plato. A catalogue of typical marriage alliances

11. "Social Mobility in England, 1500–1700," *Past and Present*, no. 33 (1966), pp. 16–55. The phrases quoted here are on pp. 16 and 17, respectively.

in eighteenth-century France would provide helpful enlightenment concerning the legal and moral bonds formed within and between different economic and geographic environments. But a considerable distance separates this general affirmation from Mousnier's belief that the formation of a marriage was a result and a sign of the anterior creation of a group united by shared interests and mutuality. It appears that the formation of a marriage then, as now, was an economic and human transaction affected by a totality of forces properly considered as a market. A marriage between social equals with a similar economic contribution from each side might be desirable because of its apparently low risk, economically and emotionally. The calculation of risk and prospective gain is a classic theme of historical writing on the bourgeoisie, and it seems premature to assume that low risk was the principal objective in the formation of bourgeois marriages, especially when mésalliance occasionally took place in noble families. Furthermore, a marriage was ordinarily intended to last for most of the lifetime of each partner and might have a divisive effect as readily as a unifying effect on the groups in which the marriage partners had originated.[12]

Divergence among historians over definitions and methods is especially troublesome because of local differences in the kinds of source material available and in the actual character of the bourgeoisie in each town. It is almost impossible to derive a useful general description from the separate studies of Albi, Marseille, Grenoble, Pontivy, and Evreux, which were prepared

12. After the death of one or both marriage partners, the inheritances might give rise to new or additional difficulties, exacerbated by a branch of law that produced especially voluminous litigation in the eighteenth century. In a debate on inheritance laws, on 6 April 1791, Jean-Denis Lanjuinais remarked, doubtless with some exaggeration, that half the treatises on jurisprudence, half the lawsuits and sources of hatred and discord were created by testaments: *Gazette nationale ou le Moniteur universel,* 8 April 1791 (in the reprint edition, VIII, 65).

in 1939, in response to Georges Lefebvre's suggestions.[13] At the congress where Labrousse delivered his report in 1955, experts on eighteenth-century Beauvais, Le Havre, Montauban, and Grenoble attempted a comparative analysis of the provincial bourgeoisie.[14] They found that the upper bourgeoisie was a small minority, cohesive, wealthy, active in lending money and sometimes in collecting royal taxes or seigneurial dues, as well as in manufacturing or trade, but above all intent upon owning land. They also found that after the middle of the eighteenth century the bourgeois groups became stable in composition and that, except where there was a parlement, the great merchants and *négociants* formed the leading element. But they also recorded important diversity. The amount an individual paid in taxes had a social significance that was purely local. The character of the bourgeoisie depended on the local economy. The merchant manufacturers of woollens, linens, and silk in Beauvais and Montauban differed from the négociants and *armateurs* of Grenoble and Le Havre. The possibilities of social ascent within the bourgeoisie also varied. In Beauvais the upper bourgeoisie was closed almost completely to newcomers after the early eighteenth century, and in Montauban the upper bourgeoisie, predominantly Calvinist, revealed an exclusive class spirit even in its religious observances. In Le Havre, on the other hand, a peasant who arrived in town wearing wooden shoes, or an artisan, could rise within a lifetime to the top of the merchant class. Since that report, new research on the

13. Commission de . . . la Vie Economique de la Révolution, *Assemblée générale* . . . , *1939*, I, 33–169, 209–248.
14. Pierre Léon, "Recherches sur la bourgeoisie française de province au XVIIIe siècle," *Information Historique*, 20 (1958), 101–105. Only a summary appeared in the *Relazioni del X Congresso Internazionale di Scienze Storiche*, IV, 331–335. The other contributors were Pierre Goubert (Beauvais), Robert Richard (Le Havre), and Daniel Ligou (assisted by J. Garrisson-Estèbe) whose report was published separately: "La Bourgeoisie réformée montalbanaise à la fin de l'ancien régime," *Revue d'Histoire Economique et Sociale*, 33 (1955), 377–404.

bourgeoisie has returned in the main to previous practice, confining each separate investigation to one town, with the difficulties of comparison this inevitably entails.[15]

While French scholarship struggled with these intractable problems, certain interpretive ideas developed by Aulard and Albert Mathiez, and significantly modified by Lefebvre, were subjected to close and unfavorable scrutiny by other historians. Aulard had equated bourgeois status with possession of property and explained bourgeois political interest as being powerfully affected by the desire to exclude the propertyless from politics. Interpreting the Declaration of Rights as largely a condemnation of the ancien régime, Aulard described it, as well as the Constitution of 1791, as a bourgeois document.[16] Mathiez carried this reasoning a step further, pointing out that in the Declaration of Rights itself only a limited idea of equality is to be found (since ability, which it sets forth as the requisite for access to remunerative and honorable occupations, is conditioned by wealth) and that the Declaration de-

15. Use of the same kinds of source materials does not ensure the disappearance of these difficulties. See the suggestions made by Michel Vovelle in three valuable articles, "Structure et répartition de la fortune foncière et de la fortune mobilière d'un ensemble urbain: Chartres, de la fin de l'ancien régime à la Restauration," *Revue d'Histoire Economique et Sociale*, 36 (1958), 387–398; "Formes de dépendance d'un milieu urbain, Chartres, à l'égard du monde rural, de la fin de l'ancien régime à la Restauration," 83ᵉ Congrès National des Sociétés Savantes, Aix-Marseille, 1958, *Actes*, pp. 483–512, and "Problèmes méthodologiques posés par l'utilisation des sources de l'enregistrement dans une étude de structure sociale," Comité des Travaux Historiques et Scientifiques, *Bulletin de la Section d'Histoire Moderne et Contemporaine (depuis 1610)*, fasc. iii (1961), pp. 49–106, compared with the data amassed by Jean Sentou, *Fortunes et groupes sociaux à Toulouse sous la Révolution (1789–1799). Essai d'histoire statistique* (Toulouse, Edouard Privat, 1969).

16. "Bourgeoisie et démocratie," *Revolution Française*, 35 (1898), reprinted as the third chapter of his *Histoire politique de la Révolution française* (Paris, Librairie Armand Colin, 1901).

fined property as an imprescriptible right.[17] For Lefebvre, the word "bourgeoisie" implicitly referred not only to a social category, whose diversity he was careful to point out, but also to a conception of life and society which was shared, he believed, by most bourgeois. This conception emphasized the need to increase earthly happiness and human dignity by means of knowledge and wealth, characteristic creations of the bourgeoisie. Political values and interests consistent with that conception of life seem to be primarily involved in his use of the word "bourgeoisie" to refer to an ideological tendency.[18]

In a doctoral dissertation on "Business Enterprise and the French Revolution," George V. Taylor showed that few merchants and financiers were leaders in the reform movements of the late eighteenth century, that the lists of grievances drawn up by businessmen in 1789 emphasized the needs of business and slighted political reform, and that businessmen sitting as deputies in the first National Assembly, as well as those attempting to influence it as lobbyists, behaved mainly as representatives of privileged groups intent upon keeping their privileges.[19]

Later, in a paper, Taylor emphasized that any attempt to relate revolutionary thought and action to an economic base ought to begin with an awareness of the pluralistic diversity of capitalism under the ancien régime.[20] He described three kinds of capitalistic activity, each with its distinctive historical roots

17. *La Révolution française*, 3 vols. (Paris, Librairie Armand Colin, 1922–1927), I, chap. 6.
18. *Quatre-Vingt-Neuf* (Paris, 1939), trans. Robert R. Palmer as *The Coming of the French Revolution* (Princeton, Princeton University Press, 1947), pp. 41–91.
19. *University of Wisconsin Summaries of Doctoral Dissertations*, 12 (1950–1951), 218–219.
20. "Types of Capitalism in Eighteenth-Century France," *English Historical Review*, 79 (1964), 478–497. The phrase quoted later in this paragraph occurs on p. 479.

11

and economic basis: merchant capitalism, which included manufacturing, trade and banking;[21] finance or court capitalism, which consisted in exploiting the needs of the monarchy for loans and for advances against future tax receipts;[22] and an "embryonic form of industrial capitalism" represented principally by mining and metallurgical enterprises. After this demonstration, one might well wonder what basis there was for unified political action by bourgeois groups possessing different kinds of capital assets and economic interests.

In a subsequent paper, Taylor discussed a fourth kind of wealth, characterized by low risk and predictable return, hence not strictly capitalist in function, which he called "proprietary" wealth: land, urban real estate, governmental offices purchased from the crown, and annuities. He pointed out that

> there was, between most of the nobility and the proprietary sector of the middle classes, a continuity of investment forms and socioeconomic values that made them, economically, a single group. In the relations of production they played a common role. The differentiation between them was not in any sense economic; it was juridical . . . There was a clear juridical boundary that separated nobles from commoners, and a commoner crossed it by registering a legal document, his letters of nobility. On the other hand, the frontier between capitalist and proprietary wealth ran vertically through both orders. The horizontal line marked a legal dichotomy, the vertical line, an economic one. To think of them as coinciding, even roughly, is to misunderstand the situation completely.[23]

21. Ninety-eight examples were studied by Taylor in "Some Business Partnerships at Lyon, 1785–1793," *Journal of Economic History*, 23 (1963), 46–70.

22. Previously characterized by Taylor, with more detail, in "The Paris Bourse on the Eve of the Revolution, 1781–1789," *American Historical Review*, 67 (1962), 951–977; cf. the suggestive treatment by Jean Bouvier and Henry Germain-Martin, *Finances et financiers de l'ancien régime* (Paris, Presses Universitaires de France, 1964), pp. 103–126.

23. "Noncapitalist Wealth and the Origins of the French Revolution," *American Historical Review*, 72 (1967), 469–496; the passages quoted here are on pp. 488–489.

Not only was there a potential diversity of economic and political interests within the "capitalist" bourgeoisie, there was potential agreement on economic objectives between a very large part of the bourgeoisie and the nobility. The political clash between some elements of the bourgeoisie and the nobility in 1789 can therefore not be explained as a direct confrontation of economic interests.

Simultaneous with Taylor's work, a number of independent suggestions emanated from Alfred Cobban. In his inaugural lecture at the University of London in 1954, he asserted that the words "feudalism" and "bourgeoisie," commonly employed by historians in summarizing the effects of the French Revolution, were mythical. He said the accepted description is to the effect that "the feudal order passed away and the rule of the bourgeoisie took its place." To this, Cobban would reply, first, that "the so-called feudalism of the eighteenth century consisted in the survival of antiquated dues and services," and that the night of 4 August 1789 represented "an attempt by throwing overboard some of the dues to salvage the rest."

Secondly, as for the revolutionary role of the bourgeoisie, Cobban said that it consisted essentially in the work of the deputies elected by the Third Estate in 1789, because "little of what had been achieved by 1791 was to be lost, and most of what was done subsequently was to be undone." He proceeded to give an enumeration of the occupations of all 648 deputies who sat for the Third Estate. This showed that 13 percent of them were négociants, manufacturers, and bankers; 25 percent were lawyers; and 43 percent were officeholders of various kinds. (The officeholders, in Cobban's classification, included judges in the bailliages; legal practitioners like proctors and notaries; administrative-judicial officials in the special tribunals for the tax districts, the salt monopoly, the rivers, lakes, and forests; and also mayors and the intendants' local representatives, the *subdélégués*.) A similar enumeration of the 891

13

members of the National Convention yielded different proportions: 9 percent were négociants, manufacturers, and bankers; 27 percent were lawyers; 25 percent were officeholders; and 17 percent were other professional men, principally physicians, teachers, and army officers. The later careers of the men who had been deputies for the Third Estate in 1789–1791 or deputies in the Convention in 1792–1795 led 629 (about 40 percent) into government positions under Napoleon, and more than 200 of these came from the category that Cobban defined broadly as former officeholders. Asserting that "whatever else the *tiers état* of 1789 wanted, they certainly wanted *la carrière ouverte aux talents*," Cobban then concluded: "A class of officials and professional men moved up from the minor to the major posts in government and dispossessed the minions of an effete Court: this was what the bourgeois revolution meant."[24]

Finding the title of Cobban's lecture especially provocative, Lefebvre sought to establish three points in reply. First, "feudalism" in its narrow acceptation referred to obligations arising under the feudal contract and relating to fiefs (which in fact still existed), but for the revolutionaries a broader definition was convenient, covering a highly complex reality with which they were familiar. They tried to draw new distinctions within that reality, abolishing mortmain, personal servitude, rights of justice, and certain other seigneurial rights, while attempting to preserve dues which could be regarded as economic rent; even so, this reexamination of the legitimacy of property rights, in itself, had revolutionary implications. Second, "the importance of the Revolution does not result solely from the intentions of those who made it. The principal fact is that for the first time in Europe, the Revolution proclaimed freedom of enterprise without any restriction other than that necessary for

24. "The Myth of the French Revolution," reprinted in his *Aspects of the French Revolution* (London, Jonathan Cape, 1968), pp. 90–111; the phrases quoted here are on pp. 95, 96, 97, 99, 104, and 106, respectively.

public order. Thereby, it did indeed open the way to capitalism." Besides, open access to public office was merely one consequence of legal equality, which was not a myth: "the substitution, for a society founded on a corporative hierarchy and on the privileges of the dominant class, of a social structure in which juridically all citizens are equal, is a reality. On this point, one can examine the feelings of the French nobility." Third, the conception of myth suggested by Georges Sorel, promising a future ideal society which may not (Sorel thought would not) ever be realized, is more relevant and is revolutionary.[25]

In the course of this reply, Lefebvre praised Cobban's attempt to catalogue the occupations of the deputies of the Third Estate and the members of the Convention. As he had done in 1939 and 1951 in narrative histories, he affirmed that it is necessary to distinguish different categories within the bourgeoisie. He also reaffirmed the importance of political ideas, pointing out that he had said

that the progressive element of the bourgeoisie was not recruited solely from among those who, by developing production, undermined the substructure of the ancien régime, and that the intellectual renewal came to a surprising extent from families of officeholders who, newly come to ease or wealth and reinforcing their independence by the purchase of venal offices, were led to engage

25. "Le Mythe de la Révolution française," *Annales Historiques de la Révolution Française*, 28 (1956), 337–345, esp. p. 343 for the passages quoted in this paragraph. The controversy over Cobban's views was later to produce some futile guesswork and advocacy about what the revolutionaries of 4 August 1789 might have or should have meant by "feudalism." The plan of operations submitted on 4 September 1789 by Merlin, secretary of the *comité féodal* of the National Assembly (reprinted in the *Archives Parlementaires*, VIII, 574–579), shows that the revolutionary legislators' intentions were clear, defines the legal term "feudal" in its usual eighteenth-century sense, and proves that Lefebvre's first point in reply in 1956 was strictly correct. There remain the questions, incompletely answered, how burdensome the old obligations were, and by whom, how rapidly and how thoroughly they were abolished in practice; but as these are not closely related to my subject, they are ignored in what follows.

in free criticism of the existing order. In this sense, the office-holders who have attracted M. Cobban's attention contributed to the preparation of the ideology that supplied the bourgeoisie with class consciousness, without which the Revolution would be unimaginable.[26]

This passage differs from what Lefebvre had written in 1951 only in displaying the words "progressive," "substructure," "ideology," and "class consciousness." Then, he had listed a number of reforms that would promote economic rationality, and added:

This is not to say, however, that these reforms aroused such enthusiasm as to take first place in the mind of the bourgeoisie, so that businessmen were the prime movers of the Revolution. Much more effective [ideas] were the rule of law and equality of rights, which appealed to the dignity of the [bourgeoisie] as much as to its interests. The old bourgeoisie of the ancien régime, the office-holders and the men of law, relatively independent and having a certain leisure, were concerned, as much from professional interest as from professional culture, to have the law prevail over violence and arbitrariness. It was they who in this respect taught public opinion.[27]

In this position of Lefebvre's, two divergences from Cobban are noteworthy. The leadership Lefebvre attributed to the officeholders was intellectual, not political in a revolutionary sense; whereas Cobban asserted that they became an important part of a new governing class but said nothing about their participation in prerevolutionary intellectual life. The attitudes and intellectual preferences of the officeholders, according to Lefebvre, helped to create an ideology that was highly com-

26. "Le Mythe de la Révolution française," p. 342.
27. *La Révolution française* (Paris, Presses Universitaires de France, 1951; identical in the 1957 edition), p. 75. After 1944, in his research on Orléans, Lefebvre came to hold this view, it would seem from his remarks in *Annales: Economies, Sociétés, Civilisations*, 14 (1959), 569. In his early work on Cherbourg, he had noted merely the social and political predominance of the officeholders in the four jurisdictions there: *Cherbourg à la fin de l'ancien régime et au début de la Révolution* (Caen, Cahiers des Annales de Normandie, 1965), p. 63.

patible with later capitalism and therefore fundamentally representative of the future historic role of the bourgeoisie of trade and industry; whereas Cobban (though careful to allow for the possibility of some disinterested motives) was intent upon suggesting the officeholders' own economic and political interests, and he especially emphasized government career opportunities which had nothing particular to do with the development of capitalism.

An emphasis different from Lefebvre's appeared in the comments of Marcel Reinhard, who had recently written a valuable article on the period's shifting ideas about social mobility.[28] Although regarding the "consecration of the absolute right of property" as a new and revolutionary effect of the National Assembly's work, he was not content to dismiss the problem of the Assembly's intentions as unimportant. He reported having found indications that profound reciprocal mistrust divided the business world from the liberal professions before and during the Revolution. It was not the businessmen who played the leading part in the Revolution, any more than they had done beforehand; rather, it was the *hommes à talents*, lawyers, physicians, and holders of offices of intermediate or lesser rank. The social revolution, Reinhard thought, was more important than Cobban had said but more complex than others, criticized by him, had realized. The revolutionary years effected a genuine replacement of the former ruling classes as well as the social ascent of many professional men. But, he said, further research would be needed on these questions.[29]

Neither Lefebvre nor Reinhard offered any detailed comments on Cobban's analysis of the careers of revolutionary legislators. Upon it, however, depends Cobban's interpretation of the "bourgeois revolution." The analysis is incomplete in

28. "Elite et noblesse dans la seconde moitié du XVIIIe siècle," *Revue d'Histoire Moderne et Contemporaine*, 3 (1956), 5–37.
29. "Sur l'histoire de la Révolution française. Travaux récents et perspectives," *Annales: Economies, Sociétés, Civilisations*, 14 (1959), 553–570, esp. pp. 557–561.

several respects. Of the deputies in 1789, it applies only to those elected by the Third Estate, taking no account of priests who might have come from bourgeois families. It ignores the possibility that the bourgeoisie, in its variety, might not have been represented statistically by the composition of the legislature. It assumes that all the deputies for the Third Estate were revolutionaries (whereas in fact one-eighth or more were reactionaries) and ignores the question whom or what the Third Estate deputies may have represented politically. More important, the central question Cobban asked and provisionally answered was where within the old society the members of the two great revolutionary legislatures had originated. To judge the meaning of any answer to this, it would be necessary to know something of the destinies of others in the same occupations who did not enter revolutionary politics or did not rise to the national legislature. The kind of analysis Cobban carried out would necessarily emphasize whatever continuity there was within any two decades considered.

There the discussion rested until Cobban returned to it in 1962, in his Wiles Lectures at the Queen's University in Belfast.[30] He opened with a succession of pleasantries, at the expense of narrative historians (for their credulity and confusion in philosophical matters), Marxian interpreters of the past (for determinism and occasional use of a pretentious, quasi-religious rhetoric), and sociologists (for attempting to construct total theories of social evolution instead of a precise, neutral vocabulary). Cobban repeated and expanded upon his objections to using the word "feudalism" for anything in the late eighteenth century other than a system of seigneurial dues. Turning again to the bourgeoisie, and noting the diversity within it recognized by Lefebvre and Soboul, he suggested an additional differentiation, between a part of the bourgeoisie

30. *The Social Interpretation of the French Revolution* (Cambridge, England, Cambridge University Press, 1964); the first three phrases quoted here are on p. 59, the others on pp. 67, 167, and 172, respectively.

that was becoming more prosperous and another part that was "definitely not rising in wealth, and was barely holding its own in social status." Cobban said "the inevitable result was a conflict between the rising and declining groups, which particularly took the form of a struggle for control of the towns." He identified the "rising" groups as those engaged in finance and business, but expressed uncertainty about what was happening to the *rentiers* and proprietors of land. He said "the class of venal officers was declining." (This assertion rested ultimately on a letter written in 1740 by d'Aguesseau, then chancellor.[31] It is certainly questionable as a description of the state of affairs thirty to fifty years later.) Cobban went on, then, to restate a principal theme of his inaugural lecture, that "the revolutionary bourgeoisie was primarily the declining class of *officiers* and the lawyers and other professional men, and not the businessmen of commerce and industry." This idea fitted neatly, seven chapters later, with the statement that "the grievances of the lower and therefore more dissatisfied elements in town and country were not so much against the survival of an old feudal order as against the coming of a newer capitalist one." Implicitly, the reader was invited to group the officeholders with "the peasant proprietors in the country, and the lawyers, *rentiers* and men of property in the town, [who] successfully resisted the new economic trends." These groupings of men with defensive attitudes in common help to explain, in Cobban's view (with one eye on the nineteenth century), the conservative phenomena of the post-revolutionary years: the slow economic development, the firm social hierarchy, and the maintenance of individual and family property rights against interference by the state. Cobban's reasoning went far beyond Taylor's, in suggesting that social antagonisms

31. The letter was cited, in a discussion of the falling prices of judicial offices in 1715–1748, by Franklin L. Ford, *Robe and Sword. The Regrouping of the French Aristocracy after Louis XIV* (Cambridge, Mass., Harvard University Press, 1953), p. 149. In that context, it was apposite.

19

within classes (especially within the bourgeoisie) had a greater effect than did conflict between classes and had this effect on the outcome as well as the origins of the Revolution, over the long run and not simply in a brief crisis.

The writings of Taylor and Cobban are alike in concentrating on the relationships between economic development and structural social change, on the one hand, and political revolution, on the other. From an altogether different perspective, Lefebvre's narrative of the revolutionary events of 1789 was subjected to new criticism by Elizabeth L. Eisenstein.[32] It will be recalled that Lefebvre used the word "bourgeoisie" with a connotation derived from his view of its historic role, associating the bourgeoisie with the experimental rationalism of the Enlightenment. He held that the revolutionary bourgeoisie acted in behalf of all Frenchmen, indeed, of human ideals with a worldwide historic significance. In her criticism, Mrs. Eisenstein took the word "bourgeoisie" simply as a reference to individuals with certain economic and social characteristics. Where Lefebvre wrote "the bourgeoisie set the 'nation' into motion,"[33] she looked for the names of men clearly bourgeois in social position. Finding that most of the leaders Lefebvre mentioned as active in Paris were not bourgeois in that sense, Mrs. Eisenstein suspected that the provincial leaders were not bourgeois but noble or newly ennobled men.

The association or dissociation of ideology and social status was not a novel issue. More than a half-century before, Daniel Mornet had concluded his examination of the catalogues of five hundred private libraries with the observation:

In sum, it appears impossible to establish lines of resistance to the philosophic movement, or centers of attraction, according to the interests or the traditions of caste and occupation. The new ideas were diffused somewhat at random. It was a matter of temperament and consciousness, not of social groupings. The conclusion agrees

32. "Who Intervened in 1788? A Commentary on *The Coming of the French Revolution*," *American Historical Review*, 71 (1965), 77–103.
33. *The Coming of the French Revolution*, p. 56.

with what is known of the slow transformations that prepared the Revolution, the curious skepticism of the nobility, the "humanitarian" ardor which conquered the middle classes, the men of the [lawyer's] robe, the pen and the desk, the support given by the men of [government] finance to those who were to ruin the system from which they obtained their livelihood, etc. The currents that incessantly eroded the ancien régime followed fissures and lines of fracture within it which constantly seem capricious.[34]

Mrs. Eisenstein's criticism of Lefebvre was based on a novel underlying idea. Instead of associating ideology with social class, she sought to associate a conception of the body politic —equalitarian, homogeneous, quantitative—with a particular era, which she defined by social processes inaugurated by the printing press. She contrasted another kind of conception of the body politic–hierarchical, heterogeneous, qualitative—belonging, she said, essentially to an era of manuscript culture.[35] In effect she pointed to the gradual transformation of intellectual processes, and not capitalist development, as the dynamic factor preceding the revolution of 1789. She said that the revolution did not mark the rise of the bourgeoisie to political power, but rather a new degree of political participation by a "non-privileged, literate laity."

Implicitly Mrs. Eisenstein conceded that privilege was an important political issue in the revolution. The existence of privilege, in fact, signified at least a legal recognition and control of the system of social stratification. The nature of this stratification had engaged Mousnier's attention, after his criticism of Labrousse's idea and its application in the book by Mlle Daumard and Furet. In a new essay, Mousnier concentrated on three types of social stratification: castes, estates, and classes.[36] The familiar distinction between a caste system

34. "Les Enseignements des bibliothèques privées (1750–1780)," *Revue d'Histoire Littéraire de la France*, 17 (1910), 449–496, on p. 469.
35. "Who Intervened in 1788?" p. 96; cf. her "Some Conjectures about the Impact of Printing on Western Society and Thought: A Preliminary Report," *Journal of Modern History*, 40 (1968), 1–56.
36. "Problèmes de stratification sociale," written in 1964 and pub-

and a class system, Mousnier said, would not serve for an analysis of French social stratification in the seventeenth and eighteenth centuries. Instead, an intermediate but distinct type of stratification would have to be recognized for this purpose, a system of estates (*ordres* in French, *Stände* in German). Mousnier attempted to outline this social hierarchy in which status depended on the honor attached to a person's social function without reference to his economic role as a producer or a consumer. He returned to his earlier point concerning the importance of family ties and lineage and again emphasized esteem, symbols, and shared psychological traits as the basis of unity within an estate.

An opportunity to discuss all these and other ideas was presented by the colloquy on sources and methods of social history, held in May 1965 at Saint-Cloud.[37] In a paper on description and measurement, Soboul expressed skepticism as to Mousnier's most recent suggestions. He said that the surest and most valid criterion of social stratification was still, in his judgment, the relationship to the means of production, since this refers to "the most permanent and most profound human activity: work and production." In a comment, Mousnier said that much more elaborate concepts of social stratification are necessary. Soboul replied that at the end of the ancien régime, the juridical structure of estates was an imperfect mask covering the class structure, which consisted of aristocracy, bourgeoisie, and lower classes. Mousnier agreed that the estates did not represent the real social structure, but he de-

---

lished as the introduction to *Deux cahiers de la noblesse pour les Etats Généraux de 1649–1651,* eds. Jean-Pierre Labatut and Yves Durand (Paris, Presses Universitaires de France, 1965), pp. 9–49.

37. *L'Histoire sociale, sources et méthodes. Colloque de l'Ecole Normale Supérieure de Saint-Cloud (15–16 mai 1965),* introduction and conclusion by Ernest Labrousse (Paris, Presses Universitaires de France, 1967). The phrase quoted in this paragraph from Soboul's paper appears on p. 19.

nied that the aristocracy was a class, in Soboul's sense, in the eighteenth century. Labrousse intervened to distinguish social structure from political structure. He said that the French Revolution did not change the social structure from a system of estates to a system of classes, but rather changed the political structure from one based on estates to one based on classes.

At the colloquy, Jacques Dupâquier examined historians' problems in constructing a classification of socio-occupational groups. Such groups existed within each estate or within each class, whatever the stratification system of society as a whole. But the boundaries and composition of such groups in the eighteenth century are difficult to determine, and Dupâquier said it would be premature to adopt a single classification before further research has been done. He simply commented on nine classification criteria that need to be investigated in regional or specialized research.[38] This presentation stimulated extensive comments. As Soboul pointed out, a classification of socio-occupational groups is intimately bound up with the definition of various types of societies. Mousnier said he perceived greater flexibility, and thus improvement, in the classifications proposed since 1961, but still thought them valueless for the seventeenth and early eighteenth centuries. Labrousse remarked that there are two kinds of minds: those which seek solutions for difficulties, and those which seek difficulties for solutions. (He placed himself in the former category.) Labrousse observed further that a classification of social groupings ought to be related to the political and economic history of the period under study. "The French Revolution was not accomplished nor defined by leagues of families, parentages or clientages . . . These antique coalitions no longer had their

38. *L'Histoire sociale*, pp. 164–166. The criteria are: economic sector (agricultural, industrial, and services, public and private); individual occupation; social status; juridical class; income level; wealth; family situation; age; and geographic origin.

former role. The French Revolution was not made by family groups but by social groups."[39]

Cobban's arguments on the nature of these social groups were not the subject of any reported comments at the colloquy, but were widely noticed elsewhere. In the preface he had said that his criticism of "a well-established pattern, consolidated by a series of great historians," was likely to encounter resistance and that his suggested alternative might in turn be criticized.[40] His expectation was more than met by the efforts of eleven reviewers.[41] His negative remarks about sociological theory, his statements that some of the ideas he criticized were Marxist-Leninist, and his assertions and hypotheses on a number of historical questions all came under attack, from several different directions.

The most incisive criticism was by Norman Hampson, who wrote that Cobban

seems to equate social with economic. He makes no reference to religion as a social force, nor to the social status, as distinct from economic advantages, that was involved in privilege. He concedes that contemporaries thought in terms of social categories which he himself rejects. Since men presumably acted in accordance with what they *believed* to be their interests, this seems to leave him exposed to the charge of explaining the "real" significance of these actions by means of the kind of general theory which he himself has declared to be untenable. His book is, in fact, a non-Marxist economic interpretation of the revolution (p. 192).

39. *L'Histoire sociale*, pp. 176–178.
40. *The Social Interpretation of the French Revolution*, p. vii.
41. Elinor G. Barber, in *American Sociological Review*, 30 (1965), 447–448; Samuel Bernstein, in *Science and Society*, 29 (1965), 472–477; Crane Brinton, in *History and Theory*, 5 (1966), 315–320; [Richard Cobb], in the *Times Literary Supplement*, 64 (7 January 1965), 8; Leo Gershoy, in *Journal of Modern History*, 37 (1965), 242–243; Jacques Godechot, in *Revue Historique*, 235 (1966), 205–209; Albert Goodwin, in *English Historical Review*, 81 (1966), 611–612; Norman Hampson, in *Irish Historical Studies*, 14 (1964–1965), 191–192; Jeffry Kaplow, in *American Historical Review*, 70 (1965), 1094–1096; George Rudé, in *New Statesman* (2 October 1964), 504–505; and Gilbert Shapiro, in *American Historical Review*, 72 (1967), 502–511.

This was not a criticism that Cobban chose to answer, but he did reply to most of his critics, aiming witticisms at several of them and clarifying what he meant in some respects.[42] His exchanges with Richard Cobb provided in addition one of those displays of verbal agility and malice which British academic people have prudently substituted for duels.

He directed his most elaborate reply to Jacques Godechot, and presented it at a new international colloquy which was organized by Mousnier to discuss social stratification in castes, estates, and classes.[43] In his review, Godechot referred to Cobban's remarks about the need for precise definitions of many words used in France at the end of the eighteenth century. But, he said, the examples of obscurity that Cobban mentioned were ill-chosen, as those terms had particular meanings well-known to trained historians. To this, Cobban in turn replied,

Let us take some of these terms, to see if they are in fact perfectly understood. We all know, says M. Godechot, what *officier* means. But do we know the role of the *officiers* in French society, their functions and relative status, how these had been changing, and in what direction, during the course of the eighteenth century? There is a whole book to be written on this subject.[44]

The main point of Godechot's review is that in 1789 men used the word "feudalism" and knew what they meant, that the bourgeoisie as well as the peasantry wanted to abolish it, and

---

42. Cobban's replies to Cobb and the latter's rejoinders appeared as letters to the editor of the *Times Literary Supplement*, 64 (1965), 72 and 114. His reply to Godechot was first given as an oral communication at the international colloquy on social stratification, held at the Sorbonne in December 1966, and was published in his *Aspects of the French Revolution*, pp. 264–274. He directed a final reply primarily to Goodwin and secondarily to Brinton, Bernstein, Kaplow, Rudé, and Shapiro, in *History*, 52 (1967), 149–159, also included in *Aspects of the French Revolution*, pp. 275–287.

43. *Problèmes de stratification sociale. Actes du colloque international* (*1966*), ed. Roland Mousnier (Paris, Presses Universitaires de France, 1968).

44. *Aspects of the French Revolution*, p. 266.

that their alliance was successful in this. He found Cobban's alternative interpretation fundamentally unpersuasive. The theme of Cobban's reply is that Godechot was thinking of political history and employing political terminology, that underneath or behind the political struggles of the revolution there was a much more complex and slowly changing social and economic system, and that the terminology appropriate for a political narrative will not serve for analytical social history. At the colloquy, the first commentator on this reply was Robert R. Palmer, who said that Cobban had introduced too sharp a distinction between political and social history, for, after all, social problems become political problems as soon as decisions are made for action. Labrousse formulated the distinction, as he had done the preceding year, in terms of state and society: two structural systems which are different conceptually and which change at different rates of speed.

This exchange provides a convenient point at which to pause and glance back over the writings and arguments of the decade following 1955. Beginning with the proposal for an occupational and economic census of the bourgeoisie, these ramified in several directions and finally came to involve reconsideration of the subject matter of social history, the analytical conceptions required for it, and the kinds of historical processes involved in it. In these discussions, the magistrates in the bailliages are exemplary in several ways. Exercising a distinct profession, they were organized socio-occupational groups in the sense intended by Mlle Daumard, Furet, and Dupâquier. Holding offices in which they had bought property rights, they formed a part of the class of men with "proprietary" wealth as defined by Taylor. They were among the officeholders who, Lefebvre said, criticized the existing government in the eighteenth century and believed that law should prevail over violence and arbitrariness. They were also among the officeholders enumerated in Cobban's examination of the deputies for the Third Estate in the Estates General of 1789, officeholders he described as part of a "declining class," though he later indicated that little is known of their functions and relative status. They were part of the literate laity evoked by Mrs. Eisenstein. In all these respects, the magistrates in the bailliages were involved in both social evolution and political revolution.

II

Jurisdiction and Politics: The Bailliage Courts in the System of Royal Institutions

The bailliages and sénéchaussées were among the most venerable of French royal institutions. Their origins were older than the assemblies of the men of the Estates and older than the earliest extant record left by the Parlement of Paris. In the ordinance of Philip II, drawn up in 1190 when he was preparing to depart for Jerusalem on the Third Crusade, the king specified that "baillivi nostri" would have power to administer "nostra jura et nostram justitiam" at their monthly assizes.[1] During the thirteenth and fourteenth centuries, the actions of

1. *Recueil des actes de Philippe Auguste, roi de France,* ed. Henri-François Delaborde et al., 2 vols. (Paris, Institut de France, Académie des Inscriptions et Belles-Lettres, 1916–1943), I, 417.

these officers and of the institutions that grew up around them helped to shape the developing power of the monarchy. At the same time, the bailliages and sénéchaussées gradually ceased to be involved in the full range of governmental activity, and they acquired a stable character. Their functions, their geographical definition, the qualifications and rank of their personnel remained fundamentally unchanged after the middle of the sixteenth century, although their number continued to grow. Practically, limits had been set upon the ways in which the king or his men in the bailliages and sénéchaussées might be able to use these institutions for new purposes. What remained to be determined was whether they would keep all the powers they still exercised and how important these would be; whether they would be jostled aside by other royal institutions and how their relations with the latter would develop.

At the beginning of the reign of Francis I, the bailliages and sénéchaussées were primarily courts of law.[2] The bailli or the sénéchal, a man of the sword and ordinarily a noble, would preside at times, especially on ceremonial occasions, when his ignorance of the law would not be disruptive. Writs still ran in his name, although the principal judges continued to be described as his lieutenants. In fact, the *lieutenant général* presided over trials and was, in the absence of the bailli or sénéchal, the ranking personage and in effect the chief judge. He and his colleagues wore the long robes of men trained in law. Their duties, in becoming professional, had acquired more uniformity. Whatever general differences may once have distinguished bailliages from sénéchaussées had disappeared. The historic traits of French royal justice since the thirteenth century had affected all of them, imparting to each the character of a council whose work was organized in regular

2. Gustave Dupont-Ferrier, *Les Officiers royaux des bailliages et sénéchaussées et les institutions monarchiques locales en France à la fin du Moyen Age* (Paris, Bouillon, 1902).

modes of procedure and whose most important decisions were reached collectively.[3] Specialization of functions within a bailliage had become systematic to some degree. When the lieutenant général was absent, his duties would ordinarily be performed by a *lieutenant particulier*. This was the usual practice, in bailliages which held regular sessions in more than one locality, outside the principal seat of the bailliage. The king's obligation to render justice was fulfilled by these judges. His interests as lord of his domains and as protector of his subjects were represented by king's counsel, that is, a king's proctor and one or more king's advocates. These officials, too, were magistrates, members of the bailliage, although not judges.[4] Learned men, acting as groups, the magistrates were no longer itinerant except when engaged in the antique procedure of the assizes, which by the sixteenth century was steadily falling into disuse. Geographically, their jurisdiction was conceived by reference to the fixed centers where the judges sat, to which

3. The developments in France that led to an elaborate written procedure and the disappearance of the trial jury are analyzed by John P. Dawson, *A History of Lay Judges* (Cambridge, Mass., Harvard University Press, 1960), pp. 43–69.

4. Conventions of usage will be employed henceforth for simplicity. The term *lieutenant,* where it referred to the presiding magistrate (and equivalents like *juge mage* in and near Languedoc, *vibailli* in Dauphiné, *sénéchal* in Brittany, *bailli de robe longue* in scattered localities) is translated "chief judge." The term *lieutenant particulier* (and equivalents like *assesseur* in some provinces, *alloué* in Brittany) is translated "associate chief judge." The *gens du roi* are referred to as "king's counsel." The terms *avocat* and *procureur* are simply transliterated, "advocate" and "proctor." (The reason for this is that the differences in France between an *avocat,* a *procureur,* and a *notaire* do not correspond to the distinction in England between a barrister and a solicitor, nor to the designation in United States courts, "attorney and counsellor, solicitor, advocate, and proctor.")

Judges and king's counsel are referred to as "magistrates" when the difference in their functions is to be ignored, or when they are considered collectively as officeholders and fellow members of a corporate body.

The reader is reminded that "bailliages" is used as the general plural word which may include sénéchaussées, and "sénéchaussée" is used only for provinces or courts where that was the actual title.

the justiciables would come. There were enclaves, separated from the main territory of a bailliage, in many places. There were uncertainties as to which court had jurisdiction over particular parishes. The number and implications of these uncertainties are difficult to fix. It is clear, at least, that the magistrates were bourgeois in a primary sense of the term: they were townsmen, who attempted to subordinate the countryside in the king's name, and who offered professionally administered justice to the inhabitants. In doing so, they acted in their own interest as much as the king's. The fees they received from litigants made up the larger part of their financial reward. This had been true under the old system of officeholding, in which the crown farmed out each office for a term of years. It remained true under the system of venal offices, in which the officeholder purchased from the crown a lifelong proprietary right to his office and received a fixed annual payment that resembled interest upon his investment. Legal professionalism and venality of office were the most significant traits of the bailliages after the middle of the sixteenth century.

These two traits determined the general character of the bailliages but not their place among all the institutions exercising judicial authority. In rank and power, they were immediately below the parlements, to which appeals from their judgments were taken. They were above the royal *prévôtés* and similar variously titled jurisdictions, which did not have power to decide *cas royaux*. The categories of cases in which the bailliages were empowered or obliged to act had not, however, been clearly or finally specified. Territory and subject matter remained imprecisely defined and often would not by themselves determine jurisdiction. Many litigants could claim that they were personally entitled to be judged in one court rather than another. Justice was delegated to the judges by the king, and he retained the right to intervene at any stage of any proceeding. The combined effect of these principles was to provide both parties in every case with opportunities to prolong, terminate, or displace the process of adjudication and particularly to turn over to the litigants the initiative in selecting a forum. Once signified, the selection could easily become a contested issue, and then the interests of the judicial officeholders led them, too, to take the issue seriously. At all levels, therefore, judges were engaged, singly and in groups, in competition to supply their services to any person who might find advantage in bringing them a dispute to be settled. In this competition, a court's readiness to tolerate or even encourage dilatory and expensive procedures could influence the quality of its clientele. If the professional zeal and pecuniary interest of the judges consistently led them to invoke the most elaborate procedures, or if one of the contending parties, sparing no expense, adopted tactics of maximum delay, then the court would be available, in reality, only to wealthy litigants. Rapidity of decision required informality and was rewarded by smaller fees. Thus a court might become the resort of the poor and lowly. Its judicial personnel and their modes of work would reflect and steadily reinforce this state of affairs. In the mid-sixteenth-century judicial hierarchy, the bailliages had already come to occupy an intermediate position, not only in rank and power but also in formality and learning, dilatoriness and costliness.[5]

It seemed for a time that many bailliages might be elevated from this intermediate position. In 1552, edicts of Henri II conferred upon fifty-eight of them the power, where small sums were involved, to receive appeals from neighboring bailliages and to make decisions that would not be subject to appeal.[6] The selected bailliages were henceforth to be known

5. Bernard Guenée, *Tribunaux et gens de justice dans le bailliage de Senlis à la fin du Moyen Âge* (Paris, Les Belles Lettres, 1963), p. 245.
6. The edict of January 1551 (old style), defining the special authority of présidial courts, is in the *Recueil général des anciennes lois françaises,* ed. François-André Isambert et al., 29 vols. (Paris, 1821–1833), XIII, 248–254. Two months later another edict listed the towns where they were to be located.

officially as *présidial* courts. Their power to pronounce final judgment was limited to cases where the value in controversy did not exceed a capital sum of 250 *livres* or an annual income of 10 *livres*. The announced motive of the edict was to bring justice within reach of the inhabitants of the provinces. Its importance lay in two other circumstances. First, the parlements had hitherto possessed exclusive power to receive appeals from the royal bailliages and to render final judgment as "sovereign" courts. There would henceforth be no reason in principle why the jurisdiction of the présidial courts should not be expanded. This could be accomplished merely by raising the monetary limit. Second, the edict required présidial judgments to be signed by no fewer than seven judges, and ordered the creation of several new offices of judicial councillors in each bailliage chosen for présidial jurisdiction. The king might find reason for future expansion of présidial jurisdiction in the prospect of creating and selling new judicial offices. Both these points were immediately obvious to the parlements. They remonstrated against the edict, and for weeks they refused to register it. Finally, in a *lit de justice,* the king assured the Parlement of Paris that the edict was necessary for fiscal reasons but that it would not be followed by further expansion of the powers or personnel of the présidial courts. He commanded and secured registration.

The edict suggested future potentialities for the présidial courts which might have brought them a greater share of judicial business and which appeared correspondingly menacing to the parlements. In the long run, it effected instead a new distinction in prestige and division of political interest between two kinds of bailliages: the présidial courts and the others.[7] Repeatedly, the parlements had opportunities to harass the présidial courts. The monetary limits that defined their power

---

7. Ernest Laurain, *Essai sur les présidiaux* (Paris, 1896), first published as a series of articles in the *Nouvelle Revue Historique de Droit Français et Etranger,* 19 (1895), and 20 (1896).

to receive appeals and their exemption from appellate review remained unchanged for two centuries. (In real terms, those limits were reduced by half or two-thirds during the price rises of the late sixteenth century.)[8] The bailliages that had not been chosen as présidial courts nevertheless regarded the latter as rivals and sought to prevent appeals from being taken to them. It remained a fact that in some cases the présidial courts were entitled to act as final judges. The fact was not obliterated by the narrowly technical significance of this power in the actual work of the courts. Its chief effects on the courts were, however, to complicate the hierarchy of honor among royal judges, to exacerbate local rivalries, and to cause a long train of jurisdictional disputes.

The distinction between the présidial courts and the other bailliages was important to the royal fisc because it offered the possibility of creating new judicial offices for sale by first elevating a bailliage to the rank of a présidial court. The same kind of importance attached to the distinction between the principal seat of a bailliage and its other seats and also to the distinction between the bailliages and the lesser royal jurisdictions (prévôtés and the like). Both présidial courts and ordinary separate bailliages increased in number during the sixteenth and seventeenth centuries. In the territory of the Parlement of Paris, the total number of bailliages more than tripled. The rate of increase in the seventeenth century was about twice the rate of increase in the sixteenth century, in its net effect in that territory.

The multiplication of bailliages was motivated by fiscal purposes only in part. It resulted also from the crown's acquisition of domains formerly held in appanages or by royal

8. The index constructed by Paul Raveau suggests a 50 percent decline in the purchasing power of the livre between 1551 and 1593. Henri Hauser reached a similar conclusion. Paul Raveau, "La Crise des prix au XVIe siècle en Poitou," *Revue Historique*, 162 (1929), 1–44, 268–293; Henri Hauser, "La Question des prix et des monnaies en Bourgogne dans la seconde moitié du XVIe siècle," *Annales de Bourgogne*, 4 (1932), 7–21.

vassals. In many of these territories, justice was administered by seigneurial courts from which appeals went directly to a parlement, never to a royal bailliage. Seigneurial courts with this privilege continued to exist in considerable numbers throughout the period when the administrative monarchy was being built up.[9] Every monarch created new ones. These facts illustrate the point that seigneurial justice under the Bourbon kings was far more than a vestige. Yet the number of seigneurial courts answerable only to the parlements declined, especially in the sixteenth and seventeenth centuries, and the number of royal bailliages grew correspondingly.

Outside the territory subordinate to the Parlement of Paris, the number of bailliages increased through additions of whole provinces to the kingdom as well. To the seven parlements in France at the beginning of the sixteenth century, there were thus added subsequently six parlements with their contingents of bailliages. Almost one-fifth of the bailliages in France in 1789 were in territorial additions subordinate to the parlements of Metz (1633), Besançon (1674), Douai (1686), and Nancy (1775); and this reckoning is not entirely complete, because it does not include the lesser royal jurisdictions from which appeals went to the sovereign council of Roussillon or that of Alsace or the provincial council of Artois. The final result of all these expansions and additions, at the end of the eighteenth century, was a total of approximately 2,700 magistrates in the royal bailliages, constituting probably between 40 and 50 percent of all the judges in the kingdom.[10]

9. About 1730, in the territory of the Parlement of Paris, thirty-six of them were included in a *Liste alphabétique des pairies et autres justices seigneuriales ressortissantes au Parlement, auxquelles on envoye ordinairement les édits, déclarations et arrests* (s.l., n.d., B.N., 4° Lf[23].156). In the 1750's, in the territory of the Parlement of Dijon, seven were listed by Claude Courtépée, *Description générale et particulière du duché de Bourgogne,* 2nd ed., 4 vols. (Dijon, 1847–1848), I, 364–365.

10. In 1730, a well-informed social critic estimated that in the whole kingdom there were about 6,000 judges, including all levels of the

Bailliages were not equally important, nor magistrates equally numerous, in every province. Lorraine had a larger population of bailliage magistrates than any other region of comparable size. This was in part an accident of the institutional history which led to the existence of two parlements there, at Metz and Nancy. But if we ignore the Parlement of Metz and consider only the bailliages subordinate to the Parlement of Nancy, the enumeration still shows an exceptionally large number of bailliage magistrates in relation to either the total number of inhabitants or the area of Lorraine. The only large province similar to it in this respect was Normandy, where bailliage magistrates were more than two-and-one-half times as numerous as in either Languedoc or Brittany. Another very dense concentration of bailliage magistrates was in Franche-Comté, where there were more than twice as many as in Dauphiné, a province of similar size.

These contrasts were part of a wider differentiation between provinces in their historical relations to the crown. Its fiscal motive for creating and selling judicial offices was operative everywhere. The process amounted to a sort of taxation. During the seventeenth century, the great age of expansion in the venality of offices, provincial leaders and institutions tried to forestall this process. They were relatively successful in Languedoc, Brittany, Dauphiné and, it would seem, Provence.

The availability of judicial offices in the bailliages during the eighteenth century was a result mainly of a province's inability to prevent their creation in earlier centuries. The

---

judicial hierarchy, not counting the advocates, the proctors, the court clerks, the bailiffs, or the other court functionaries, who were altogether much more numerous than the judges. Charles-Irénée Castel, abbé de Saint-Pierre, *Annales Politiques,* ed. Joseph Drouet (Paris, Champion, 1912), p. 19.

The principal event modifying this total after 1730 was the incorporation of Lorraine into the kingdom in February 1766, with about 40 magistrates in the Parlement of Nancy, nearly 200 in the bailliages, and unknown numbers in royal prévôtés and seigneurial courts.

Table 1. Number of Bailliages and Number of Magistrates
in Bailliages, by Territorial Jurisdictions of Parlements, 1789.

Parlement	Bailliages				Magistrates		
	Présidial	Nonprésidial	Total	Enumeration of members lacking for	Présidial	Nonprésidial	Enumerated total
Paris	42	101	143	13	619	426	1,045
Toulouse	15	9	24	0	212	70	282
Grenoble	1	11	12	0	11	49	60
Bordeaux	13	12	25	9	151	20	171
Dijon	6	14	20	0	67	65	132
Rouen	6	31	37	0	79	191	270
Aix	0	12	12	5	0	45	45
Pau	0	7	7	0	0	14	14
Rennes	4	23	27	0	54	59	113
Metz	5	10	15	0	52	26	78
Besançon	6	7	13	0	76	48	124
Douai	1	5	6	0	11	37	48
Nancy	4	28	32	0	40	153	193
Total	103	270	373	27	1,372	1,203	2,575

Sources: see Appendix below.

Table 2. Départements Ranked by Relative Size of Judiciary in Bailliages, 1790, with Data on Urbanization and Literacy.

Département	Number of bailliage magistrates per 100,000 inhabitants[a]	Urbanization,[b] if exceptionally great or slight (in percent)	Minimal literacy,[c] if exceptionally extensive or limited (in percent)
Meurthe	28	Urban (>15)	Very extensive (>80)
Vienne	23	—	Very limited (<20)
Vosges	21	Nonurban (<6)	Very extensive (>80)
Doubs	20	—	Very extensive (>80)
Meuse	19	Nonurban (<7.5)	Very extensive (>90)
Moselle	19	—	(No data)
Jura	18	—	—
Manche	18	—	(Data insufficient)
Marne	17	—	(Data insufficient)
Haute-Marne	17	—	Extensive (>70)
Calvados	16	Urban (>15)	Very extensive (>80)
Loiret	14	Urban (>20)	Limited (<40)
Côte-d'Or	14	—	—
Gers	14	Nonurban (<7.5)	(Data insufficient)
Cher	13	—	Limited (<30)
Aisne	13	Nonurban (<7)	Extensive (>60)
Oise	13	Nonurban (<7.5)	Extensive (>70)
Corrèze	13	Nonurban (<7.5)	Limited (<30)

In half the départements, the number of bailliage magistrates per 100,000 inhabitants was less than 13 but more than 6.

Gard	6	Urban (>25)	—
Loire-Inférieure	6	Urban (>20)	Limited (<30)
Gironde	5	Urban (>15)	Limited (<30)
Bouches-du-Rhône	5	Very urban (>60)	Limited (<40)
Ariège	5	Nonurban (<4)	(Data insufficient)
Nièvre	5	Nonurban (<5)	Very limited (<20)
Hautes-Pyrénées	5	Nonurban (<4)	(Data insufficient)
Ille-et-Villaine	5	—	Very limited (<20)
Haute-Loire	5	—	Limited (<40)
Isère	4	Nonurban (<7.5)	Limited (<40)
Haute-Garonne	4	Urban (>15)	Very limited (<20)
Vendée	4	Nonurban (<6)	Limited (<30)
Tarn	2	Urban (>15)	(Data insufficient)
Côtes-du-Nord	1	Nonurban (<7)	(Data insufficient)
Lozère	0	Nonurban (<4)	—

number of offices actually occupied was, however, determined by the demand for this kind of economic and psychological investment. The demand varied, not only between provinces but also within them. The division of the provinces into *départements* in 1790 made possible statistical comparison of small regions, and this reveals intraprovincial differences in the relative size of the judiciary in the bailliages (Table 2). The effective demand for judicial offices in the bailliages was not uniformly great even in Lorraine, nor uniformly slight even in Brittany.

Large and small numbers of bailliage magistrates were distributed geographically in a pattern that does not entirely correspond with any single demographic, economic, or social factor. Three factors deserve scrutiny because they illuminate some characteristics of the bailliage judiciary in the last phase of the ancien régime. First in importance is the extent of minimal literacy. An imaginary line from Mont Saint Michel to Geneva seems to have marked a boundary between the comparatively literate northeast and the comparatively illiterate southwest, during the whole period from the late seventeenth century to the late nineteenth century. Broadly, the same line separates the area of many bailliage magistrates from the area of few bailliage magistrates: Lorraine, Franche-Comté, Champagne, and Normandy are northeast of the line; Brittany, Languedoc, and most other provinces with few magistrates, are

---

Appendix, below, and population data of 1790 given by Marcel Reinhard, *de de la population pendant la Révolution et l'Empire. Instruction, recueil de ?es et notes* (Gap, Commission d'Histoire Economique et Sociale de la ᵒolution, 1961), pp. 26–28.

Indicated by the proportion of the population resident in communes with ɾe than 5,000 inhabitants, which is calculated from data of 1794 given by nhard, pp. 48–49.

Indicated by the proportion of men capable of signing their names at the ᵉ of marriage, data of 1786–1790 given by Michel Fleury and Pierre Valɾy, "Les Progrès de l'instruction élémentaire de Louis XIV à Napoléon III ᵓrès l'enquête de Louis Maggiolo (1877–1879)," *Population*, 12 (1957), 92, on p. 86.

southwest of it. The importance of minimal literacy in causing the growth of the judiciary is twofold. To the degree that elementary education created opportunities for more advanced education, it spread both the capacity and the potential desire for a judicial career, and thereby enlarged the number of possible purchasers of judicial offices. On the other hand, elementary education may have made the legal process more accessible to laymen and encouraged numerous lawsuits, thereby providing fees which made judicial offices less unattractive as investments.

The second factor related to the number of bailliage magistrates is the size of the town population. Where the bailliage judiciary was exceptionally large, the urban population was typically average or slightly below average in size. Where the bailliage judiciary was somewhat larger than average (thirteen or fourteen magistrates per 100,000 inhabitants), the urban population was usually somewhat smaller than average (6 to 9 percent of the whole population). These general statements are not, however, universally applicable. In Lorraine, every département had a large number of bailliage magistrates, whether the urban population was large (Meurthe), average (Moselle), or small (Meuse, Vosges). In Normandy, both a large judiciary and a considerable urban population were to be found in the Calvados département. These exceptions may perhaps best be explained by reference to the unusual extent of literacy in these départements.

Where the bailliage judiciary was small, most commonly the urban population was not near average size but was either large or very small. It was difficult for a large judiciary to form within a small bourgeoisie, if only because few families possessed the resources needed for the purchase of office. In very large towns, there was a tendency for members of the bourgeoisie to enter other careers, whether business opportunities or higher-ranking offices, and this placed an upper limit on the expansion of the bailliage judiciary. Here again, exceptions must be noted. In ten départements, the urban population exceeded 20 percent of the total population, and in five of these départements (Seine, Hérault, Nord, Seine-Inférieure, Rhône-et-Loire, and Loiret), there was an average or even an above-average number of bailliage magistrates in relation to the total population. In ten départements, the urban population was less than 5 percent of the total population, and in at least four of these (Deux-Sèvres, Ardèche, Ain, and Haute-Saône) the bailliage judiciary was near average size in relation to the total population. (The number of magistrates could not be ascertained in Charente and Landes). It remains true that typically at the end of the eighteenth century, the demand for offices was effective in maintaining a large judiciary in those regions where towns, amidst a rural population, were prospering yet were neither very numerous nor very large.

The third factor related to the number of magistrates in a département is the presence or absence of a provincial capital. For example, the disparity between the Vienne département, with twenty-three magistrates per 100,000 inhabitants, and the Vendée département, with four magistrates per 100,000 inhabitants, seems best explained by the fact that Poitiers, the center of provincial life, is in Vienne. Neither royal administration nor élite group life had penetrated far into the western part of Poitou. The same kind of contrast, in less extreme degree, is visible between the Cher and the Indre départements in Berry, and between the Marne and the Aube départements in Champagne.

The end of the eighteenth century is the most convenient point in time for a census of bailliage magistrates and an analysis of their geographic distribution. The reason is simply that information was accumulated at that point through the effects of royal legislation, the extension of almanac-publishing in the provinces, and revolutionary reforms. But these findings cast light on earlier periods also. At no time, probably, were there many more than the 2,700 magistrates estimated to be holding office in the bailliages in the 1780's. Two centuries earlier, certainly, there were many fewer: a total between 500 and 1,000 would seem a reasonable guess. Let us turn back to that point, in order to trace the changing political and juris-dictional position of the bailliage magistrates during the seven-teenth and eighteenth centuries.

In relation to the national political community, the most important function that devolved on the bailliages was their use as electoral circumscriptions for the Estates General dur-ing the sixteenth century and in 1614. The royal letters of convocation were addressed to the bailli or sénéchal. His suit-ability to preside over the process was determined in part by his long-standing authority to command the attendance of clergymen and noblemen for cas royaux and of noblemen for the *ban* and the *arrière-ban* as well. But usually the bailli or sénéchal was in no way expert in procedural matters. Or-dinarily, the king's proctor presented the letters of convocation to the chief judge, who had them read aloud in the court room and made public in the jurisdiction at large. The convocation letters contained only the most general instructions to the chief judges of the bailliages concerning whom to summon to the electoral meetings and by what procedure.[11] In fact, during the sixteenth century, in much of northern France, they tended to summon increasing numbers. Three motives for their extension of the suffrage can be imagined. In the first place, the electoral assemblies were quasi-judicial proceedings in that they were meant to provide information for the king in the *cahiers de doléances,* as well as persons deputized to provide

11. For instance, to proceed immediately, to hold the electoral assembly in the principal town of the bailliage and within the shortest possible time, and to convoke "all those of the three estates in your territory and under your jurisdiction as is accustomed and has been done in similar cases," in the example of a royal letter of convocation published by Yves Durand in his edition of the *Cahiers de doléances des paroisses du bailliage de Troyes pour les Etats Généraux de 1614* (Paris, Presses Uni-versitaires de France, 1966), pp. 301–302.

further information and empowered to give consent. The king's judges might have conceived it to be their duty to the king to involve as many persons as possible. Secondly, some equitable principle may have suggested that parish priests, lesser noblemen, and peasants ought to be consulted because they would be affected by the decisions taken. Thirdly, the participation of the lesser towns and villages had the effect of supplying the king's judges with allies against their political opponents, the oligarchies installed in the municipal councils of the greater towns.[12]

Within the Third Estate, there were disputes over political participation. At issue was the proper content of the term "Third Estate," and particularly whether it referred to the bourgeois notables of the large towns or included the inhabitants of small towns and even villages. The issue activated classic rivalries, between large and small towns, between town and countryside. The local outcome depended in great part on whether there were provincial estates, regularly convoked, with well-established electoral procedures in which the large towns predominated or even excluded the others. Where this was the state of affairs, the municipal officials of the large towns preserved this position, in Dauphiné, Provence, Languedoc, Brittany, most of Burgundy, and much of Guyenne. In many other places, extension of the suffrage was actually followed by an increase in the number of bailliage magistrates elected deputies. As a proportion of all the deputies for the Third Estate, their number rose to 18 percent in 1576, to 24 percent in 1588, to 39 percent in 1614. Most of those elected were chief judges.[13]

12. J. Russell Major, *The Deputies to the Estates General in Renaissance France* (Madison, University of Wisconsin Press, 1960), concluded that extension of the suffrage occurred notably in Picardy, Champagne, Normandy, Ile de France, Orléanais, Berry, Touraine, Maine, Anjou, and Poitou, and suggested (pp. 125–126) the second and third of the possible motives mentioned in this paragraph.

13. Major, *Deputies*, pp. 164–165.

The political importance of the bailliage magistrates and other holders of royal offices in this period, particularly in 1614, is difficult to interpret. Historians have duly confused the matter by implicitly presupposing nineteenth- and twentieth-century notions of electoral politics. One should begin by asking why many bailliage magistrates were willing to serve as deputies, since most townsmen at the time would not have wanted to undertake a dangerous, expensive journey and remain away from home for several months. Evidently, bailliage magistrates commonly found these negative aspects outweighed by the opportunity to uphold their interests as officeholders and as provincial notables. Included among their interests, certainly, were their legal rights and prerogatives as officeholders. It is difficult to say why historians have so often overlooked the emphasis, in various orations at the Estates General, on the honor properly due to royal judges.[14] Their very eminence within the Third Estate would create an obligation to represent the Third Estate and an opportunity to defend their eminence against the competition of mayors and town councillors. This kind of obligation and opportunity was perhaps as important to them as material interest.

The simple fact that bailliage magistrates were willing to serve as deputies was one reason why the electors chose them, but there were other reasons, too. First, the conception of royal judgeships as peculiarly honorable was not held by bailliage magistrates alone, but was widely shared. Secondly, to the extent that the electors regarded the adoption of a grievance list as their own most important task, and the list itself as a set of controlling instructions, it would be natural to choose as a deputy the chief judge of the bailliage, for he had presided over the process of adopting the grievance list. The chief judge might then have served as an emissary more than a maker of law, and as a representative, not in the sense

14. See, for example, the statements quoted by Durand in his introduction to the *Cahiers de doléances de Troyes*, pp. 61–62.

that he was typical of the electors but rather in the sense that he was the weightiest personage they could choose to present the "remonstrances, complaints and grievances, and the proposals and advice" requested by the king. In some regions, the bailliage magistrates, especially the chief judges, were powerful because each stood at the center of a network of lesser royal and seigneurial courts. Where the preliminary electoral assemblies in these lesser jurisdictions chose their local judges as delegates to the assembly for the bailliage, this alone might determine the election of the chief judge as a deputy for the bailliage.[15] Some bailliage magistrates tended to be royalist in their political sentiments, opposed by merchants and lawyers sympathetic to the Catholic League and the popular attitudes which it had expressed and which subsisted for years.[16]

Whatever the reasoning of the electors who chose bailliage magistrates, it did not determine their conduct as deputies in the Estates General. There they had to respond to the diverse initiatives of the crown, the clergy, and the nobility, as well as the Third Estate deputies elected in places dominated by provincial estates. Even within the Third Estate, political issues would have been complicated and difficult to resolve. Ecclesiastical policy, confronted with a choice between Gallican and ultramontane tendencies, was connected with the contest over the prerogatives of the crown as against those of the parlements and, in 1614, the respective powers of the regency and the king's cousins. These questions in turn affected mercantile and fiscal policy. Every issue was placed in a new perspective when all three Estates assembled. The responses of the bailliage magistrates sitting with the Third Estate were

15. This occurred in the bailliage of Troyes in 1614, according to Durand, pp. 47–48.
16. For example, at Angers, according to Albert Meynier's introduction to the *Cahiers des gens du Tiers Estat du pays et duché d'Anjou en 1614* (Angers, 1905).

not dictated only by their position as bailliage magistrates and are difficult to characterize briefly and accurately. One historian says they were an important part of a forward-looking political movement supporting the parlements' ambitions to share power with the monarchy.[17] Another says they were for the most part at odds with the interests of the merchant oligarchies in the great towns.[18] Still others have discussed whether they were in some way controllable by the crown.[19]

The bailliage magistrates were not politically dependent on the crown nor susceptible to its immediate control by any practicable action. Their property rights in their offices could be liquidated through repayment or seized as a penalty for individual malfeasance, but outright confiscation appeared almost out of the question. Like other royal officeholders, the bailliage magistrates could be influenced. There was nearly always some privilege or other that they desired to safeguard or obtain. In the late sixteenth and early seventeenth centuries, the right of an officeholder to transfer the property in his office by inheritance was not firmly established. To secure inheritability of offices would entrench the whole system of venality that had been denounced by the clergy, the nobility, and the Third Estate in 1560 and 1576. In 1588, all three estates again asserted that officeholders ought to be elected. The clergy and the nobility remained consistent in opposing sale and inheritance of office, but the Third Estate diverged from them. It suggested that a judicial office which had been long established should be allowed to pass to the officeholder's close

17. Claude Alzon, "Quelques observations sur les Etats Généraux français de 1614," Commission Internationale pour l'Histoire des Assemblées d'Etats, *Journeés Internationales, Paris, 1957*, pp. 35–42.

18. Major, *Deputies*, p. 9.

19. George A. Rothrock, "Officials and King's Men: A Note on the Possibilities of Royal Control in the Estates General," *French Historical Studies*, 2 (1962), 504–510; J. Michael Hayden, "Deputies and *Qualités*: The Estates General of 1614," *French Historical Studies*, 3 (1964), 507–524.

relatives (son, son-in-law, brother, or nephew). Resignation in favor of a successor was already possible, but was limited by a requirement that the old officeholder resign at least forty days prior to his death: the Third Estate asked that the requirement be waived for these judicial offices. The request was not granted, but it indicates one of the ambitions of bailliage magistrates who constituted almost one-fourth of the Third Estate deputies.

The forty-day survival requirement was evidently disadvantageous to royal officeholders; so much so, they could be expected to pay for its elimination. After prolonged debate among his advisers, Henry IV finally decided to exempt every officeholder who paid an annual tax amounting to 1⅔ percent of the assessed value of his office. By paying a small premium, the holder of a royal office could thus insure its inheritability. The new arrangement was promulgated in a royal declaration at the end of 1604. At the same time, a six-year franchise to collect the annual tax and to resell vacant offices on which it was not paid was assigned to Charles Paulet, who agreed to pay more than a million livres a year to the royal treasury. From his name the annual tax acquired the denomination *paulette* by which it was known thereafter throughout the seventeenth and eighteenth centuries. A few important offices were not permitted to be inherited in this simple way but were reserved for royal appointment whenever vacant through death or resignation. The offices of first president and proctor-general in a parlement were the principal ones ineligible for the paulette. The office of chief judge in a bailliage with présidial jurisdiction was likewise ineligible at first, but in 1611 was made inheritable under the paulette system.[20]

The royal government's practice of selling offices, reinforced as it was by the new arrangement for their inheritability,

20. The authoritative account of these matters is by Roland Mousnier, *La Vénalité des offices sous Henri IV et Louis XIII* (Rouen, Editions Maugard, [1945]) pp. 208–243.

was a pivotal issue in the Estates General of 1614. The clergy and especially the nobility wanted the whole system to be abolished and they repeated their desire for election of office-holders. The Third Estate, led by bailliage magistrates who constituted more than one-third of its representatives, maneuvered to protect officeholders against becoming the sole victims of fiscal reform. The Third Estate was willing to see the paulette eliminated if at the same time there were reductions in the sum devoted to pensions for noblemen and in the amount collected in the major landed property tax, the *taille*. It was willing to see the royal government cease selling offices if at the same time it eliminated the forty-day survival requirement: this combination would still have permitted office-holders to sell their offices, and would have freed them to leave the offices to their heirs. These conditions, on which the Third Estate insisted, may have been calculated to make any change impossible or merely to ensure that noblemen would sacrifice and property tax payers would benefit. Whatever the motives, the Third Estate's program was unacceptable to the clergy and the nobility. The stalemate left the royal government in the position of arbiter. In the end, none of the fiscal reform proposals suggested by the Estates was implemented.[21]

After 1614, judiciary and administration confronted each other directly. There was no longer any intervening national representative institution in which either might find allies and antagonists. The king's ministers sought to protect their policy-making and especially their fiscal powers and to establish and maintain subordinate agents. The parlements likewise had subordinates, the bailliages and lesser courts, which they both dominated and protected. They exercised a quasi-legislative authority, issuing regulatory orders on a wide variety of subjects. At times they interposed a kind of veto, refusing to permit royal edicts to be copied into their records, thereby rendering

21. Mousnier, *La Vénalité des offices*, pp. 569–587.

unenforceable the policies of the king's ministers. In general, the latter came to terms with the parlements by recognizing and enhancing their superiority over the other institutions composed of proprietors of offices. Inherent in the system of venal offices was permanent competition among these institutions. Success in the competition was not determined by a single standard but involved jurisdictional authority, ceremonial honor, and exemption from fiscal burdens. The royal government could exploit this competitive situation in order to make officeholders pay for their relative power and relative rank. In the long run, during the seventeenth century, the effect on the bailliages was to reduce their jurisdictional authority, while leaving their rank and fiscal exemptions essentially unchanged.

Elevating an ordinary bailliage to the power and rank of a présidial court was one way of creating new judicial offices. This would necessarily involve reducing the territorial jurisdiction of an existing présidial court. Its magistrates might be willing to provide a substantial loan to the royal treasury, in order to obtain agreement from the crown to withdraw the edict creating a new présidial court.[22] Alternatively, the edict might be put into effect, and the new offices sold. This occurred especially during 1634–1642, years of preparation for war and actual war against Spain, when sixteen bailliages were enlarged into présidial courts.[23]

Other ways of marketing new offices had different effects. Instead of distinguishing one bailliage from its neighbors, the

22. See, for example, "Pièces relatives au présidial projeté à Fontenay-le-Comte en 1598 et en 1644," ed. Maurice Pouliot, *Archives Historiques du Poitou*, 47 (1939), 167–188.

23. In 1634, at Lectoure; 1635, Guéret, Rodez, and Le Puy; 1636, Tulle and Valence; 1637, Châlons-sur-Marne; 1638, Montargis; 1639, Auch, Château-Gontier, Châtillon-sur-Indre, Libourne, and Mâcon; 1641, Langres and Sarlat; 1642, Limoux. The legislation is listed in the *Catalogue général des livres imprimés de la Bibliothèque Nationale: Actes Royaux*, II, 404, 436, 461, 482, 506, 513, 546, 555, 561, 563, 579, 599, 635.

crown could reduce the jurisdictional authority of all the bailliages in order to assign particular duties to other institutions. It did so on three occasions in the seventeenth century. In 1627, the power to hear and decide in first instance all lawsuits affecting the royal domain or the public roads and bridges was taken from the bailliages and assigned to the *bureaux des finances;* at the same time six new offices were created in each of the twenty-one bureaux.[24] In 1679, the power to decide disputes between noblemen over hunting rights and the honorific rights derived from fiefs, where there had been insulting words or offenses against the honor of a gentleman, was taken from the bailliages and assigned to the *maréchaux de France* sitting in the *tribunal du point d'honneur* in Paris. The process of adjudication of such disputes was later decentralized, by edicts of 1693 and 1704 creating two judicial offices for this purpose in the territory of every bailliage.[25] For thus cutting away part of the jurisdiction of the bailliages, one motive was the prospect of selling new offices. There were also other motives: administrative convenience in the one case, effective prevention of duelling in the other. Better performance of governmental tasks was stronger still as a motive for yet another jurisdic-

24. The origins of the Trésoriers de France were medieval. In the course of the sixteenth century, the performance of their duties was decentralized, their positions were converted into venal offices and steadily multiplied, and in 1577 they were assigned collective responsibilities as bureaux des finances. Details and references are given by Jean-Paul Charmeil, *Les Trésoriers de France à l'époque de la Fronde* (Paris, Editions A.&J. Picard, 1964).

25. Legislation of Henri IV and Louis XIII defined as a distinct category all disputes between nobles involving their honor, and assigned jurisdiction to a new, special tribunal composed of the maréchaux de France, who continued to sit also, and ordinarily, as the judges of the *connétablie* deciding civil and criminal cases involving military personnel. The offices created in 1693 and 1704 were those of *lieutenant des maréchaux de France* and *conseiller rapporteur du point d'honneur.* See the article "Point d'honneur," in the *Répertoire universel et raisonné de jurisprudence,* ed. Joseph-Nicolas Guyot, 2nd ed., 17 vols. (Paris, 1784–1785), XIII, 151–153.

tional change, which had a greater impact on the bailliages, the creation of the office of police magistrate.

An edict of March 1667 established the office of police magistrate for the city of Paris. An edict of October 1699 established such an office in every town where a bailliage sat.[26] The office holder was entitled *lieutenant général de police*, by analogy with the chief judge for civil and criminal cases. As a member of the bailliage, he was to have the second rank, immediately after the chief judge for civil cases. The safety and economic welfare of the town were placed mainly in the hands of the police magistrate, and he was given wide powers to investigate, issue regulations, and render judgments. The matters that came within his jurisdiction included the cleaning of streets and public spaces, maintenance of street lighting, and damage resulting from fires and floods. He was given responsibility for the provision of adequate supplies of food and for limitation of the prices of food. He had jurisdiction over riots, disorders, and illegal assemblies. He was to inspect markets, inns, and other establishments and determine their hours of opening and closing, and to supervise manufacturing, apprenticeships, elections of masters and journeymen, and enforcement of the statutes and regulations concerning artisans. He had the right, also, to attend and vote in assemblies of the municipal authorities.

Jurisdiction over town affairs aroused keen interest among the officeholders already involved, the bailliage magistrates and the municipal officials. Delineation of distinct authority in these matters, and sale of the office having the authority, stirred up the old rivalry between bailliages and municipalities. It was as if the royal government had decided to auction a nicely calculated slice of authority, knowing that there would

26. The edicts were reprinted in Guyot's *Répertoire*, 2nd ed., X, 564–565 and 567–568. The functioning of the institution in one town is treated in detail by Julien Ricommard, *La Lieutenance générale de police à Troyes au XVIIIe siècle* (Paris, Hachette, 1934).

be at least two avid bidders. There ensued obscure intrigues and struggles between would-be purchasers of the new office. Wealthy corps like the sénéchaussées at Poitiers and Riom were able to buy the office of police magistrate and rotate its duties among their members. In some bailliages a judge already in office, in others a newcomer to the bench, succeeded in acquiring it. These results wrought little change, since the police magistrate had to reach a practical understanding with the other judges in order to carry out his duties and take part in the corporate life of the court, from whose rank was derived much of the honor accruing to his office. Another specialized title was added to an array of offices which might already include a chief judge and an associate chief judge for civil cases, a chief judge and an associate chief judge for criminal cases, a presiding judge for présidial cases, a number of councillors, a king's proctor, and one or two king's advocates. But none of these offices attracted the interest of the municipal officials as did the office of police magistrate. In some towns, therefore, the new offices escaped the control of the existing membership of the bailliage and was acquired by the mayor or the town councillors. Where this occurred, the bailliage suffered a real loss of jurisdiction. The general effect of the creation of this office, therefore, was to establish a new differentiation among the bailliages: between those that had some control over the office of police magistrate and those that did not.

These differences in jurisdiction—between the présidial courts and the other bailliages, and between the courts with municipal police jurisdiction and those without it—were laid down on a common base which consisted of a broad jurisdiction in both civil and criminal matters. [27] In first instance, all bailliages had exclusive jurisdiction of four important categories of civil cases. One category consisted of lawsuits over

27. See the article "Cas royaux," in Guyot's *Répertoire,* 2nd ed., II, 722–726.

rights to fiefs and noble lands, including the possession and definition of the honorific rights and the existence of remunerative rights. A second category consisted of lawsuits where one of the contending parties was a noble and where moveable property or personal rights were in dispute. A third category included certain ecclesiastical property rights, such as possession of a benefice, rights of patronage, and landed rights of parish churches, hospitals, and other institutions. A fourth category, consisting of disputes arising over contracts bearing the royal seal, included matters in which a document drawn up by a royal notary was at issue. The jurisdiction of the bailliages in criminal cases extended generally to the crimes and misdemeanors committed in their respective territories. Every priest, noble, or royal judge implicated in any offense had to be tried by a bailliage if not by a parlement. Certain offenses had to be prosecuted before a bailliage: lèse-majesté in the second degree, premeditated murder, kidnapping, rape, armed assault, duelling, embezzlement of municipal funds, and heretical preaching, almost all to be classed, in a later age, as felonies.

The main jurisdictional lines, relatively neat and firm in the definitions of the eighteenth-century legal manuals, were deflected and blurred by exceptions duly noted in the same manuals. Some judges could extend the scope of their operations by claiming a preferential right (*prévention*) empowering them rather than other judges to hear and decide a particular case.[28] The exercise of this right depended on receiving the complaint prior to its reception by the judge who would ordinarily hear the case and was conditional upon the latter's failure to ask that it be remanded. A bailliage could exercise the right of prévention over lower royal judges (*prévôts* and others with different titles) and over seigneurial judges within its territory. As an encouragement of competition for judicial business, the right of prévention might be regarded as useful

28. Jean Riollot, *Le Droit de prévention des juges royaux sur les juges seigneuriaux* (Paris, Rousseau, 1931).

in ensuring that justice would be done by someone. Jurisdictional rules depended not only on the rights of some judges as against other judges but also on the personal privilege of certain litigants guaranteed in royal letters of *committimus*. This privilege permitted the holder to obtain trial in first instance before a particular court, either the Parlement of Paris, the parlement of the province, or even a présidial court. The practical effect was to remove from the bailliages all the cases that involved peers of the realm, councillors of state, officers of the royal household, members of the parlements, *secrétaires du roi,* and various other high-ranking personages. Thus, throughout the judicial hierarchy, it was often possible for a royal judge to reach downward and deprive his subordinates of judicial business. The bailliages were appellate courts, reviewing the decisions of seigneurial and lower royal judges, but they could expand their jurisdiction most readily by increasing the number and importance of trials in first instance.

Many bailliages stood in continuing need of more judicial business, for financial reasons. Judges of their rank were still required to pay the paulette in order to ensure the inheritability of their offices. But the forced loans imposed on them from time to time by the monarchy were far more burdensome. When Louis XIV sanctioned their exemption from the taille in 1674, he ordered "moderately assessed sums" to be collected from them for this privilege.[29] The monarch sometimes required his judges in the bailliages to increase the capital sums they had invested in their offices and to accept in exchange increased annual interest payments, *augmentations de gages.* The judges in a bailliage could act as a group to borrow the total sum required of them. They could seek to pass on the burden of their corporate debt by obtaining larger revenue from the fees paid by litigants—in effect, an excise on lawsuits. In order to achieve this shifting of the fiscal burden, the judges

29. Edmond Esmonin, *La Taille en Normandie au temps de Colbert* (Paris, Hachette, 1913), p. 249.

usually needed both a richer crop of lawsuits and a larger field in which to harvest them.

An elaborate mechanism enabled the French monarchy to obtain money from its subjects for the satisfaction of their *goût des offices* and their *esprit processif*. The operation of the mechanism depended on the subjects' continued willingness to pay for these luxuries. During the last years of Louis XIV, the taste for office and the litigious spirit were made too costly to support. The prices of judicial offices fell. As there developed serious difficulty in keeping competent officeholders, the reliability of judicial decisions declined and, with it, the volume of judicial business.[30] In 1718, an inquiry by the proctor-general of the Parlement of Paris, undertaken in the performance of his general supervisory responsibility for the bailliages subordinate to the Parlement, evoked some reports like the following, from Mâcon:

Nearly half [the offices] are vacant and there is no hope of their being filled. The extraordinary debts, which the company has been obliged to assume in order to pay the taxes with which it has been burdened, the suppression of privileges which it was forced to acquire at a high price . . . the capitation [tax], collected with unheard-of rigor . . . render these offices suspect and unmarketable . . . Only the *lieutenant général civil*, the *lieutenant particulier*, and one *conseiller* are rich . . . Those in office are so discouraged that they are abandoning their offices and attempting to provide for their subsistence by careful management of their lands. The result is that we pass whole months without being able to find enough judges to hold présidial hearings.[31]

The downward spiral had worse effects on the bailliages more vulnerable than that of Mâcon, where, after all, half the offices continued to be filled, three judges were rich, and from

30. This is merely a restatement of the analysis written in 1729 by the chancellor, d'Aguesseau, in his memorandum "Sur les vues que l'on peut avoir pour la réformation de la justice," *Oeuvres,* ed. Jean-Marie Pardessus, 16 vols. (Paris, 1819), XIII, 200–229.
31. Viard, *procureur du roi* in the bailliage of Mâcon, to the *procureur-général,* 23 March 1718 (B.N., ms. Joly de Fleury 2156).

time to time seven judges would meet to act as a présidial bench. A number of lesser bailliages maintained during the eighteenth century only a marginal existence. Even in the 1770's, under greatly improved general economic conditions, one of the small sénéchaussées in Brittany held only thirty-five hearings and decided ten cases in an average year; consisting of two judges and a king's proctor, it met in a room with cracking plaster and a rotting floor, in a building rented from the former chief judge, Pic de la Mirandole, who insisted on having his own coat of arms displayed in the courtroom.[32] There was a vast difference between such a court and the sénéchaussée at Riom or the bailliage at Orléans, where a score of judges wearing the red robes of the high magistracy filed into a veritable palais de justice on the day after Saint-Martin's to hear the annual harangue by the king's proctor. They were based on a sufficiently large territorial jurisdiction or were composed of judges sufficiently wealthy to withstand the financial pressure imposed on them during the wars.

The construction of the administrative monarchy during the seventeenth century involved a relative weakening of the royal judiciary in political terms. This is a well-known fact in the history of the parlements.[33] Its counterpart is that the weakening of the bailliages occurred at the same time and was more serious. The monarchy reduced and complicated the jurisdiction of the bailliages while exploiting the magistrates for fiscal purposes. The differences in jurisdictional authority between présidial courts and other bailliages, and between bailliages with and those without municipal police power, were troublesome in themselves. The economic differentiation among the

32. Raymond Delaporte, *La Sénéchaussée de Châteauneuf-du-Faou, Huelgoat et Landelau, et les juridictions seigneuriales du ressort* (Paris, Pedone, 1905), pp. 61–62, 77, 137.
33. Franklin L. Ford, *Robe and Sword. The Regrouping of the French Aristocracy after Louis XIV* (Cambridge, Mass., Harvard University Press, 1953), p. 82.

companies of bailliage magistrates was aggravated in the later years of Louis XIV, with further divisive effects.

After 1715, as the parlements recovered and extended their power, the bailliages also began in general to revive. Tentatively and unsteadily, the central government changed its practices toward the bailliages and began to consider ways of making their administration of justice more effective. At first this occurred on the initiative of men like d'Aguesseau and Joly de Fleury, who owed their prominence to their membership in the Parlement of Paris, the natural ally and patron of the bailliages as long as the interests of the whole judiciary were undivided and due subordination was maintained. During the two decades when d'Aguesseau was chancellor, he contemplated several reforms in the judicial system which in combination would have had far-reaching effects.[34] His taste for argumentation led to the development of elaborate plans, but his emphasis on political practicability, falling nearly always on the side of inaction, rendered most of them visionary. The only result of his work that was important to the bailliages

34. D'Aguesseau envisioned a single body of law for the whole kingdom, a simple, expeditious procedure, and a rational organization of the courts with qualified personnel and effective discipline. All of this was to be achieved gradually.

About 1742, he proposed to enlarge the subject matter over which the royal bailliages and sénéchaussées exercised jurisdiction, at the expense of the royal prévôtés (and equivalents) and of the seigneurial courts; to raise the monetary limits on the jurisdiction of the présidial courts; to diminish the total number of judgeships; and to intensify the competition among royal judges by making the right of prévention more widely applicable. He proposed to let the parlements determine the reforms that would affect them. These proposals were set forth in his undated "Idée générale ou plan abrégé de l'usage que l'on pourrait faire des états envoyés par les intendants pour former un meilleur arrangement des sièges ordinaires de judicature," ed. by Paule Combe as *Mémoire inédit du chancelier Daguesseau* (Valence, Imprimeries Réunies, 1928). He had asked the intendants for pertinent information in 1740. Three related memoranda by an intendant, dated February 1742, are quoted by Edouard Evérat, *La Sénéchaussée d'Auvergne et siège présidial de Riom au XVIII⁰ siècle* (Paris, 1885), p. 93 and *passim*.

was the abolition of the royal prévôtés and similar jurisdictions in the towns where the bailliages were located. Even this was done with characteristic caution, beginning in five towns near Paris in the early 1740's, proceeding to others in 1747 and 1748, and culminating in April 1749 in a general edict.[35]

In the middle years of the century, the judges in the larger and wealthier bailliages themselves began to express their interest in widening the subject matter over which they had jurisdiction and obtaining greater privileges. In their minds, the two objectives were closely related, for both would help to attract able and reputable men to the judicial offices. A flurry of correspondence was stimulated among some présidial courts by the edict of 1750 that provided for ennoblement of army captains and lieutenants, which naturally suggested that nobility might be conferred on présidial judges after sufficiently long service.

A more extensive and better organized effort developed in 1762 in the atmosphere of reform encouraged by the comptroller of the finances, Bertin, who is known to historians mainly for his sympathy for physiocratic doctrines.[36] In that year the system of justice was entrusted to a newly appointed keeper of the seals, Feydeau de Brou, an old man with more than forty years' experience as an intendant in various provinces, where he had had many opportunities to consider the needs of the bailliages.[37] A committee was formed to prepare legislation concerning the présidial courts, which quickly learned of the committee's existence. The magistrates of Angers suggested that all the présidial courts prepare statements for the committee. The bailliage of Tours suggested that

35. *Catalogue général des livres imprimés de la Bibliothèque Nationale: Actes Royaux*, V, 906, 943, 983, 1007, 1017, 1078, 1096, 1100, 1102, 1120, 1123.

36. Georges Weulersse, *Le Mouvement physiocratique en France (de 1756 à 1770)*, 2 vols. (Paris, Félix Alcan, 1910), I, 78–83.

37. His son, the intendant at Rouen, delivered a speech in July 1761 showing traces of physiocratic doctrine (Weulersse, II, 337, 405, 453).

they jointly request Jousse, the well-known legal writer, who was a judge in the bailliage of Orléans, to present their views. Both proposals were accepted by a large number of présidial courts.[38] Diagnoses and prescriptions circulated among them during 1763. The proctor-general of the Parlement of Paris added his own recommendations.[39] But then the whole business came to a sudden halt. The parlements' hostility to Bertin led to his removal from the comptroller-generalship and his replacement by Laverdy, a councillor in the Parlement of Paris. Feydeau de Brou was replaced as keeper of the seals by old Maupeou, former first president of the Parlement of Paris, whose son was appointed first president. When Jousse sought an interview with the new keeper of the seals, the latter wrote that no spokesman was desired and that if any information were ever needed it would be requested.

The activity of the magistrates indicates a nascent willingness to cooperate across provincial and jurisdictional boundaries that had not previously been characteristic of bailliages. At the same time, the specific proposals advanced by the présidial courts were extremely various and even conflicting, and they show that the historic atmosphere of particularist competition had by no means evaporated.[40] The strongest desire of the présidial courts, on which they generally agreed, was to obtain ennoblement for sufficiently long service. This suggestion was adopted by the proctor-general of the Parlement of Paris, as well. Both the objective of the présidial courts and its acceptance in principle by a leading member of the Parle-

38. In the archives of the sénéchaussée of Vannes are copies of 77 replies to the proposal from Tours, of which 48 agreed to it. Albert Macé, "La Réforme des présidiaux au XVIIIᵉ siècle," *Bulletin de la Société Polymathique du Morbihan*, 36 (1890), 127–137, and offprinted.

39. B.N., ms. Joly de Fleury 2154.

40. The proposals of 12 présidial courts are analyzed by Evérat, *La Sénéchaussée d'Auvergne et siège présidial de Riom*, pp. 267–276. Cf. André Chenal, *Etude sur le présidial d'Orléans* (Orléans, A. Gout & Cie., 1908). pp. 149–151.

ment of Paris indicate that what was forming was not a battle between the noble judges in the parlement and the commoners in the bailliages. It was to be, instead, an alliance between the high-ranking and the middle-ranking judges for the benefit of the whole judicial branch. Important obstacles stood in the way of such an alliance. Not only were there the weary contests for territorial jurisdiction between neighboring présidial courts. There was also the general desire of those courts to extend their right to receive appeals and their exemption from appellate review, by raising the monetary limit from 250 livres to 1,000 livres as a capital sum. This suggestion was not incorporated in the memorandum by the proctor-general of the Parlement of Paris. It ran directly counter to the interests of the parlements.

The results of the discussions concerning the présidial courts were meager compared with the proposals made. A royal declaration in July 1763 affirmed exemption from the taille for the magistrates in the bailliages. An edict of August 1764 ordered the abolition of the office of presiding judge for présidial cases, long recognized as a needless duplication of the chief judgeship. Legislation of August 1768 provided that nobility would be conferred on the magistrates in the Châtelet of Paris for sufficiently long service or upon death in office. No other court of the bailliage type at that time received any privilege of ennoblement through office holding.[41]

The line of development that had originated after the death of Louis XIV and that had led to the activity of the 1760's was interrupted radically by the chancellorship of the younger Maupeou. In 1769, soon after receiving the seals, he saw one of the memoranda drawn up by d'Aguesseau with its elaborate

41. The only other such court ever to obtain the privilege of ennoblement was the sénéchaussée of Marseille, in August 1700 (revoked in August 1715) and again in July 1780 (maintained until 1790). For this and the Châtelet of Paris, details are given by François Bluche and Pierre Durye, *L'Anoblissement par charges avant 1789* (2 fasc., Paris, Les Cahiers Nobles, 1962), II, 34.

plans for reorganizing and improving the bailliages. His own plans, prepared with the assistance of Lebrun, took a very different shape. He explained his reasoning on the subject of the bailliages twenty years later:

The membership of these bodies, long since enfeebled, subject at so many points to the influence of the parlements, the nature of their jurisdiction itself, so difficult to define precisely, finally their multiplicity, offered me only a precarious and uncertain resource in these courts; to give them the requisite weight and composition, it would have been necessary to change their nature, remake them, reduce their number; and I felt that it would cost less to build more majestic and more useful edifices.[42]

Maupeou was a political architect. He saw clearly the political weakness of the bailliages. He did not intend to reform their administration of justice except indirectly, through the effects of supervision by the reorganized parlements and the new provincial courts of appeal that he desired primarily for political reasons. For the same reasons, his intentions in choosing new judges seem to reflect a fixed belief in the value of rank, whether or not it was accompanied by ability. He wanted to avoid filling up the appellate bench with judges from the bailliages and was especially determined not to rely on them for the chief judgeships but on intendants instead. In the vast territorial jurisdiction of the Parlement of Paris, which was to be divided among five new courts of appeal and a reorganized parlement, this determination dictated the location of four new courts: at Clermont-Ferrand, where he could draw on the membership of the *cour des aides,* rather than at Riom or Moulins, where there were distinguished sénéchaussées; at Blois, where there was a *chambre des comptes,* rather

42. The passage quoted is from Maupeou's memorandum of 1789 addressed to Louis XVI, published in full by Jules Flammermont, *Le Chancelier Maupeou et les parlements* (Paris, 1883), appendix. It was largely copied from his plan of 1769, in the opinion of his latest biographer, Jacques de Maupeou, *Le Chancelier Maupeou* (Paris, Editions de Champrosay, 1942), p. 126.

than at Orléans, where the bailliage that counted Pothier and Jousse among its recent members had earned a greater reputation; at Poitiers and Châlons-sur-Marne, where there were bureaux des finances. The location of the fifth new court was an obvious choice, Lyon, the second city of the realm, where the sénéchaussée had been combined with a *cour des monnaies*.

Most bailliages accepted the reform of Maupeou as passively as he could have hoped. For them, there was no effort to liquidate the property rights in the offices or the system of compensation in the form of fees paid by litigants. The few bailliages that resisted were confronted by Maupeou in vigorous fashion, with the same tactics as toward the provincial parlements: securing the adherence of some of the judges and removing the rest from office. The resistance was strongest in the Châtelet of Paris, which was bound to the Parlement by a number of ties of family and friendship. But Maupeou obtained help from the chief civil judge, Dufour de Villeneuve, who secured the judges' vote to accept the reorganization edict and continued thereafter to preside over the civil branch, from which thirty-eight of the forty-three judges remained absent. New venal offices, created to replace those of the protesting judges, were slowly bought up while the Châtelet continued to function. Outside of Paris, the opposition was strong at first in Champagne and in the West. But in no province were the bailliages united in opposition to Maupeou. After the exemplary treatment accorded to the Châtelet of Paris, most opponents yielded. In only five towns was it necessary to replace some or all of the judges in the bailliage: Troyes, Auxerre, Villefranche in Beaujolais, Mâcon, and Blois. The reasons for their special tenacity are partly obscure. A sharp division of opinion within the bailliage was manifest at Auxerre. It represented a continuation of rivalry between the leading families which had previously erupted in disputes over the administration of the hospital and over expressions of Jansenism in the *collège*.[43] Resistance in the bailliages was eliminated or silenced, at all events, before the end of 1771. Many positions in the new courts of appeal were filled, in fact, by bailliage magistrates, whose devotion to the parlements proved to be less than unswerving. Except for this detail, Maupeou's assessments were borne out by the events of 1772 and 1773, and it is clear in retrospect that his dismissal in 1774 was brought about not by any failure of his plan but by machinations among courtiers and the new king's political incapacity.[44]

The reestablishment of the parlements was followed by a renewed effort to enlarge the power of the présidial courts. An edict of November 1774 permitted them to receive appeals and render final judgments in cases up to a value of 2,000 livres where they had previously been limited to values of 250 livres or less.[45] Judges in ordinary bailliages protested against this extension of their rivals' jurisdiction. The new keeper of seals, Hue de Miromesnil, a creature of the parlements, readily reconsidered the matter. An edict of August 1777 established a special procedure, to be applied in every case, for determining whether a présidial court which asserted jurisdiction was entitled to do so. The edict also listed a variety of subjects on which the présidial courts could not render final judgment and reminded them that they did not have power to issue regulatory orders or to require any judge within their territories to register any royal enactment.[46] Then followed in their turn the protests of the présidial courts. The bailliage of Sens issued a printed statement urging their claims, which was ordered quashed by the Parlement of Paris. The sénéchaussée of Guéret circulated a letter attacking the new edict as injurious to the honor of the

43. Rapport du subdélégué sur les divisions qui règnent à Auxerre, 1773 (A.D. Yonne, C 7).
44. Robert Villers, *L'organisation du Parlement de Paris et des conseils supérieurs d'après la réforme de Maupeou (1771–1774)* (Paris, Sirey, 1937).
45. *Recueil général des anciennes lois françaises*, XXIII, 57–58.
46. *Ibid.*, XXV, 86.

présidial courts and to the welfare of litigants. A renewed effort to organize a combined assertion of their interests, led this time by the sénéchaussée at Riom, was markedly less successful than in 1763, since it attracted the support of only sixteen présidial courts. In the end, it was the chief judge of the bailliage of Reims, Lévesque de Pouilly, recently appointed a *conseiller d'état,* who served as their spokesman. In August 1778 a royal declaration rescinded or interpreted away some of the provisions of 1777 that were most objectionable to the présidial courts.[47]

In the last decade of the ancien régime, the bailliages with présidial jurisdiction had been restored to a semblance of the position outlined for them by Henri II, but it had been made clear that the parlements would be able to prevent them from being further strengthened. The position of the other bailliages, protected by the parlements from real subordination to the présidial courts, had improved measurably because the number of judicial offices had ceased to expand. The bailliages exercised jurisdiction over a slightly narrower subject matter than in the sixteenth century, but they retained their main functions as the ordinary courts for civil and criminal trials. In some 370 towns, it was they who, chiefly if not solely, represented the King's justice.

The professional life of the judges in the bailliages provided them with a broad knowledge of the functions and problems of all the important local institutions. Municipal affairs, the activities of the intendant and especially of his subdelegates, the hospitals and collèges, were all subjects on which the judges had direct knowledge either through litigation or through personal action based on their standing as notable personages. In political life within the locality, they were in a special position from which they could readily assist in the maintenance of existing rights or help to preserve the estab-

47. *Ibid.,* XXV, 391–392.

lished order. To it they brought not only their special education as men of law but a particular experience derived from listening to the complaints of others, conferring privately in their council chambers, and arriving, in one way or another, at a collective decision which was only afterwards announced. Judges who took their duties seriously would tend to become imbued with an attitude toward social life generally and toward decision-making in particular that was distinctive. Where caution and procedural exactness were needed, it could be constructive. But the subjects on which they were accustomed to making decisions, as distinct from those concerning which they were well informed, were narrow in scope: landed rights and a variety of crimes were certainly the most important. The responsibilities they actually exercised provided only slight training in political and governmental processes, compared with that obtained, for example, by the English justices of the peace in the period from 1625 to 1640, a comparison that in retrospect seems appropriate because of the ensuing historical events. Only an extraordinary occurrence, such as the convocation of the Estates General, could engage them intensively in politics.

III

Bailliage Magistrates in the Social Order of the Late Eighteenth Century

Judicial authority and political influence were exercised by bailliage magistrates collectively for the most part. But a magistrate's participation in the decisions of a court or a corporate group affected a social order in which his position as an individual was very much involved. Social, economic, and intellectual characteristics contributed to defining the significance of official actions, just as office formed an aspect of identity. This has not escaped the attention of historians of the royal government under Louis XIII and Louis XIV. Hence a thoughtful article describes the bailliage magistrates in the seventeenth century.[1] It provides a point of comparison in

1. Pierre Goubert, "Les Officiers royaux des présidiaux, bailliages et

treating particularly their social, economic, and intellectual characteristics.

Both family origin and individual career contributed to fix a man's place in the intricate social order of the late eighteenth century. The two criteria might conflict. The need to reconcile their dictates had long before helped to determine that the social hierarchies would be subject to explicit legal rules. The distinction between noble and commoner was dependent on the idea of monarchy and was defined by law, enforced by privileges and sanctions. Within each of the two legal classes, rank was regulated by judicial decisions of the parlements and the king's council. It is possible, accordingly, for historians to specify the relative legal rank of many social categories, especially those which were defined by occupations. But a classification based on legal rules may be anachronistic. Its apparent precision is likely to be misleading and, at best, it fails to reflect processes of interaction between groups and elements of personality that always counted in real life. The legal rules therefore provide indications which must be scrutinized in the light of other evidence.

Nobles and commoners were separated by a social space that was never empty but was always being crossed by individuals moving upward or downward on the paths marked out by occupational success and failure. This ceaseless traffic was regulated by the laws concerning *anoblissement* and *dérogéance*. Together their effect was to assign each occupation to one of three levels, in accordance with whether it would confer nobility on a commoner, would leave a man's class position un-

---

élections dans la société française au XVIIe siècle," *XVIIe Siècle,* nos. 42–43 (1959), pp. 54–75, based on detailed research in Beauvais and sampling elsewhere, especially in Amiens, Coulommiers, Melun, and Bourges. Broad comparisons with my findings are not vitiated by the fact that most of my detailed research was in Burgundy and Poitou (the magistrates in those two provinces constituted altogether 8 percent of the total in the kingdom in 1789); my sampling extended to Languedoc, Lorraine, Bourges, Limoges, and La Rochelle.

changed, or would lower a noble into the commonry. A judge-ship in a bailliage, like most kinds of service to the king, was an intermediate occupation entailing neither ennoblement nor derogation. A judgeship in a parlement was by law an enno-bling occupation.

The division of the royal judiciary, by the differentiation be-tween the two classes, had begun in reality before Louis XIV was born.[2] In the seventeenth century, certain parlements, in Paris, Rennes, and doubtless elsewhere, tended to deny com-moners admittance to office.[3] In this sense, the so-called "noble reaction" began in the parlements more than a century before the Revolution of 1789. The exclusive tendency strengthened and spread. Meanwhile the distinction between the classes was recognized, clumsily, in the law: it provided in general that nobility would be conferred on a family for two generations' service in a parlement or other sovereign court (20 years' service or death while in office, in each generation). At Gren-oble (after 1639), Paris (after 1690), Besançon (after 1694), and Douai (after 1713), one generation's service in the parle-ment was legally sufficient to ennoble a family.[4] The eight-

2. Roland Mousnier, *La Vénalité des offices sous Henri IV et Louis XIII* (Rouen, Editions Maugard, [1945]), pp. 507–517, describing shifts in the social stratification of officeholders in Normandy, says that the Parlement seems to have detached itself from and increasingly looked down on the others.

3. In 1715, in the Parlement of Paris, 59 percent of the magistrates were grandsons of nobles (among them, the dean, Le Nain, in office since 1655); and many of these could trace their nobility further back. In all, 81 percent of the Paris magistrates in 1715 had fully attained noble status before taking office. François Bluche, who discovered these facts, found the exclusive tendency at work as early as 1659. See his theses: *Les magistrats du Parlement de Paris au XVIIIe siècle (1715–1771)* (Paris, Les Belles Lettres, 1960), pp. 76–83, and *L'origine des magistrats du Parlement de Paris au XVIIIe siècle (1715–1771). Dictionnaire géné-alogique* (Paris, constituting vols. 5 and 6 of *Paris et Île-de-France, Mém-oires publiés par la Fédération des Sociétés Historiques et Archéologiques de Paris et de l'Île-de-France*, 1953–1954).

4. François Bluche and Pierre Durye, *L'Anoblissement par charges avant 1789*, 2 fasc. (Paris, Les Cahiers Nobles, 1962), ii, 21–25, list the

eenth-century situation seems paradoxical: noble status was ordinarily treated by the parlements as a prerequisite for entering office but was designated by law as a reward for holding office in a parlement. The law of ennoblement had even come to equate the effect of judicial office in a few of the parlements with that of the office of secrétaire du roi in a chancellery, although the latter office was altogether different in other respects. The governmental functions of a king's secretary required no legal training and constituted no obstacle to financial and commercial activity. The social significance of the office of king's secretary lay in its very openness to wealthy commoners, for whom it was a normal means of access to noble status.

There were other offices which would ennoble a family for a single generation of service, notably in the cour des aides, the chambre des comptes, and the cour des monnaies in Paris, and which were neither as closed to commoners as were the parlements nor as open as the chancelleries. These offices could be used as a detour, more or less difficult, which enabled some ambitious commoners, starting from a bailliage or from law practice, to circumvent the exclusiveness that usually blocked the professional path directly upward into the parlements in the eighteenth century.[5] There were, besides, many offices—in

---

ennobling offices and specify exceptions and modifications introduced at various times; they note details not discussed here.

5. In the cour des aides in Paris, 24 percent of the councillors were sons of magistrates in lower-ranking financial or judicial companies (including bailliages) and 7 percent were sons of advocates, in the period 1724–1790, according to Guy d'Arvisenet, "L'Office de conseiller à la cour des aides de Paris au XVIIIe siècle, d'après les mémoires inédits de Louis-Achille Dionis du Séjour," *Revue Historique de Droit Français et Etranger*, 4th ser., 33 (1955), 537–559, on p. 539.

In the cour des monnaies in Paris, one-sixth of the councillors were sons of magistrates or had themselves been magistrates in bailliages, as can be seen from the list drawn up by François Bluche, *Les Magistrats de la cour des monnaies de Paris au XVIIIe siècle, 1715–1790* (Paris, Les Belles Lettres, 1966), esp. pp. 30, 33, 35, 36, 40, 41–43, 50, 51, 54, 58, 60, 61, 63–65, 69, 70, 75.

The complicated career lines and corporate relations among the

the provincial chambres des comptes, cours des aides, and bureaux des finances—which conferred noble status after two generations' service and offered a slower alternative to persistent and lucky families. The anxieties of these families are easy to imagine. What was easily overlooked, until it was pointed out in an illuminating paper,[6] was the anxiety of the officeholders already in place to ensure that their corps would be "well-composed." The comment written in 1780 by a member of the *cour des comptes, aides et finances* of Provence is revealing:

There is a mean to be observed between too much and too little rigidity. We must recognize that our offices do not require the proof [of nobility needed for the Order] of Malta, since they are designated as ennobling. There are some benches for which a name is needed; others where a mixture is needed, a name or wealth; others, finally, where talent and wealth ought to carry the vote. It would be desirable to include only [such families as] Castellane, but this is not possible. The condition of [being a] magistrate has declined; the high nobility believes itself above it, the poorer nobility cannot be transplanted or it serves badly . . . the magistrate ought to be rich, otherwise the thirst for wealth consumes him.

The social distance between the parlements and bailliages was therefore not a chasm never to be crossed. Some parlements would admit no commoners; but others required only that newcomers display wealth and the determination to make themselves acceptable as noblemen, with the understanding that always they would constitute a small minority.

The parlements refused admission to most commoners, even

sovereign courts in 1715–1748 are described briefly by Franklin L. Ford, *Robe and Sword. The Regrouping of the French Aristocracy after Louis XIV* (Cambridge, Mass., Harvard University Press, 1953), pp. 41–52.

6. Charles Carrière, "Le Recrutement de la cour des comptes, aides et finances d'Aix-en-Provence à la fin de l'ancien régime," 81ᵉ Congrès National des Sociétés Savantes, Rouen-Caen, 1956, *Actes*, pp. 141–159. The passage quoted below appears on p. 153.

though they would have been ennobled. Membership in a bailliage did not attract most nobles, even though they would have retained their noble status. Both these prejudices must be borne in mind in order to explain the division of the royal judiciary between a noble bench and a commoner bench. Indeed, it was apparently the nobles' reluctance to enter the lesser judgeships which was more widespread. From 1774 to the revolution, 14 percent of all the new magistrates entering the parlements were not legally noblemen beforehand.[7] For the bailliages, evidence of the legal status of the magistrates is not available in such a massive and well-ordered way. But participation in the electoral assemblies of the nobility in 1789 indicates at least that other nobles failed to object to a significant assertion of noble status. This was not a legal proof of noble status, but it is an indication that entails only a small risk of error.[8] According to this indication, noblemen constituted 7 percent of

7. This was the proportion of new magistrates who were unable or did not trouble to prove their noble descent so as to be exempted from a tax, the *marc d'or de noblesse*, payable by everyone entering an office that would eventually confer noble status. The records of exemptions were edited by Robert de Roton, *Les arrêts du Grand Conseil* [*sic*, for *conseil du roi*] *portant dispense du marc d'or de noblesse* (Paris, Société du Grand Armorial de France, 1951). Using them, Jean Egret, "L'Aristocratie parlementaire française à la fin de l'ancien régime," *Revue Historique*, 208 (1952), 1–14, provided numerical data concerning the noble or commoner status of all new magistrates except *conseillers clercs* (and including the *conseils souverains* at Colmar and Perpignan, which are omitted from my calculations).

In a comment on Egret's article, Ford inadvertently used as divisor the total number of magistrates in 1790 and as dividend the number of new magistrates in 1774–1789; hence his quotient, 42 percent, indicates the extent of replacement in the fifteen years before the Revolution and not, as he thought, the proportion of commoners among all the new magistrates. Ford's conclusion is strengthened by correcting this mistake. (*Robe and Sword,* pp. 145–146).

8. Philippe Du Puy de Clinchamps, *La Noblesse* (Paris, Presses Universitaires de France, 1959), p. 45, estimates that 6 to 7 percent of those voting in the assemblies of the nobility in 1789 did not possess noble status in the full legal sense.

Table 3. Apparent Proportion of Non-Nobles among New
Councillors in Parlements, 1774–1789.

Parlement	Number of new *conseillers laïcs*, 1774–1789	Number exempted from marc d'or de noblesse	Proportion presumably not yet noble (in percent)
Paris	71	63	11
Toulouse	27	22	19
Grenoble	19	16	16
Bordeaux	40	26	35
Dijon	42	33	21
Rouen	38	29	24
Aix	21	21	0
Pau	28	18	36
Rennes	52	52	0
Metz	21	13	38
Besançon	31	27	13
Douai	14	9	36
Nancy	10	10	0
Total	414	339	18

Source: Jean Egret, "L'Aristocratie parlementaire française à la fin de l'ancien régime," *Revue Historique,* 208 (1952), 1–14, footnotes. Omitted here, but included by Egret, are 85 new presidents and 34 new king's counsel in the parlements, all of whom were exempted from the marc d'or de noblesse.

the magistrates in the sénéchaussées in Poitou and 6 percent of those in the bailliages in Burgundy.[9]

9. In Poitou (including Loudun, which was not part of the *généralité*), there were 95 magistrates in office (see Appendix, *infra*), of whom 7 were nobles and one held simultaneously another office that would ennoble his family: Gustave Bardy, "Les Electeurs de la noblesse du Poitou en 1789," *Mémoires de la Société des Antiquaires de l'Ouest,* 25 (1858–1859), 325–543, on pp. 384, 387, 425, 471, 491; Henri Beauchet-Filleau, Paul Beauchet-Filleau, and Joseph Beauchet-Filleau, *Dictionnaire historique et généalogique des familles du Poitou,* 2nd ed. (Poitiers, Oudin et Cie., 1891–1915, and Fontenay-le-Comte, Lussaud frères, 1963–   , in progress), III, 433; IV, 239; V, 110, 134.

In Burgundy, there were 129 magistrates in office (see Appendix,

The reluctance of nobles to hold office in a bailliage court varied in different provinces and localities. Doubtless the percentage of noblemen among all the bailliage magistrates in the kingdom was slightly higher or lower than that in Poitou and Burgundy. Yet those provinces were more typical than was Languedoc, where there was a preponderance of présidial courts and a comparatively small number of magistrates, of whom 14 percent were noblemen. Concentrations of noblemen like those in the bailliage of Orléans (44 percent of the magistrates) or the sénéchaussée of Lyon (55 percent of the magistrates) were certainly exceptional, and are to be explained principally by the wealth of those families and the opportunities to secure ennoblement through holding other offices in those localities.[10]

---

infra), of whom 8 were nobles and 3 others held ennobling offices simultaneously: Louis de La Roque and Edouard de Barthélemy, *Catalogue des gentilshommes qui ont pris part ou envoyé leur procuration aux assemblées de la noblesse pour l'élection des députés aux Etats Généraux de 1789*, 32 fasc. (Paris, 1861–1865), *Bourgogne*, pp. 6, 9–11, 30, supplemented by Adrien Arcelin, "La Noblesse du bailliage de Chalon-sur-Saône en 1789," *Mémoires de la Société d'Histoire et d'Archéologie de Chalon-sur-Saône*, 8 (1895–1901), 303–320, on pp. 10, 12; André Bourée, *La Chancellerie près le Parlement de Bourgogne* (Dijon, Bellais, 1927), pp. 253–254, 266; Roger de Lurion, *Notice sur la Chambre des comptes de Dôle* (Besançon, Jacquin, 1892), pp. 246, 257, 258, 279, 313; Alfred de Curzon, *La Chancellerie près le Parlement de Franche-Comté* (Paris, 1933; first published in *Mémoires de la Société d'Emulation du Doubs*, 1930–1932), p. 83.

The term "Burgundy" in this chapter refers generally to the area governed by the provincial Estates rather than that under the jurisdiction of the Parlement but is modified to exclude the *comté adjacent* of Bar-sur-Seine and to include the Mâconnais and is thereby made equivalent to the départements of Côte-d'Or and Saône-et-Loire together with the districts of Auxerre and Avallon.

10. In the eight sénéchaussées in Languedoc, there were 110 magistrates, of whom 15 were nobles (5 in the sénéchaussée of Toulouse, 4 in the sénéchaussée of Montpellier, and a scattering elsewhere). In the bailliage of Orléans, there were 16 magistrates, of whom 7 were nobles, and in the sénéchaussée of Lyon there were 22 magistrates of whom 12 were nobles. See the almanacs mentioned in the Appendix, below, and the

The Châtelet of Paris was the court in which magistrates were noblemen in the greatest numbers, and it represents an exception of a different kind. There, the class distinction corresponded approximately to the difference in professional rank between the principal judges and the king's counsel, on the one hand, and the councillors on the other. In 1768, three of the four presiding judges, the police magistrate, the king's proctor, and all four king's advocates were nobles; but only five of the councillors were nobles, although others were sons of holders of ennobling offices. In that year, a royal edict provided for ennoblement of magistrates in the Châtelet. Twenty years' service or death while in office would suffice for one of the principal judges or king's counsel; forty years' service, or twenty years' service followed by death while in office, were required for a councillor. Thus the edict registered existing distinctions. It does not seem to have wrought much change. In the years 1775–1788, one-third of the new councillors were already nobles before they entered office. For the majority of nobles, however, this office was an apprenticeship; for most of the commoners, it was a career. Half the noble councillors held office in the Châtelet for less than six years, while four-fifths of the commoners remained longer. Of the sixty-four councillors on the bench in 1790, only eight had entered office as nobles.[11]

In provincial towns, nobles were to be found especially in the présidial courts, primarily in the offices of chief judge of civil cases, secondarily in those of king's proctor. These were the offices that provided the widest opportunities for individual responsibility and the greatest freedom from subordination in

---

Catalogue by La Roque and Barthélemy: *Languedoc (généralité de Montpellier)*, pp. 5, 15–18, 23, 27; *Languedoc (généralité de Toulouse)*, pp. 5, 22, 24, 25; *Orléanais, pp.* 36, 39, 40, 42, 44; *Lyonnais,* pp. 6–11.

11. Réceptions au Châtelet (A.N., Y 1869); Liquidation des offices du Châtelet (A.N., D XVII 9, no. 126); *Almanach royal,* 1768–1790; Roton, *Les arrêts;* Bluche, *L'Origine des magistrats.*

the functioning of the courts. Yet for a noble even the office of chief civil judge in the sénéchaussée of Poitiers, a présidial court with a distinguished history, seemed hardly worth acquiring.[12] There, and in many other présidial courts, a chief judgeship had belonged to the same family for generations. Most commonly, although not in Poitiers, the family had meanwhile acquired nobility by holding some other office as well. To exercise the functions of the inherited chief judgeship was less troublesome than to try to overcome the general unwillingness of fellow noblemen to buy that expensive and unremunerative office. In 1789, there were ninety-nine chief civil judges in office (and four such offices vacant) in the présidial courts. Forty of these magistrates were noblemen.[13]

The line that separated the royal courts into two classes of judgeships was not an undeviating horizontal. Men not yet fully ennobled were admitted to 18 percent of the councillorships in the parlements. Noblemen occupied 40 percent of the chief civil judgeships in the présidial courts; smaller numbers of noblemen held lesser offices in présidial courts and a few of the principal offices in ordinary bailliages. But having noted

12. Angélique-Séraphime de Ferrières (Mme Lecomte de Médel), "Correspondance (1770–1789)," ed. Henri Carré, *Archives Historiques du Poitou*, 47, (1931), 1–166, on p. 135.

13. The names of 57 chief civil judges are conveniently given in the *Recueil de documents relatifs à la convocation des Etats Généraux de 1789*, ed. Armand Brette, 4 vols. (Paris, Imprimerie Nationale, 1894–1915), III and IV, in the comments on the respective présidial jurisdictions. The sources for the names of the other 42 are listed in the Appendix, *infra.*, notes. Those who were noblemen are indicated in the *Catalogue* by La Roque and Barthélemy: *Auvergne et Rouergue*, p. 23; *Bourgogne*, pp. 6, 11, 12; *Champagne*, pp. 22, 25, 29, 37, 39, 50; *Franche-Comté*, pp. 11, 13; *Isle de France*, p. 68; *Lyonnais*, p. 10; *Languedoc (généralité de Toulouse)*, p. 5; *Lorraine*, 1e livraison, p. 43; *Lorraine*, 2e livraison, p. 6; *Marche et Limousin*, pp. 12, 17, 30; *Normandie*, pp. 14, 32, 73, 87; *Orléanais*, p. 36; *Poitou*, p. 14; *Picardie*, p. 11; *Périgord, Aunis, Saintonge et Angoumois*, pp. 18, 31, 41; *Roussillon, Foix*, p. 19; *Touraine et Berry*, p. 19; *supplément*, p. 32; and by Arcelin, p. 310, and Jean Meyer, *La Noblesse bretonne au XVIIIe siècle* (Paris, S.E.V.P.E.N., 1966), pp. 301, 361.

these details, we should not let them obscure the dominant fact. For the great majority of royal magistrates, the line between nobles and commoners ran below the parlements and above the bailliages.

Whether its members originated as nobles or commoners, every occupational group had prerogatives that pertained to the occupation itself. Among the most significant of these were rights of precedence. The rank of every occupation in a town or city was visibly displayed in the processions that accompanied celebrations of thanksgiving and important events in the Christian calendar. These ceremonies were controlled by rules of precedence which gave rise, especially in the seventeenth century but also in the eighteenth century, to a mass of lawsuits. By the 1780's, merely to report the decisions seemed an endless task.[14] Such proceedings were characteristic of a monarchical and litigious society, just as competitive exhibitions of courtesy had been characteristic of the chivalrous company surrounding the late medieval dukes of Burgundy.[15]

In many lawsuits over precedence, one issue was the precise nature of the functions whose honorific value was being contested: how directly they had been delegated by the king, how closely they resembled acts that were essentially royal. The solution handed down on this issue sometimes helped to determine the powers and duties that would devolve on a single office or corps amid the loosely organized, ceaselessly shifting collection of groups which exercised public authority.[16] For example, the establishment of the présidial courts led, through

14. "We would never finish if we attempted to report all the decisions of the parlement or the [King's] council or the Grand Conseil concerning precedence." Jacques-Vincent Delacroix, "Préséance," *Encyclopédie méthodique: Jurisprudence*, ed. Lerasle, 8 vols. (Paris, 1782–1789), VI, 700–706, on p. 703.

15. Johan Huizinga, *The Waning of the Middle Ages*, transl. F. Hopman (London, Edward Arnold & Co., 1924), pp. 34–38.

16. This point is illustrated by Pierre Perrenet, "Préséances," *Mémoires de la Société pour l'Histoire du Droit et des Institutions des Anciens Pays Bourguignons, Comtois et Romands*, 3 (1936), 209-215.

a tangle of lawsuits and decisions, to the discovery of a distinction between the councillors in a présidial court and the councillors in a bailliage unadorned by présidial jurisdiction. The former were entitled to the qualification of *conseiller du roi,* because like a parlement they acted as a group, whose number and authority were fixed by particular legislation: "Les gens tenans le présidial." In a simple bailliage, the ordinary judges were conseillers not of the king but of the bailli or his lieutenant; hence a lawyer pleading a case there addressed himself to the presiding judge, who announced the court's decision in the singular: "M. le bailli ordonne."[17] From this distinction in turn arose a line of decisions giving precedence to the présidial courts but not to the simple bailliages in contests between judges and other officeholders.

Royal legislation seldom defined powers and duties in sufficient detail to foreclose every opportunity for this species of indirect aggrandisement. In reassigning public tasks, therefore, the central government initiated many contests over precedence. The transfer of certain judicial powers over the royal domain, from the bailliages to the bureaux des finances, was followed by a succession of lawsuits over precedence. In these struggles, the présidial courts were generally victorious during the 1680's, but the echoes continued to form part of the atmosphere in the eighteenth century.[18] Even more persistent were the contests between the judges and the mayors and town councillors of their localities. At almost any time between the middle of the sixteenth century and the end of the eighteenth century, several such lawsuits were pending. In the earlier part of the period, when the mayors were generally elected, there was a line of decisions holding that the présidial

17. Delacroix, "Préséance," p. 705.
18. Jean-Paul Charmeil, *Les Trésoriers de France à l'époque de la Fronde* (Paris, Editions A.&J. Picard, 1964), p. 208, comments on the conflicting treatises by Regnard de Gironcourt, a member of a bureau des finances, and Jousse, a judge in the présidial court at Orléans, published in 1776 and 1777, respectively.

courts, at least, had precedence.[19] Legislation of 1692 and 1702, which established the mayors as holders of royal offices sold by the crown, permitted the question to be reopened.[20] The town officials did not initiate all the lawsuits. In practice, they were often able to take advantage of their responsibility for the arrangements for ceremonial processions and their control over the town crier. The judges were quick to bring suit when the arrangements and announcements prevented their superior rank from being displayed.

Precedence was a representation of place in the order of public affairs. It could be asserted legitimately by judges only when wearing robes, by other officials only when bearing the distinctive marks of their duties; and it was a local right, confined to the town or the parishes where those duties were performed. A judicial decision concerning precedence was sometimes guided by reasonings of constitutional solemnity, and if these could be summarized in a familiar and sonorous Roman phrase, so much the better. Thus the precedence of the *robe* before the *épée,* although subject to various exceptions, was elevated into a principle: *Cedant arma togae.*[21] Rulings which gave precedence to laymen before clergymen, and to the holders of ennobling offices before nobles who held no office, were, as Delacroix noted, "in contradiction with the most strongly established opinions." Yet the right of precedence, diligently enforced as it was, affected public opinion regarding the status of occupations and was spread deliberately into circumstances that were not controlled by judicial decisions. This, too, is confirmed by Delacroix, indirectly, for he pointed out that precedence "cannot be demanded in private ceremonies where individuals are indiscriminately invited, such as

19. *Encyclopédie méthodique: Jurisprudence,* VI, 712.

20. *Répertoire universel et raisonné de jurisprudence,* ed. Joseph-Nicolas Guyot, 2nd ed., 17 vols. (Paris, 1784–1785), XI, 176–181.

21. Cicero, *De officiis,* I, 77. (This work was included in a selection for school use published in Paris in 1711 and reprinted in 1725 and 1744.)

marriage celebrations or burials."[22] Probably the public that had opinions on these matters regarded the magistrates of the royal bailliages as standing almost on the high level where the rules of precedence placed them. Tradition would support this view. In the seventeenth century, the magistrates occupied the first place in the provincial Third Estate.[23] Geographic differences were in this respect almost nonexistent. At Toulouse, at the end of the eighteenth century, the magistrates formed the occupation easiest to classify in a study of social stratification: they were at the pinnacle of the Third Estate.[24]

Recognition of the magistrates' elevated place in a social hierarchy did not exclude a feeling that their elaborate titles and honors were exaggerated. Such a feeling is perceptible in the joking salutations addressed to one of them, Rouget de Gourcez of Niort, by a man who had married one of his cousins and had become his friend, as well as a town councillor and intendant's subdelegate in nearby Saint-Maixent. Rouget de Gourcez's title was lieutenant genéral civil. In familiar letters, the subdelegate addressed him as "mon général" and "mon cher généralissime."[25] It was not difficult for a bailliage magistrate to attract the attention of gossips and critics like the royal prison warden's son in Reims, Hédoin, who served as a proctor's clerk, then a junior officer of dragoons, and ultimately as a judge in the tribunal du point d'honneur at Epernay. He disliked the meddlesome activity of the chief civil judge at Reims: "l'ubiquiste de toutes les affaires bonnes ou mauvaises";

22. "Préséance," pp. 702, 705.
23. Goubert, "Les Officiers royaux," pp. 58–62. Indeed, in the eighteenth century, the primacy of the bailliage magistrates seems even more definite, since they no longer maintained such close relations as Goubert found with the officeholders of the *élections*.
24. Pierre-Henri Thore, "Essai de classification des catégories sociales à l'intérieur du tiers état de Toulouse," 78⁰ Congrès National des Sociétés Savantes, Toulouse, 1953, *Actes*, pp. 149–165.
25. André Levieil, "Correspondance de Picoron de la Pergellerie avec Rouget de Gourcez," *Bulletin de la Société Historique et Scientifique des Deux-Sèvres*, 6 (1931–1934), 341–347.

on another occasion, "l'universel Lévesque de Pouilly." He had no admiration for the other judges at Reims, referring to one as "l'idiot" and to another as "ce singe de magistrat" and noting with scarcely concealed pleasure in 1788 that the bailliage of Reims was investigating to determine who had led a donkey onto the magistrates' bench and left it there.[26] Ridicule and hostility of this type are ordinarily directed toward socially prominent men, and they tend to confirm indirectly the elevated position of the bailliage magistrates, just as the tenacity of the mayors and town councillors and the Trésoriers de France, in disputes over precedence, tends to confirm it.

The magistrates of the bailliages clearly held a place of high honor in the bourgeoisie. In contrast, their economic rewards were small and are very difficult to estimate precisely. One reason for the difficulty is that part of their compensation was received collectively by a bailliage and then divided among the judges. Merely as a problem in accounting, calculation of a judge's professional income would be complicated; the paucity and the dispersal of sources of information reduce it to a matter of examples and tentative interpretation. As an investor in a royal office, a magistrate received interest, denominated *gages,* which had generally been fixed since the early seventeenth century at an annual rate of 3 percent, or less, on the investment. As a professional man rendering a service, a judge was paid by the parties to the disputes that he helped to decide. For taking part in the judgment of a case in which written pleadings were submitted, he received *épices;* for other kinds of work, especially fact-finding by interrogation or by inspection of a locale, he might receive *vacations.* Which types of cases entailed these fees, and how large they should be, were frequently disputed questions. The fees for a case were usually assessed by the presiding judge, sometimes by all the partici-

26. Joseph-Antoine Hédoin de Pons Ludon, "Journal," ed. Pol Gosset, *Travaux de l'Académie Nationale de Reims,* 151 (1936–1938), 20–132. The phrases quoted are from pp. 76, 106, 108, 111, 128, and 129.

pating judges, but when a judgment was appealed the fees might be revised by the court above. The matter was regulated by royal legislation, and complaints and revisions had gradually created additional rules. In the first place, judges were not entitled to collect fees for judgments by default, summary judgments, civil cases in which only the king's counsel was a party, or cases decided without written pleadings. These exclusions created an incentive for the judges in first instance to press every case into the most elaborate, time-consuming, and costly procedural framework. The remedy available to litigants was to accept default judgments wherever the outcome was reasonably predictable. As a result, not only did this rule deny the judges compensation for expeditious decisions, simply reached, but it also effectively limited the number of slow and complicated proceedings from which they could exact compensation. Secondly, the fees were supposed to be in proportion to the difficulty of the work and the number of sessions required to reach a decision, irrespective of the value in controversy and the wealth or standing of the parties. This principle constituted an invitation to aggrieved litigants to attack the assessments by the original judges, hence another incentive for appellate proceedings. The regulations concerning judges' fees therefore increased the volume of paper work in the administration of justice, the delays, and the costs.[27]

Judges' fees were a nuisance and sometimes a major obstacle to justice. If they had a compensating advantage, it did not consist in steady or generous payment of the judges for their work. Pagart d'Hermansart, a judge at Boulogne-sur-Mer in the years 1777–1789, received an average income from all his professional activity of 1,900 livres annually, which rose

27. An informative and extremely critical discussion of judges' fees appeared in the *Traité des droits, fonctions, franchises, exemptions, prérogatives et privilèges annexés en France à chaque dignité, à chaque office et à chaque état,* ed. Joseph-Nicolas Guyot and Philippe-Antoine Merlin, 4 vols. (Paris, 1786–1788), III, livre ii, pp. 140–166.

or fell by as much as 600 livres from year to year, according to his grandson.[28] With gages of 200 livres in addition, this income represented a rate of return averaging nearly 6 percent on his investment, which had amounted to 36,000 livres for the property rights in the office and the lawbooks of its previous holder. But the annual tax on the inheritability of the office and the capitation tax incurred by holding the title would make the net rate of return about 4½ percent. This was better than average for a judge in a bailliage. Not only was Pagart d'Hermansart the chief civil judge, he was also the only one in Boulogne able to conduct judicial business, since one judge was in failing health and the other was too old.

The number of judges in office was practically decisive for judicial incomes in almost every locality, for it had long been extremely difficult to expand the jurisdiction of a bailliage. The fragmentary information relating to the sénéchaussée of Poitiers, territorially one of the largest in the kingdom, suggests the importance of the relationship between the number of judges in office and their incomes. In the early years of the eighteenth century, the professional income of judges in Poitiers declined greatly. At the same time, the number of judges in office decreased from forty to twenty-two, as old judges died and their offices were not taken up. Between 1735 and 1760, the economic position of the court appears to have been partially retrieved. The number of judges thereafter remained stable. Still, 300 livres annually in the form of épices was a greater sum than any except perhaps the chief civil judge could hope to receive.[29] The conclusion that épices amounted

28. Emile Pagart d'Hermansart, "Note sur la valeur pécuniaire de la charge de lieutenant-général en la sénéchaussée à la fin du XVIIIe siècle," *Bulletin de la Société Académique de l'Arrondissement de Boulogne-sur-Mer*, 3 (1879–1884), 385–387.

29. For its civil judgments, the sénéchaussée of Poitiers collected épices amounting to an annual average of 220 to 240 livres for each judge between 1697 and 1707. Thereafter, the épices declined. In 1734, they averaged 100 livres each, for judges only half as numerous. Between

to no more than a few hundred livres annually for the busiest judges is reinforced by the accounts of the sénéchaussée at Moulins.[30] Indeed, a judge in the sénéchaussée at Riom remarked, in a letter to a colleague, that it was in the public interest for justice to be rendered by rich or well-to-do men, less susceptible than others to improper influences, better able to maintain the necessary dignity.[31] It is noteworthy that in the agitation of 1763 the présidial courts, although eager to obtain enlarged jurisdiction and new privileges, especially ennoblement through officeholding, did not press for increases in the fees they were permitted to collect.

The magistrates in the bailliages purchased the right to perform an especially honorable service. They paid a high price, in relation to the pecuniary rewards to be expected. Perhaps a better measure of the cost they sustained is to be found by comparing the capital invested in a judgeship and the judge's income from other sources. Neither sum is easy to determine. The purchase price of a judicial office was by no means the

---

1740 and 1757, a special account was kept for the épices collected by the lieutenant-général civil for those cases on which he served as *rapporteur*. The total recorded was 6,803 livres, of which he received 2,268 livres as rapporteur and 453 livres simply as a member of the court: altogether an annual average of 151 livres for him from those cases. (The chief civil judge was entitled to choose, by *préciput*, the cases on which to serve as rapporteur, and probably obtained a large proportion of all his épices from them.) In the same period, the *lieutenant particulier criminel* served as rapporteur for 33 criminal cases in 15 years, bringing in a total of 4,067 livres, an annual average of 271 livres to be divided among the judges participating in criminal judgments. Charles de Gennes, "Notice sur le présidial de Poitiers," *Mémoires de la Société des Antiquaires de l'Ouest*, 26 (1860–1861), 359–528, on pp. 444–445.

30. A.D. Allier, B 731.

31. Letter from Rollet d'Avaux to Chabrol, 24 July 1763, quoted by Edouard Everat, *La Sénéchaussée d'Auvergne et siège présidial de Riom au XVIII* siècle (Paris, 1886), p. 59. Of the judges in the Parlement of Paris, Bluche writes that they necessarily appeared rich because it was necessary for them to be rich (*Les Magistrats du Parlement de Paris*, p. 149); for the judges in the bailliages, it seems, a much smaller fortune was sufficient but it was even more necessary.

sole cost incurred in obtaining it.[32] Even a notarized contract of sale did not always state the purchase price itself accurately.[33] As for the determination of any person's income in the eighteenth century, the difficulties are well known: the crudeness of tax assessments, the exemption of the well-to-do (including royal judges) from important taxes, and the complexities in the interpretation of notaries' deeds.

The magistrates in the bailliages and sénéchaussées were not exempt from the *vingtième*, and no property-owner was exempt from the *contribution foncière* after 1790. But my attempts to locate the magistrates' tax assessments in these records, in Dijon, yielded very incomplete results, mainly, it would appear, because assessments for the vingtième in various localities are dispersed throughout an entire series of documents, and because the matrices for the rolls of the contribution foncière are largely missing. In any case, more weight can be placed on information derived from deeds drawn up by notaries. Usually, one signatory or another had an interest in accurate statement of the material facts. The purposes

32. Gabriel Lepointe, "L'Acquisition d'un office de magistrature judiciaire, au Mans, à la fin de l'ancien régime," *Province du Maine*, 2nd ser., 33 (1953), 196–209, examined in detail the process by which Ménard de la Groye secured his office of councillor in the sénéchaussée of Le Mans in 1768. Lepointe discovered in Ménard's papers a kind of handbook enumerating 25 steps from the purchase of property rights in such an office to installation on the bench. Lepointe also lists the costs of Ménard's office: 7,000 livres capital value; a gift to Ménard's predecessor worth 300 livres; a fee of 149 livres for issuance of royal letters granting the predecessor *emeritus* standing; cost of notarized documents for the acquisition of the office, 59 livres; and 35 other taxes, fees, and gratuities amounting in all to 2,291 livres. Ménard declared, a few years thereafter, that the annual revenue from the office was less than the annual tax on its inheritability.

33. Where the purchase price of an office was higher than the maximum allowed by the edict of February 1771, the contract of sale might understate the price in order to appear in conformity with the law. For what seems to be an example of this, see my note "Sur le prix des offices de judicature à la fin de l'ancien régime," *Revue d'Histoire Economique et Sociale*, 42 (1966), 192–196.

set forth in the document itself provide tests of the probable exactness or mere conventionality of the facts recited. And notarized documents are chronologically specific; indeed, one of their important functions was to fix a precise date for the obligations defined. This makes it indispensable for the historian to choose among the various points in a family's life cycle at which its wealth, incessantly changing, might be measured. For the question at hand, the most pertinent document is clearly the marriage contract, because a judicial office in a bailliage was acquired at the age of twenty-eight, on the average, hence about the time of marriage. The acquisition of office and the establishment of a new household were two aspects of the preservation, or improvement, of a family's position in the social order of a locality.

The marriage of Louis Mallet de Fois and Julie Babinet de Santilly, in Poitiers in 1787, exemplified a traditional ideal. Each was the child of a retired conseiller in the sénéchaussée of Poitiers and was provided with ample landed wealth by the terms of the marriage contract.[34] It specified that Mallet would receive from his father (a widower) landed property estimated at a total value of 34,600 livres. The principal element in this fortune was the estate of la Rondelle in the parish of Vouillé.[35] Including the house, barn, storehouses, wine cellars, and the meadows, vineyards, *métairies*, and rents that pertained to it, this property was valued at 30,000 livres, which implies that it produced an income of 1,500 livres a year. To this were added the household furnishings and the supplies on hand, together with the debts of the *métayers* and arrears of rents, evaluated at a total of only 600 livres because it was expected that the debts and arrears might be difficult to collect. Secondarily, there was the métairie of la Vouge, in the parish of Thurageau.[36] It was evaluated at 4,000 livres, indicating an income

34. Ms. minute, A.D. Vienne, E⁴/27–429 (17 March 1787).
35. Nineteen kilometers west-northwest of Poitiers.
36. Twenty-seven kilometers north-northwest of Poitiers.

of 200 livres a year. Finally, it was agreed that the young couple would live in Mallet's father's house in Poitiers, would be provided with food, fuel, a domestic servant, and a horse and would retain ownership of any furnishings they purchased, marking their linens with the letters M and B. In case they were compelled by incompatibility with Mallet's father, or any other reason, to move out, the latter undertook to pay them 1,000 livres annually during his lifetime, as an alternative equivalent to the specified living arrangements. In effect, Mallet was to be free to spend the income from the rural property, an income which was presumably more than one-and-one-half times as large as the annual sum required for the essential costs of his new household in town—and those costs were to be met independently.[37]

The fortune bestowed on the *demoiselle* Babinet appeared approximately equal to that of her future husband. Her mother (a widow) turned over all the rights and property to which she was entitled by succession from her father and his family in Poitou and her maternal relatives in Touraine. The capital value of this was estimated at a total of 40,000 livres, indicating an income of 2,000 livres annually. In addition, she received the house and estate of Chaumelonge, in the parish of Andillé.[38] This property was evaluated at only 4,000 livres net, because it was burdened with two twenty-year *rentes*, of 100 and 200 livres annually, due to other individuals, as well as a perpetual rente of 400 livres annually, due to her mother. From the property in Touraine, the bride was to pay her mother an additional 400 livres annually during the latter's lifetime, in lieu of *douaire*. The total value of the bride's marriage portion thus depended on how soon her mother's death extinguished obligations amounting to 800 livres annually. Most of the real

37. In addition, Mallet received the office of conseiller, evaluated at a low figure, 6,000 livres including the costs incurred five years previously when he became a judge.
38. Twelve kilometers south of Poitiers.

estate on the bride's side, as on the groom's, was reserved eventually to the family of origin; each contributed only 1,500 livres to the new household's community property. Yet the total landed wealth with which the couple began their married life—yielding a net annual income of 3,500 livres, according to their parents—remains the truest measure of their affluence.

The Mallet-Babinet contract was especially noted by an alert observer, the sister of the marquis de Ferrières, as "un très riche mariage dans la bourgeoisie."[39] The truth of her phrase is confirmed by comparison with five marriage contracts of judges holding the same kind of office in Poitiers in the years 1774–1786. Only the marriage of Faulcon (a friend of Mallet's since their school days) provided a similar economic basis for the new household.[40] In each of three other contracts,[41] the landed property, rentes, and cash bestowed on the bride and groom totalled 45,000 to 50,000 livres, indicating an annual income of 2,200 to 2,500 livres, which can be considered nearer normal for judges in Poitiers at the time of marriage.

It was possible to begin a judicial career there with much slenderer resources. This is exemplified by the marriage contract of Joseph Nicolas and Marie-Anne Durant de la Pastellière.[42] His father was a councillor in the sénéchaussée, her

39. Mme de Médel, "Correspondance," p. 119.

40. Ms. minute, A.D. Vienne, E⁴/13–190 (5 January 1783). The bride was promised a total of 40,000 livres; the groom declared that he would enter the marriage with all the property rights he had inherited from his father, notably the house, estate, and dependent *métairies* of la Grande Fenêtre in the parish of Biard (two kilometers west of Poitiers), but these were not evaluated in the contract.

41. Mss. minutes, A.D. Vienne, E⁴/27–387 (19 January 1774, Dutillet–*demoiselle* Dansays), E⁴/12–279 (4 April 1777, Rampillon–*demoiselle* Robert), and E⁴/21–43 (17 June 1781, Dansays–*demoiselle* Delavergne). In two of these, the groom received in addition an office of councillor: for Dutillet, it was evaluated at 8,000 livres; for his brother-in-law, Dansays, at 12,000 livres.

42. Ms. minute, A.D. Vienne, E⁴/12–297 (26 March 1786). From his

father was a king's advocate in the bureau des finances; both were dead at the time of the marriage. Altogether, Nicolas's financial resources amounted to a capital sum of 14,500 livres, and his annual income was presumably about 700 livres. The bride declared that she would bring to the marriage all her inherited property rights, but she did not trouble to specify them or to demonstrate, what was probably the fact, that they were greater than those of her future husband. Nicolas and his bride were better off than his father and mother had been at the time of their marriage, when each received 8,000 livres worth of real estate and household furnishings.[43] The Nicolas family was not experiencing an economic decline. Yet young Nicolas and his bride possessed only one-third to one-half as much income from landed property as some other recently married councillors his age.

These six councillors whose incomes can be estimated had obtained their offices at various times by inheritance or by purchase. The evaluations of the offices in their marriage contracts, which have been noted, varied widely and should perhaps be regarded as subject to modification depending on certain other provisions of the contracts. The market value of the office of councillor in the sénéchaussée of Poitiers can be independently determined. A careful purchaser in 1780 recorded in his journal the steps in the bargaining and the price

---

mother, Nicolas received a house in the *bourg* of Champigny-le-Sec, 25 kilometers northwest of Poitiers. With its lands and rents in money and kind, it was evaluated at 9,000 livres, indicating an annual income of 450 livres, and it constituted the main element of his fortune. He was also to receive furnishings, firewood, and agricultural implements estimated to be worth 1,500 livres, and the rents due from the tenants of two houses in Poitiers totalling 150 livres annually. From his uncle, a canon of the collegiate church of Saint-Hilaire-le-Grand in Poitiers, he received a gift of 1,000 livres. In addition, he received the office of councillor which had been held by his father and which was evaluated at 12,000 livres.

43. Ms. minute, A.D. Vienne, E⁴/27–301 (10 August 1752).

he was to pay: 10,840 livres.[44] Doubtless this price was higher than would be usual because the buyer came from a family never before represented among the magistrates and because the seller was reluctant. Considering 9,500 livres as a more normal price, and comparing this with the income to be received by the husband in accordance with a typical marriage contract, we may conclude that the office of councillor in Poitiers ordinarily represented about eight years' income from other sources (but might represent as little as five years' or as much as fourteen years' income) to those who held the office.

In smaller and less important courts, judicial office was less expensive. A judge's other property, too, was lower in value, but not always very much lower. An advantageous marriage might suffice to put a small-town judge on the same economic level as a judge in a provincial capital. An example is provided by the marriage contract of a future revolutionary politician and imperial prefect, Cochon de Lapparent.[45] His office of

44. Simon-Pierre Coutineau, ms. journal, entry dated 10 June 1780. He had decided to buy an office of conseiller two years before, had attempted to negotiate with an officeholder early in 1780 but had lost hope of reaching agreement with him. Then, Coutineau wrote, another councillor, Venault, "se décida à vendre parce qu'il n'avait pas payé le centième denier qui se trouvait monter à 960 livres. Il paraît plus traitable, mais comme ce n'était qu'à la solicitation de sa famille qu'il s'en défaisait il n'y eut point de délais qu'il ne demanda pour se décider. Il prit le parti d'augmenter son office de 15 louis, qu'il réduisit avec beaucoup de peine à 10 [louis = 200 livres] et nous terminâmes le sujet à 8 heures du soir à raison de 10,840 livres, savoir, 9,840 livres que je lui payait et 1,000 livres que je réservai pour payer les 9 années de centième denier qu'il devait." The preceding year, another purchaser, Babinet (son and great-grandson of councillors), had paid 8,600 livres for a councillor's office and 3,000 livres in fees and gratuities for the issuance of documents and the costs of formal installation, according to his great-nephew, Charles Babinet, "Le Présidial de Poitiers, son personnel de 1551 à 1790," *Mémoires de la Société des Antiquaires de l'Ouest*, 2nd ser., 25 (1901), 151–341, on p. 296.

45. Ms. minute, A.D. Vendée, III E, étude 8 (19 April 1774), a document not mentioned by Paul Boucher in *Charles Cochon de Lapparent, Conventionnel, Ministre de la Police, Préfet de l'Empire* (Paris, Editions A.&J. Picard, 1969). The contract specified that neither the bride nor the

councillor in the sénéchaussée of Fontenay-le-Comte counted as part of his marriage portion at its purchase price of 3,000 livres. In addition, his father, a widower who was the seigneurial judge at Champdeniers, promised to pay him 600 livres annually until the time when he would turn over to him property evaluated at 12,000 livres. Cochon's judicial office represented five years' income to him from all his other property. His bride, Anne-Henriette-Félicité Queré, daughter of the king's proctor in the municipality of Fontenay-le-Comte, received an advance against her inheritance consisting of the sum of 1,200 livres and an annual income of 1,000 livres. The economic position of the new Cochon household was thus closely comparable to that of Nicolas and his wife in Poitiers twelve years later.

This sampling of marriage contracts of judges in Poitou is susceptible of a limited comparison with others drawn up elsewhere. In the contract of marriage, various future contingencies were envisaged: the rights of inheritance from parents might or might not have been conferred in their entirety; the death of one spouse might or might not permit the other to invoke certain clauses (*gain de survie* with or without *préciput, douaire préfix, renonciation à la communauté*); above all, the contract balanced the economic independence of the new conjugal community against the reserved property rights of the parents, brothers, and sisters of each spouse. In these matters, the *coutume* (or some variant of Roman law) influenced the choices of the contracting parties.[46] The total

---

groom would have the freedom (usual under the coutume of Poitou) to dispose by testament of one-third of the assets provided by his or her family; instead, all except the community property was to revert to the family of origin. It was primarily the bride's family that was protected by this exceptional arrangement.

46. The choice of contractual provisions was not inflexibly determined. See Jacques Lelièvre, *La Pratique des contrats de mariage chez les notaires au Châtelet de Paris de 1769 à 1804* (Paris, Editions Cujas, 1959), and Georges Chevrier, "Le Régime matrimonial en Mâcon-

economic value of two contracts drawn up under different coutumes can therefore be compared only by an elaborate analysis. But the immediate significance of the marriage contract was that it provided for the new household's income during at least the first few years of marriage. These arrangements can reveal something of the general nature and range of magistrates' fortunes at the beginning of the judicial career.

The marriage contracts of judges in the bailliage and présidial court of Bourges justify conclusions similar to those derived from Poitiers. For a young man holding the office of councillor and recently married, annual income between 2,200 and 2,500 livres was normal a decade before the Revolution. The range of incomes among councillors was considerable, the highest income being nearly three times as great as the lowest. The predominance of rural land and local rentes among the assets of young councillors and their brides is notable. Urban real estate was occasionally an income-producing asset, sometimes, if the new couple was not to begin by residing in one or the other parental household (as for Grandjean de la Coudraye), a dwelling. A man holding one of the principal judgeships in a bailliage ordinarily received a greater income than a councillor at the time of his marriage. At Bourges in 1786, the associate chief civil judge, Rapin, was promised 500 livres from rural land and income of 2,500 livres from his father, former comptroller in the local court of coinage (*siège de la monnaie*). His bride, demoiselle Sapiens, daughter of a councillor in the tax court (*élection*), was to receive an income almost as large (from rural land, 917 livres; from urban real estate, 190 livres; from rentes, 312 livres and two hens; and directly from her parents, 1,379 livres). The combined total of 5,798 livres income does not include whatever Rapin would obtain from his office, evaluated at 15,000 livres and

nais aux XVII⁰ et XVIII⁰ siècles," *Mémoires de la Société pour l'Histoire du Droit et des Institutions des Anciens Pays Bourguignons, Comtois et Romands,* 25 (1964), 77–95.

Table 4. Annual Incomes, in Livres, Provided in Marriage Contracts of Four Councillors in the Bailliage of Bourges, 1775–1781.

Names of groom and bride	Domaine(s) et terres	Maison(s) à Bourges (5% of valuation)	Rente(s)	Cash (5% of total)	Totals	
Grandjean	54	500	150	21	725	2,919
Bonnardet[a]	1,086	395	209	504	2,194	
Brisson	790	0	10	0	800	1,100
Labbé[b]	300	0	0	0	300	
Ragu	398	0	390	38	826	2,688
Delavarenne[c]	1,862	0	0	0	1,862	
De Beauvoir	900	80	775	0	1,755	2,555
Albert[d]	0	0	800	0	800	
Averages { groom	535	145	331	15	1,026	2,315
{ bride	812	99	252	126	1,289	
{ total	1,347	244	583	141		

[a] Ms. minute, A.D. Cher, E 8060 (12 April 1776). Grandjean's father, a *marchand de draps et soie*, and mother were both living; in addition to the sources of income specified, they bestowed on him the office of councillor, valued at 5,500 livres. Demoiselle Bonnardet's father, seigneur of la Planche, Presly, Dournon, Hissy, and other places, was dead. She received, in addition to the income and cash specified, assets totalling 14,548 livres (tenants' debts, arrears of rentes, and promissory notes amounting to 9,866 livres, livestock valued at 3,631 livres, and household furnishings valued at 1,050 livres).

[b] Ms. minute, A.D. Cher, E 6818 (21 October 1776). Both Brisson's father, a professor in the faculty of medicine of Bourges, and demoiselle Labbé's father were dead. The contract concluded: "lesquelles dots ci-dessus sont tous les biens que les dits futurs possèdent actuellement."

[c] Ms. minute, A.D. Cher, E 2813 (22 May 1781). The parents of both were living. Ragu received, in addition to the income and cash specified, the office of councillor, valued at 3,000 livres, and livestock valued at 500 livres. Demoiselle Delavarenne received, in addition, livestock valued at 2,760 livres and the promise that she would inherit real estate valued at 10,000 livres from her aunts.

given to him by the terms of the contract.[47] He began his judicial career with twice the initial income of the most well-to-do councillor on the same bench.

At Auxerre, in an earlier period, the range of incomes among magistrates beginning their careers in different offices was a little narrower. With its wheat and white wine, Auxerre was generally a wealthier locality than Poitiers or Bourges. It is therefore not surprising that, even before the rise in agricultural prices of the 1770's, the least well-to-do councillor concerning whom information is available was better off than his counterparts in Poitiers and Bourges. Among the magistrates at Auxerre, rural property (including vineyards) was important but constituted a smaller proportion of total assets, particularly those contributed by the bride's family, than at Bourges. On the other hand, rentes constituted a larger proportion of the magistrates' assets at Auxerre and were not purely local investments: Housset de Champton held one, of 10,000 livres, on the Clergy of France, and Mme Grasset had inherited seven *reconnaissances* totalling 48,000 livres issued by the colony of Canada. These details modify only slightly the broader conclusions. As was true of the bailliage magistrates in the seventeenth century, the composition of their incomes reveals them as exceedingly careful proprietors of land and circumspect lenders of money, for whom judicial office was in economic terms a secondary investment.[48] In the second half of the eighteenth century, at the beginning of a career in a présidial court, an ordinary income for a councillor would be between 2,200 and 2,900 livres. A high income, characteristic of one of the principal judges or the king's proctor, would approach 6,000 livres.

In the light of these conclusions, the economic position of young Jean-Charles Danse, at his installation as a councillor in the bailliage and présidial court of Beauvais in 1787, ap-

---

47. Ms. minute, A.D. Cher, E 8621 (12 March 1786).
48. Goubert, "Les Officiers royaux," p. 66.

Table 5. Annual Incomes, in Livres, Provided in Marriage Contracts
of Five Magistrates in Auxerre, 1761–1774.

Names of groom and bride	Domaine(s), labourage(s)	Maison(s) à Auxerre (5% of valuation)	Vignes	Rentes	Totals	
Hay	45	0	95	380	520	1,690
Villetard[a]	233	40	301	596	1,170	
Grasset	900	0	0	150	1,050	5,609
Imbert[b]	0	839	0	3,720	4,559	
Housset	40	0	60	2,392	2,492	3,758
Baudesson[c]	250	0	267	749	1,266	
Martineau	1,550	0	0	0	1,550	3,020
Disson[d]	446	0	396	628	1,470	
Robinet	415	0	130	860	1,405	3,997
Despatys[e]	0	0	0	2,592	2,592	
Averages { groom	590	0	57	757	1,404	3,616
bride	186	176	193	1,657	2,212	
total	776	176	250	2,414		

[a] Ms. minute, A.D. Yonne, étude Guimard, liasse 270 (11 January 1761). The parents of both were living. In addition to the income specified, Hay received the office of *conseiller sur le fait des tailles*, evaluated at 11,600 livres. Demoiselle Villetard was promised, in addition, 4,938 livres in cash and *lettres de change* to be paid within one year. (This and the other contracts represented in this table were governed by the coutume of Auxerre.)

[b] Ms. minute, A.D. Yonne, étude Guimard, liasse 176 (14 February 1767). The father of each was dead. In addition to the income specified, Grasset received books valued at 1,500 livres and the office of

procureur du roi, valued at 30,000 livres. (Twelve years later, when he sold the office, he was paid 30,600 livres for it by his successor, Rémond, according to the inventory postmortem of Grasset's personal property: étude Guimard, liasse 293, December 1783.) Demoiselle Imbert's father had been *trésorier principal* of Canada; of her income, 1,920 livres consisted of interest on *reconnaissances* issued by the colony. She received, in addition to income, a trousseau valued at 5,697 livres and household furnishings valued at 2,131 livres.

[c] Ms. minute, A.D. Yonne, étude Guimard, liasse 277 (16 September 1768). Housset's parents were not mentioned; his uncles were present. In addition to the income specified, he brought to the marriage the office of lieutenant particulier civil, evaluated at 16,000 livres, and cash and arrears of rentes totalling 3,000 livres. Demoiselle Baudesson's father, who was the mayor of Auxerre, bestowed on her, in addition to the income specified, a trousseau valued at 3,000 livres and arrears of rentes totalling 1,670 livres.

[d] Ms. minute, A.D. Yonne, étude Guimard, liasse 283 (6 November 1774). Martineau's father was dead. In addition to the income specified, he received, from his father's succession, the office of *avocat du roi*, valued at 5,000 livres, and his books and desk valued altogether at 1,200 livres. (Five years later, he acquired the office of chief criminal judge.) Demoiselle Disson received, in addition, household linens valued at 1,500 livres.

[e] Ms. minute, A.D. Yonne, étude Guimard, liasse 283 (29 December 1774). Robinet received from his parents the office, evaluated at 11,000 livres, of *commissaire des gardes et suisses* in the service of the comte de Provence; later he was to succeed his father as conseiller in the bailliage and as proprietor of the domain of Pontagny (evaluated in this marriage contract at 15,000 livres). Demoiselle Despatys's father, former mayor of Clamecy, was dead. Of her income, 2,300 livres consisted of the interest on property to be transferred to her in a future settlement of her father's and mother's successions.

pears exceptional. It is true that his parents and then his grandfather had died, leaving him the town's finest fortune, whose history has been reconstructed with an appropriate wealth of detail.[49] His bride brought 80,000 livres, and he contributed 227,000 livres to the community property, figures which would indicate a joint annual income in excess of 11,000 livres, nearly triple that of the wealthiest councillor entering the bailliage of Auxerre in the 1770's.

The economic position of bailliage magistrates at the time of marriage can be compared with that of other occupational categories, thanks to the recent statistical work of historians on marriage contracts. For this purpose, it is necessary to employ the measure they have utilized, despite its merely approximate character: the combined total assets contributed to each marriage in behalf of the groom and the bride. This sum is discoverable in the *enregistrements* of marriage contracts of nineteen magistrates in Burgundy in the decade before 1789, all marrying for the first time at the ages of twenty-six to thirty-four years. (That is 15 percent of all the magistrates then in office in Burgundy in the bailliages other than Auxerre.) The total value of assets in these contracts averaged 82,623 livres. Two-thirds of the contracts specified total assets between 35,000 and 110,000 livres and were fairly evenly distributed between those two figures.

A generation earlier, in Paris, less than 3 percent of all marriage contracts drawn up in the year 1749 involved assets totalling more than 100,000 livres. Less than 5 percent of all marriage contracts involved assets totalling 30,000 to 100,000

49. Pierre Goubert, *Familles marchandes sous l'ancien régime: les Danse et les Motte, de Beauvais* (Paris, S.E.V.P.E.N., 1959); for "the richest of the Danse," see p. 161. Another comparison (in the inverse sense): the estimates of the tax assessing authority at Toul, the interim commission of the provincial assembly, may have understated the annual incomes of 10 of the 13 magistrates there, since they averaged 1,015 livres, and ranged from 600 to 2,000 livres. Robert Laurent, "La Fortune des privilégiés du bailliage de Toul en 1789," *Annales Historiques de la Révolution Française*, 21 (1949), 340–345.

Table 6. Assets Bestowed in Marriage Contracts of
Nineteen Magistrates in Burgundy, 1779–1788.

Magistrate's title, location of bailliage, date	Office (if included) valued at	Groom's other property	Bride's property	Combined total
ief civil judge[a]				
Auxonne, 1780	—	32,000	20,000	52,000
Montcenis, 1787	—	80,000	28,000	108,000
Avallon, 1788	22,500	7,500	14,000	44,000
ief criminal judge[b]				
Mâcon, 1782	—	92,000	52,000	144,000
Semur-en-Auxois, 1783	3,000	33,000	21,500	57,500
Chalon-sur-Saône, 1785	—	Unspecified	35,000	—
sociate chief judge[c]				
Châtillon-sur-Seine, 1784	—	40,800	41,017	81,817
Dijon, 1784	10,700	11,300	25,000	47,000
uncillor[d]				
Mâcon, 1782	—	50,000	44,000	94,000
Mâcon, 1783	10,000	60,000	70,000	140,000
Dijon, 1783	—	25,000	50,000	75,000
Beaune, 1784	—	Unspecified	25,000	—
Beaune, 1784	3,000	29,000	33,880	65,880
ng's proctor[e]				
Châtillon-sur-Seine, 1779	15,000	12,000	30,000	57,000
Avallon, 1780	—	20,000	17,000	37,000
Autun, 1787	—	85,000	63,000	148,000
ng's advocate[f]				
Mâcon, 1784	12,000	75,000	53,000	140,000
Châtillon-sur-Seine, 1785	12,000	42,000	41,000	95,000
Auxonne, 1786	3,000	3,600	11,800	18,400

[a] A.D. Côte-d'Or, C 8782 (19 December 1780), C 8798 (15 February 1787); D. Yonne, C 743 (6 May 1788). (None of these was a présidial court.)
[b] A.D. Saône-et-Loire, C 3049 (19 March 1782); A.D. Côte-d'Or, C 8788 (19 nuary 1783); A.D. Saône-et-Loire, C 1617 (26 January 1785). (All were présidial urts.)
[c] A.D. Côte-d'Or, C 8441 (enregistrement, 31 October 1784), E 868 (ms. grosse, December 1784, Fyot family papers). (Both were présidial courts.)
[d] A.D. Saône-et-Loire, C 3049 (7 October 1782), C 3050 (17 January 1783, nership of the office of councillor was bestowed on the bride by her father— e unique example of this I encountered); A.D. Côte-d'Or, C 8788 (11 February 83); A.D. Saône-et-Loire, C 1000 (14 June 1784), C 1001 (17 September 1784). eaune was not a présidial court.)
[e] A.D. Côte-d'Or, C 8434 (14 June 1779); A.D. Yonne, C 736 (3 April 1780);). Saône-et-Loire, C 1003 (19 April 1787). (Avallon was not a présidial court.)
[f] A.D. Saône-et-Loire, C 3053 (12 October 1784); A.D. Côte-d'Or, C 8442 (3 tober 1785), C 8000 (17 July 1786). (Auxonne was not a présidial court.)

livres. In this second category of wealthy new households, various occupations were represented. The richest of the *maîtres-marchands* constituted 30 percent of these households. Some of the wealthier holders of offices in the royal judiciary or administration constituted 20 percent. Commoners practicing no occupation, some described as "bourgeois," constituted 19 percent, and unusually well-to-do members of the liberal professions, 10 percent. Nobles, of median economic position within their class, formed 13 percent of these marriages.[50] In Dijon, at the same time, the economic categories defined by marriage contracts were far less heterogeneous. Less than 4 percent of all the contracts drawn up in the year 1748 involved assets totalling more than 100,000 livres, and these were exclusively for marriages of nobles. Only one noble's contract involved assets totalling less than 100,000 livres (and it was worth more than 50,000 livres). Only three bourgeois had assets totalling more than 20,000 livres (and each was worth less than 50,000 livres). Eighty-five percent of the merchants and bourgeois possessed total assets of less than 20,000 livres. Thus, in Dijon, a generation before the Revolution, the statistics of marriage contracts reveal a hiatus rather than an overlap between the economic position of the commercial bourgeoisie and that of the nobility.[51] It was this space which might have been occupied by magistrates in the bailliages if any had married in Dijon in 1748. In interpreting these figures, it is necessary to recall that agricultural prices and land values rose considerably after the middle of the eighteenth century. Yet it seems still true at the end of the eighteenth century that most bailliage magistrates were in the

50. Adeline Daumard and François Furet, *Structures et relations sociales à Paris au milieu du XVIII* siècle (Paris, Librairie Armand Colin, 1961), p. 19, table analyzing a total of 2,002 marriage contracts.

51. Maurice Garden, "Niveaux de fortune à Dijon au milieu du XVIII* siècle," *Cahiers d'Histoire,* 9 (1964), 217–260, on p. 227, table analyzing a total of 165 marriage contracts.

wealthiest part of the bourgeoisie and were comparable with the middle economic strata of the nobility.

The magistrates of the bailliages did not constitute a single economic category defined by either freedom from anxiety, or inability to acquire riches. An impression of a range of wealth could have been derived cumulatively from the marriage contracts of judges in Poitou in 1774–1787, at Bourges in 1775–1781, and at Auxerre in 1761–1774. The marriages of magistrates in the rest of Burgundy, in 1779–1788, enable us to confirm and extend this as a conclusion. The range there was from 18,400 to 148,000 livres in total assets at marriage: the king's proctor in Autun had a fortune eight times as large as did the king's advocate in Auxonne at the same stage of life (and practically the same age, since the former was thirty and the latter twenty-eight). The economic contrasts within the judicial profession can be explained in part by the differences in power and prestige between a présidial court like the one at Autun and a simple bailliage, like the one at Auxonne, little more than a prévôté. In effect, the marriage contracts reveal two overlapping ranges of wealth, one for the présidial courts, and another for the simple bailliages. In one, the figures, representing one-sixth of all the présidial magistrates in office, indicate average total assets at marriage of 98,120 livres, with a range from 47,000 to 148,000 livres. In the other, the figures represent one-eighth of all the magistrates in office in the simple bailliages, and indicate average total assets of 54,213 livres, with a range from 18,400 to 108,000 livres. The two overlapping ranges of wealth are still fairly wide.[52] To them might

52. In the bailliages without présidial jurisdiction, the difference between the wealthiest and the poorest magistrates appears extremely great because of the chances of documentation. The wealthiest magistrate discovered in the simple bailliages was the chief justice at Montcenis, whose father, as *seigneur engagiste* of the royal barony of Montcenis, was to receive a rente of 18,000 livres annually on his lease of the mine of Montcenis to Perier, Bettinger & Cie., under an agreement

be added a third range of wealth overlapping with that of the judges in the bailliages. The magistrates in the Parlement of Burgundy in this period, according to gossip in Dijon, married demoiselles whose fortunes varied from 30,000 to 260,000 livres.[53] A bailliage judge's bride brought a fortune, on the average, in excess of 35,000, and might possess as much as 70,000 livres. As in the parlements, the nonpecuniary benefits of the judgeships in the bailliages attracted some young men who could scarcely afford to own them and continued to attract others whose wealth and prospects could have supported more costly offices.

The royal judiciary, in the bailliages as well as in the parlements, represented sufficient distinction to serve as one of those fixed points in a social hierarchy that could sustain a positive belief in stability from generation to generation. In Moulins, the associate chief civil judge, Vernin, was the son, grandson, and great-grandson of holders of the same office, and his great-great-great-grandfather had been king's proctor, under Louis XIII, in the same sénéchaussée.[54] It would be possible to bring forward examples of judicial families whose establishment in their positions was as antique as that of the Bourbon monarchs in theirs. The marquis de Roux, with his sympathetic comprehension of the ancien régime, wrote that in the proof of long maintenance of a standing rigorously defined and carefully differentiated there stood revealed the social ideal of old Poitou, "épris de durée et de hierarchie minuti-

of 10 May 1786 [Charles Ballot, "La Révolution technique et les débuts de la grande exploitation dans la métallurgie française. L'introduction de la fonte au coke en France et la fondation du Creusot," *Revue d'Histoire Economique et Sociale,* 5 (1912), 29–62, on p. 49]. On the other hand, the chief civil judges of the présidial courts in Burgundy are not represented in the marriage contracts analyzed here.

53. Albert Colombet, *Les Parlementaires bourguignons à la fin du XVIIIᵉ siècle* (Dijon, chez l'auteur, 1937), pp. 73–74.

54. André Delavenne, *Recueil généalogique de la bourgeoisie ancienne,* 2 vols. (Paris, Société du Grand Armorial de France, 1954–1955), I, 431–432.

euse."[55] But the ideal was embodied by a very small minority of the magistrates in the bailliages at the end of the eighteenth century.

In Poitou, in 1788, there were 96 judges and king's counsel in office: the fathers of 23 had held the same offices, and the fathers of 4 others had held other offices in the same sénéchaussées.[56] Thus 72 percent were newcomers to the ordinary royal judiciary in Poitou. Only 3 magistrates represented lineages of long distinction.[57] At Poitiers, the chief civil judge's father was the fourth successive chief criminal judge in a direct line descended from a councillor in the Parlement of Brittany under Henri IV and, further back, from Robert Irland, a Scot who settled in Poitiers before 1500 and was a celebrated professor of law in the first half of the sixteenth century. The king's proctor's father was the fourth king's advocate in a direct line, the first having been Jean Filleau, simultaneously a professor of law and commentator on the coutume, in the last decade of Louis XIII's reign. At Civray, the chief civil judge, Fradin, was the fifth in succession of his family to hold the office since the time of Louis XIII, and was descended from a fifteenth-century mayor of Saint-Jean-d'Angély.

In Burgundy, in 1788, there were 130 judges and king's counsel in office: the fathers of 23 had held the same offices, the fathers of 6 had held lesser offices in the same bailliages,

55. Marie de Roux, *La Révolution à Poitiers et dans la Vienne* (Poitiers, 1910, as *Mémoires de la Société des Antiquaires de l'Ouest*, 3rd ser., 4), p. 28.

56. Beauchet-Filleau, *Dictionnaire*, I, 345, 520, 608, 688, 708; II, 208, 328, 362; III, 53, 251, 558; IV, 100, 239; Babinet, "Le Présidial de Poitiers, son personnel," pp. 287–299; parish registers, Loudun (Saint-Pierre-du-Marché), baptism 21 January 1752, Montmorillon, baptism 16 April 1741; *lettres de provisions*, for Saint-Maixent, 27 June 1787 (A.N., V¹ 529); marriage contracts, Fontenay-le-Comte, 16 May 1775 (A.D. Vendée, III E, étude 2) and Montmorillon, 25 January 1790 (A.D. Vienne, dépôt 129, no. 137).

57. Beauchet-Filleau, *Dictionnaire*, III, 428–433, 557–558; V, 134–138.

and the fathers of 6 others had held greater offices in the same bailliages.[58] Altogether, 73 percent were newcomers to the ordinary royal judiciary in Burgundy. The most distinguished lineage was that of Marie d'Avigneau, chief civil judge at Auxerre, the fourth of his family to hold the office since their ennoblement, in 1660, by letters patent.[59]

The magistrates whose fathers had not been magistrates were newcomers in only a limited sense. Most came from landowning families which regarded university training in law as the usual higher education even for young men who might subsequently enter the priesthood. Their economic and intellectual experience was already similar to that of the families represented in the royal judiciary. Some of the fathers of the new magistrates had themselves exercised other official or professional occupations. The greater bailliages with présidial

58. The principal sources for these figures are minutes of *lettres de provisions*, A.N., series V¹: for Auxerre, cartons 362 (23 September 1750), 384 (5 March 1755), 430 (15 January 1766), 440 (13 July 1768), 478 (18 December 1776), 484 (20 August 1777), 486 (15 January 1777), 500 (23 February 1780), and 519 (6 April 1785); for Châtillon-sur-Seine, 508 (13 March 1782) and 511 (29 January 1783); for Saulieu, 425 (27 May 1765); for Nuits, 526 (23 August 1786); for Beaune, 519 (25 May 1785); for Saint-Jean-de Losne, 429 (24 April 1765); for Autun, 427 (5 June 1765) and 430 (2 July 1766); for Montcenis, 519 (22 June 1785); for Bourbon-Lancy, 440 (23 June 1768); for Charolles, 515 (11 February 1784); for Chalon-sur-Saône, 335 (13 August 1743) and 529 (15 November 1787); for Mâcon, 423 (1 August 1764) and 516 (15 December 1784). Not all such documents mentioned it when the subject had been preceded in office by his father; the following auxiliary sources were used here: marriage contracts, A.D. Yonne, étude Guimard, 3 January 1758, and enregistrements in C 730 (26 September 1776) and C 743 (6 May 1788); A.D. Côte-d'Or, C 8445 (19 February 1790); A.D. Saône-et-Loire, C 955 (7 September 1761) and C 3053 (12 October 1784); parish registers, Dijon (Notre-Dame), baptism 8 June 1733; Chalon-sur-Saône (Saint-Vincent), baptism 24 January 1761; Mâcon (Saint-Pierre), baptism 7 July 1757, marriage 22 July 1788, burial 1 November 1791; also, Laroche, "Le Bailliage de Charolais," *Annales de Bourgogne*, 5 (1933); Boussand, "Notes de la famille Perret," *Bulletin de la Société d'Etudes du Brionnais*, 2 (1932); and Bourée, *La Chancellerie*, p. 79.

59. Bourée, *La Chancellerie*, p. 254.

Table 7. Occupations of Fathers of the Magistrates
in Office in the Sénéchaussée of Poitiers in 1788.

Occupation	Number
Judiciary and law	
Same office	6
(one of these also held office simultaneously in the bureau des finances of Poitiers)	
Lesser office in the sénéchaussée	1
Advocate practicing before the sénéchausée	1
Finance	
Comptroller of finances for the généralité	1
Trésorier de France in the bureau des finances	1
(also held office simultaneously in the sénéchaussée)	
Collector of *décimes* for the diocese	1
Other occupations	
Subdelegate at Melle for the intendant of Poitou	1
Valet de chambre ordinaire et gouverneur des pages de la chambre du roi, in Versailles	1
Docteur-régent in the faculty of medicine, Poitiers	1
Imprimeur and *juge consul,* in Poitiers	1
Undetermined	5
Total	20

Sources: Marriage contracts, A.D. Vienne, E⁴/27–313 (6 June 1748), E⁴/27–384 (11 December 1771), E⁴/27–287 (19 January 1774), E⁴/12–279 (7 April 1777); Beauchet-Filleau, *Dictionnaire*, II, 712; III, 352.

jurisdiction attracted recruits from families in a number of occupations. At Poitiers, the occupations of the fathers of newcomers were various: law practice, medicine, publishing, and royal and ecclesiastical finance were included; royal administration was represented by an intendant's subdelegate in an agricultural market town, the elaborate hierarchy around the throne by the governor of the pages in the king's chamber. All the magistrates, except one king's advocate who came from Limoges, were members of notable families of Poitou.

In the other eight courts in Poitou, the occupations of the magistrates' fathers were less varied and less distinguished. Of the seventy-six magistrates in those courts in 1788, twenty were sons of magistrates. Fifteen were sons of practitioners of another occupation in the judiciary or the law; seven advocates, six judges or attorneys holding office in seigneurial courts, two notaries. Four magistrates were sons of officeholders in special royal tribunals: the élection of Châtellerault, the *grenier à sel* of Loudun, and the *maîtrise des eaux et forêts* of Niort. Many other magistrates' fathers were neither officeholders nor professional practitioners but simply landed proprietors. Still more than in Poitiers, the continuation of families in judicial offices was characteristic of a minority, and a large influx of families was moving upward within the legal and officeholding bourgeoisie or adding the public dignity of magistrates to the private capacity of notable landowners.[60]

In Burgundy, a sharp contrast between the bailliages of Auxerre and Dijon was manifest in the origins of their magistrates. At Auxerre, almost half the magistrates were sons of magistrates in the bailliage. More than one-third were grandsons of magistrates in the bailliage. Not only was the chief civil judge a fourth-generation noble, but four other magistrates were sons of king's secretaries ennobled simply upon certification of twenty years' incumbency or death while holding office. The bailliage of Auxerre was unusual for the wealth that enabled several magistrates' families to purchase costly ennobling offices and for their persistence in Auxerre while advancing toward membership in the local nobility. The magistrates in the bailliage of Auxerre occupied a local peak; those in the bailliage of Dijon stood on a stepping-stone. The councillor Petitot, son of a widely known king's proctor in the bailliage, alone represented continuity from the previous generation. Only three other magistrates' fathers were trained in

60. Marriage contracts, Fontenay-le-Comte, A.D. Vendée, III E, étude 8 (19 April 1774, 23 January 1780, and 24 November 1789); parish registers, baptisms, Civray, 20 January 1749, Loudun (Saint-Pierre-du-Marché), 31 October 1737, 31 August 1742, 20 September 1750, 19 August 1754; Beauchet-Filleau, *Dictionnaire*, I, 476, 725; II, 444, 740; III, 185, 244, 265, 427; IV, 475, 741; V, 111.

Table 8. Occupations of Fathers of the Magistrates
in Office in the Bailliage of Auxerre in 1788.

Occupation	Number
Judiciary and law	
Same office	6
Lesser office in the bailliage	2
(one of these also held office simultaneously as king's secretary in the chancellery at Dijon)	
Office in the prévôté of Auxerre	1
(until its abolition in 1749; afterward held office as king's secretary in the chancellery at Besançon)	
Advocate practicing before the bailliage	2
Special royal tribunal	
Councillor in the *maréchaussée of Auxerre*	1
Other occupations	
Physician	1
Wholesale merchant	1
(held office as king's secretary in the chancellery at Besançon)	
Négociant, in Switzerland	1
Wine dealer (*commissionnaire en vins*)	1
(held office as king's secretary in the chancellery at Dôle)	
Undetermined	1
Total	17

Sources: Francis Molard, "Le Bailliage d'Auxerre," *Annuaire Historique du Département de l'Yonne,* 3rd ser., 5 (1891), pt. iii, pp. 94–138; Curzon, *La Chancellerie,* p. 83; Lurion, *Notice sur la Chambre des comptes de Dôle,* p. 313; Bourée, *La Chancellerie,* p. 253; A.D. Yonne, étude Guimard, 289 (14 April 180); A.N., V¹ 519 (6 April 1785), and F⁷ 5236.

law. None was a noble. At least one-third of the magistrates were born outside the Dijonnais. The bailliage of Dijon was marked by exceptional social and geographic mobility, and the market for its offices was relatively extensive. As bailliage offices generally became easier to sell toward the end of the eighteenth century, Dijon was especially affected. Half the magistrates in the bailliage of 1756 had failed to pay the

Table 9. Occupations of Grandfathers of the Magistrates
in Office in the Bailliage of Auxerre in 1788.

Occupation	Paternal grandfathers	Maternal grandfathers
Judiciary and law		
Office in the bailliage	5	1
Office in the prévôté of Auxerre	1	0
Judicial office in a seigneurial court	0	1
Advocate practicing before the bailliage	1	0
Special royal tribunal		
Provost in the maréchaussée of Auxerre	0	1
Finance		
Collector of décimes for the diocese and simultaneously subdelegate at Auxerre for the intendant of Dijon	1	1
Collector of décimes for the diocese	0	1
Collector of *aides* at Chablis	0	1
Other occupations		
Wood merchant	0	2
Wine dealer (commissionnaire en vins)	0	1
Undetermined	9	8
Totals	17	17

Sources: Same as for Table 8.

paulette and had died still possessing their offices, which thereupon reverted to the crown.[61] In contrast, during the 1780's, four offices were sold by incumbents who had held them, on the average, for only eleven years, and who then pursued their careers in some other occupation.[62]

The other sixteen bailliages in Burgundy were intermediate

61. *Almanach du Parlement de Bourgogne*, 1756; A.N., V¹ 445 (3 July 1769), 450 (24 January 1770), 451 (8 August and 31 December 1770), and 458 (9 December 1772), letters of appointment to offices "vacant aux parties casuelles."

62. A.N., V¹ 450 (31 August 1770), 456 (7 August 1771), 458 (21 October and 9 December 1772), 503 (2 May 1781), 507 (30 January 1782), 515 (15 December 1784), 516 (15 September 1784), letters of appointment of magistrates who resigned their offices after 1780, and of their successors.,

Table 10. Occupations of Fathers of the Magistrates
in Office in the Bailliage of Dijon in 1788.

Occupation	Number
Judiciary and law	
Greater office in the bailliage	1
Attorney representing the seigneur in his court, at Cussey-les-Forges	1
Notary, in Dijon	2
Other occupations	
Bailiff (*huissier*), Parlement of Dijon	1
Négociant, in Paris	1
Bourgeois of Dijon	1
Grocer (*marchand épicier*), in Dijon	1
Bourgeois of Seurre	1
Bourgeois residing at Pierre, steward (*fermier*) of Authunies	1
Undetermined	2
Total	12

Sources: Parish registers, baptisms: Dijon (Notre-Dame, 23 January 1731, and 8 June 1733; Saint-Michel, 1 November 1747, and 9 April 1758; Saint-Pierre, 27 October 1752); Cussey-les-Forges, 26 October 1735; Pierre, 2 March 1756; marriage: Dijon (Saint-Jean, 11 February 1783). Marriage contract: 6 December 1784 (A.D. Côte-d'Or, E 868, Fyot family papers). La Sicotière, "Deux poètes excentriques: l'abbé Gérard des Rivières et Frécot Saint-Edme," *Bulletin de la Société Historique et Archéologique de l'Orne,* 12 (1893), 449–475, for Frécot, chief civil judge in the bailliage of Dijon from 1784 to 1790.

The places in Burgundy referred to here are: Cussey-les-Forges, 40 kilometers north of Dijon; Seurre, 40 kilometers south-southeast of Dijon; and Pierre, 23 kilometers southeast of Seurre.

between Auxerre and Dijon in social composition. The bailliage of Mâcon, with four magistrates' sons one of whom was the grandson of a king's secretary in the chancellery at Grenoble, resembled that of Auxerre more than did any other.[63] The

63. Parish registers, Mâcon (Saint-Pierre), marriages 5 October 1784 and 22 July 1788, burial 1 November 1791; A.N., V[1] 423 (1 August 1764), 515 (9 June 1784), and 537 (17 June 1789); François Perraud, *Les Environs de Mâcon, anciennes seigneuries et anciens châteaux* (Mâcon, Protat frères, 1912) p. 141.

bailliage of Châtillon-sur-Seine had three members whose fathers had been magistrates in the bailliage, and another member who simultaneously held office himself as a Trésorier de France in the bureau des finances at Dijon and whose son in turn was a magistrate in the Parlement of Dijon.[64] At Chalon-sur-Saône, the bailliage included two magistrates' sons and two holders of ennobling offices; at Autun, two magistrates' sons and one holder of an ennobling office; at Avallon and at Charolles, two magistrates' sons, no holders of ennobling offices. Each of the other bailliages in Burgundy included at most one son of a magistrate. In this respect, the fluidity characteristic of the bailliage of Dijon was fairly common. But, at Semur-en-Auxois and at Beaune one bailliage magistrate was the son of a holder of an ennobling office, and at Saulieu one magistrate held an ennobling office himself, and the presence of these men advancing toward noble status indicates an element of local stability. This range of social characteristics in the different localities is evidently not to be explained solely by the presence or absence of a provincial parlement. The wealth of the local economy and its openness to economic and social currents outside the locality were generally important.

The magistrates of the bailliages in the late eighteenth century did not form a single social category defined by the occupations their fathers had exercised. The overwhelming majority came from families which had been engaged, one, two, or three generations previously, in law practice, the administration of justice in seigneurial courts, the collection and supervision of tax payments, or the management of landed estates. The existence of numerous judicial offices in the bailliages, therefore, did not draw investment capital away

64. Marriage contract, enregistrement 19 February 1790 (A.D. Côte-d'Or, C 8445); A.N., V¹ 508 (13 March 1782) and 511 (29 January 1783); Jean Thomas-Collignon, "Le 'Monde du Trésor' en Bourgogne," *Mémoires de la Société pour l'Histoire du Droit et des Institutions des Anciens Pays Bourguignons, Comtois et Romands*, 9 (1943), 131–179, on p. 170 (note); Colombet, *Les Parlementaires bourguignons*, p. 46.

from trade and industry so much as from agriculture, royal and ecclesiastical finance, and activities in the judicial and legal professions.[65]

The families that acceded to bailliage offices did not all remain in them for the same period of time. Frequently the result was a social disparity between members whose families had long been represented there and others who were newcomers. This could only be aggravated where some magistrates were noblemen and some were commoners. Surely not all the magistrates in the sénéchaussée of Poitiers, for example, were invited to those social occasions when the chief judge, Irland de Bazôges, was host to the nobles in Poitiers and their ladies, who arrived at Le Fief Clairet in a half-dozen carriages, bringing their own dinner for a "picnic," and afterward went to the intendants' mansion for dancing and a light supper.[66]

Diversity of lineage and social mobility of the magistrates' families were characteristic of the bailliages in the late eighteenth century. Inherent in this fact were infringements of such ideals as the stability of the social composition of a bailliage, the eminence of the magistrates in the bourgeoisie, and their capacity to function as a group of professional colleagues. Kinship ties between magistrates in a bailliage might counteract these disintegrative potentialities. Existing kinship ties might be supplemented and new ones created for the next generation of magistrates by the formation of marriage alliances between magistrates' families. In the seventeenth century, such marriage alliances were an important source of solidarity in some bailliages in northern and central France.[67]

65. This point, although incidental here, deserves emphasis because it partly contradicts the interpretation of Henri Hauser, "Les Caractères généraux de l'histoire économique de la France," *Revue Historique,* 173 (1934), on pp. 317–318, followed by several other historians.

66. Mme de Médel, "Correspondance," p. 141; Raymond de La Guéronnière, "Le Fief-Clairet et les Irland," *Bulletin de la Société des Antiquaires de l'Ouest,* 3rd ser., 8 (1928–1930), 398–420.

67. Goubert, "Les Officiers royaux," pp. 60–61.

But in the late eighteenth century, it was far more common for magistrates in a bailliage to be unrelated than related to one another through either kinship or marriage. In Poitiers, for instance, there were twenty magistrates in office and there might therefore have been 190 relationships of kinship or alliance if each magistrate had been related to every other magistrate. In fact, there were two kinships and four alliances.[68] The ratio of the actual to the possible number of relationships, which we may call the coefficient of interrelatedness, was 0.03 in the sénéchaussée of Poitiers. In Auxerre, the continuity with late seventeenth-century notable families had left a deposit of remote kinship ties in the bailliage. These remained perceptible in the frequency of family names borne mostly by second or third cousins. The Marie family was represented by three magistrates, the Housset family by three magistrates, and the Robinet family by two magistrates.[69] Closer ties had been created in the early and middle eighteenth century and were continually being created at its close, through marriage formation. There were three sets of first or second cousins, and 8 relationships defined by marriage alliances.[70] Among the seventeen

68. Dansays and Nicolas were cousins, the former's mother being the sister of the latter's father. Dutillet married a sister of Dansays, and when Robert and De Cressac entered office their sisters' husbands, Rampillon and Lamarque, respectively, were already councillors. Later, Rampillon's mother's brother, Tranchant, entered the sénéchaussée as chief judge of criminal cases, and Robert married a daughter of another magistrate, Baguenard. (This does not include the marriage of Mallet de Fois to the daughter of the late ex-magistrate Babinet de Santilly, referred to previously.)

69. The king's advocate Marie and the councillor Marie de la Forge descended from the same grandfather, the former from his first wife and the latter from his second wife; each was a third cousin of the father of the chief civil judge, Marie d'Avigneau. The associate chief civil judge, Housset de Champton, the councillor Housset's father, and the king's advocate Housset's father were all second cousins. Robinet de la Coudre and Robinet de Pontagny's father appear to have been second cousins.

70. Robinet de Pontagny was a second cousin of Martineau (his paternal grandmother having been a sister of the latter's paternal grandfather) and a first cousin of Thierriat (who was the son of Robinet's

magistrates in the bailliage of Auxerre, there could have existed 136 relationships of kin or alliance. The actual interrelatedness is indicated by the coefficient 0.08, more than twice that for Poitiers and more than ten times that for Dijon. Where many magistrates were sons or grandsons of magistrates, as was true at Auxerre, there was usually also a relatively high frequency of marriage alliances. Family continuity and interrelatedness thus appear as two aspects of the success of this kind of occupational group in conserving its position in local society.

A bailliage magistrate was a member of a judicial company, but more fundamentally he was a representative of a family. His career choice itself was guided in his family's interest, and so was his property management and his marriage arrangement. The magistrate's distinctive social position was mainly defined by his membership in the two intersecting groups, family and judicial company. Yet his individuality was not submerged in group membership and could burst forth disruptively. It was encouraged to do so by the rules and expectations implanted in the bailliage courts. Each magistrate had a particular institutional position, defined first of all by his title, and even the councillors were supposed to stand in clear relations to one another by reason of seniority. Disputes within a bailliage over the respective rights of members were frequent and nowadays are often bewildering for historians.[71] Where compre-

---

father's sister). One of Villetard's sisters was Hay's wife, and another was Martineau's mother. The king's advocate Marie was the husband of Robinet de la Coudre's sister. The king's proctor Rémond was the husband of the councillor Housset's sister. Three magistrates, Thierriat, Raffin, and Villetard, had married the Germain sisters, whose father was a prosperous wood merchant. Two other magistrates, Robinet de Pontagny and Soufflot, married the daughters of a former king's advocate, Despatys.

71. In an essay on the king's proctor at Châtellerault, an expert on eighteenth-century Poitou characterizes such a dispute excellently: "one of those extremely tangled affairs which are remarkable for telling us almost nothing about the subjects with which they are concerned." Pierre Massé, "Le Constituant Dubois," *Bulletin de la Société des Antiquaires de l'Ouest,* 4th ser., 2 (1954), 825–842, on p. 826.

hensible, the disputes were usually over ceremonial or symbolic issues. Since the rights of precedence and similar prerogatives affected the economic values of bailliage offices, such disputes involved material interests indirectly. In the privacy of the magistrates' deliberations, judicial restraint sometimes disappeared, as in the sénéchaussée of Poitiers, where there was a heated argument over whether the chief judge of criminal cases should also sit and vote in civil cases.[72] Having won this point, the same judge sought to preside, in the absence of the chief civil judge, over the consideration of a civil case. He tried to drag the associate chief civil judge out of the chair and, having failed in this, he sat on top of him.[73] In Poitiers, and elsewhere, the rights of the chief police magistrate's office were a particular source of discord where the office was owned by the judicial company as a whole and exercised by turns.[74] Any ambiguity, however, concerning precedence, the distribution of the judges' fees, the respective rights of any two or three competing officeholders, the corporate payment of the taxes on the offices, or the details of various kinds of proceedings was capable of kindling or inflaming a disagreement.

Individual characteristics were also manifested in the in-

72. Coutineau, ms. journal, 7 May 1781: "Il y eut beaucoup de propos fort vifs et fort indécents de la part de MM. Tranchant [lieutenant criminel] et Dutillet [conseiller] que l'on eut beaucoup de peine à calmer." On another occasion, Dutillet called another councillor "vieux salaud, vieux bougre, vieux jean-foutre."

73. Coutineau, 18 February 1784.,

74. The chief civil judge, Irland de Bazôges, was concerned to eliminate diversity of judgments by magistrates taking turns in the police court and sought to exercise special prerogatives over it. Tranchant, his nephew (Rampillon), and the latter's brother-in-law (Robert), and others protested. Irland took the matter before the Parlement of Paris. The youngest councillors tried to remain neutral. The topic fills many pages of Coutineau's journal from 1784 to 1789. See also Félix Faulcon, *Correspondance,* ed. Gabriel Debien, 2 vols. (Poitiers, 1939–1953, as *Archives Historiques du Poitou,* 51 and 55), I, 234, 246–249. At Troyes, there was likewise the formation of factions, though with less bitterness: Julien Ricommard, *La Lieutenance générale de police à Troyes au XVIIIe siècle* (Paris, Hachette, 1934), pp. 303, 529.

tellectual life of the magistrates. So much so that it is not easy to describe in general terms. The professional work of a bailliage magistrate, we have seen, was highly honorable but not materially profitable. For some men, and in some ways, it was interesting. To be sure, the bailliage magistrates had no constitutional claim to exercise political authority through remonstrances and regulatory orders, as the parlements did. But their tasks were not all narrowly technical. In many cases, they were primarily judges of factual questions, and these sometimes had considerable interest for anyone disposed to observe his fellow men. The application of the provincial coutume or of royal legislation to a particular case was always capable of raising difficulties which had to be resolved by a bailliage. A considerable number of the major commentaries on coutumes and royal legislation were the work of bailliage magistrates, and this traditional activity continued unabated during the eighteenth century. A well-known commentator on Louis XIV's procedural ordinances was the chief criminal judge in the bailliage of Autun, Serpillon, who was succeeded in office by his son in 1765. Another, more celebrated, commentator was Jousse, councillor in the Châtelet of Orléans from 1734 until his death in 1781. One of Jousse's colleagues in that court was Pothier, until he accepted the professorship at Orléans in which he turned out his treatises on French private law. The editor of the principal encyclopedia of jurisprudence, Guyot, had begun his career as a bailliage judge in Lorraine.[75]

---

75. The *Répertoire universel et raisonné de jurisprudence* first appeared in 64 octavo volumes beginning in 1775. Its editor, Joseph-Nicolas Guyot (1728–1816), had been a councillor in the bailliage of Bruyères, 1757–1768, and was later a judge in the tribunal of cassation for ten months in 1795. (The Bibliothèque Nationale catalogue of authors attributes the book to Pierre-Jean-Jacques-Guillaume Guyot, but this is an error. Louis-Hector Chaudru de Raynal and Augustin-Charles Renouard, *Le Tribunal et la Cour de cassation. Notices sur le personnel (1791– 1879)* (Paris, 1879), p. 41, provide an accurate list of J.-N. Guyot's major publications.) The second edition, in 17 quarto volumes, appeared in 1784–1785, and cost a large sum, 168 livres (Faulcon, *Correspond-*

Among his collaborators, besides many advocates in Paris, were two magistrates, Boucher d'Argis *fils,* a councillor in the Châtelet of Paris from 1772, and Guesnard de Lisle, a councillor in the bailliage of Chaumont-en-Bassigny from 1774. The commentator's spirit can be discerned also in the compilation of precedents and documents concerning the Estates General which was prepared in 1788 by Lalourcé and Duval, councillors in the Châtelet of Paris.[76]

As the last example suggests, a few magistrates had wider horizons than the administration of justice. This had long been true. From Bodin through Loyseau to Domat, some of France's most influential political theorists held bailliage offices. They expended their intellectual energies in efforts to discern the substantive rationality of the whole political system rather than to improve the functional rationality of their own profession. The same general description applies equally to an eighteenth-century writer like Le Trosne, who performed his duties as a bailliage magistrate with evident seriousness yet at the same time contributed greatly to the development and the diffusion of physiocratic ideas.[77] He was not a continuator of

---

ance, I, 229). Many articles were copied from Guyot's *Répertoire* for the *Encyclopédie méthodique: Jurisprudence,* edited by Lerasle and published in 1782–1789.

76. Charlemagne Lalourcé (1751–?) and François-Alexis Duval (1762–1791) were councillors in the Châtelet of Paris from 1777 and 1784, respectively. Their work, *Forme générale et particulière de la convocation et de la tenue des assemblées nationales ou Etats Généraux de France,* 3 vols. (Paris, 1789), was accompanied by 2 collections of documents in 13 additional volumes.

77. Guillaume-François Le Trosne (1728–1780), king's advocate in the Châtelet of Orléans, wrote *Les Effets de l'impôt indirect prouvés par les deux exemples de la gabelle et du tabac* (1770), *De l'ordre social* (1777), *De l'administration provinciale et de la réforme de l'impôt* (1779), and several shorter works. From 1764 onward, he made an invaluable contribution to the physiocratic movement, bringing to it "an honorable name and position, a vigorous juridical and philosophical talent, and even a sober yet elegant prose style," in the judgment of Georges Weulersse, *Le Mouvement physiocratique en France (de 1756 à 1770),* 2 vols. (Paris, Félix Alcan, 1910), I, 100.

earlier political theory, for he did not address himself to the kinds of problems with which it had been preoccupied: the nature of sovereignty, the prerequisites for political unity, and the hierarchies of authority. As a political economist and a follower of Quesnay, he sought to analyze economic production, exchange, and taxation, and the ways in which political institutions might best respond to these material processes. In a sense, then, Le Trosne's professional and intellectual lives exemplify a distinctively eighteenth-century dichotomy between juridical scholarship and political philosophy.[78] But it would be a mistake to see this in exclusive terms, for in his actual environment Le Trosne was a colleague of Jousse and an acquaintance of Pothier in a bailliage that was exceptionally active in both spheres.

The intellectual activity of bailliage magistrates generally in the eighteenth century evokes two principal observations. First, as might be expected, the magistrates whose nonprofessional intellectual life left any trace were a small minority. Second, those who were active did not restrict their interest to professional subject matter or to questions arising from it, such as the nature of law or the means of resolving conflict in society. In La Rochelle, for example, Seignette demonstrated his electrical experiments in 1777 before a distinguished tourist, the "comte de Falkenstein," Joseph II of Austria.[79] In

78. William F. Church, "The Decline of the French Jurists as Political Theorists, 1660–1789," *French Historical Studies,* 5 (1967), 1–40, contends that in general men trained in law, working as lawyers or judges, and adhering to traditional legal concepts, yielded intellectual leadership to political philosophers untrained or uninterested in professional legal work but committed to a new version of natural law doctrine. The article pertains both to intellectual tendencies and to the identity of the intellectual leaders who best illustrated the tendencies, none of whom was a bailliage magistrate in the period after Louis XIV.

79. Pierre-Henry Seignette (1735–1807), *assesseur criminel* from 1762 and lieutenant particulier from 1779 in the sénéchaussée of La Rochelle, principal secretary of the local Academy from 1770, and mayor in 1771–1775, became a judge in the tribunal of cassation in 1795.

Limoges, Juge de Saint-Martin labored over prior decisions of the Parlement of Bordeaux and wrote books on silviculture and meteorology.[80] In Nîmes, Delon wrote plays, poetry, and an essay on Rousseau's *Confessions* before undertaking a campaign for the construction of a canal for the town.[81] In every province there was to be found, among the bailliage magistrates, some experimenter, observer of nature, historical scholar, essayist or versifier.

Similarly, in the work of organizing provincial intellectual life, a small minority of the bailliage magistrates was active. Seignette was the principal secretary of the Academy of La Rochelle. Haillet de Couronne was the permanent secretary for belles lettres of the Academy of Rouen. Riboud was the founder and permanent secretary of the Emulation Society of Bourg-en-Bresse. In Moulins, the director of the agriculture society was the chief civil judge in the sénéchaussée, Grimauld, who seemed to the travelling Arthur Young to be "a man of considerable fortune, of information and knowledge, agreeable and polite," although unable to respond satisfactorily to Young's attempt to discuss methods for improving agriculture in the province.[82] In all, few magistrates were actively involved in the corporate intellectual life of provincial academies and agriculture societies. When Dubois de Fosseux became perma-

80. Jacques-Joseph Juge de Saint-Martin (1743–1824), councillor in the sénéchaussée of Limoges from 1774, prepared an annotated edition of Abraham Lapeyrère, *Décisions sommaires* [du Parlement de Bordeaux], which remained in manuscript, and wrote a *Traité de la culture du chêne* (Paris, 1788), a description of *Arbres du Limousin* (Limoges, 1790), and *Observations météreologiques faites pendant l'hiver de 1789* (Limoges, 1790), and later works.

81. Alexandre Delon (1753–1825), councillor in the sénéchaussée of Nîmes from 1776, was the author of many writings.

82. *Travels during the Years 1787, 1788, and 1789, Undertaken More Particularly with a View of Ascertaining the Cultivation, Wealth, Resources, and National Prosperity of the Kingdom of France*, 2nd ed., 2 vols. (London, 1794), I, 170, entry of 7 August 1789. The remark refers to Jacques Grimauld, seigneur of Panloup, Lagrange, Monchenin, and Le Péage, who succeeded his father as chief judge in Moulins in 1782.

nent secretary of the Academy of Arras in 1785, he began to inundate other learned societies with letters offering to exchange correspondence. He received many more responses from clergymen and physicians than from bailliage magistrates. This was perhaps to be expected, since the clergy and the profession of medicine far outnumbered the bailliage magistracy; but many of the magistrates never replied, and only ten became reliable correspondents.[83]

The academies were hierarchical groups of social and intellectual elites in the provinces. They were doubtless more receptive to noblemen than to commoners and in Bordeaux and Dijon were dominated by magistrates in the parlements. But they were also open to well-educated, energetic members of the upper bourgeoisie.[84] In Châlons-sur-Marne, where there were only eight magistrates in the bailliage, three of them were members of the academy. The experience of Dubois de Fosseux indicates, however, that in the academies those bailliage magistrates who were members contributed to the social distinction of the audience more than to the volume or the quality of the presentations and derived from membership the pleasure of association with inquisitive minds more than the satisfaction of accomplishment.

Members of academies and learned societies in the eighteenth century were in general very greatly outnumbered by Freemasons. This was true also among bailliage magistrates in particular. For one reason, Freemasonry was more accessible

83. Léon-Noël Berthe, *Dictionnaire des correspondants de l'Académie d'Arras au temps de Robespierre* (Arras, chez l'auteur, 1969), nos. 72, 121, 172, 329, 533, 543, 678, 744, 848, 943.

84. Daniel Roche, "Milieux académiques provinciaux et société des lumières. Trois académies provinciales au XVIIIe siècle: Bordeaux, Dijon, Châlons-sur-Marne," *Livre et société dans la France du XVIIIe siècle*, ed. François Furet (Paris, The Hague, Mouton & Co., 1965), pp. 93–184. In analyzing the social composition of these three academies, Roche counted bailliage magistrates as noblemen; it would be more correct, in the absence of precise information about individual status, to count them as bourgeois.

to them than academy membership. In 160 of the towns where bailliage courts were located in 1789, there were Masonic lodges.[85] The total number of bailliaage magistrates who were members of these is unknown. Between 1775 and 1789, seven lodges in provincial towns sent bailliage magistrates as their deputies to the Grand Orient.[86] Nineteen other bailliage magistrates, in various towns, were members of one or another of the lodges in Paris; preponderantly, these were magistrates in the eastern provinces, Burgundy, Franche-Comté, Lorraine, and Champagne.[87] Because the membership of the Paris lodges is known, greater significance attaches to the statistics concerning Freemasons among the magistrates in Paris. Of the seventy-one in office in the Châtelet in 1789, sixteen were members of at least one Paris lodge affiliated with the Grand Orient.[88] The proportion, 22 percent, exceeded that for the Parlement of Paris, of which one-sixth of the presidents and councillors in office in 1789 were in Paris lodges affiliated with the Grand Orient. The magistrates were not all members of the same lodge but formed groups concentrated in a small number of lodges. The lodge Les Cœurs Simples de l'Etoile Polaire was the one for which the largest number of magistrates showed a predilection, since it included six councillors in the Parlement (among them d'Amarzit de Sahuguet d'Espagnac and two other ecclesiastics), and five of the older councillors in the Châtelet. The middle-aged councillors in the Châtelet (be-

85. Alain Le Bihan, *Loges et chapitres de la Grande Loge et du Grand Orient de France (seconde moitié du XVIIIᵉ siècle)* (Paris, Commission d'Histoire Economique et Sociale de la Révolution Française, *Mémoires et documents*, XX, 1967), pp. 3–259, 451–455.

86. Alain Le Bihan, *Franc-Maçons parisiens du Grand Orient de France (fin du XVIIIᵉ siècle)* (Paris, Commission d'Histoire Economique et Sociale de la Révolution Française, *Mémoires et documents*, XIX, 1966), pp. 44, 76, 79, 209, 249, 367, 440.

87. *Ibid.*, pp. 46, 47, 49, 100, 126, 132, 148, 190, 209, 257, 260, 316, 347, 356, 361, 384, 414.

88. *Ibid.*, pp. 64, 86, 90, 127, 128, 263, 308, 312, 315, 356, 372, 373, 378, 393, 436, 482.

tween the ages of thirty and fifty) were members of other lodges, principally Thalie and Le Zèle, in which there were no magistrates of the Parlement. In Paris, then, Freemasonry did not provide an inclusive professional association of magistrates. In the Châtelet, the Freemasons were mostly old or middle-aged, and some degree of diversity between groups is surely represented by differences in lodge membership. Whether any particular intellectual affinities were involved remains, however, an unanswerable question. The intellectual content of Freemasonry was diffuse and for the magistrates who were Freemasons was probably less important than the sociability it facilitated.[89]

A substantial minority of bailliage magistrates readily joined the associations and clubs that were accessible to them. Corporate membership was an unavoidable characteristic of their profession, and the proclivity for group life was far more widespread among them than the solitary perseverance of the scientist or scholar. Yet many who were not members of associations nonetheless gave some attention to the varied intellectual life of the late eighteenth century. The diversity of their interests constitutes a major contrast with the magistrates of

89. Le Bihan's comment on a paper by André Bouton summarizes the results of an enormous amount of scholarly work: "Freemasonry's diffuse influence: immense. Its immediate influence, as a body, at some moment or other in the Revolution: null. Yet no pre-1789 organization can be compared to the Masonic organization; there were about 900 lodges and some tens of thousands of Masons in relations with Paris through officers and deputies . . . Masonic activity was more important than it has been described, but it was purely Masonic. The Masons conducted initations, they concerned themselves with philanthropy . . . But it is necessary to extend to all of France what has been found for Paris, and to introduce nuances into the conclusions where appropriate." *Annales Historiques de la Révolution Française*, 41 (1969), 500.

An antirevolutionary Masonic lodge, in which one of the leaders was the chief civil judge in the bailliage, is described by Marcel Henriot, "La Loge maçonnique de Semur-en-Auxois à la veille de la Révolution," *Annales de Bourgogne*, 6 (1934), 78–82, and, with a very different emphasis, Régine Robin, "Franc-Maçonnerie et lumières à Semur-en-Auxois en 1789," *Revue d'Histoire Economique et Sociale*, 43 (1965), 234–241.

the seventeenth century. During the first three quarters of that century, bailliage magistrates typically possessed a high degree of intellectual culture, of an old type based on humanist learning and legal training. In the late seventeenth and early eighteenth centuries, their collections of books reveal the presence of three new categories of interests: travel literature, theater (especially the French classics), and critical or polemical writings.[90] By the late eighteenth century, the array of available subject matter had widened very greatly, and so had the range of intellectual interests to be found among magistrates. A thorough statistical analysis of this is precluded by the paucity of the documentation. Lists of the books owned by magistrates were generally included in postmortem inventories of personal property, but under most coutumes these documents were drawn up only in certain circumstances and are accordingly rare.

In four magistrates' personal-property inventories that I found, the salient common characteristic of the libraries is their moderate size, large enough to merit the notary's attention but not large or fine enough to require really expert evaluation. A notary called in a local bookseller to evaluate the 450 volumes left by Baudy de Feuillé, king's advocate in the sénéchaussée of Châtellerault.[91] The bookseller noted that more than half the books lacked bindings and did not trouble to record most of the titles or authors. This magistrate, whose father and grandfather had held the same office since the last decade of the seventeenth century, had contracted very large debts as a young man.[92] At his death, his personal property aside from his books was valued at only 572 livres. It seems probable that he had inherited his copies of Corneille, Racine,

90. Goubert, "Les Officiers royaux," pp. 70–73.

91. Inventaire après décès de Jean-René-Marie Baudy, A.D. Vienne, E⁴/34–14 (19 January 1790).

92. Within a year after marriage, in 1768, his wife obtained a judicial order dissolving the community of property between them in order to protect her property from his creditors, according to the inventory.

Molière, Voltaire, Bayle's *Dictionary,* and about 30 folio volumes of lawbooks.

Even less information is available about the 832 volumes possessed by Housset, a wealthy councillor in the bailliage of Auxerre, for the *Grand Dictionnaire historique* of Louis Moreri and *La Maison rustique* are the only works named in the inventory.[93]

The king's proctor at Auxerre, Grasset, owned 653 volumes, most of which were identified by title.[94] This library is remarkable for range and diversity, not depth. It seems to reflect a mind drawn by active curiosity in various directions. There are Demosthenes' orations in Greek, the works of Cicero, Vergil, Ovid, and Persius in Latin, and Franch translations of Homer, Horace, Seneca, Juvenal, and Plutarch. There are the works of Petrarch and the *Colloquies* of Erasmus. There are the French dramatists and poets of the seventeenth and eighteenth centuries: Corneille, Racine, Molière, Boileau-Despréaux, Saint-Evremond, Prosper Crébillon, J.-B.-Louis Gresset, Regnard, and Voltaire's *Henriade.* Grasset had Rollin's treatise, *De la manière d'enseigner et d'étudier les belles-lettres,* and Rousseau's *Emile;* Domat's *Les Loix civiles dans leur ordre naturel* and Montesquieu's *De l'esprit des lois;* Fontenelle's *Entretiens sur la pluralité des mondes,* Pluche's *Spectacle de la nature* and *Histoire du ciel,* as well as popularizations of physics by Nolet and Renaud. He had Vauban's *Projet d'une dîme royale,* Mirabeau's *Théorie de l'impôt,* and works of the agronomists Duhamel du Monceau and Buc'hoz. In religion, the Jansenist tendency strong in Auxerre throughout the eighteenth century is represented by Pascal's *Lettres à un provincial,* by the *Logique de Port-Royal* and other writings of Arnauld and Nicole, and by Quesnel's translation of and reflections on the New Testament.

93. Inventaire après décès de Claude-Etienne Housset, A.D. Yonne, étude Coste, 88 (1 April 1788).

94. Inventaire après décès de Pierre-Edme-François Grasset, A.D. Yonne, étude Guimard, 293 (15 December 1783).

An interest in antiquity is revealed by the presence of Rollin's histories of the ancient Near East and the Roman republic, an interest in modern history by that of histories of France by Mézeray, Liniers, Boulainvilliers, Larrey, and Hénault, various biographies and memoirs, and Voltaire's *Histoire de Charles XII.* Besides several accounts of travels in exotic lands and geographic descriptions, Grasset had Raynal's *Histoire philosophique et politique des établissements et du commerce des Européens dans les deux Indes.* Polemical writings related to the parlements' prosecution of the Jesuits and to Maupeou's reform of the parlements were in his library. Some of the diversity in it is doubtless to be accounted for by differences between Grasset and his father, who had been an advocate and a seigneurial judge, but the publication dates of some of the editions preclude the possibility that Grasset inherited them. There were limits, however, to his taste for novelty. Among several dictionaries, including Moreri's, he did not have the *Encyclopédie* of Diderot. He had none of the works of the materialists. He had only one novel, Rousseau's *Nouvelle Héloise.* Above all, it was the library of a serious professional magistrate, in which the necessary codes and commentators predominated.

A different family history and a different intellectual predisposition are apparent in the collection of books left by Bailly, a well-to-do councillor in the minor bailliage of Issoudun, in Berry. Of his 320 volumes, 50 were unbound and in disrepair, and hence only 165 titles were inventoried.[95] Bailly's father had occupied a post in the king's household, as *gentilhomme de la vénerie du roi.* His grandfather, after being trained as a lawyer, had held office as king's proctor in the court of coinage in Bourges. The contents of Bailly's library indicate that the absence of a strong family tradition of extensive learning in the law was not compensated by zeal on his part. His important

95. Inventaire après décès de Louis Bailly, A.D. Indre, E 2237 (13 January 1789).

law books were three editions of the coutume of Berry, two editions of that of Paris, a treatise on successions and one on French law, one volume of a two-volume dictionary, two collections of maxims, three books on procedure, and a minimum of commentators: Coquille, Louet, Bornier, Duplessis, Thaumas de la Thaumassière. This was feeble compared with Grasset's library, which included Justinian's *Code, Digest,* and *Institutes,* and glosses, as well as reports of court decisions, all in Latin, and a much fuller collection of French ordinances, commentators and reports of decisions. Bailly, on the other hand, had a relatively large collection of memoirs and biographies of great personages in sixteenth- and seventeenth-century European history, and French translations of a few ancient authors: Euclid's *Elements,* Vergil, Ovid, Petronius, Pliny's *Natural History,* Martial, Lucan's *Pharsalia,* and Suetonius' life of Caesar. Amongst them were seven editions of the *Almanach royal* published during the fifteen years before his father's marriage, and so it appears that these books belonged to the social context of a minor courtier rather than that of a magistrate. Bailly himself had almost none of the books published during his own lifetime, neither legal commentators like Jousse, Du Rousseaud de la Combe, and Pothier, nor the characteristic productions of the Enlightenment. Rousseau's *Nouvelle Héloïse* was the only book that he could not have inherited.

Both Grasset's and Bailly's book collections were much smaller than the libraries of members of the Parlement of Paris. Nevertheless, it is instructive to compare the libraries owned by the lesser magistrates with those typical of the parlement. Seven magistrates in the Parlement who died after 1780 had libraries that were catalogued in the usual way for sale by bookdealers, and these catalogues have been analyzed. For comparison, Grasset's and Bailly's books can be classified in the same categories.

In relation to the numbers of their other books, Grasset and Bailly both had more legal and religious writings than did the

Table 11. Composition of the Libraries of Seven Magistrates
in the Parlement of Paris and Two Magistrates
in Bailliages after 1780.

Categories	Seven members of parlement	Grasset	Bailly
Law	11 %	27%	21%
History	35	12	26
Belles lettres	32.5	20	24
Sciences & arts	15.5	19	7
Theology & religion	6	15	13
Unclassified	0	7	9

Source: Régine Petit, "Les Bibliothèques des hommes du Parlement de Paris au XVIIIᵉ siècle," unpubl. mémoire submitted at the Sorbonne in 1954 and cited by Bluche, *Les Magistrats du Parlement de Paris,* p. 291. The members of the Parlement involved here appear to include Berthelot de Saint-Alban, Durey de Meinières (distinguished for his work as a compiler of jurisprudence), Dionis du Séjour (a noted astronomer), Douet de Vichy, Goislard de Montsabert, and Marquet. Mlle Petit also analyzed 7 library catalogues drawn up in 1734–1765 and 15 drawn up in 1766–1780.

members of the Parlement of Paris. The bailliage magistrates' libraries, growing slowly from a basis provided by their fathers and grandfathers, had not extended far into humanistic and contemporary literature. In simple numbers, the magistrates in the Parlement commonly owned more books on law and theology than the bailliage magistrates owned, but had greatly expanded their collections of history and belles lettres and thus had shifted the weight of their libraries into these categories. The difference between Grasset's and Bailly's libraries is also noteworthy. Grasset's library contained relatively more science than the libraries of the members of the Parlement. Bailly's library contained much less science. Most of the books associated with one or another of the intellectual tendencies constituting the Enlightenment were classified as science. This contrast between Grasset and Bailly provides, therefore, a rough measure of the difference between their responses to the

Enlightenment. In short, an interest in eighteenth-century intellectual innovations could be combined with a serious attitude toward the professional work of a magistrate, as appears in Grasset's library, and, on the other hand, lack of interest in the law did not necessarily lead to a strong interest in recent innovations in other disciplines.

Intellectually active magistrates were interested in a wide variety of subjects, which often included jurisprudence and sometimes expanded from it to include political philosophy and political economy. Neither in the associations they joined nor in the books they acquired did they reveal any primary intellectual concerns. No distinctive ideological position was characteristic of them. This fact ought not to be surprising, since, in the stable circumstances of most of the eighteenth century, economic interests and social aspirations did not unite them, and their intellectual interests led in many different directions. Yet the bailliage magistrates did occupy a particular position in the royal judiciary, a position which ultimately would involve them in the prerevolutionary debate over the constitution of the French monarchy.

The true character of the constitution was a political issue —one might almost say the political issue—for years before 1789, on which many volumes were written with Montesquieu's great work by no means the first. It is important to note that the issue was also, and inescapably, a professional question for judges and lawyers. This was so because during the eighteenth century the parlements sought to redefine their ambiguous constitutional role, and to use it in a way which critics then and since viewed as merely self-promoting. Thereby a new ambiguity was created. As François Bluche writes,[96]

Perhaps no society was as strictly attached to its prerogatives and its egotistical interests as that handful of men, proud of their origin,

96. *Les Magistrats du Parlement de Paris,* p. 383.

of their social and political power, of their capacity to block the exercise of governmental authority.

And yet, these magistrates used the words "liberties," "common good," "people's interest," with a sincerity that cannot be altogether denied. This involuntary ambiguity—which long sustained the deceptive image of a liberal Parlement—formed part of the social reality of the Parlement.

The contradictions perceptible in the conduct of the parlements, especially the Parlement of Paris, caused uncertainties and disagreements among bailliage magistrates and advocates. At times these troubling matters rose to the forefront of their consciousness and left traces in their writings. In the autumn of 1783, for example, a rumor circulated in Poitou that a high court of appeal would soon be established in Poitiers, similar to the one instituted there by Maupeou in 1771. A councillor in the sénéchaussée of Poitiers, Félix Faulcon, then twenty-five years old, exchanged letters on this subject with two of his correspondents, Texier, with whom he had studied law, and Rangeard de la Boissière, an uncle by marriage. All three men favored the creation of a high court of appeal in Poitiers. They recognized that it would diminish the territorial jurisdiction of the Parlement of Paris and agreed that this would benefit ordinary litigants. They also agreed that the Parlement of Paris ought to employ remonstrances and refusal to register legislation in order to block attempts at despotic action by royal ministers. Finally, they agreed that in fact the Parlement of Paris was using remonstrances and refusal to register legislation, not as it ought to do but merely in defense of its own prerogatives. In view of this, Faulcon thought that the institutional position of the Parlement of Paris was not worth preserving. He wrote:

Certainly there was a time when the magistrates of that august tribunal, animated by love of the public weal, energetically sustained the nation's rights . . . forcefully opposed the ministers' ruinous plans. Then, also, studious and just, they did their own work and rendered decisions that were always equitable at little cost.

Such they were, my friend, but such they are no longer. Today, dissipated by the pleasures of a voluptuous life, guided by ambition, they subscribe with a blind deference to the monarch's will. They will still evince some firmness if one attacks their privileges; but they will readily sacrifice the nation's interests rather than incur a disgrace which would cover them with glory. Besides this pusillanimity, you know their administration of justice and the painful experiences of the wretched litigants n Paris.[97]

In reply, Texier reaffirmed that even with its abuses of the ordinary processes of justice, the Parlement still represented a "shadow, and often the effect, of the intermediary power, capable of preventing the excess of despotism at which we should immediately arrive" otherwise. The existence of abuses, Texier argued, was in fact a reason to preserve the Parlement's institutional position. For, "I expect, from the excess of public miseries, a necessary revolution, which would tend toward the people's ruin and toward despotism if there did not remain to us at least the shadow of the intermediary power," but a revolution which, with the Parlement protecting "our fundamental laws, cannot fail to turn to our relief." Texier went on to present a garbled version of Montesquieu's *Esprit des lois.* Faulcon's other correspondent, Rangeard de la Boissière, agreed with Faulcon. It is tempting, but would be erroneous, to see in these exchanges of letters a disagreement between the magistrates Faulcon and Rangeard, on the one hand, and the advocate, Texier, on the other. In actuality, some of the other magistrates in the sénéchaussée of Poitiers disagreed entirely with Faulcon, as he remarked himself in one of his letters,

97. Faulcon, *Correspondance,* I, 171–179, 183, for this passage and the replies quoted hereafter. Texier was in law practice as an advocate in Loudun, where he had married into the prominent family of Dumoustier de la Fond (his wife's uncle, king's advocate in the bailliage, was to be elected a deputy for the Third Estate in 1789). Rangeard de la Boissière was a councillor in the bailliage of Blois, having previously been proctor general in the chambre des comptes there which had been transformed by Maupeou into a high judicial council and, after the revocation of Maupeou's reforms, had been abolished in 1775. Rangeard's wife was the aunt of Faulcon's wife.

and, on the other side, there were lawyers who disagreed with Texier. Thus the major issue over which the bailliage magistrates might have formed a unifying ideology before 1787 did not draw a united response from them. Instead, it fostered political divisions within each bailliage, as well as within the legal profession.

The predominant characteristic of the bailliage magistracy in the 1780's appears in retrospect to be multiple potentiality as yet unrealized. Wealth, local social position, a wide scattering of intellectual capacity and interest, and an ambiguous relation to the parlements which constituted the natural leadership of the royal judiciary, all traits that we have considered, combined to justify expectancy in the face of impending political change.

IV

The Political Mobilization of the Bailliage Magistrates, 1787–1789

The right to participate in politics was a major issue throughout the revolutionary years in France, and one of the themes of their history is the initiation of one group after another into actual political experience. The process might be visualized as successively descending the social scale, from the aristocrats in the parlements, recalcitrant if not revolutionary as early as 1787, to the peasants and to the shopkeepers and artisans who gave the term *sans-culotte* a new—political— meaning in 1792. But it is important to avoid a schematic view of these manifold changes. In particular, for the magistrates in the bailliages, it is useful to distinguish between 1787, when the monarchy called upon a few of them to participate in reforms, and the year between May 1788 and May 1789. In the latter period, all the magistrates in the bailliages were brought into politics. This initiation was, in accordance with temperaments and circumstances, unnerving or exhilarating.

In obtaining the king's agreement to convoke an assembly of notables, Calonne appears to have been trying to circumvent the obstructive power of the clergy and some elements in the parlements. At the same time, he did not want to call into being an independent legislative body. To the extent that he intended to appeal to a third political force, which would support fiscal reforms, this force was to consist of the highest-ranking nobility and a fraction of the Third Estate: in fact, he called upon a dozen dukes, eight venerable marshals of France (whose average age was 75), and sixteen other titled nobles, together with the mayors of twenty-five important towns.[1] Among these mayors, as it happened, were six magistrates— in the bailliages of Bourges, Orléans, Tours, and Troyes, and the sénéchaussées of Limoges and Nantes—and two former judges, from Clermont-Ferrand and Metz.[2] Heavily outnumbered in the assembly of notables by magistrates of the parlements and distributed among five of the bureaux into which the assembly was divided, these eight bailliage magistrates played no distinctive part in the deliberations. In the bureau over which the count of Artois presided, the mayors of Bourges and Limoges followed Lafayette's lead.[3] Like him, and like the proctor-general of the Parlement of Provence, the mayor of Limoges invoked the necessity for consent by the Estates General to new taxation. In the bureau headed by the duke of Bourbon, the mayor of Troyes shared the suspicion with which

1. Jean Egret, *La Pré-Révolution française* (*1787–1788*) (Paris, Presses Universitaires de France, 1962), pp. 16–18.
2. *AP*, I, 185. All these bailliage magistrates, except the mayor of Troyes and the procureur syndic of Nantes, were members of families ennobled in the 18th century or in the course of ennoblement.
3. Jean Egret, "La Fayette dans la première assemblée des notables," *Annales Historiques de la Révolution Française*, 24 (1952), 1–31.

many of the notables regarded Calonne, and he reported that in the whole assembly only nine members supported the minister in the days before the latter's dismissal.[4] The mayor of Orléans, who was in the bureau headed by the duke of Orléans and was reputed to be entirely loyal to Calonne,[5] was thus exceptional among the bailliage judges in the assembly. Unlike him, they generally followed the lead of the assembly's dominant figures.

The circumspection of the judges in the assembly of notables, and their tendency to align themselves with the intransigence of the parlements on the issues under consideration there, supported the preconception that the bailliages were the creatures of the parlements. This had been the belief of Maupeou, and in 1787 it was still current in governmental circles. When Loménie de Brienne was appointed a minister, in May, one of the first pieces of advice he received concerning the new provincial assemblies, which were to be established during the summer, was to limit the role that might be played in them by bailliage magistrates. Otherwise, these men, "experienced in public affairs, would acquire a dangerous influence: it is to be feared that the assemblies would soon be dependent on the Parlement [of Paris]."[6] The way proposed to limit the bailliage magistrates' role was to restrict the Third Estate to half the membership of each provincial assembly. The warning against

4. "Lettres de Claude Huez, maire de Troyes, député à l'Assemblée des Notables (1787)," ed. Octave Beuve, *La Révolution dans l'Aube*, 1 (1908), 49–60, on p. 59. These letters are disappointingly meager. Huez said (p. 58) that if he included details of the assembly's operations his letters would probably be intercepted.

5. Etienne-Charles de Loménie de Brienne, *Journal de l'Assemblée des Notables de 1787*, ed. Pierre Chevallier (Paris, Librairie C. Klincksieck, 1960), p. 52.

6. Quoted by Pierre Renouvin, *Les Assemblées provinciales de 1787* (Paris, A. Picard, 1921), p. 95. The warning was offered by Louis-Hardouin Tarbé, an important functionary in the *contrôle générale des finances*, who collaborated in drafting the regulations that established the provincial assemblies in the summer of 1787. Renouvin, p. 243 (note).

the bailliage magistrates was perhaps formulated as a pretext for the proposed remedy, or perhaps from a belief that the judicial hierarchy still gave the parlements effective means of controlling the bailliage magistrates in this new, nonjudicial political institution. In either case, the warning was not a realistic appraisal of the bailliages' place in local politics. They had certainly not exercised strong leadership in the two provincial assemblies established by Necker, at Bourges in 1778 and at Montauban in 1779. In the former, the twenty-three members for the Third Estate included three bailliage magistrates, and in the latter, the twenty-six members for the Third Estate included six bailliage magistrates.[7] The assemblies were as weak and timid as Necker had intended them to be.

As a member of the assembly of notables, Loménie de Brienne had urged that the Third Estate be permitted to elect two-thirds of the members of each provincial assembly. As a minister, he acted in accordance with current governmental fear of the judiciary. He restricted the Third Estate to half the membership and, instead of making the assemblies entirely elective at once, began with royal appointment of half the members for each Estate and co-optation of the remaining half. The men appointed for the Third Estate were primarily businessmen and landowners and included very few bailliage magistrates. But these men of substance co-opted a disproportionate number of bailliage magistrates for the remaining half of the representation of the Third Estate. The ministerial policy of excluding bailliage magistrates was largely counteracted, and in the end they constituted a considerable proportion of the Third Estate membership of the provincial assemblies, generally about one-fifth.[8]

7. *Etrennes curieuses et utiles de la province de Berri,* 1789; Gérard Boscary, *L'Assemblée provinciale de Haute-Guyenne, 1779–1790* (Paris, 1932), p. 71.

8. *Almanach de la ville et du diocèse de Troyes,* 1789; *Calendrier de l'Orléanais,* 1788; Henry Fromont, *Essai sur l'administration de l'assem-*

The effects of the provincial assemblies on the attitudes and participation of the bailliage magistrates in politics are not easy to ascertain because they were variable and, in general, undramatic, like the assemblies themselves. From this particular viewpoint, Tocqueville's characterization of the reform seems certainly to overemphasize the degree of change it actually wrought.[9] Yet there is some basis for thinking that the reform implied to contemporaries a fundamental modification of the principles of government. A former magistrate in Blois, Rangeard de la Boissière, would not accept cooptation as a member of the provincial assembly at Orléans because he was too old to travel easily. But, he wrote, he could not refuse membership in the subordinate assembly for the Blois region, "thinking that decent citizens ought to contribute to the success of an establishment which is to bring about a fortunate revolution in the interest of the peoples. One must hope that time and the useful knowledge that can be acquired by the members of these assemblies will give them the solidity they are capable of possessing." Three months later he remarked: "The ancien régime

---

blée provinciale de la généralité d'Orléans (1787–1790) (Paris, Imprimerie de la Faculté de Médecine, 1907), p. 605; Marie de Roux, *La Révolution à Poitiers et dans la Vienne* (Poitiers, 1910, as *Mémoires de la Société des Antiquaires de l'Ouest,* 3rd ser., 4), p. 85; *Procès-verbaux des séances de l'administration provinciale de la généralité de Lyon,* ed. Georges Guigue (Lyon, 1898), pp. 2, 7; Félix Mourlot, *La Fin de l'ancien régime et les débuts de la Révolution dans la généralité de Caen* (Paris, Société de l'Histoire de la Révolution Française, 1913), pp. 35–36; Désiré cardinal Mathieu, *L'Ancien régime dans la province de Lorraine et Barrois* (Paris, 1879), pp. 356–358.

9. "It was above all the radical reform that the administration, properly so-called, underwent in 1787, which, having brought disorder into public affairs, came to disturb each citizen even in his private life . . . Public administration had suddenly changed all its agents and reformulated all its maxims. The state had not at first appeared to receive a great shock from this immense reform; but every Frenchman had felt a small private commotion." *L'Ancien Régime et la Révolution,* ed J.-P. Mayer and André Jardin, 2 vols. (Paris, Librairie Gallimard, 1952–1953), I, 236, 243.

left no hope of obtaining tax reductions by making it known that others were not being taxed. Now everyone will be able to denounce his neighbor, without embarrassment."[10] These statements identify what was surely one important element of new experience for the magistrates who were members of provincial assemblies, the information amassed about economic and fiscal affairs and with this the discussion of the politics of taxation. Another aspect of the assemblies is suggested by Rangeard's feeling of obligation to become a member. Membership in one of these assemblies gave official recognition to the political prominence of many men. This identified a kind of political élite, in the minds of its members and also of a larger public. If elections were to be held, there would be some obvious candidates.

The operative value of the provincial assemblies, and especially of the bailliage magistrates within them, was not very great. The sessions were brief, and the assemblies' affairs were guided during most of 1788 by interim commissions, particularly by the two *procureurs syndics* chosen by each assembly. Few bailliage magistrates were members of these commissions, and even more rarely was one named procureur syndic. On the whole, for bailliage magistrates as for the general public, the importance of the provincial assemblies lay not in what they accomplished, or could have accomplished, but in the issues that were stirred up by the effort to establish them. Above all, the problems of representation was presented in terms very similar to those of 1788 and 1789. The proportion of the membership representing the Third Estate was fixed at half, but, more important, it was explicitly and widely considered as a question to be settled. The selection of half the members by royal appointment not only eliminated, for the

10. Félix Faulcon, *Correspondance*, ed. Gabriel Debien, 2 vols. (Poitiers, 1939–1953, as *Archives Historiques du Poitou,* 51 and 55), I, 302–303, 317 (Rangeard de la Boissière to Faulcon, 26 October 1787, and 19 January 1788).

time being, the free choice of the electors but also raised general questions concerning eligibility for selection as a representative. The bailliage magistrates, like other educated, property-owning town dwellers, were thereby given matter for reflection much more than for action.

The next large-scale measures of royal reform, undertaken by Lamoignon, had practically an opposite impact on the bailliage magistrates. Instead of attempting to keep them from exercising political choice, Lamoignon confronted them and the parlements with the two simple alternatives of supporting or opposing a drastic program of institutional change. His plans were prepared during a lull in political activity in Paris and Versailles, in an atmosphere of relative calm, during the early months of 1788. The international crisis occasioned by Prussian intervention in the United Provinces had ended with the restoration of the Prince of Orange. The fiscal crisis had declined in urgency since the Parlement of Paris had registered an edict delaying the expiration of the second vingtième tax, and the rentes issued in January had quickly been bought up by investors and speculators. The cold and the mud of winter were having their usual effects on governmental machinery dependent on scribes and messengers. It is true, some members of the Parlement of Paris were slowly proceeding to draft new remonstrances, which were finally published in March and April, against the royal session of 19 November 1787 and against *lettres de cachet*. But public discussion in the capital continued at a slower pace, measured by the publication of pamphlets at the rate of one a week.[11]

The legislation presented by Lamoignon to the Parlement of

11. Between 1 July and 19 November 1787, the rate of publication of new pamphlets in Paris had been 2.2 per week. Between 19 November 1787 and 8 May 1788 it was 1.1 per week. (In the rest of France as a whole, in contrast, the rate of publication rose from 1 pamphlet a week to more than 3 pamphlets a week.) Ralph W. Greenlaw, "Pamphlet Literature in France during the Period of the Aristocratic Revolt (1787–1788)," *Journal of Modern History*, 29 (1957), 349–354, Table 1.

Paris on 8 May 1788 emanated from a divided ministry and did not form a coherent whole.[12] It had three major objectives: the reform of criminal procedure, the reorganization of the law-courts, and the creation of a new constitutional form, the plenary court. Each of these aspects of Lamoignon's program was designed for a distinct sector of opinion and by a distinct group of governmental advisers.

Concerning revisions of law and procedure for criminal cases, Lamoignon sought advice from a committee of six Paris lawyers. The principal figure in the committee was Target, who was on close terms with Malesherbes, Lamoignon's older cousin and fellow-minister, a noted humanitarian.[13] In the declaration modifying criminal procedure, the preamble asserts that "the progress of enlightenment would alone suffice" to suggest the need to reconsider Louis XIV's ordinance.[14] Announcing that all the king's subjects may address advice to Lamoignon on this matter, the preamble declares that the conclusions of public opinion, after mature examination, will be given the force of law. The reforms themselves required specific description of every offense charged, required a three-vote plurality of the

12. Texts reprinted in the *Recueil général des anciennes lois françaises*, ed. François-André Isambert et al., 29 vols. (Paris, 1821–1833), XXXVIII, 525–567. In the judgment of Marcel Marion, *Le Garde des sceaux Lamoignon et la réforme judiciaire de 1788* (Paris, Hachette, 1905), p. 7, the legislation came at an inopportune time but was a well-ordered and well-considered whole, realistically practicable. Less optimistic and more credible descriptions are presented by Charles-E. Séeger, *Essai sur les grands bailliages établis en 1788 en Normandie* (Caen, E. Domin, 1911), and Paul Metzger, *Le Conseil supérieur et le grand bailliage de Lyon (1771–1774, 1788)* (Lyon, A. Rey, 1913), pp. 361–442.

13. Egret, *Pré-Révolution*, p. 123 (note); Pierre Grosclaude, *Malesherbes, témoin et interprète de son temps* (Paris, Fischbacher, 1961), pp. 299 and 567.

14. The preamble goes on to state that "l'esprit systématique" will never evoke anything but suspicion on the ministers' part. But this seems no more than a ritual condemnation of ideology and contrasts with Maupeou's denunciation of "l'esprit de système" as the essential cause of the parlements' egregious resistance to royal authority. (*Recueil général des anciennes lois françaises*, XXII, 501–506.)

judges voting for conviction in a capital case and a month's delay thereafter to permit appeals and acts of clemency, and abolished humiliating and painful procedures in the interrogatory after conviction. These were all applications of enlightened and humanitarian principles.

The task of proposing reorganization of the bailliages was entrusted primarily to a councillor of state, Philpin de Piépape, former chief judge of the bailliage of Langres. He sought information and suggestions from at least two of the principal judges in other bailliages.[15] The resulting ordinance on the administration of justice embodied a traditional ideal of provincial town dwellers: to reduce the delays in obtaining judgment, the costs of lawsuits, and the crowds of litigants in the royal and provincial capitals. The preamble states that "the wisest of all the laws" previously enacted on this matter was the edict of Henri II creating the présidial courts in 1552. The new ordinance originated, in effect, in the program for strengthening the présidial courts contemplated by d'Aguesseau in the 1740's and timidly begun in the aftermath of Maupeou's dismissal in the 1770's. Lamoignon abandoned the gradual timing characteristic of d'Aguesseau. His ordinance defined a new category of tribunals, the *grands bailliages*, and gave them power to render final judgment in most civil and criminal cases. The only cases reserved to the parlements were those in

15. A letter from a councillor of state to Chabrol, chief criminal judge at Riom, 31 January 1788, is quoted by Edouard Evérat, *La sénéchaussée d'Auvergne et siège présidial de Riom au XVIIIᵉ siècle* (Paris, 1885), p. 294. Another letter, from Irland de Bazôges, chief civil judge at Poitiers, writing from Paris to a colleague in Poitiers, 15 January 1788, provides some details: "The ministry is no longer concealing that it is engaged in making our courts and even the lower ones more useful to the provinces. This is being worked on seriously, but it is a big operation: it will be examined by M. [Philpin] de Piépape, royal commissioner for legislation, and M. [Dufaure] de Rochefort, [*maître des requêtes*,] who is *rapporteur* for the *bureau des réunions* [*des sièges et offices royaux, du conseil d'etat du Roi*]. I am being asked for additional details; send me what you have ready." Quoted by Roux, p. 115.

which the value in controversy exceeded the very large sum of 20,000 livres, or a crime was charged against a privileged person exempt from judgment other than by a parlement, or the issue concerned regalian rights, the royal domain, the rights of peers, or the legal status of individuals. The Châtelet of Paris, forty-four other bailliages, and the judicial councils of Alsace and Roussillon were designated to become grands bailliages. This reorganization of the judiciary was in no way a reform of guiding principles. Venality of offices, fees paid by litigants to judges, ennoblement of officeholders—these traditional practices were not affected. The reassignment of powers and duties among existing institutions was an extreme version of a reform long contemplated and was responsive to desires expressed by the small-town bourgeoisie in 1614 and thereafter.

The third principal measure associated historically with Lamoignon was the edict establishing the plenary court. This was initially not his idea. Indeed, it was inconsistent with his conduct in opposition to the Maupeou parlement, and it rested on principles incompatible with those underlying his tradition-minded decentralization of the lawcourts. The idea for the plenary court came from Loménie de Brienne or someone who advised him.[16] Like the assembly of notables, and like Loménie de Brienne's plan for a national assembly chosen indirectly by the provincial assemblies, the plenary court might make it possible to avoid convoking the Estates General.

As described in the edict, the plenary court was to have 142 members, approximately as many as the Parlement of Paris or

16. "I do not know what short-sighted man proposed to M. de Brienne at the same time the plan for the plenary court . . . The keeper of the seals, who had fought against the plan, was obliged to give way to the ascendancy of M. de Brienne, whom he needed." Jean-Paul Rabaut de Saint-Etienne, *Précis historique de la Révolution française,* 6th ed. (Paris, 1813), p. 76. Cf. Antoine-François-Claude Ferrand, *Mémoires,* ed. H. de Broc (Paris, 1897), p. 25. Egret, *Pré-Révolution,* p. 247, ascribes, I believe, insufficient emphasis to this evidence.

the assembly of notables of 1787. In composition, the plenary court was a hybrid of the Parlement and the assembly of notables. Its nucleus was to be the forty-seven magistrates of the *grand'chambre* of the Parlement of Paris, with the addition of sixteen magistrates from other parlements, the Paris chambre des comptes and the Paris cour des aides; the actual members of these sovereign courts would comprise 44 percent of the membership of the plenary court. The other members were to include the seven princes of the blood royal, thirteen archbishops and bishops, thirty-seven nobles not in the magistracy (twenty-eight of these being the lay peers), four councillors of state, and four *maîtres des requêtes*. All this was much the same as in the assembly of notables. The plenary court would differ from it principally in not including the twenty-five mayors of important towns and the twelve deputies from the *pays d'états* who had sat among the notables.[17]

The plenary court's duties were to register all general legislation common to the whole kingdom and to adjudicate forfeiture of office by magistrates guilty of disobedience. It would be empowered to draw up remonstrances, but only within two months after receiving the royal act in question. Its registration of new taxes would be provisional, until a subsequent meeting of the Estates General: here again, the hybrid nature of the plenary court appears, in that provisional approval would be appropriately given not by a court of law but by an assembly of notables.

The preamble of the edict set forth practical and constitutional justifications for the plenary court. It pointed out that the ministry's program had met with resistance from some of the

17. The plenary court was to include, finally, the six honorary councillors in the Parlement of Paris, four "other qualified persons" appointed by the King, and three great officers of the crown (grand almoner, grand master of the king's household, and grand chamberlain). The chancellor or, in his absence (as in 1788), the keeper of the seals would preside, and the proctor- and advocates-general of the Parlement of Paris would serve as king's counsel.

provincial parlements, that provincial assemblies, freedom of the grain trade, conversion of the *corvée* into a monetary payment, and continuance of the second vingtième tax could therefore not be put into effect in all parts of the kingdom. To overcome this resistance by exercising the royal authority in a lit de justice would be repugnant to the king's paternal goodwill; besides, it would spread anxiety and undermine investors' confidence in the royal credit. Thus the practical need for a single court to register all general legislation. Further, such an institution had existed some five centuries before and, according to the preamble, had never ceased to exist: an assembly of persons entrusted with verifying and publishing the laws was part of the French constitution. The plenary court had been and would henceforth be this assembly.

Such a description of the French constitution might seem, in retrospect, an ironic joke on those theorists of the history of the parlements who had written of the May fields of the Frankish monarchy. But it was surely more than that. It represented, on the one hand, a departure from the position "C'est légal, parce que je le veux," which Louis XVI had asserted in the Parlement of Paris on 19 November 1787. On the other hand, in view of the extreme novelty of the plenary court as an institution, the edict asserted in effect that the king and his ministers could and would define and redefine not only ordinary law but constitutional forms. The edict was being prepared for publication at precisely the time when the Parlement of Paris was adopting the remonstrance of 11 April 1788, containing a new, extreme challenge to royal rights.[18] The correctness of either position could be determined only by a long and elaborate study of precedents. What is more important, in the present context, is

18. *Remontrances du Parlement de Paris au XVIIIᵉ siècle*, ed. Jules Flammermont, 3 vols. (Paris, 1888–1898), III, 721–734, discussed by John F. Ramsey, "The Judicial Reform of 1788 and the French Revolution," in *Studies in Modern European History in Honor of Franklin Charles Palm* (New York, Bookman Associates, 1956), pp. 217–238.

the simple fact that the nature of the constitution had become explicitly a political issue over which the claims of each side were clearly escalating.[19]

The political strategy implied by the creation of the plenary court likewise seems clear. It was an effort to come to terms with the moral center of the large and complex world of judges and lawyers, the grand' chambre of the Parlement of Paris, and an effort to destroy the political power of the impulsive youths in the *chambres des enquêtes* of Paris and also, especially, to destroy the power of the provincial parlements. This strategy would have had a greater chance of success if, in each province where there was an important parlement, provincial estates had been established as a kind of political equivalent to the plenary court.[20] In the event, the parlements differed in their responses but were able to unite in resistance to an unprecedented degree and were strongly supported by many advocates in their localities.[21]

The issue was referred in the first instance to the magistrates in the forty-five bailliages that had been selected as grands bailliages. Lamoignon and his collaborators had tried to choose dependable allies among the courts. He had to rely on the in-

19. A remote but in some ways similar set of circumstances is described by Sir David Keir in his chapter on "The Decline and Fall of Conciliar Government" in early seventeenth-century England: "The reigning house and its opponents alike proved destitute of the gifts of intellect and character which would have made a gradual adjustment of constitutional ideas possible . . . There was much bad law and worse history in the appeals which each side made to the constitutional practice of the past . . . Because it proved impossible any longer to agree as to how the constitution should be worked, each side strove to alter its structure so as to make its own will prevail." *Constitutional History of Modern Britain*, 7th ed. (London, Adam and Charles Black, 1964), pp. 159–161.

20. This is suggested by Egret, "La Prérévolution en Provence, 1787–1789," *Annales Historiques de la Révolution Française*, 26 (1954), 97–126: the mildest opposition of any parlement was in Provence, where the magistrates had already received the satisfaction of seeing some of their number sit in the revived provincial estates, in January 1788.

21. Egret, *Pré-Révolution*, pp. 251–280, gives a good account.

tendants to effectuate the judicial reorganization and, where possible, chose présidial courts in the towns where the intendants resided. In the territory of the Parlement of Paris, all thirteen intendants' towns except La Rochelle were assigned grands bailliages, and all sixteen grands bailliages were in intendants' towns except those at Angoulême, Le Mans, Beauvais, Sens, and Langres. In Normandy, the three grands bailliages were in the three intendants' towns. But in the territories of the other provincial parlements, there were not as many intendants as grands bailliages; their surveillance and protection were readily available almost exclusively in the very towns that were seats of the parlements so adversely affected by the creation of the plenary court.[22]

The designated grands bailliages were confronted with an agonizing choice, which could not be unequivocally settled either by reference to constitutional principles and the impulses of professional zeal or by calculations of self-interest. The parlements having protested against the legislation of 8 May, and the King having commanded its implementation, they had to accept the risks of disobedience to one or the other. These risks could not readily be measured. It was impossible to know whether or when Lamoignon would follow Maupeou into private life and only too easy to predict the attitude of the parlements thereafter. The first reaction, characteristic of most grands bailliages, was to hesitate, watching for the assertion of leadership within the most influential companies of

22. Toulouse, Grenoble, Bordeaux, Dijon, Aix, Rennes, Metz, Besançon, Nancy. On the other hand, in these provinces no intendant resided in fourteen localities where grands bailliages were to be established: in Languedoc, Carcassonne, Nîmes, and Villefranche-de-Rouergue; in Dauphiné, Valence; in Guyenne, Condom, Dax, and Périgueux; in Burgundy, Chalon-sur-Saône and Bourg-en-Bresse; in Provence, Digne; in Brittany, Nantes and Quimper; in Franche-Comté, Vesoul; and in Lorraine, Mirecourt. A list of all the jurisdictions is given by Marion, pp. 263–269.

magistrates or awaiting decisive action by the intendant which would lift the burden of responsibility from themselves.

The vast majority of conscientious magistrates doubtless approved the institution of the grands bailliages. The primary question for them was simply whether this reorganization of the courts was so beneficial as to outweigh whatever ill effects might be expected from the creation of the plenary court. The question thus brought into play the magistrates' attitudes on the major unresolved constitutional issue: the proper role of the parlements and the precise nature of the usual distinction between monarchy and despotism. But the answers that the magistrates gave by their conduct were far from being a clear expression of sentiment on this issue and were affected by previous relations with a parlement and personal allegiances of every sort as well as by anxiety over the consequences of their actions. Something of the atmosphere in which their decisions were formed is conveyed by a letter from Faulcon, the young councillor in the sénéchaussée of Poitiers, whose antipathy to the Parlement of Paris we have already noted. The sénéchaussée had received the new legislation on 15 May; the chief judge wrote to Lamoignon indicating the difficulties that stood in the way of securing the sénéchaussée's acceptance of the legislation; Lamoignon replied that the king wanted the sénéchaussée to register it "without delay"; and the chief judge convoked the magistrates to meet at 6 A.M. on 24 May.[23] In that meeting, Faulcon wrote,

At first I thought as you do about it, and openly declared myself on the side of the opponents; but in the end, after renewed orders from the king to register without delay, after a six-hour session in which considerations for and against were fully examined, having started to pronounce against registration in my first remarks, shaken by the sensible opinions of some of my colleagues, and con-

23. Simon-Pierre Coutineau, ms. journal, entry dated 15 May 1788.

sidering that these new institutions were sure to be of inestimable value to our fellow citizens, that an overt resistance could have unfortunate results both for them and for us, by causing us to lose the rights entrusted to us, that more than half the grands bailliages had already registered, and that it was both ridiculous and illogical to refuse a valuable benefit long called for by the generality of the people, brought around, as I say, by these important reasons and several others which escape my memory, I decided to revise my opinion, and the registration passed at the end of the session by unanimous consent of the sixteen judges present.

As for the Parlement, I'll tell you frankly that I did not sympathize with it, and could never regret that it has been deprived of the capacity to register the laws. In fact, open the historical records and the archives of jurisprudence. Neither favor the Parlement . . . The magistrates of that tribunal . . . have never openly resisted our kings' despotic wishes except to the extent that these were contrary to their own prerogatives or personal interests; and if . . . we go on to consider their way of rendering justice . . . they are the people's scourges and insatiable blood-suckers . . .

Some speak of great principles; it is said that the parlements belong to the fundamental constitution of the monarchy, that they are irremovable and that the prince has no right to touch their constitution, which is part of that of the State itself. That whole display is only a contrived illusion, which however misleads credulous and uneducated folk . . .

An assembly or some tribunal was needed, solely charged with registering the laws for the whole kingdom . . . I shall say frankly that the plenary court does not fulfill my desires in that respect and that its present composition appears to me too exposed to the ministers' influence, but I hope that sooner or later it will undergo changes and that one day it will be entirely composed of the deputies of the different provinces.[24]

In this account, the multiple reasons mentioned in self-defense against a critical friend and the vague hope that the plenary court will become a representative institution in the future appear almost parenthetical beside the emotional force of Faulcon's condemnation of the Parlement of Paris. Yet this

24. Faulcon, *Correspondance*, I, 331–333 (Faulcon to Texier, 20 June 1788).

was by no means the whole story. In Poitiers, the chief judge's father had served in the judicial council established there by Maupeou, and the chief judge himself was "devoted to the Keeper of the Seals."[25] His influence in the deliberations on 24 May 1788 is not mentioned by Faulcon. Besides, the letter does not explain the absence of four judges (Dansays, his brother-in-law Dutillet, and his cousin Nicolas, as well as Vincent) and does not mention the sénéchaussée's formal decision to ask the king to conserve the Parlement "in its entire form and its power to verify the laws."[26]

In some localities, the circumstances and the results were nearly the reverse of those in Poitiers. The bailliage of Caen, for instance, had strongly resisted Maupeou's institution of a judicial council at nearby Bayeux, and in 1784 the chief judge at Caen had turned to the Parlement of Normandy for assistance in the local political struggle against the mayor of Caen. The special bonds of patron and client held firm in 1788. The magistrates of Caen wrote to Lamoignon that they were distressed by the "sudden and unexpected revolution," and they refused to act as a grand bailliage.[27]

Sharp disagreements within the judicial company occurred elsewhere. In Le Mans, the chief judge and eight other magistrates accepted the reform but were unable to overcome the determination of five colleagues who would not serve in the grand bailliage. Three of the latter were exiled, by lettres de cachet, to small towns in neighboring provinces. From Le Blanc, in Berry, one of these men wrote to his wife that he

25. Faulcon, *Correspondance,* I, 326 (Rangeard de la Boissière to Faulcon, third week of May 1788).
26. The full text is quoted by Charles de Gennes, "Notice sur le présidial de Poitiers," *Mémoires de la Société des Antiquaires de l'Ouest,* 26 (1860–1861), 359–528, on pp. 504–505.
27. Robert Carabie, "L'Enregistrement au bailliage de Caen des édits de mai 1788," *Annales de Normandie,* 9 (1959), 301–314; Jean-Claude Perrot, "Conflits administratifs et conflits sociaux au XVIIIᵉ siècle," *Annales de Normandie,* 13 (1963), 131–138.

regarded his judicial career as finished. "I have not the least desire to resume the functions I have abandoned; what made them agreeable was the unity that reigned in the company, but that unity has unfortunately been broken . . . Look at the company now, divided into two factions which are going to detest each other, for matters have been carried to the point where all the ties of confraternity have been broken. What could I have to do with men for whom I have no esteem?"[28]

The larger number of grands bailliages, however, preserved a semblance of internal unity as they moved from delay to equivocation, taking refuge in procedural formalities, registering the new measures while noting that they were forced to comply with the royal will, and avoiding any clear commitment throughout the summer. In the autumn, the proctor-general of the Parlement of Paris attempted to classify the conduct of the grands bailliages in his jurisdiction. He listed five "which absolutely refused to perform any functions" assigned to them by the reform: the Châtelet of Paris, the bailliages of Bourges and Orléans, and the sénéchaussées of Lyon and Angoulême. Seven others "appeared to have some willingness yet performed no functions" (perhaps mainly because lawyers withdrew pending cases from them): Amiens, Beauvais, Châlons-sur-Marne, Le Mans, Moulins, Riom, and Tours. Finally, four "had special reasons" for serving: Soissons, Sens, Langres, and Poitiers.[29] In all, five were adamant in their loyalty to the Parlement, and eleven obeyed the king with varying degress of hesitation and ambiguity.

In the territories of the other parlements, with very few ex-

28. Quoted by P. Ballu, *François Ménard de la Groye* (*1742–1813*), *magistrat manceau* (Le Mans, Imprimerie Jean Vilaire, 1963), p. 41.

29. B.N., ms. Joly de Fleury 2153, ff. 106–113. It may be surmised that in Langres the special reason was the collaboration of the former chief judge, Philpin de Piépape, with Lamoignon, and that in Poitiers it was the loyalty of the chief judge, Irland de Bazôges, and the king's proctor, Filleau, to him. At Sens, Loménie de Brienne had been translated to the archbishopric there, from that of Toulouse.

ceptions the grands bailliages located in towns other than those where the parlements sat accepted their new duties. The judges of the bailliage of Rouen and the sénéchaussée of Toulouse braved the disapproval of their respective parlements, the opposition of most advocates, and the coarse hostility of the local populace, but the other grands bailliages in the same towns as the parlements refused to register the legislation.

The establishment of the grands bailliages effected a new distinction in prestige and a division of political interest among judicial companies that had theretofore been nominally equals, the présidial courts. It was foreseeable that to choose forty présidial courts (as well as five ordinary bailliages) for this kind of enhancement was to invite many of the other sixty-three présidial courts to oppose the whole idea. Especially was this true when the creation of the plenary court offered a constitutional issue through which these présidial courts could transform private disappointment into civic indignation. In the territory of the Parlement of Paris, there were twenty-six présidial courts left over after Lamoignon's selection of the grands bailliages. Seventeen, generally the largest and most prestigious, reported that they registered his legislation under duress and some of them protested more actively; the remaining nine présidial courts in the jurisdiction appear to have acquiesced in silence.[30] In the territories of the other parlements, there were thirty-seven présidial courts not elevated to

30. According to a letter from the proctor-general of the Parlement of Paris to the first president, 29 October 1788 (B.N., ms. Joly de Fleury 2153, ff. 6–15), the présidial courts reporting a registration with protest or under duress were at Angers, Aurillac, Auxerre, Blois, Château-Gontier, Chaumout-en-Bassigny, Clermont-Ferrand, Guéret, Laon, La-Rochelle Mâcon, Mantes, Meaux, Melun, Saint-Pierre-le-Moutier, and Troyes. (Egret, *Pré-Révolution*, p. 286, adds Reims to this list on the basis of B.N., mss. Joly de Fleury 1099–1100.) It can be presumed that no protest emanated from the other nine présidial courts: La Flèche (in Anjou); Châtillon-sur-Indre (in Touraine); Chartres, Montargis; Abbeville and Senlis (in Picardy); Château-Thierry and Provins (in Brie); and Vitry-le-François (in Champagne).

grands bailliages. In the territory of the Parlement of Toulouse, there were ten such courts and all protested the legislation, as did all three such courts in Burgundy. In Normandy only the présidial court of Coutances followed the lead of the grand bailliage of Caen, and in Lorraine the présidial court of Saint-Dié protested, but that of Dieuze did not.[31] In all, probably at least half of these thirty-seven courts protested.

Among the lesser bailliages without présidial jurisdiction, there was little desire to risk an independent political expression opposed to the ministers and the intendant. A campaign by the parlements and their adherents was needed to stir up protests. As the five magistrates in the small town of Avallon, in Burgundy, observed, when they finally published a protest on 12 June, they were obliged to do so because otherwise "one might deduce from our silence a culpable indifference, or a still more culpable circumspection."[32] Even so, protests emanated from only a minority of the nonprésidial bailliages.[33]

31. Egret, *Pré-Révolution*, p. 287; Christian Pfister, "Les Préliminaires de la Révolution à Nancy. L'agitation parlementaire de 1788," *Mémoires de l'Académie de Stanislas*, 6th ser., 7 (1909–1910), 88–161, on p. 121.

In the jurisdiction of the Parlement of Bordeaux, the présidial court at Agen was not chosen as a grand bailliage. Its judges disagreed over whether to register the edicts. On 18 August 1788, meeting in their council chamber, those present voted 8–3 in favor of doing so; but thereafter a quorum could not be secured for a public session and the registration had still not been effected in November when withdrawal of the edicts was announced. Aristide Douarche, "Notes sur la justice et les tribunaux à Agen pendant la Révolution," *Révolution Française*, 22 (1892)–24 (1893), in vol. 22, pp. 245–247.

32. B.M. Dijon, fonds de Juigné, 57, XIII. The Parlement of Burgundy had met on 4 June and declared all who accepted places in the new tribunals to be "traitors to the king and to the nation, perjured and reputed infamous." Thereafter the bailliages of Saint-Jean-de-Losne, Saulieu, Montcenis, Avallon, and Beaune, as well as the présidial courts of Châtillon-sur-Seine and Semur-en-Auxois, issued pamphlets stating their protests.

33. In his letter of 29 October 1788, cited above, the proctor-general in Paris listed 22 bailliages "qui ont enregistré comme forcés," 19 "qui paraissent avoir enregistré purement et simplement," and 56

For the magistrates in the most prominent courts and the largest towns, the inner turmoil of conflicting duties, the anxiety over the future actions of parlements and royal ministers, and the factional divisions in the judicial profession were all intensified in their effects by being presented to public criticism. It was the explosion of pamphlets during the spring and summer of 1788 which especially marked the entrance of the leading bailliage magistrates on the political stage, where many of them were cruelly treated by the audience. The diatribes against the bailliage magistrates of Rouen and Toulouse, who betrayed their parlements and therewith their cities, were particularly extreme. In the kingdom as a whole, the rate of publication of new pamphlets increased from about six per week in the period before 8 May to about thirty-three per week during the two ensuing months.[34] Most of the pamphlets appeared in provincial cities and towns and argued more or less vehemently against the plenary court. Doubtless the mass of pamphlets represented a frightened and angry minority, defending its political principles and material interests and attacking the ministers who threatened them. Although about half, perhaps more, of all the bailliage magistrates may have genuinely supported Lamoignon's entire program, a far greater number were profoundly troubled by the necessity of making an important political choice and frightened or irritated by the violence of political passions swirling around them. After Lamoignon's dismissal and the suspension of his reform institutions, there remained, at the end of 1788, yet another new experience for the magistrates, in what can be described as consensus politics.

---

which had not informed him whether they had protested and which we can presume did not do so. In Brittany, 14 of the 23 nonprésidial sénéchaussées protested, according to Augustin Cochin, *Les Sociétés de pensée et la Révolution en Bretagne,* 2 vols. (Paris, Librairie Plon, 1925), II, 169–170. In Lorraine, 15 of the 28 nonprésidial baillages protested, according to Pfister, pp. 119–123.

34. Greenlaw, "Pamphlet Literature," p. 352, and Table 1.

It is scarcely an exaggeration to assert that early in 1789 everyone in France wanted the Estates General to meet. Away from Versailles, and especially among educated town dwellers, political agreement went far beyond that simple desire. An era of regeneration seemed about to open. Among magistrates in the bailliages, anticipation must have risen to a high pitch when the electoral regulation of 24 January 1789 was published. It defined the electoral districts for most of the kingdom as the territories of the bailliages. It specified the election procedures and placed them under the supervision of the chief civil judges and the king's proctors. All the magistrates could reasonably view the elections as public business for which they might have to exercise a particular responsibility. Where the office of chief civil judge or that of king's proctor was vacant, or where it was possible to argue that the officeholder was ineligible to perform his duties, a contest often ensued. The chief criminal judge, or the associate civil judge, or the dean among the councillors, would attempt to take over the duties of the chief civil judge, while the king's advocate would attempt to replace the king's proctor. The correspondence of the keeper of the seals and the comptroller-general of the finances relating to the elections is, in fact, full of claims, counterclaims, and rulings on questions of this kind.[35] The legal points at issue are of interest primarily in relation to the earlier history of these offices. The frequency of the disputes reveals the strength of the old habit of turning to the crown for the award of an honorable duty, even at the time when a new way of obtaining such a duty was being opened by the imminent elections.

In 290 localities, which included all the most important provincial cities and towns, the election procedure was to begin with assemblies of occupational and professional groups. Each corporation or association was required to elect one or more

35. *Recueil de documents relatifs à la convocation des Etats Généraux de 1789,* ed. Armand Brette, 4 vols. (Paris, 1894–1915), esp. I, xxxi–xlvi.

representatives to an electoral assembly for the town as a whole.[36] The regulation neither required nor forbade such a group to draw up its own cahier of complaints and requests for presentation in the assembly for the town, and in most places these groups did not do so. The judicial company of the bailliage in one of these towns was entitled to elect two representatives. The magistrates prepared written cahiers of their own even more rarely than other occupational groups.[37] In themselves, these written cahiers indicate concern for political issues and awareness that interests may be threatened or ideals achieved and that political opportunity can be seized and shaped in one way rather than another. There were six judicial companies of which a member had participated in the assembly of notables in 1787; four of these companies adopted written cahiers two years later.[38] But the absence of a written cahier does not prove that concern and awareness were lacking. Nor is any particular attitude or opinion necessarily represented especially heavily in the documents. Certainly the proposals

36. *Recueil de documents relatifs à la convocation des Etats Généraux,* I, 77 (electoral regulation, art. 26), and 101–102, 107, 120, 122, 125, 131, 137, 163, 169, 177, 182, 192, 199, 201, 206, 207, 209, 210, 217, 222, 233, 242, 264 (lists of towns thereby required to hold preliminary assemblies of corporate groups). In reality, some towns not included in any of these lists nevertheless proceeded under art. 26 of the regulation: for example, Provins. The total of 290 towns is therefore smaller than the actual number.

37. The corporate groups adopted preliminary cahiers in fewer than one-eighth of the towns where such groups were required to meet, if we may conclude from the surviving documents. In a number of places, however, most groups did so but not the bailliage magistrates. Beatrice F. Hyslop, *Répertoire critique des cahiers de doléances pour les Etats Généraux de 1789* (Paris, Leroux, 1933), pp. 158, 181, 232, 294, 327, 430, 517, and *Supplément* (Paris, 1952), pp. 27, 28, 127, 130, 141.

38. The cahiers adopted by the magistrates of Bourges and Limoges have been published, but those of the magistrates of Orléans and Troyes have not been recovered. [*Cahiers de doléances du bailliage d'Orléans pour les Etats Généraux de 1789,* ed. Camille Bloch, 2 vols. (Orléans, 1906–1907), II, 4; *Cahiers de doléances du bailliage de Troyes (principal et secondaires) et du bailliage de Bar-sur-Seine pour les Etats Généraux de 1789,* ed. Jules-Joseph Vernier, 3 vols. (Troyes, 1909–1911), I, 7.]

that might be made were not fixed merely by the belief that a corporate cahier would be useful for advancing them in the assembly for the town. In short, even a small number of cahiers, each of which was considered and adopted by a group of bailliage magistrates, may represent the opinions of many or even most of the magistrates who did not adopt corporate cahiers.

The extant cahiers of the bailliage magistrates are geographically well distributed, except that they do not come from the peripheral provinces which had their own parlements: in the east, Lorraine, Franche-Comté, and Burgundy; in the south, Dauphiné, Provence, Languedoc, and Guyenne; and, in the west, Brittany. Few cahiers drawn up by magistrates were prepared by the smaller bailliages which lacked présidial jurisdiction, and which had political interests that were in some ways distinct as well as economic and social circumstances different from those of the présidial courts. The opinions of magistrates in the présidial bailliages are set forth in ten extant cahiers.[39] Seven of these documents were pre-

39. Four texts adopted by présidial magistrates are in manuscript: at Beauvais (in A.D. Oise, B 57), La Rochelle (in A.D. Charente-Maritime, C 266 bis), Moulins (in B.M. Moulins, ms. 111), and Provins (in B.M. Provins, ms. 176).

Six texts have been published: *Cahiers de doléances des corps et corporations de la ville d'Alençon pour les Etats Généraux de 1789*, ed. René Jouanne (Alençon, 1929), pp. 3–14; *Cahiers de doléances des corporations de la ville d'Angers et des paroisses de la sénéchaussée particulière d'Angers pour les Etats Généraux de 1789*, ed. Arthur Le Moy, 2 vols. (Angers, 1915–1916), I, 87–99; *Cahiers de doléances du bailliage de Bourges et des bailliages secondaires de Vierzon et d'Henrichement pour les Etats Généraux de 1789*, ed. Alfred Gandilhon (Bourges, 1910), pp. 599–613; "Doléances des corporations et corps constitués de Limoges, 1789," ed. Alfred Leroux, *Archives Historiques de la Marche et du Limousin*, 12 vols. (Limoges and Tulle, 1887–1912), I, 1–126, on pp. 3–14; *Cahiers de doléances pour les Etats Généraux de 1789. Bailliage de Reims*, ed. Gustave Laurent (Reims, 1930), pp. 15–20; *Cahiers de doléances du tiers état du bailliage de Rouen*, ed. Marc Bouloiseau, 2 vols. (Paris, 1957–1960), I, 4–6.

[The manuscript identified in Miss Hyslop's *Répertoire* as the cahier

pared in towns in the territory of the Parlement of Paris; two were prepared in Normandy; and one was prepared in Limousin, subordinate to the Parlement of Bordeaux. In all, the political views of one-tenth of the présidial courts are recorded in the subsisting cahiers. These views do not consist merely of support or opposition for specific legislative and administrative actions. They include persuasive elaborations with a variety of nuances of phrasing which, for the magistrates who adopted the cahiers, may have been as important as the specific recommendations themselves. The principal positions and the details can best be considered together in relation to a few general topics.

As to the constitution, the cahiers of the présidial magistrates agreed on three fundamental propositions. They said that there should be regular meetings of the Estates General every few years, that its right to give or withhold consent to taxation must be recognized, and that provincial estates should be established. On each of these points, however, the magistrates of Beauvais adopted an opinion differing in emphasis from those of magistrates elsewhere and tending to indicate greater confidence in the administrative monarchy as it presently existed.[40] The difference in emphasis appears especially sharp where the cahiers set forth objectives to be accomplished before approval

---

of the magistrates of Quimper (A.N. B^a 26) is actually a protest written by six of them after the electoral assembly of the Third Estate there.]

40. The regular meetings of the Estates General were envisaged by most judicial companies as automatic. The magistrates of Beauvais indicated willingness to depend on the king to convoke them: "Le Roi sera supplié d'assembler les Etats Généraux tous les cinq ans." Most judicial companies put major stress on the principle of consent to taxation; the magistrates of Beauvais omitted the idea altogether. The other magistrates all called for the establishment of provincial estates; those of Beauvais did not mention them. In discussing tax reform, the magistrates of Beauvais implied that the nature and amount of taxation were for the king to determine: "Il sera très humblement supplié de diminuer le prix du sel." And they expressed confidence in the provincial assemblies set up in 1787. Ms. Beauvais (arts. 28, 34, 38).

of new taxes. Three cahiers urged that the deputies refuse to grant taxes until constitutional principles had been established to assure that the Estates General would meet regularly in the future.[41] The magistrates of Beauvais did not give priority to the establishment of constitutional principles. They said the deputies should simply ask the king "to ordain that no vote relating to taxes will be taken until in his wisdom he has considered the wishes and grievances of his people concerning religion, justice, and police."[42] The magistrates who insisted on control by the Estates General, and those of Beauvais who were inclined to rely on the royal ministers, differed in their attitudes to current affairs and immediate prospects rather than in terms of well-developed theories. The magistrates who especially emphasized the constitutional right to grant or refuse taxation were silent or vague concerning the relationship between the Estates General and the king's legislative power. The magistrates of Limoges said that a new constitution was needed in order to eliminate existing uncertainty as to "the power of the sovereign" and "the rights of the nation in general." Their own description of the future legislative branch provided a new example of ambiguity: "the Estates General with His Majesty." The same notion was expressed by the magistrates of Reims. A clear conception of a royal right to veto proposed legislation, and of the king's obligation to obey enacted law, was outlined by the magistrates of Alençon.[43] But in none of these cahiers is there an idea of sovereignty as an absolute

41. Ms., La Rochelle (arts. 1–4); *Cahiers Alençon*, p. 11; *Cahiers Reims*, p. 16. Similarly, but more vaguely, ms., Provins (art. 41): "Que . . . les députés ne s'occupent des impôts que lorsque les loix qui tendent à l'administration, lesquelles doivent amener le bonheur et la tranquillité de l'état, auront reçues leur sanction et auront été promulguées."

42. Ms., Beauvais (avant-propos).

43. *Archives Historiques du Limousin*, I, 4; *Cahiers Reims*, p. 15; *Cahiers Alençon*, p. 4.

right, whether of the people or of the ruler. The magistrates readily imagined conflict between the Estates General and the royal ministers over taxation. They did not foresee a contest leading to a stalemate over other legislative objectives. Not only would the king continue to take part in the legislative process but he would continue to choose his ministers. They would be required to supply information to the Estates General, and could be prosecuted and punished for malfeasance; but they could not be removed simply through losing the confidence of the legislature.[44] The political limitations on the monarchy indicated in these cahiers consisted at most in two points: to repose in the Estates General the right to refuse to provide economic resources; and to entrust the provincial estates, rather than royal commissioners, with apportionment of the fiscal burden.

The purposes as well as the amount of government expenditure were to be subject to broad control by the Estates General. The magistrates saw the evident necessity to obtain precise information about existing state debt and to provide for its reduction. Five of their cahiers suggested selling the royal domain, except the forests, in order to extinguish debt.[45] Three cahiers suggested using some of the revenues of wealthy ecclesiastical benefices for this purpose.[46]

In proposing reforms to control future expenditures, the magistrates aimed at reducing unjustifiable enrichment of those who profited from royal generosity and administrative inefficiency. The item of expenditure that was almost universally suspect in their eyes was the pension list. Nine cahiers, all except the one adopted by the magistrates of Reims,

44. *Cahiers Alençon,* p. 9; *Cahiers Rouen,* I, 5.
45. Ms., La Rochelle (art. 5); *Cahiers Alençon,* p. 10; *Cahiers Bourges,* p. 604; *Cahiers Rouen,* I, 4; *Archives Historiques du Limousin,* I, 10.
46. Ms., Moulins (art. 15); *Cahiers Angers,* I, 92; *Cahiers Bourges,* p. 609.

specifically called for careful scrutiny with a view to reductions in it.[47] Two cahiers display overt hostility to the nobles in Versailles and the financial intrigues from which they benefited.[48] The profits of tax collectors, treasurers, and contractors—all those financiers whose widespread unpopularity was both historic and symbolic—constituted another item of government expenditure to be reduced or eliminated. Seven of the magistrates' cahiers mentioned this or made a request, which can be taken as an equivalent, for direct payment of taxes to the provincial estates and thence into the royal coffers.[49] A minority of the magistrates included various other suggestions: cautious retrenchment in the expenses of the royal households;[50] reductions in the emoluments of generals and admirals;[51] elimination of the intendants and hence of their salaries;[52] limitation of the profits of postal administrators.[53]

What these magistrates said about government expenditure is less significant than what they failed to say. They omitted any mention of military costs as a whole, except the magistrates of Angers, who said that the Estates General ought to determine the number of troops to be maintained in peace-

47. The chief civil judge at Reims, Lévesque de Pouilly, was one of 7 bailliage magistrates in the entire kingdom to receive a pension. [Etat des magistrats qui ont des pensions sur le Trésor royal, 1788 (A.N., BB[30] 62).] His pension was listed as 3,000 livres.

48. *Cahiers Angers,* I, 92; *Cahiers Bourges,* p. 605.

49. Mss., Beauvais (arts. 29–31), La Rochelle (art. 6), Moulins (art. 8), Provins (art. 50); *Cahiers Angers,* I, 92; *Cahiers Reims,* p. 16; *Archives Historiques du Limousin,* I, 6.

50. Mss., La Rochelle (art. 5), Moulins (art. 11); *Cahiers Angers,* I, 91.

51. Ms., Moulins (art. 12); *Cahiers Angers,* I, 93.

52. *Cahiers Angers,* I, 90.

53. Ms., Beauvais (art. 32): "Les administrateurs des postes faisant des bénéfices immenses, et le produit de cette partie des finances ne pouvant qu'augmenter chaque jour par l'étendue des correspondances et l'usage d'écrire qui s'est introduit dans tous les ordres de l'Etat."

time.[54] Only the magistrates of Alençon displayed any conception of a power to be exercised by the Estates General to determine the purposes for which public funds would be expended. They did not speak of the positive objectives of government expenditure, again with the exception of the magistrates of Alençon, who anticipated action to meet "the costs of establishments necessary and advantageous to society."[55] Altogether, the magistrates' cahiers fail to show real comprehension of those causes of the national debt which were quantitatively most important, of the sweeping measures needed to surmount the financial crisis, or of the opportunities for policy determination that might come with control over the expenditures of government.

For government revenues, the magistrates favored a principle of equality of taxation. They varied in the emphasis and rigor with which they stated this, in their selection of existing privileges that appeared particularly unjust, and in the methods they wished to see adopted for the future. The magistrates of Limoges and Moulins formulated their ideas briefly and in absolute terms: taxes must bear upon both wealth and income of every sort; they must be proportional and irrespective of political power or social rank; and they must be assessed as shares of definite sums granted by the Estates General.[56] This position implied a fiscal policy which would be as neutral as possible, economically, politically, and socially, between various elements in the population, but which was to be administered so as to reinforce the control of the Estates General over the royal ministers. Such a policy was favored by the magistrates of Alençon also, but they showed themselves anxious to postpone any confrontation with defenders of the fiscal privileges of the clergy and nobles. First, the Estates

54. *Cahiers Angers,* I, 91.
55. *Cahiers Alençon,* p. 10.
56. Ms., Moulins (art. 4); *Archives Historiques du Limousin,* I, 6.

General should consider the present exemption, in practice, of incomes from commerce: "the capitalists" ought perhaps to pay as much as landed proprieters. Then the assembly should decide whether all kinds of property and income ought to be taxed proportionally. Only afterward would it be urged to declare that privileges for the clergy and the nobles were unconstitutional.[57] This strategy evidently reflects fear that the Estates General might shatter into factions. The magistrates of Alençon exhibited less confidence than those of Moulins and Limoges, while favoring the same fiscal policy.

The element in this policy that was specifically favored by all the other cahiers was to strike down the immunities of the clergy. All exemptions of the nobles, too, were clearly designated for elimination, except by the magistrates of Bourges. The latter, indeed, considered that "all the citizens of a State ought to contribute to public expenses," but derived from this a condemnation of favored treatment for wealth other than land and for "speculators in money." On this they agreed generally with the magistrates of Angers, Provins, and Reims, who also desired taxation to bear effectively on wealth other than land.[58] The magistrates of Bourges, Angers, Provins, and Moulins, asked specifically for abolition of the tax collected from commoners who purchased noble estates (*francs fiefs*), a symbol of fiscal privilege.[59]

57. *Cahiers Alençon,* pp. 10, 13–14.

58. The magistrates of Bourges saw that it would be difficult to "penetrate the obscurity surrounding this moveable wealth." The magistrates of Angers suggested a tax on income from loans: they said that a person who in effect borrowed money, by contracting to pay a *rente constituée,* should withhold 5 percent from the payments; but they did not indicate how the tax collectors would make sure of obtaining the sums deducted. The magistrates of Reims simply urged the institution of a proportional tax on wealth other than real estate, and those of Provins merely "que le commerçant . . . paye une tax en raison de la force de son commerce." Ms., Provins (art. 67); *Cahiers Bourges,* p. 605; *Cahiers Angers,* I, 92; *Cahiers Reims,* p. 16.

59. It was only with reference to "this humiliating mark for which the reason no longer exists" that the magistrates of Bourges mentioned fiscal

The force behind these equalitarian statements concerning taxation was an indignant hostility, first of all to existing privileges for land held by the clergy and the nobility and, secondarily, to the failure of the tax system to draw upon commercial wealth. The elimination of privileges and exemptions, translated into positive principle, seemed to mean simply proportional taxation. Where the magistrates discussed other positive objectives and practical details, they diverged into various kinds of imprecision and incoherence.

Whether taxes were to be assessed on wealth or on income was not carefully examined in any of these ten cahiers. The magistrates of Angers, Bourges, and Reims, like those of Limoges, Moulins, and Alençon, mentioned both without distinguishing sharply between them; those of Beauvais and La Rochelle mentioned only wealth. In seven cahiers, it was stated or assumed that taxes should be apportioned in the old way as shares of a fixed total burden. The magistrates of Angers and Bourges, on the other hand, implied their readiness to accept a method of assessment as a percentage of income for certain taxes, notably a reformed version of the existing vingtièmes; those of Provins wanted to substitute the *impôt territorial* paid in kind for the existing taxes.[60] Whether equity required applying the same system of collection to all taxpayers or extending special treament to some was considered in five cahiers, with divergent results.[61] Whether all taxes or

---

equality of commoners and nobles. The magistrates of Angers simply included it in a list of taxes to be abolished, but those of Moulins called it "un reste de servitude" and those of Provins called it "un reste des anciens abus de la féodalité et contraire à l'intérêt même de l'impôt, à l'intérêt de la noblesse et au droit de propriété." Mss. Moulins (art. 8), Provins (art. 72); *Cahiers Angers*, I, 90; *Cahiers Bourges*, p. 613.

60. Ms., Provins (art. 67); *Cahiers Angers*, I, 92; *Cahiers Bourges*, p. 603.

61. The Angers magistrates believed that service as a local tax collector was too demeaning for the clergy, the nobles, and the holders of royal offices and wished to preserve their exemption from such service. Those at La Rochelle said that local tax collectors might be incapable of fair

only certain ones should be abolished was another question that was variously answered. The magistrates of Alençon placed special emphasis on the total abolition of all existing taxes and the rebuilding of the tax structure on the basis of new grants of authority by the Estates General.[62] The magistrates of Bourges argued for the retention of existing taxes, except the *aides*, the excises on wine that were collected on consumption by producers, on transport, and on wholesale and retail sale. Of all taxes, the aides were a major target for criticism by the judicial companies. Six asked for outright abolition,[63] and a seventh, for sharp reduction of their amounts.[64] Only the *gabelle* appeared comparably pernicious. Six cahiers asked for its abolition[65] and one, for thorough reform.[66] Both wine and salt were necessities,[67] equalled or surpassed in importance

---

treatment of parish priests, seigneurs, and others "whom in any other circumstance they are obliged to respect"; such persons should be listed on a special tax roll and permitted to pay directly to the treasury of the provincial estates. Those at Beauvais said that the same system of collection should be applied to all taxpayers, particularly to prevent separate ecclesiastical assessments from overburdening the parish priests. The magistrates of Limoges and Provins simply asserted that in each locality there should be one tax roll for all taxpayers. Mss., Beauvais (art. 28), La Rochelle (art. 6), Provins (art. 9); *Cahiers Angers*, I, 91; *Archives Historiques du Limousin*, I, 6.

62. *Cahiers Alençon*, p. 8.

63. Mss., Beauvais (art. 31), La Rochelle (art. 7), Provins (art. 52); *Cahiers Angers*, I, 90; *Cahiers Bourges*, p. 602; *Archives Historiques du Limousin*, I, 6.

64. Ms., Moulins (art. 5 bis).

65. Mss., Beauvais (art. 34), Moulins (art. 5), Provins (art. 52); *Cahiers Angers*, I, 90; *Cahiers Rouen*, I, 4; *Archives Historiques du Limousin*, I, 6.

66. *Cahiers Bourges*, pp. 599–602.

67. The magistrates of Bourges estimated that people drank wine at an annual rate of four-fifths of a *poinçon*, Paris measure, for each man, woman, and child in the kingdom. *Cahiers Bourges*, p. 602. This would amount to about 3 liters per week per person. Cf. Armand Machabey, *La Métrologie dans les musées de province et sa contribution à l'histoire des poids et mesures en France depuis le XIII⁰ siècle* (Troyes, Grande Imprimerie de Troyes, 1962), pp. 159, 178.

for most households only by bread, and these taxes were correspondingly unpopular. Their heavy incidence on the poor was, however, not the main reason generally given by the magistrates for wanting them abolished.[68] The chief objections were to the ceaseless vexation of taxpayers in collecting these taxes and the excessive profits of the tax collectors.[69] Underlying these objections, in the magistrates' minds, general ideas were compounded which they did not make explicit but which can be inferred. There was the assumption that taxes ought to be based on individual wealth or on income considered as a measure of wealth. Correspondingly, there was the tendency to regard taxes on consumer expenditures as unfair, mingled with the recognition that such taxes are both inflexible and difficult for the taxpayer to keep distinct in his accounts. Finally, most judges disliked the *gens de finance*, and favored administrative simplicity.[70]

68. The magistrates of Beauvais observed that the amount exacted in aides was "ruineuse pour les redevables," those of La Rochelle that the whole system of the aides was "ruineux pour les campagnes," and the magistrates of Moulins urged "que le sel soit à la portée des facultés de la classe la plus pauvre des citoyens." Mss., Beauvais (art. 31), La Rochelle (art. 8), Moulins (art. 5). But the other magistrates did not comment on the regressive incidence of these taxes.

69. The aides subjected "les citoyens de toutes classes aux recherches les plus honteuses, à des saisies et aux peines qui en sont la suite" (Bourges), and produced "une multitude de vexations arbitraires qui échappent à l'oeil de la justice" (La Rochelle). The gabelle was "l'impôt le plus odieux et le plus vexatoire" (Moulins), and the occasion of "recherches vexatoires qui ne tournent qu'au profit des fermiers généraux, et désolent les gens de la campagne" (Angers). Both taxes "ont plus contribués à enrichir des particuliers qu'à fermer les plaies de l'Etat" (Provins).

70. At Provins the magistrates said: "Que les impôts . . . au lieu et place de ceux dont la suppression devient nécessaire par les frais énormes de perception qu'ils entrainent au préjudice du Trésor royal, soient simples, sous une seule dénomination, et sans aucun accessoire. Que la durée des dits impôts soit toujours fixée, que la charge en devienne presque volontaire en frappant sur des objets purement de luxe, sur le nombre de domestiques de chacun, de croisées sur rue, portes cochères

The belief that the royal government should cease to impose needless complexity was expressed in straightforward fashion by those who called for the elimination of internal customs barriers. This step was suggested in six cahiers, with the objective of removing obstacles to commerce.[71] There was no other discussion of commerce or industry except by the magistrates of La Rochelle. The latter offered those engaged in commerce "the benevolence that is due to a class of citizens as useful as they are estimable." For the masters of trades, they wished to solicit the king's favor "for so worthy and numerous a part of his subjects." The patronizing tone suggests how far these judges were from mingling on equal terms with men in business and the trades. These sentiments were accompanied not by a statement of convictions about economic policy but by an offer of support for the demands of the local chamber of commerce and by three particular recommendations for local benefit.[72] In none of this was there a hint of devotion to freedom of enterprise as a principle. It showed, on the other hand, concern for local prosperity and willingness, certainly, to accept electoral support from businessmen.

The agricultural economy received similarly limited attention from the magistrates. A general adherence to physiocratic

---

. . . Que tout citoyen saisisse du premier coup d'oeil ce qu'il peut devoir au fisc, et alors il payera sans murmure l'impôt lorsqu'il aura la certitude qu'il doit tourner à l'avantage de l'État." Ms., Provins (art. 48, 49, 52).

71. Mss., Beauvais (art. 35), La Rochelle (art. 9), Moulins (art. 6), Provins (art. 52); *Cahiers Angers,* I, 90; *Archives Historiques du Limousin,* I, 13.

72. The magistrates of La Rochelle recommended lowering the duties on exports from the kingdom and on imports into France from the colonies; they objected to the importation of sugar from foreign refineries in competition with sugar refined in La Rochelle, and they proposed restoring the rules, abolished in 1777, which had permitted masters' widows to enter their occupations without paying fees and their sons and sons-in-law to pay reduced fees. The magistrates of Provins, it is true, briefly expressed the desire that trade be encouraged in their town, "as it has everything that can contribute to trade." Mss., La Rochelle (arts. 8, 9, 19), Provins (art. 65).

doctrine is displayed in the recommendation of the magistrates of Moulins that the Estates General should be concerned with "everything that is capable of favoring commerce and above all agriculture, on which depends the true wealth of the State."[73] But most judicial companies merely singled out one or two particular abusive practices that had adverse effects on agriculture. The problem that most commonly caught their attention was that of seigneurial hunting rights. Four cahiers recommended limitations on these rights, to allow cultivators to kill off wild creatures or require seigneurs to have this done.[74] The magistrates of Limoges were the only ones to record specific suggestions for economic development: temporary tax benefits to encourage land clearing and reclamation, reliance on private initiative instead of royal administration to carry on and improve horse-breeding. They also called for outright abolition of seigneurial monopolies, which they considered to be based on serfdom. The magistrates of Beauvais and Rouen recognized real property rights in the seigneurial monopolies, and suggested extinguishing them by indemnifying the proprietors. The magistrates of Bourges were the only ones who suggested eliminating perpetual dues in money and in kind, which ought to be redeemed, they said, for a sum twenty-five times the annual value.[75] The magistrates of Angers, although denouncing at length the usurpations of seigneurs, held a more conservative position. Their cahier condemned those seigneurs who had been taking rights of common from the villagers, cutting down trees along the country roads, collecting excessive fees upon the sale of rights to land within their seigneuries, or arranging for the registers of obligations due them to be revised by commissioners whom they appointed. It

73. Ms., Moulins (art. 21).

74. Mss., Beauvais (art. 25), Provins (art. 10); *Cahiers Angers*, I, 98; *Cahiers Rouen*, I, 6.

75. *Archives Historiques du Limousin*, I, 6, 10; ms., Beauvais (art. 24); *Cahiers Rouen*, I, 6; *Cahiers Bourges*, p. 606.

is noteworthy that the magistrates of Angers said nothing in opposition to the existence or the principles of the seigneurial régime itself. What they did say would, however, appeal to many rural electors in Anjou, where seigneurial usurpations had recently been the subject of an uproar.[76]

As important to most villagers as the seigneurial régime was the condition of the church and its effect on the practice of religion. Four cahiers adopted by magistrates merely comment on two or three particular aspects of this topic;[77] the magistrates of Alençon simply recommended disbanding most monastic orders, for "society will gain more from having good judges, good soldiers, and good cultivators than from keeping men who are supposed to have no occupation but the contemplative."[78]

The recurrent tone of these scattered comments and the paucity of their number reveal no keen interest in the problems affecting the practice of religion or the main facts defining its actual position in the society. In contrast, the magistrates of Beauvais, Bourges, Limoges, and Provins intended thorough and coherent reforms.[79] They all urged the provision of a decent minimum income for every parish priest, the figure of 1,200 livres being suggested at Bourges and Limoges. At Beau-

76. Le Moy, "Introduction," *Cahiers Angers,* I, xxxv–xxxix.

77. Elimination of all holy days except Sunday: ms., Moulins (art. 14). Criticism of parish priests who enforced payment of burial fees by refusing to celebrate subsequent marriages involving members of families that had not paid, criticism of *vicaires* begging for subsistence: *Cahiers Angers,* I, 93–94. Emphasis on maintaining liberties of the Gallican church, and desire for repairs of church buildings to be paid for by recipients of the tithe: *Cahiers Reims,* p. 15. Cessation of all kinds of payments to the papal curia and the *déport* paid by parish priests to bishops; prohibition of holding more than one benefice; simplified definition of the tithe: *Cahiers Rouen,* I, 5.

At La Rochelle the magistrates said nothing about religion or the church.

78. *Cahiers Alençon,* p. 10.

79. Mss., Beauvais (arts. 1–7), Provins (arts. 1–8); *Cahiers Bourges,* pp. 606–609; *Archives Historiques du Limousin,* I, 12.

vais, Bourges, and Limoges the magistrates said that election as a canon ought to be reserved for parish priests who had served for a certain number of years. All four cahiers called for the enforcement of existing laws which required bishops and archbishops to reside in their dioceses or forfeit part of their incomes. The Limoges magistrates wanted to apply these requirements to abbots and other benefice-holders also, and added a paragraph against the holding of more than one benefice. The magistrates of Beauvais and Bourges, like those of Alençon, recommended eliminating some monastic communities; but unlike them, they aimed explicitly at bringing the communities into conformity with religious purposes. The establishments with few members were the ones to be closed. The Beauvais magistrates said: "Either they have large incomes, and abuses are almost inevitable, or they have not enough for subsistence, and evil is perhaps still more to be feared." The Bourges magistrates said that if the monastic life were reduced to its former simplicity, it "would still have virtues, and there are a few pure souls who deserve asylum." The magistrates of Beauvais, Bourges, and Limoges included proposals concerning primary and secondary education, designed to improve its financing, or to take it out of the hands of the religious orders altogether in order to improve the quality of instruction or to spread its benefits through the countryside. The magistrates of Beauvais and Provins expressed concern for improvement of hospitals.[80]

The administration of justice was the subject that evoked most fully both the ideals and the interests of the magistrates in the présidial courts. They discussed in considerable detail the functioning of the system of justice as a whole and the relations among its parts, the protections to be afforded individuals, and the needs of judges in general and of the bailliages

80. Mss., Beauvais (art. 17), Provins (arts. 69–71); *Cahiers Bourges,* p. 608; *Archives Historiques du Limousin,* I, 14.

especially. Two contrasting attitudes on this subject are discernible in their cahiers. One attitude was particularist, hierarchical, and jurisdictional in its arguments and usually opposed in its conclusions to drastic change. The other attitude was generally civic, equalitarian, and principled in its arguments and ready to contemplate sweeping away an established practice or institution. Which attitude was adopted by the magistrate who drafted the cahier, and in turn by the whole judicial company, depended partly on local conditions that affected their interests or that might be relevant to the election of deputies to the Estates General. It also depended on less tangible matters, which can be called, summarily, the dominant intellectual atmosphere of the judicial company itself.

The two attitudes are well illustrated in the discussion of lettres de cachet. The majority of the judicial companies were critical of their use. One line of argument against them started from the need to guarantee the liberty of the individual against arbitrary action and the right of every individual to retain his personal freedom subject only to the decisions of his "natural judge." This argument concluded with the demand for abolition of lettres de cachet.[81] Another reason for objecting to them was judicial independence, which was seen to be impaired by the practice of royal ministers who decided on the propriety and duration of imprisonment. This sort of objection implied judicial control over the ministers, not elimination of the prac-

81. Ms., La Rochelle (art. 17); *Archives Historiques du Limousin*, I, 14; *Cahiers Alençon*, p. 7, where the issue is stated broadly: "The citizen, not being susceptible to being judged except in conformity with the law to which he has subjected himself through the general will, cannot be deprived of his freedom except when he is accused of an action that the law has characterized as an offense."

Only the magistrates at Alençon used the term "natural judge" in opposing the procedure of lettres de cachet. But the magistrates at La Rochelle used the term (art. 18) in condemning *évocations,* and those at Limoges used it in calling for abolition of administrative tribunals (I, 8). The term does not appear anywhere in the other magistrates' cahiers.

tice.[82] The magistrates of Angers adopted a still more narrowly conceived objection, to the effect that lettres de cachet should not be used against magistrates of the parlements who opposed registering new taxes or other royal legislative acts, because "such constraints occasion too much disorder in the State."[83]

The impact of local interests of the bailliages themselves is exemplified in the discussions of seigneurial justice. In their cahiers, the magistrates in the présidial courts commonly omitted this topic. Where they chose to comment on it they could adopt either of two attitudes. Their own interests prompted recommendations for procedural changes that would transfer judicial business from seigneurial courts to the royal bailliages. Civic improvement, envisaged more generally, might lead toward reforms within the seigneurial courts themselves or, alternatively, to their complete abolition. In the five cahiers that address themselves to the topic, the magistrates of Beauvais, Reims, and Provins gave great weight to their own interests; those of Limoges and Rouen emphasized the functioning of the system of justice as a whole.

The présidial courts of Beauvais and Reims had each been engaged in a long struggle against a seigneurial court belonging to a great lord of the Church, and the présidial court of Provins was at odds with a number of smaller seigneurial jurisdictions. The magistrates of Beauvais said that many enormous abuses were inescapable in seigneurial courts, which ought to be restricted to the adjudication of cases involving the law of fiefs or requiring speedy decision. Until this could be accomplished, their recommendation was for a wholesale transfer of judicial business to the royal judges. One of the measures they indi-

---

82. Ms., Provins (art. 34); *Cahiers Bourges,* p. 599; *Cahiers Reims,* p. 16; *Cahiers Rouen,* I, 5, asking also for maintenance of the *puissance paternelle,* for which lettres de cachet commonly served as a method of enforcement.

83. *Cahiers Angers,* I, 89.

cated was to require appeals to be taken before royal bailliages from all seigneurial judges, in particular those of peerages. This would have the effect of inserting an additional level of appellate jurisdiction between the larger, more effective seigneurial courts and the parlements; it would be of no obvious advantage to the subjects.[84] At Reims, the magistrates of the royal bailliage asked for the abolition of all seigneurial justice, but in case this failed to be adopted they urged all the same measures as the magistrates of Beauvais were indicating.[85] In Beauvais and Reims the royal judges in effect called for the help of the Estates General to secure victory for them in old contests with the judges of the count-bishop of Beauvais or the archbishop and duke of Reims.

Seigneurial justice was treated in a very different way by the magistrates of Limoges and Rouen.[86] Briefly, and in moderate terms, the cahier at Limoges insisted on reform of the abuses in the practice of justice before the seigneurial courts. It urged that every seigneur with rights of *haute justice* be required to provide a courtroom, a clerk's office, and a prison, that his judges be law graduates, and that the principal officeholders reside in the locality. It added that persons bringing lawsuits should be permitted, if they chose, to proceed directly before royal judges. The magistrates of Rouen set forth the general principle that a person proceeding upward through the appellate jurisdictions ought to be faced with the same number of

84. The other principal measures recommended were: to prohibit the seigneurial judges from exercising any police jurisdiction in the towns, even those where they were situated; and to confer on the royal judges an unconditional right of prévention, empowering them to proceed to decide a case, ordinarily subject to seigneurial jurisdiction, in which they had asserted royal jurisdiction, even if the seigneurial judges asked that it be remanded. Ms., Beauvais (arts. 7, 8).

85. *Cahiers Reims,* pp. 17, 18; similarly, but much less elaborately, ms., Provins (art. 68).

86. *Archives Historiques du Limousin,* I, 9; *Cahiers Rouen,* I, 5.

courts no matter where he lived. Therefore, they said, the seigneurial courts exercising haute justice should be eliminated and their proprietors compensated.

Not only local interests, but the probabilities of their being satisfied were at work in shaping the demands in the cahiers. Three sénéchaussées, situated in provincial capitals far from the parlements to which they were subordinate, called for division of the territory of their parlement into smaller appellate jurisdictions. In doing so, the magistrates of Angers, Limoges, and Moulins all but avowed the long-standing ambition of many présidial courts to become high courts of appeal.[87] (That their ambitions were credible is suggested by the selection, eleven years later, of Angers, Limoges, and Moulins as locations for courts of appeal.) But in 1789, at Beauvais, Bourges, La Rochelle, Provins, and Reims, the magistrates' emphasis was on increasing the powers of the présidial courts as against the parlements. They recommended raising the monetary limits on the cases they could adjudicate and eliminating the costly futilities which the edict of 1777 had injected into their procedures.[88]

In some localities the magistrates enjoyed, or wished to establish, friendly relations with other groups in the *monde du palais*, the professors of law, advocates, proctors, notaries, clerks, and process-servers. With the high-ranking professions, relations of courtesy, at least, were almost universal. Where there was a faculty of law, the magistrates refrained from

87. The magistrates of Moulins and Limoges said that their own cities would be proper locations for parlements. Ms., Moulins (art. 17); *Archives Historiques du Limousin,* I, 8. Those of Angers suggested the establishment of "conseils supérieurs" in the cities furthest removed from the Parlement of Paris, although in 1771 they had opposed Maupeou's creation, the *conseil supérieur* at Blois, nearer Paris. *Cahiers Angers,* I, 98.

88. Mss., Beauvais (art. 12), La Rochelle (art. 16), Provins (arts. 12, 3); *Cahiers Bourges,* p. 611; *Cahiers Reims,* p. 17.

issuing public criticism of the professors.[89] Outside the university towns there were no such local relations to restrain the magistrates from harsh comments on legal education: "empty formulas" or "a mere ceremony" in which "money is substituted for knowledge."[90] But toward lower-ranking practitioners of law, the magistrates of Angers, Bourges, Reims, and Beauvais were notably less considerate. The notaries' training as clerks was said to be too brief, the existing controls over the honesty of their work too loose, their fees unjustifiably large.[91] The proctors were described as defrauding their clients both directly, by charging fees in excess of the tariff, and indirectly, by grossly inflating the written pleadings for which they were paid a fixed sum per line.[92] Similarly for the clerks, the magistrates of Angers, Beauvais, and Bourges recommended reductions in fees.[93] The magistrates of Beauvais and Bourges denounced the lowly process-servers for avarice and fraud, while those of Angers and Reims, too, called for rules or for judicial authority to limit their fees.[94]

89. In Angers and Reims, the magistrates said nothing about legal education. In Bourges, they condemned law faculties elsewhere, naming that of Reims, for selling degrees. *Cahiers Bourges,* p. 609.

90. The phrases quoted are from, respectively, mss., La Rochelle (art. 15), Beauvais (art. 14), Moulins (art. 20). Similarly, *Cahiers Rouen,* I, 5, *Archives Historiques du Limousin,* I, 8–9.

91. Ms., Beauvais (arts. 10, 23); *Cahiers Reims,* p. 18; *Cahiers Bourges,* p. 612; *Cahiers Angers,* I, 96.

92. *Cahiers Angers,* I, 95; *Cahiers Reims,* p. 19; *Cahiers Bourges,* p. 610, where the magistrates observed that "their profits are such that one is tempted to wonder whether procedure was created to guide the judges or to facilitate new fortunes."

93. Ms., Beauvais (art. 18); *Cahiers Angers,* I, 96; *Cahiers Bourges,* p. 611. The magistrates of Limoges recommended a very different sort of change: reducing those fees which were paid to court clerks but assigned to the royal domain. *Archives Historiques du Limousin,* I, 8.

94. "Les infidélités des huissiers sont le fléau de la justice." Ms., Beauvais (art. 11). The magistrates of Bourges said that in selling off moveable property the huissiers concocted delays to enable them to keep the proceeds, which they were often unable thereafter to repay because of their "insolvabilité ordinaire." *Cahiers Bourges,* p. 610. Cf. *Cahiers Angers,* I, 96; *Cahiers Reims,* p. 19.

The magistrates' relations with practitioners in their town were controlled by facts very different from those that shaped their relations with the judicial structure outside it. To the présidial courts, the administration of justice appeared dominated by the parlements. Some of them were restive under the burdens they felt in conducting their own judicial business. Five of their cahiers attacked the privilege of committimus, which allowed the parlements to exercise jurisdiction over high-ranking subjects when otherwise their cases would have been heard first by a bailliage.[95] In the attitudes of all présidial magistrates toward the parlements, however, much more than jurisdictional rivalry was involved.

The parlements' power to refuse to register new laws was objectionable to those who put their faith in the Estates General. Especially this was so because the parlements were not elected and were able to exclude prospective new members. To leave them a fragment of legislative authority would be to keep it not only from the king but from popularly elected representatives as well. It was logically possible to preserve the parlements' veto while destroying their power to exclude prospective members. To do so would tend to legitimize the parlements' authority to maintain boundaries beyond which lawmaking could not go. But the parlements' power to exclude prospective members affected other issues besides the legitimacy of any refusal to register new laws. Two other issues were important: the proper nature of judicial authority itself, and the opportunities and rewards in the judicial career. One view of these issues held that judicial authority was originally and essentially royal; that the king could delegate it suitably by selling proprietary rights to judgeships and permitting them to be resold by his subjects; and that it was proper—justified by the constitutional interdependence of the monarchy and the nobility—to exclude the low-born from judgeships and to re-

95. Mss., Beauvais (art. 11), Provins (art. 19); *Cahiers Reims,* p. 18; *Cahiers Alençon,* p. 6; *Cahiers Rouen,* I, 5.

ward respectable commoners with ennoblement for judicial service which was distinguished in one way or another. In opposition to this view, it was held that every person was entitled to choose his "natural judge" and obey no other; that giving judgment was a profession requiring ability, learning, character, and experience; and that to these qualities the distinction between noble and commoner was irrelevant.

These were troublesome and divisive issues for the magistrates in the présidial courts, accustomed as they were to wield a fraction of royal judicial power, believing that their profession was a public trust, proprietors of their own offices, and sustaining more or less intense ambitions. In the minds of some, there occurred a fusion of ideas that defined at once the future constitution of legislative power, the essential character of judicial office, and the nature of the opportunities and rewards proper to a professional career. The combined force of these ideas propelled them from a limited purpose, of delivering a blow against the parlements' dominance, to the objective, more far-reaching perhaps than they realized, of securing the abolition of all the venal offices in the judiciary, including their own offices, through repurchase by the Treasury. The magistrates in Alençon, Rouen, and Limoges called for popular election of judges instead of sale of judicial office, and those of Moulins said that venality should be eliminated in order to entrust judgeships to men of merit and experience.[96]

96. Ms., Moulins (art. 19); cf. art. 17 stating as a principle "que les magistrats sont au peuple et que les peuples ne sont pas aux magistrats"; and *Archives Historiques du Limousin*, I, 8; *Cahiers Alençon*, p. 6; *Cahiers Rouen*, I, 5.

Incidentally it should be noted that in some other towns, where the présidial court magistrates did not prepare corporate cahiers, their representatives were willing to join in a recommendation for liquidating the venal offices in the judiciary. In Limoux, near Carcassonne, the town cahier called for abolition of venality and was signed by Captier de Vallete, associate chief criminal judge, and Bonpieyre, king's proctor, representing the présidial court. [A.M. Limoux, AA 86, on deposit in A.D. Aude.] The same demand appears in the town cahier of Nîmes

Such proposals were too much for the présidial courts elsewhere. At Beauvais, Bourges, Provins, and Reims, the magistrates made this clear in their cahiers by asking for the exemption of their offices from the annual tax on inheritability.[97]
Their property rights in the offices would thus become unconditional. Three of those companies (Beauvais, Bourges, and
Provins) joined this request to a proposal to abolish the fees
paid by litigants to judges. The net effect would have been to
eliminate part of the costs of lawsuits, most of the judges'

---

signed by Ricard and Griolet representing the présidial court, and in the
town cahier of Autun signed by Serpillon and Pigenat representing the
présidial court. [*Cahiers de doléances de la sénéchaussée de Nîmes pour
les Etats Généraux de 1789*, ed. Edouard Bligny-Bondurand, 2 vols.
(Nîmes, 1908–1909), I, 572, 579; "Cahiers des paroisses et communautés
du bailliage d'Autun pour les Etats Généraux de 1789," ed. Anatole
Desplaces de Charmasse, *Mémoires de la Société Eduenne*, 3 (1874), on
pp. 232, 237.]
In the town cahiers I have seen, this occurs in a minority, just as it
does in the subsisting corporate cahiers of présidial magistrates. The
signatures must represent genuine agreement: in Angoulême, the town
cahier included a precise and emphatic condemnation of venality of judicial offices, with the consent of one representative of the présidial court,
Lagrézille, and a recorded protest by the other representative, Cousturier
du Chastelard. [*Cahiers de doléances de la sénéchausée d'Angoulême et
du siège royal de Cognac pour les Etats Généraux de 1789*, ed. Prosper
Boissonnade (Paris, 1907), pp. 66, 69.]
97. Mss., Beauvais (art. 20), Provins (art. 21); *Cahiers Bourges*, p.
611; *Cahiers Reims*, p. 18. Probably this was also the desire of many
judicial companies in the lesser royal bailliages without présidial jurisdiction. It was stated by the magistrates of the sénéchaussée of Morlaix,
in Brittany. On the other hand, the 3 magistrates at Pontoise, near Paris,
said nothing pertaining to the question; those of Rochefort-sur-Mer proposed eliminating the fees paid by litigants to judges and compensating
the latter in salaries paid out of provincial tax funds, a reform which
was compatible with either the continuation or the liquidation of property
rights in judicial offices. [Henri Legohérel, "Les Cahiers de doléances de
la ville de Morlaix," *Revue Historique de Droit Français et Etranger*,
4th ser., 39 (1961), 180–247, on p. 229; Ernest Mallet, *Les Elections du
bailliage secondaire de Pontoise en 1789* (Pontoise, Société Historique
du Vexin, 1909), pp. 105–108; "Cahiers de doléances des communautés
de Rochefort-sur-Mer en 1789," ed. Philippe Rondeau, *Archives Historiques de la Saintonge et de l'Aunis*, 16 (1888), 340–479, on p. 443.]

professional income, and part of the royal treasury's revenue from the venal offices: the existing system would be simpler, more rational, and less burdensome for persons involved in lawsuits, but unchanged in its fundamentals. Two other cahiers refrained entirely from discussing the venal offices in the judiciary. In Angers, the magistrates seem to have wanted to keep their offices, although their cahier did not say so.[98] The magistrates of La Rochelle, expressing a general desire for reform in the judiciary, implied that they approved the project commenced by Lamoignon ten months before, in which venality of office was maintained.[99]

The future of the venal offices in the judiciary was the central issue, for the présidial magistrates, in a tangle of questions that ran to the problem of legislative power and to that of equal opportunity in professional careers. The four abolitionist judicial companies, which favored cutting through the central knot by liquidating the venal offices, did not all give the same emphasis to the other strands in the tangle. Two of those companies selected the parlements' power to refuse to register new laws and condemned it as merely an illegitimate privilege. The magistrates of Alençon and Limoges urged that the parlements be deprived of this power, in order to entrust legislative authority exclusively to the Estates General and the king.[100] The other two companies selected the exclusion of commoners

98. *Cahiers Angers*, I, 48, 61.

99. They favored "toutes les demandes et représentations qui peuvent tendre à la réforme des abus ou à la perfection dans l'ordre judiciaire." They expected that "la révolution salutaire qu'on espère à cet égard" would diminish the number of appeals and the restrictions on the power of certain tribunals. Ms., La Rochelle (art. 20). The only "salutary revolution" they had any reason to expect was the one planned by Lamoignon and suspended by the royal declaration of 23 September 1788. To be sure they had rejected it when it was promulgated in conjunction with the creation of the plenary court.

100. *Cahiers Alençon*, pp. 5–6; *Archives Historiques du Limousin*, I, 4. No statement on this issue appears in the magistrates' cahiers at Moulins and Rouen.

from most offices in the parlements as artificial and unjust. The magistrates of Moulins and Rouen called for the admission of commoners as well as nobles to the highest dignities in the judiciary, on the basis of merit. Those of Limoges, though not mentioning the exclusion of commoners from the parlements, made essentially the same point with reference to the army and the church.[101]

The six conservative judicial companies, which did not favor liquidating the venal offices, were not unanimous on the related questions. Four of these companies said that the parlements' power to refuse to register laws was necessary in order to preserve the constitution. The magistrates of Angers specified that the enactments of the Estates General should be submitted to the parlements for registration, without which they would be unenforceable.[102] Those of Beauvais, Provins, and Reims shared the opinion that the power to refuse to register should be maintained.[103] The problem presented by noble exclusiveness in the parlements could be ameliorated in a classic manner by conferring nobility on the magistrates in the bailliages. This idea had been proposed before and in 1763 was the main proposal uniting the présidial courts. It is noteworthy, then,

101. Ms., Moulins (art. 10); *Cahiers Rouen,* I, 5; *Archives Historiques du Limousin,* I, 13.

102. *Cahiers Angers,* I, 89.

103. Ms., Beauvais (art. 27) suggesting that on new enactments the parlements obtain comments from any interested bailliages before consenting to register; ms. Provins (arts. 38, 39), that only the Estates General and not the parlements ought to have power to grant taxes and loans, but that the parlements should examine all laws concerning "l'administration, la grande police, la justice et autres auxquelles les circonstances pourroient donner lieu," and further that registration in lit de justice should be null and void, as "contraire au droit de la Nation." The magistrates of Reims sought to extend the requirement of registration so as to include the decisions of the king's council; it is to be presumed that they meant the *conseil des parties,* but even so this would have considerably strengthened the parlements' dominance over the judiciary. (*Cahiers Reims,* p. 18.)

No statement on the parlements' power to register laws appears in the magistrates' cahiers at Bourges and La Rochelle.

that only two of these ten cahiers of présidial courts in 1789 revived the idea. The magistrates of Reims recommended ennoblement as a reward for distinguished service on any lower bench; those of Beauvais asked for automatic ennoblement for long service in a présidial court, as was provided for the judges in the Châtelet of Paris.[104] Such proposals were compatible with the admission of commoners to the highest dignities in the judiciary, the army, and the church. The magistrates of Beauvais said that bishoprics should not be reserved for noble lineage but for knowledge and virtue. Those of Provins said that commoners who had held offices in présidial courts should be permitted to do so in parlements "if their fortune enables them to maintain the rank."[105] Resentment of noble exclusiveness in the parlements was not confined to the présidial courts that called for liquidating the judicial offices but was to be found among the conservative présidial courts as well.

Both the problem of the power to legislate and the question of equality of opportunity were logically related not only to the future of the existing judicial offices but also to the voting procedure to be adopted in the Estates General. This issue was whether the Estates General should count the votes of all individual deputies, and thereby give full effect to the doubled numerical representation of the Third Estate, or count one vote for each of the three Estates. It was already the subject of pamphlets and slogans, and was the hottest political issue for the educated population in early 1789. In the cahiers of the présidial magistrates, six judicial companies said that the votes of the individual deputies should be counted in the Estates General, and four said nothing about the issue.

104. Ms., Beauvais (art. 12); *Cahiers Reims,* p. 20. At La Rochelle, the magistrates did not comment on the provisions of Lamoignon's plan which would have conferred nobility automatically for sufficiently long service in the grands bailliages.

105. Mss., Beauvais (art. 3), Provins (art. 59), the latter including the upper ranks of the army and the bishoprics in the commoners' claim for career opportunities.

The probable meaning of silence on the voting issue, and the sense in which this indicated conservatism, can be elucidated by reference to the cahier adopted by the magistrates of Alençon. They stood firmly for counting the votes of individual deputies, not of the three orders. But they opposed making this the first item of business, either in their cahier or in the Estates General, as the magistrates of Beauvais, Rouen, La Rochelle, and Limoges desired to do.[106] The magistrates of Alençon began with the statement that "France ought to be regarded as an immense family brought together by common interests." They asserted that the general interest, rather than any particular interest ought to determine not only the outcome of debate on every issue but the sequence in which the issues would be taken up. When they came to the question of voting procedure, at the end of their cahier, the magistrates of Alençon warned that "the fear of kindling the fire of discord" should prevent the Third Estate from pressing for an immediate decision to count the votes of individual deputies.[107] The

106. At Beauvais, at Rouen, and at La Rochelle, the first sentence in the magistrates' cahier demanded that the Estates General count the votes of its individual members, not of the three orders. At Limoges, the magistrates' cahier began with a brief preamble and then these demands: that the Estates General define the constitution; that the Estates General meet regularly; that its enactments, when sanctioned by the king, become law despite restrictive mandates of any of its members and without reference to the parlements; and that in the Estates General the votes of individual members, not of the 3 orders, be counted.

107. *Cahiers Alençon*, pp. 3, 12. Similarly, the magistrates of Moulins said, in their preamble: "Notre souverain a pour objet le bien du peuple, maxime la plus importante de tout gouvernement légitime; il sait que la réussite dépend de la volonté générale et pour se la procurer il demande le résultat des volontés particulières. Puissent les obstacles disparaître! Puissent le vil interêt et les préjugés céder à la raison! Puissent tous les ordres se faire un point d'unité dans la cause commune! Surtout que l'affreux égoïsme n'isole plus les individus! Que chaque Français se pénètre de cette vérité que l'on est homme, que l'on est citoyen avant d'être prêtre, noble, ou magistrat! Pour nous que l'on appelle le troisième ordre, mais qui sommes le vrai corps de la Nation, redoublons d'amour pour la patrie, que ce sentiment vif et doux échauffe nos âmes; mettons

four judicial companies which said nothing about the issue perhaps included some members who agreed with the Parlement of Paris that voting should be by the three Estates. It is barely conceivable that in each of these companies a majority favored counting the votes of the three orders in the Estates General. It is likely that in each company a majority favored counting the votes of individual deputies but was reluctant to offend the opinions of nobles or to appear in the guise of partisans of a militant faction, thereby impairing the political unity of the locality in opposition to the central government and what was called "ministerial despotism." Silence on this issue thus represents significant disagreement with the magistrates of Beauvais, Rouen, La Rochelle, and Limoges, who revealed their willingness to offend nobles and their readiness to adopt a partisan stance. Doubtless their partisanship reflected belief in the justice of the position adopted and pessimism as to the future political conduct of nobles. A display of partisanship was also, implicitly, an offer of political alliance to electors of the Third Estate.

This question of the voting procedure in the Estates General tended to polarize nobles and commoners in the politically active population in general. It threatened, one might suppose, to divide any judicial company which included both nobles and commoners among its members. But in fact none of these judicial companies was divided along class lines in whatever arguments may have occurred over their corporate cahiers. Where the magistrates took an emphatic stand for counting the votes of individual deputies in the Estates General, the corporate cahier was signed by two noblemen and nine commoners while another nobleman and a commoner were absent (La

---

de la justice dans nos prétentions, de la générosité dans les sacrifices qu'il conviendra faire; joignons à nos réclamations tant de sagesse et d'union qu'il résulte des vœux du troisième ordre une nouvelle preuve que la volonté la plus générale est toujours la plus juste, et que la voix du peuple est en effet la voix de Dieu."

Rochelle) or by three noblemen and eleven or twelve commoners (Beauvais, Limoges).[108] Where the magistrates refrained from mentioning the issue, either there were no noblemen in the judicial company (Angers, Provins), or three noblemen and nine or ten commoners signed the cahier while two other noblemen and a number of commoners were absent (Bourges, Moulins), or two noblemen and five commoners signed while one other nobleman was absent (Reims).[109]

The magistrates in the présidial courts disagreed, then, over whether the existing judicial offices should be liquidated and over the degree to which they themselves should take sides in and thereby exacerbate a contest between the nobility and the Third Estate. It is a reasonable hypothesis that the magistrates' corporate opinion on one issue correlates with that on the other issue. In fact, such a correlation exists but is not very strong. Three of the four judicial companies that favored liquidating the venal offices called for voting by individual deputies in the Estates General; half of the other judicial companies made that demand. Of the judicial companies that called for voting by individual deputies in the Estates General, half recommended liquidating the venal offices in the judiciary; of those that withheld comment on the voting procedure in the Estates General, three out of four expressed or implied a conservative attitude toward the venal offices in the judiciary.

It was the sequence of later events that brought out, in fact, the implicit connection between these two issues. The establishment of voting by individual deputies and the transforma-

108. Louis de La Roque and Edouard de Barthélemy, *Catalogue des gentilshommes qui ont pris part ou envoyé leur procuration aux assemblées de la noblesse pour l'élection des députés aux Etats Généraux de 1789*, 32 fasc. (Paris, 1861–1865), *Isle de France*, pp. 68–69; *Périgord, Aunis, Saintonge, Angoumois*, pp. 18, 19, 23; *Marche et Limousin*, pp. 22, 23; cf. Gustave Desjardins, *Le Beauvaisis, le Valois, le Vexin Français, le Noyonnais en 1789* (Beauvais, 1869), p. 40 (note); and *AP*, III, 465–470, 552–556 for La Rochelle and Limoges.

109. La Roque and Barthélemy: *Touraine et Berry*, pp. 28–30; *Bourbonnais et Nivernais*, pp. 7–9, 12, 13; *Champagne*, pp. 38, 39.

tion of the Estates General into the National Assembly was to block the aspirations of noblemen, led by the parlements, to exercise a veto over the legislative process. The liquidation of the existing offices in the judiciary was to be the means of destroying finally not only the parlements' power but the parlements themselves. The later counterrevolutionary attack on these actions joined them together under the aegis of a liberal, equalitarian, and revolutionary ideology. But in late February and early March 1789, when the corporate cahiers de doléances were written and adopted, this association of ideas had not occurred to many magistrates in the présidial courts. Any effort to classify their cahiers as revolutionary or counterrevolutionary is made difficult by the diversity that would be characteristic of moderate temperaments in the midst of any new and rapidly changing political situation.

Nevertheless, it is possible to concentrate on the issues relating to the nature of the political order and the place of the judiciary within it, and to examine each cahier for evidence of civic idealism as contrasted with self-interest and for determination to effect reforms as contrasted with willingness to leave the existing order unchanged. Reading these ten cahiers in this way reveals a range of political positions held by the magistrates in the présidial courts. At one end of the scale are the partisans of liberal and equalitarian reform, the magistrates in Rouen and Limoges; tending in that direction, those in Alençon and Moulins; near the midpoint of the scale, the magistrates in La Rochelle; tending in a conservative direction, those in Beauvais and Provins; and exhibiting a fairly clear conservative attitude, those in Angers, Bourges, and Reims.

Recognition of a range of political positions should not be allowed to obscure the attitudes and opinions expressed with near unanimity in these documents and undoubtedly representative of most présidial court magistrates all over the kingdom. To limit the monarchy, by empowering the Estates General to prevent the imposition of taxes; to reduce the impact of central administration on the provinces, by establishing institutions of provincial government which should have genuine authority to collect, allocate and expend public funds; to cut away the excessive profits of tax collectors and to stop the frivolous disbursement of pensions and emoluments; to eliminate the fiscal privileges of clergy, nobility, and businessmen: these were objectives that présidial court magistrates shared with most of the politically articulate, including many clergymen and noblemen. The achievement of these objectives would necessitate resolution of issues, especially the nature and extent of reform in the judiciary, on which the présidial court magistrates were divided.

The cahiers adopted by the magistrates in these ten cities and towns became part of a larger political context that took shape rapidly thereafter. Several further steps in the convocation process, during March 1789, led finally to the electoral and deliberative assemblies of the clergy, the nobility, and the Third Estate of the ten respective bailliages.[110] Similar bailliage assemblies met in most other places in the kingdom at about the same time. On the principal issues over which the magistrates in these ten présidial courts disagreed, the nobility and the Third Estate disagreed more strongly and more consistently, as the accompanying chart reveals.[111]

In the bailliages of Beauvais and Provins and in the sénéchaussées of Angers and La Rochelle, the Third Estate called for liquidation of the venal offices in the judiciary, although the magistrates in those présidial courts had presup-

110. Except for the two bailliages in Normandy, summaries of these proceedings appear in the *Recueil de documents relatifs à la convocation des Etats Généraux*, III, 224–229, 324–327, 351–354, 473–482, 507–515, 559–566; IV, 395–404, 619–631.

111. The general cahiers of the nobility and the Third Estate of these bailliages are in *AP*, I, 710–720; II, 32–45, 294–309, 319–325, 444–449; III, 471–486, 564–572; V, 447–455, 526–537, 594–597, and, for the Third Estate of Rouen, *Cahiers Rouen*, I, 229–254, supplemented by II, 457–473.

Venal offices in the judiciary and voting procedure in the Estates General of 1789; opinions expressed in cahiers de doléances of présidial magistrates, Third Estate, and nobility in ten towns.*

	Estates General voting by individual deputies	Estates General voting: no comment or ambiguous opinion	Estates General voting by Estates
Liquidate venal offices in judiciary	Alençon, *Alençon, Angers, Beauvais,* La Rochelle, *Limoges,* Moulins, *Provins,* Rouen, *Rouen*	BEAUVAIS, Moulins	ANGERS, LA ROCHELLE, LIMOGES, MOULINS, PROVINS, REIMS, ROUEN
No comment on venal offices in judiciary	Bourges, La Rochelle, *Limoges*	Angers	
Maintain venal offices in judiciary	Beauvais, Provins, *Reims*	Bourges, Reims	ALENCON, BOURGES

* (There were 9 possible combinations of comments or lack of comments; each combination is represented by location on the chart. Présidial magistrates are indicated by place-names in roman type; the Third Estate, by place-names in italic type; the nobility, by place-names entirely in capital letters.)

posed the continuing existence of venality.[112] In the sénéchaussée of Limoges, the Third Estate did not mention the
issue, despite the magistrates' recommendation that the offices
be liquidated and the judiciary thenceforth elected.[113] The
nobility in these ten bailliages commonly refrained from mentioning this issue at all. It was not the power and dignity of
judges but membership in the noble class which they wished
to see made unavailable to mere wealth, and so (except in
Reims) they all asked for abolition or severe limitation of
ennoblement through officeholding. Only in the bailliage of
Beauvais did the nobles call also for liquidation of the venal
offices in the judiciary. In the sénéchaussée of Angers, the
nobles said that venality of offices was one of several questions
"too delicate, susceptible to a discussion involving too many
considerations,"[114] to permit instructing their deputies in advance of the meeting of the Estates General. As for the voting
procedure in the Estates General, this was now clearly a subject
of class conflict in these localities, except Beauvais. There the
nobles said that the three orders should vote separately, but
that if all three orders failed to agree on a question it should
be submitted to a vote by the individual deputies: the nobles

112. In Angers, the impetus for demanding liquidation of the venal
offices in the judiciary came from the advocates and, especially, the law
faculty. In La Rochelle and Provins, however, the idea was not suggested
by the advocates in their cahiers; where it came from is not evident. It
could have been suggested by a rural notary preparing a cahier for his
village, as occurred at Troissereux, near Beauvais. [Desjardins, *Le
Beauvaisis*, p. 152. Some other comparisons of cahiers of présidial court
magistrates, advocates, proctors, and notaries may be found in my
article, "The *Bourgeoisie de Robe* in 1789," *French Historical Studies*, 4
(1965), on pp. 17 and 19.]

113. Why the topic was omitted from the final cahier of the Third
Estate is not clear. The 5 commissioners who drew it up included
Montaudon, syndic of the advocates in Limoges (their corporate cahier,
like that of the magistrates, called for liquidation of the venal offices in
the judiciary), and the chief judge, Grégoire de Roulhac, both of whom
were elected deputies for the Third Estate.

114. *AP*, II, 34.

of Beauvais were willing to give up the legislative veto on which most nobles insisted. Those of La Rochelle, it is true, would have consented to voting by individual deputies on all matters concerning taxes and fiscal legislation but not on matters concerning the constitution or legislative questions generally. In short, where the magistrates' corporate opinion was conservative with respect to the venal offices, the Third Estate commonly overruled it. Where the magistrates hesitated to take one side or the other on the voting procedure to be followed in the Estates General, both the Third Estate and the nobility were typically adamant.

Neither within the Third Estate nor within the nobility were bailliage magistrates as individuals excluded from participation in formulating cahiers. The influential position which had crumbled was rather that of the judicial company, part of the corporative organization of social and political life which was dissolving visibly as the process of convoking the Estates General created new forms of deliberation and choice. What remained for bailliage magistrates was the possibility of testing their individual convictions and abilities in these new, competitive forms. Some of them did so, and the degree of their success varied greatly from one town to another. At Alençon, the cahier drafted by the associate chief judge, Demées, for the présidial magistrates, served as the basis of the cahier of the town of Alençon and finally of the entire Third Estate of the bailliage. Similarly at Angers, the cahier drafted by the king's advocate, Brevet de Beaujour, for the law faculty (of which he was a member) became eventually the Third Estate cahier for all five sénéchaussées of Anjou. On the other hand, in Beauvais the cahier of the Third Estate was a fair summary of all the urban corporate and village cahiers in the bailliage.[115] The magistrates' contribution, dealing with the church and the

115. My statement here summarizes the interpretation of Desjardins, *Le Beauvaisis*, pp. 141–154. Most of the urban corporate cahiers in Beauvais examined by Desjardins were destroyed in 1940.

administration of justice, amounted to less than one-eighth of the text. In Moulins, the cahier of the Third Estate was largely based on that of the advocates, who contributed all the major constitutional demands and about one-third of the whole text, while the contribution from the magistrates' cahier amounted to less than one-tenth of the text. In still other towns, the magistrates had no visible effect on the Third Estate cahier, as at Rouen, where it was essentially the work of Thouret, an advocate.

The magistrates' participation was likewise variable but generally less noticeable in the deliberations of the nobility. In Bourges, Limoges, and Moulins, the commissions drafting the nobles' cahiers included no bailliage magistrates, although in those towns some of the magistrates were noblemen. In La Rochelle, the chief civil judge, Griffon de Romagné, and the former king's proctor, Rougier, were among the ten commissioners. In Beauvais, eight commissioners drafted the cahier of the nobility. One was the former chief judge, Borel, and their secretary was his son, the current chief judge, Borel de Brétizel; yet it is probably right to attribute the unusual liberalism of the final document to the leadership of the comte de Crillon, who presided over the nobility, as much as or more than to the participation of these magistrates.

A cahier de doléances was, in 1789, an important statement of both ideology and program, far more controversial than the party platforms issued for elections under later political régimes in which stability and apparent consensus gave full effect to habitual loyalties. The adoption of the final cahier for the Third Estate was especially an occasion for negotiations among the drafting commissioners.[116] In some provincial capi-

---

116. The atmosphere of such negotiations is evoked in a letter from 1 of the 24 commissioners who produced the final cahier for the Third Estate of the province of Maine, by combining the cahiers of the principal sénéchaussée and the 6 secondary bailliages. To a friend, he wrote: "Only with difficulty could we obtain the votes of the secondary bailliages. It was really necessary to give in on a number of articles that

tals, there was heated debate, in which local and personal pride of authorship and political influence, as well as fundamental principles, were felt to be at stake.[117] In these discussions, bailliage magistrates fairly commonly participated. The whole business of preparing drafts of cahiers and reconciling them with one another was only half the task entrusted to these assemblies preparatory to the Estates General, and only half the opportunity for those with political ambitions. The other was the election of deputies, and in this, too, many bailliage magistrates entered into competitive political activity.

In the elections, 127 magistrates in office in various bailliages were elected deputies for the Third Estate.[118] This number amounted to one-fifth of the total representation of the Third Estate when the Estates General first met. Five other magistrates, who had been chosen by the Third Estate as alternate deputies, were called upon before the end of 1789 to take seats in the National Assembly.[119] In addition, 4 bailliage magistrates were elected deputies for the nobility, and 3 others, chosen by the nobility as alternates, were called upon before the end of 1789 to take seats.[120] One bailliage magistrate,

sound policy ought to have eliminated. But how can one expect moderation from a composite of three hundred minds, from men who believe firmly that the cahier is a collection of adopted laws which deliver them from every constraint . . . I encountered much impatience, and many difficulties, in striving for conciliation." Michel-René Maupetit, "Lettres," ed. Emile Queruau-Lamerie, *Bulletin de la Commission Historique et Archéologique de la Mayenne*, 2nd ser., 17 (1901), on p. 313.

117. The contest over the choice between the cahier of Fontenay-le-Comte and that of Poitiers, in the final Third Estate assembly for Poitou, for example, is described briefly by Roux, *La Révolution à Poitiers et dans la Vienne*, pp. 149–154.

118. *Recueil de documents relatifs à la convocation des Etats Généraux*, II, 36–331; III, 743–753. The total, 127, does not include former bailliage officeholders, of whom there were a good many.

119. *Ibid.*, II, 99, 120, 160, 167, 305. One of these was Riffard de Saint-Martin, councillor in the sénéchaussée of Villeneuve-de-Berg (A.N., V¹ 504), whose judicial office is not mentioned in the *Recueil*.

120. The deputies were de Burle, chief judge in the sénéchaussée of Sisteron, in Provence; David de Ballidart, king's proctor in the bailliage

chosen as an alternate deputy for the clergy, was similarly seated in the National Assembly.[121] Altogether, one-twentieth of the bailliage magistracy sat in the new national legislature in 1789. No other occupation saw so large a proportion of its members selected to take part in the deliberations that would open a new era.

This striking outcome resulted partly from a factor that was, in a sense, accidental. The elections were carried out in assemblies, which required presiding officers. As in 1614, the royal instructions determined that the chief civil judge of the bailliage should preside over each Third Estate electoral assembly. In the clergy and the nobility, as well as in the Third Estate, many electoral assemblies chose their presiding officers as deputies. The deputies were to stand for the most notable elements, the natural spokesmen, of the provinces and towns. This was the counterpart of the great importance that was still attached to the cahiers de doléances, even though the deputies were given a broad mandate and full power to act and even though the royal regulations suggested the identity of the natural spokesmen in advance of the choice. The quantitative effect on the election results can be circumscribed by observing that forty-eight bailliage magistrates, three-eighths of those elected for the Third Estate, had actually presided, in either secondary or principal bailliages, over the electoral assemblies that chose them as deputies. This was by no means as common a practice as it was to become in 1791, when the electoral assemblies chose their own presiding officers, and two-thirds of the assemblies then elected their presiding officers to the na-

---

of Vitry-le-François; Gleises de Lablanque, chief judge in the sénéchaussée of Béziers; and Seurrat de Laboulaye, councillor in the bailliage of Orléans. The alternates seated in 1789 were Chabrol, chief criminal judge in the sénéchaussée at Riom; Irland de Bazôges, chief civil judge in the sénéchaussée of Poitiers; and Talon, chief civil judge in the Châtelet of Paris.

121. This was de Lespinasse, prior of Saint-Pierre-le-Moutier and ex officio councillor in the bailliage there.

tional legislature.[122] In 1789, it was, however, widespread throughout the kingdom. In every généralité except those of Rouen, Alençon, and Lyon, at least one judge who had presided over a bailliage assembly was elected.

More important in securing electoral victories for bailliage magistrates was the political leadership that had devolved on them in certain provinces. Half of those elected for the Third Estate came from the West, the East, and a few smaller regions near the center of the kingdom. As defined in Table 12, these regions had in common the absence of any great commercial city, except for Nantes in Brittany, and the absence of a parlement with its large contingent of advocates. In addition, it seems that these regions shared some intangible qualities of political atmosphere. Many men in the bourgeoisie evidently looked in the bailliage magistracy for political leaders, and a considerable number of magistrates expected to act as leaders. In this connection, it is noteworthy that eight of the ten présidial courts whose corporate cahiers de doléances we have examined were located in the regions of magistrates' electoral popularity. It may be surmised that, especially in these regions, magistrates who expected to exercise political leadership tended to think of doing so by means of a cahier. The cahiers in particular did not secure them electoral victories. But their intuition that the immediate political environment was receptive to their leadership was broadly accurate.

On the other hand, a full analysis of the regional concentrations of bailliage magistrates' electoral victories would have to elucidate their defeat in large areas—including Languedoc and Champagne. In such regions, there was a total of 625 bailliage magistrates, only 16 of whom were elected.

122. Auguste Kuscinski, *Les Députés à l'Assemblée législative de 1791. Liste par départements et par ordre alphabétique des députés et des suppléants* (Paris, 1900). Ten executive officers of départements, 8 bishops, and 36 other local officials were doubly elected in this way.

Table 12. Electoral Popularity of Bailliage Magistrates
in the Third Estate, 1789, by Regions.

Index of magistrates' popularity[a]	Region	Number of magistrates elected
6.9	Vosges	4
3.8	Anjou + Poitou + Aunis	12
2.4–2.9	Généralité of Paris (excluding prévôté and city of Paris)	8
	Brittany (excluding Rennes)	10
	Franche-Comté (excluding Besançon)	6
	[Lorraine (excluding Nancy) + Barrois	8]
	Limousin + Périgord	5
1.6–1.9	Berry + Bourbonnais	4
	Normandy (excluding Rouen)	11
	Lorraine (excluding the Vosges) + Barrois + Trois Evêchés	9
0.7	Languedoc (Béziers, Carcassonne, Castelnaudary, Castres, Limoux, Montpellier, Nîmes, Toulouse)	5
0.6	Champagne (généralité of Châlons)	4
0.4	Burgundy (Auxerre, Dijon, Autun, Chalon-sur-Saône, Semur-en-Auxois, Châtillon-sur-Seine, Charolles, Mâcon)	3
0.2	Picardie + Vermandois (généralités of Amiens and Soissons)	3
0.02	Guienne (including Agenais, Condomois, Albret, and Bazadois) + Quercy + Rouergue	1

Source: Appendix, below, and *Recueil de documents relatifs à la convocation des Etats Généraux de 1789,* ed. Armand Brette, 4 vols. (Paris, Imprimerie Nationale, 1894–1915), II, 481–538.

[a] This index is the product of two fractions (the number of bailliage magistrates elected by the Third Estate in the region ÷ the total number of Third Estate deputies from the region) × (the number of bailliage magistrates elected by the Third Estate in the region ÷ the total number of bailliage magistrates in the region), multipled, for convenience, by 100. A region where all the bailliage magistrates were elected and all the Third Estate deputies were bailliage magistrates would have an index of 100. For the kingdom as a whole, the index was $(127 \div 611) \times (127 \div 2700) \times 100 = 0.98$. According to this index, bailliage magistrates enjoyed an electoral popularity in Poitou and adjacent provinces, for example, that was nearly four times as great as in France generally.

Having registered the effects of the electoral procedure and of the distinctive qualities of political life in particular regions, we must finally notice the very widespread desire of a great number of bailliage magistrates to leave the judiciary, at least temporarily, for a new political vocation. There is much evidence on this point. It was generally thought unseemly to put forward one's own candidacy and indecent to organize voters in behalf of a candidate. Some magistrates did both, and when they were indiscreet this was noticed. At the first stage of the electoral process, a magistrate might begin a political career by being chosen to represent his judicial company in the assembly for the town. Here is Coutineau's record of the election of two representatives of the présidial court in Poitiers: "Baguenard and Lanot were elected. They had ten votes, against six for Lamarque, who much desired to be named and had for this purpose asked each of us for our votes on the first ballot, offering his vote on the second."[123] Once chosen as a member of the electoral assembly for the town, it was possible to obtain support from other corporate groups. In Saint-Maixent, for instance, the cotton stocking manufacturers instructed their representatives to vote for two judges, Chaudreau and Agier, "whose character and patriotism are known to us," as the town's representatives in subsequent electoral assemblies.[124]

There was an alternative route to the electoral assembly for the bailliage, beginning not in the town but in the countryside. Cochon, a councillor in the sénéchaussée of Fontenay-le-Comte, attended the electoral assembly of the village of Ardin, where his estate of Lapparent was located, and there he was chosen as a representative to the electoral assembly for the

123. Ms. journal, 2 March 1789.
124. *Cahiers de doléances des sénéchaussées de Niort et de Saint-Maixent et des communautés et corporations de Niort et Saint-Maixent pour les Etats Généraux de 1789,* ed. Léonce Cathelineau (Niort, 1912), p. 339.

sénéchaussée of Niort.[125] But this was very unusual. It was unnecessary: the final electoral assemblies were not required to choose from among their own members in electing the deputies to the Estates General and did not always do so. Furthermore, villages commonly chose local men as their representatives, not magistrates from a nearby town. In Poitou, for example, there was a total of twenty-nine magistrates in the sénéchaussées of Civray, Niort, and Saint-Maixent, and a total of 201 villages in their jurisdictions; besides Cochon de Lapparent, only one magistrate, Delaroy de la Grange, a councillor at Niort, was chosen by a village to be its representative in the electoral assembly of the sénéchaussée.[126] For bailliage magistrates in general, the easier way into electoral politics started in the town and proceeded through some kind of conciliation of the interests of town and villages.

Later, when the rural and urban electors of the Third Estate gathered for the assembly of the bailliage, there were new possibilities for mobilizing support. In Chalon-sur-Saône, the king's proctor and the chief civil judge were both elected to the Estates General, and a disgruntled observer wrote: "All their friends and all their following, all those dependent on the tribunal and its adherents . . . colleagues in office, retired magistrates who came in from the country expressly for this, the practitioners in all the villages who had been named electors . . . did not hesitate to solicit, seek, and demand votes for them."[127] Another complaint said that "letters had been addressed to the electors asking for their votes, and ballots had

125. Paul Boucher, *Charles Cochon de Lapparent, Conventionnel, Ministre de la Police, Préfet de l'Empire* (Paris, Editions A. & J. Picard, 1969), p. 24.
126. *Cahiers Niort et Saint-Maixent*, p. 212; *Cahiers de doléances de la sénéchaussée de Civray pour les Etats Généraux de 1789*, ed. Prosper Boissonnade and Léonce Cathelineau (Niort, 1925).
127. Letter to Cérutti, 19 April 1789, unsigned (A.N., B^a 31^4). Joachim Cérutti, a Jesuit teacher in Lyon and a friend of the encyclopedists, founded the newspaper *La Feuille Villageoise*.

been passed around on which were designated the individuals to be chosen."[128] Even after allowance for exaggeration, these comments help to explain how two of the three bailliage magistrates elected deputies in Burgundy secured their election.

In the assembly of the Third Estate for the bailliage, the electoral procedure gave the chief civil judge and the king's proctor a special advantage in forwarding their candidacy without seeming to do so. The king's proctor had the duty of formally requesting that the proceedings begin, and the chief civil judge had the duty of formally ordering them to begin. These duties offered occasions for declamatory speeches on the obligations of deputies in the Estates General and of the electors who were about to choose them. Armand Brette remarked, after his diligent study of the elections, that such speeches were opportunities of unequalled importance.[129] It would be a wearisome task to read them all, but a sampling suggests that many contained two significant themes, the essential unity of the kingdom and the need for its regeneration. These themes were appropriate expressions of men holding the place in society that was held by bailliage magistrates, and exercising their occupation, but were not a very explicit guide for future political action. In particular, uncertainty necessarily lingered as to the political conduct of bailliage magistrates if it should come about that regeneration could not be achieved with unity.

128. Protest by Claude Lambert, elector from Chagny, quoted by Paul Montarlot, *Les Députés de Saône-et-Loire aux assemblées de la Révolution* (Autun, 1905), p. 149.

129. *Recueil de documents relatifs à la convocation des Etats Généraux,* III, 26. Besides 48 presiding judges, 20 king's proctors were elected deputies for the Third Estate.

V

Bailliage Magistrates as Deputies in the Estates General and National Assembly, 1789–1791

The creation of a national legislature was in itself a revolutionary achievement, acclaimed as such in advance. But neither the form of the National Assembly nor its principal enactments were foreseen. While the Assembly evolved as an institution, its membership was divided over issues that shifted, sometimes with bewildering suddenness. The pressure of events and unavoidable decisions created groupings, allegiances, and antipathies. These, in turn, affected the functioning of the Assembly.

Trained and experienced in legal analysis, accustomed to pronouncing judgment, those deputies who were magistrates in bailliages had opportunities both to help in shaping the new legislative institution and to cast their weight for or against particular legislation. Their opportunities changed as the institution evolved and its political experience accumulated. The role of the magistrates as deputies became significantly different from what it had been when the Estates General first met.

To extract the magistrates' role from the history of the National Assembly is a difficult enterprise promising uncertain results. For this difficulty there are two principal reasons. The history of the National Assembly has received relatively little attention from historians since Aulard. The important contributions in the last half-century make a very brief list: a couple of suggestive articles by Gustave Rouanet; valuable studies of two leaders and their policies, by Georges Michon and Jean Egret, respectively; and the documents prepared for the royal sessions of 5 May and 23 June 1789, published in a definitive edition.[1] The sparseness of the historical writing reflects in part the nature of the sources. An improvised institution, the National Assembly began without the regular procedures that would have generated a complete body of records. Its majority rejected the idea of publishing or even preserving lists showing how individuals voted in each roll-call vote.[2] Only the numbers voting on each side were recorded, not always reliably. The Assembly entrusted the task of preparing minutes of proceedings to secretaries elected from the membership in political contests for four-week terms of office. The process of approving the minutes readily degenerated into an occasion for reopening debate on the matters recorded. The secretaries were therefore

1. Rouanet, "Les Débuts du parlementarisme français," *Annales Révolutionnaires,* 8 (1916), 173–211, and "Les Séances de la Constituante après le 14 juillet 1789," *Annales Révolutionnaires,* 9 (1917), 433–455, 610–628; Michon, *Adrien Duport. Essai sur l'histoire du parti feuillant* (Paris, Payot, 1924); Egret, *La Révolution des notables. Mounier et les monarchiens* (Paris, Librairie Armand Colin, 1950); *Recueil de documents relatifs aux séances des Etats Généraux, mai–juin 1789, tome Ier,* ed. Georges Lefebvre and Anne Terroine, 2 vols. (Paris, Centre National de la Recherche Scientifique, 1953–1962).

2. *Procès-verbal de l'Assemblée Nationale,* 9 July 1789, pp. 2–3.,

under steady pressure to seek impartiality through brevity and dry formality.[3] The sessions were open to the public, but contemporaries saw them as dramatic spectacles, clashes in debate over principles, competitions in eloquence. Only a few deputies, and only their highly visible activities, were reported in newspapers, some of which were improvised, as hastily as the Assembly itself, for this very purpose. The National Assembly had the equivalent of corridors and cloakrooms, but the political activity there remained largely concealed, both because anything resembling factional alignment was thought to be indecent and because the public audience, in the galleries and in the newspaper columns, was ruthless.

The documentation published contemporaneously is unbalanced in such a way as to obscure particularly the bailliage magistrates, who were men of the conference room rather than the podium. A partial remedy can be found because a number of deputies, well aware that they were witnesses of great events, kept their own records, especially in order to report to family, friends, or constituents. For the purposes of this chapter, voluminous evidence is provided by the letters of two magistrates who sat as deputies from the province of Maine: a judge from the capital, Le Mans, and the king's proctor from a small town, Mayenne.[4]

3. This observation is due to Rouanet, in vol. 9, pp. 442–446.

4. François-René-Pierre Ménard de La Groye, 222 letters to his wife in Le Mans (25 April 1789–21 June 1791, and 4–16 October 1791, an additional 32 letters written during the summer of 1791 having apparently been lost), mss., A.D. Sarthe, 10 J 122; and Michel-René Maupetit, 253 letters to Dupont-Grandjardin, a seigneurial judge and political figure in Mayenne (25 April 1789–27 September 1791), ed. Emile Queruau-Lamerie in twenty-one installments in the *Bulletin de la Commission Historique et Archéologique de la Mayenne*, 2nd ser., 17 (1901)–23 (1907). (Maupetit held the office of king's proctor in the bailliage of Bourgnouvel sitting in Mayenne, a jurisdiction from which all appeals were carried to the sénéchaussée at Le Mans, and therefore not a bailliage in the strict sense used for the electoral regulations of 1789 and for this study, Appendix; but it would be quixotic to ignore his letters for a technical reason of this kind.)

These are supplemented by some of the reactions of the chief judge of Draguignan, in Provence, and the king's advocate from Guéret, in the Marche, in letters scattered throughout the period of the National Assembly's existence.[5] For the early months of the Assembly, there are also the writings of the chief judges of Saint-Brieuc, in Brittany; Sarrelouis, in Lorraine; and Châtellerault and La Châtaigneraie, in Poitou.[6] And, for the later months, there are the letters of the chief judge of Lannion, in Brittany, and Faulcon, the judge from Poitiers whom we have encountered in earlier chapters, who had been elected an alternate and was called upon in April 1790 to take a seat as a deputy.[7]

5. Jacques-Athanase Lombard de Taradeau, 33 letters to the municipal council of Draguignan (5 August 1789–19 September 1791), ed. Louis Honoré, *Var Historique et Géographique,* 2 (1925–1928), 230–248, 255–278, 322–342, 347–365; and Jean-Baptiste Grellet de Beauregard, 21 letters to the marquis de La Celle at his château of Ajain near Guéret (12 June–14 September 1789, and 29 May 1790–19 April 1791), ed. Dardy, *Mémoires de la Société des Sciences Naturelles et Archéologiques de la Creuse,* 2nd ser., 7 (1899), 53–117.

6. Julien-François Palasne de Champeaux, 23 letters to the correspondence committee in Saint-Brieuc (1 May–16 October 1789), ed. D. Tempier, *Mémoires de la Société d'Emulation des Côtes-du-Nord,* 26 (1888), 210–263; Nicolas-Théodore-Antoine-Adolphe de Lasalle de Berweiller, 105 letters to the electors of the bailliage of Sarrelouis (9 June 1789–22 January 1790) and to the municipal council of Sarrelouis (15 February–31 July 1790), ed. R. Herly, *Bulletin de la Société des Amis des Pays de la Sarre,* 4 (1927), 195–307; Jacques-Antoine Creuzé de Latouche, *Journal des Etats-Généraux et du début de l'Assemblée Nationale (18 mai–29 juillet 1789),* ed. Jean Marchand (Paris, Librairie Henri Didier, 1946); and Louis-Prosper Lofficial, 22 letters to his wife in La Châtaigneraie (18 May–24 October 1789), ed. C. Leroux-Cesbron, *Nouvelle Revue Rétrospective,* 7 (1897), 73–120, 169–192. (Lofficial was chief judge in the bailliage of Vouvant sitting at La Châtaigneraie, a jurisdiction from which all appeals were carried to the sénéchaussée at Poitiers, and therefore not a bailliage in the strictest sense; the same comment applies to his letters as to those of Maupetit, above, n. 4.)

7. Gabriel-Hyacinthe Couppé, 18 letters to the district administration of Lannion (4 September 1790–19 June 1791), ed. D. Tempier, *Mémoires de la Société d'Emulation des Côtes-du-Nord,* 27 (1889), 22–61; and Félix Faulcon, *Correspondance,* ed. Gabriel Debien, 2 vols. (Poitiers, 1939–1953, as *Archives Historiques du Poitou,* 51 and 55), II, 147–463.

These letters and memoranda represent, with varying degrees of incompleteness, the views of about 8 percent of the bailliage magistrates serving as deputies for the Third Estate. As a sample of opinion, this proportion is not negligible. It is, however, systematically under-representative of the conservatives among the bailliage magistrates. The conservatives fairly rapidly came to disagree with many politically influential men in their respective provinces and towns and accordingly were not much inclined to send reports to correspondence committees or political letters to their wives for transmission to acquaintances at home. Allowance can be made for this element of bias in the evidence, since other sources permit discovery of the identity and the views of these conservatives.

Bailliage magistrates were not the only deputies who wrote letters. Their political evolution can be compared, at some points, with that of other deputies who were not magistrates. Five lawyers, in particular, left interesting materials that have been published.[8] Still other perspectives may be discerned in the writings of two other deputies, a physician and an intellectual nobleman, both from Poitou.[9]

8. Jean-Pierre Boullé, 32 letters to the municipal council of Pontivy in Brittany, ed. Albert Macé in 18 installments in the Documents section of the *Revue de la Révolution*, 10 (1887)–16 (1889); Adrien Duquesnoy, *Journal sur l'Assemblée Constituante, 3 mai 1789–3 avril 1790*, ed. Robert de Crèvecœuer, 2 vols. (Paris, 1894); Jean-François Gaultier de Biauzat, *Correspondance*, ed. Francisque Mège as vol. II of the biography, *Gaultier de Biauzat*, 2 vols. (Paris, 1890); Jean-Baptiste Poncet-Delpech, *La première année de la Révolution vue par un témoin (1789–1790). Les "Bulletins" de Poncet-Delpech*, ed. Daniel Ligou (Paris, Presses Universitaires de France, 1961), and "La Suite des papiers de Poncet-Delpech," ed. Daniel Ligou, *Annales Historiques de la Révolution Française*, 38 (1966), 426–446, 561–576; René-Antoine-Hyacinthe Thibaudeau, "Correspondance," ed. Henri Carré and Prosper Boissonnade, *Mémoires de la Société des Antiquaires de l'Ouest*, 2nd ser., 20 (1897), 5–203.

9. Jean-Gabriel Gallot, journal (21 April–31 July 1789) and 17 letters to his wife in Saint-Maurice-le-Girard (21 May 1789–26 January 1790), ed. Dr. Louis Merle in the biographical study, *La vie et les œuvres du Dr. Jean-Gabriel Gallot* (Poitiers, 1961, as *Mémoires de la Société des*

The establishment of the National Assembly was a difficult, complicated, and lengthy process. The point at which it was completed depends to a considerable degree upon a historical judgment. The formal opening of the Estates General was on 5 May; the first session in which clergymen, nobles, and commoners voted in a single roll call was that of 30 June; the rules of procedure were adopted 29 July; important standing committees were created in August; and the future of the Assembly remained uncertain throughout the whole period until 6 October, at least.

Among the deputies of the Third Estate, political disagreement was manifest even before the formal opening session. The issues were what conduct to expect from the nobles (including the bishops) and what attitude to adopt toward them. Initially, the deputies of the Third Estate grouped themselves by provinces, because of prior acquaintanceships and distinct provincial interests. The lines of disagreement concerning the nobles coincided with certain provincial groupings, because recent political experience had taught contrasting lessons in different provinces. The men from Dauphiné had reasons to hope for the union of nobles and commoners in order to achieve a constitutional monarchy. The men from Brittany expected the nobles to obstruct every reform and were prepared, in general, to match or exceed their obstinacy. These deputations were coherent, although not unanimous, minorities at the outset and were to remain so during most of the summer. One of the processes involved in the formation of political groups was to be the clustering of deputies from other provinces round their leaders: Mounier, from Dauphiné; and several, chiefly Le Chapelier, from Brittany.

The majority of the Third Estate deputies coalesced only gradually in support of a policy which was not the same as that

---

Antiquaires de l'Ouest, 4th ser., 5), pp. 59–102 and 104–136; Charles-Elie, marquis de Ferrières, *Correspondance inédite, 1789, 1790, 1791,* ed. Henri Carré (Paris, Librairie Armand Colin, 1932).

of either the Dauphinois or the Bretons. This occurred as the Third Estate deputies attempted to settle a series of particular questions. Whether the deputies' elections were to be certified by each Order or by all three in common was a question distinct from whether to debate and vote on other matters thereafter as three Orders or as one assembly of individual deputies. The ultimate fate of church property, seigneurial rights, and nobles' honorific prerogatives was still another issue. The relationship between these questions and the speed with which they should be decided were additional matters of disagreement and individual tergiversation. The course taken by the majority of the Third Estate during May and June is defined by three essential coordinates: the recorded votes of 18 May, 10 June, and 17 June.

On 18 May, after four days of debate, the question was how to respond to what the nobles and the clergy had already voted to do. The nobles had decided to proceed to certify the elections of the deputies of their Order separately. The clergy had suggested conferences among conciliation commissioners drawn from all three Orders. The deputies of the Third Estate had to choose between the motion of Rabaut de Saint-Etienne, to agree to designate 16 individuals as spokesmen in the conferences, and the motion of Le Chapelier, ignoring the suggestion for conferences, to summon the clergy and the nobility to join in a general assembly to certify the elections of all the deputies. At the time of the vote in the Third Estate, the 20 deputies from the city of Paris had not yet arrived and about 150 others were absent. The result was 360 for Rabaut's motion, and 66 (including all 44 deputies from Brittany, and a scattering from elsewhere) for Le Chapelier's motion.[10]

The conferences produced no agreement between the Third Estate and the other two Orders, and were succeeded by a second round of conferences in the presence of royal commis-

10. Gaultier de Biauzat, *Correspondance*, p. 68; Maupetit, vol. 18, p. 136.

sioners ending 9 June in a confirmed stalemate. The vote in the Third Estate on 10 June was on whether to adopt or to discuss further a motion of Sieyès. His motion was to invite the clergy and the nobility to join the Third Estate in order to certify the elections and to call the roll of electoral circumscriptions recording the absence of all deputies who did not answer. The result of the vote was 493 for adoption, 41 for further discussion.[11]

In the subsequent roll call of electoral circumscriptions, held accordingly, no nobles or clergymen responded except 3 parish priests from Poitou, who were joined during the ensuing week by 17 other parish priests from various provinces. The roll call having been completed, the question was how the assembled deputies should entitle themselves. The vote of 17 June was to adopt or reject five motions, each specifying a different title. During debate, Sieyès had amended his motion to specify the title "National Assembly." His motion was the first to be acted on, and by a vote of 491 to 90 it was adopted.[12]

In the impatient minority of 18 May, magistrates were as important in numbers and in leadership as they were in relation to the whole Third Estate. Ten of the forty-four deputies from Brittany were magistrates. A few magistrates from other provinces were prominent spokesmen for intransigence in the face of the nobility and for decisive action. Such were Le Grand, king's advocate in the bailliage of Châteauroux,[13] and Milscent, a judge at Angers, who were both chosen on 19 May among

11. These were the numbers counted by Camus, as noted by Creuzé de Latouche, *Journal*, p. 94. The other teller, Populus, reported 487 for adoption, 34 for further discussion, according to Gaultier de Biauzat, *Correspondance*, p. 104.

12. *Recueil de documents relatifs aux séances des Etats Généraux*, II, 57 (n. 76); *Point du Jour*, I, 3; Gallot, "Journal," p. 82. The tellers reported that 2 other votes were unrecorded [perhaps inaudible].

13. Two characterizations: "Le Grand, the most annoying, the most insufferable of all the prattlers, dangerous through this in itself and because of his pride" (Duquesnoy, *Journal*, I, 27); "Le Grand . . . very firm and a good orator" (Creuzé de Latouche, *Journal*, p. 8).

the commissioners for the Third Estate in the conferences with the clergy and the nobility. It was Le Grand who, on 16 June, first strongly urged the title "National Assembly" upon his fellow-deputies of the Third Estate.[14] The anger of the Breton faction against its opponents also emerges clearly in the intemperate language of the chief judge of Saint-Brieuc, reporting to his fellow townsmen.[15]

In the dilatory and conservative minorities in the Third Estate votes in June, other bailliage magistrates were included. On 10 June, besides Dupont de Nemours and three lawyers from Paris, the minority consisted of "magistrates, men of privilege, and other deputies who are generally suspected of being devoted to the Nobility."[16] The minority on 17 June was twice as large, and benefited from the constitutional ideas and the personal prestige of Mounier. In his view, the deputies of the clergy and the nobility, although they had no right to deliberate as separate Orders, still represented part of the nation, and therefore the title of "National Assembly" could not legitimately be assumed by the Third Estate deputies and a score of parish priests. His view was shared by other influential and persuasive commoners, notably Thouret. The deputies in the minority on 17 June were not a random aggregation; they had already, during the session the evening before, been gathered in

14. Le Grand's motion, proposed as a substitute for that of Sieyès, appears in *AP*, VIII, 122. According to Duquesnoy, *Journal*, I, 99–100, a previous speaker had already said that Sieyès's original motion was weak and that the Third Estate deputies ought to take the title of National Assembly; Duquesnoy wrote that this speaker was the king's proctor in a bailliage in Lorraine, a description which would fit no one but Petitmengin of Saint-Dié.

15. "We have among us some *jean-foutre* (slackers) devoted to aristocracy . . . Parish priests come over to us every day . . . but as yet only three Bretons . . . If those beggars of parish priests fail us . . . we are determined to denounce them to the nation as beggars, as traitors to their country." Palasne de Champeaux, letter of 16 June (during the session), p. 234.

16. Creuzé de Latouche, *Journal*, p. 94.

one part of the chamber.[17] Outstanding among them, besides Mounier, were former or current associates of royal ministers and celebrated lawyers from Paris, Rouen, Bordeaux, and Nancy.[18] The bailliage magistrates who voted with these men were not the leaders of the minority.

More than two-thirds of the deputies for the Third Estate swung from the conciliatory position of 18 May to the adamant position of 17 June. Some found the first round of conferences sufficient proof that attempts at conciliation were futile: among these, at the end of May, was the chief judge of Châtellerault, Creuzé de Latouche, who recorded his trenchant criticisms of bishops, nobles, and ministers.[19] But it was in the first days of June that the course of action which had been advocated all along by the Bretons attracted majority support.

In attitude, the mass of the Third Estate deputies remained moderates, though in differing degrees and for distinct reasons. One who professed moderation as a coherent policy was Maupetit, the king's proctor from Mayenne. After the vote of 18 May, he wrote a long report to his friends and constituents at home, forestalling criticism and counteracting unrealistic expectations which might lead to impatience or despair.[20] Maupetit said that the Third Estate had made clear its determination to secure individual voting in a single assembly, that its moderate tone and conciliatory proceedings would convince the nobles they need have no fear for their just rights, and that some time would be required to put an end to the division between the three Orders. If this policy proved in-

17. Boullé, letter dispatched 19 June, vol. 13, Documents, p. 12.
18. Creuzé de Latouche, *Journal*, pp. 124, 126, mentioned "nearly all" the 20 deputies from Paris; Malouet (who was in close touch with Necker at this time); Thouret and the other 7 deputies from Rouen; Prugnon and Régnier from Nancy; Lebrun, from Dourdan, who had been Maupeou's secretary; Dupont of Nemours, formerly an adviser of Calonne; and the Garat brothers from Bordeaux.
19. *Journal*, pp. 30, 33–35.
20. Letter of 21 May 1789, vol. 18, pp. 137–143.

sufficient, he said, then an actual crisis would be required. For three weeks, however, he held steadily to optimism, patience, reluctance to see the Third Estate take a decisive step, and readiness to accept royal mediation. He did not change his mind even when the nobility announced itself organized as a separate Order and declared its separate status to be a fundamental principle of the monarchy. While Maupetit was critical of the deputies from Brittany, because of their vehemence, extreme proposals, and intolerance of disagreement, he nevertheless wrote that "les têtes exaltées" were needed to keep the Third Estate always watchful. He was moderate even on the subject of extremists.[21]

Maupetit presented the Sieyès motions adopted in June as a logical continuation of the previous moderate policy.[22] In reporting the first motion to his constituents, he pointed out that the clergy and the nobility would always be free to join the Third Estate, even after the latter had certified the elections of its deputies as representatives of the greater part of the nation. This kept open the way to eventual union. At the same time, it would make action possible. The clergy and the nobility would join sooner or later, "since it is established that we are all in agreement as to the substantive matters." At first Maupetit thought that the Third Estate would not assume the title of National Assembly, "which would lead one to believe that we claimed to represent the whole nation." But after the debates of 15 and 16 June, he reported with no adverse comment that Sieyès was proposing that title, and in the end he voted for it. In presenting the decision of 17 June as consistent with that of 18 May, he disagreed with both minorities, intransigent and conciliatory, and their respective leaders, Le Chapelier and

21. Letters of 26 and 30 May and 5 June 1789, vol. 18, pp. 147–156.
22. Letters of 13 and 17 June 1789, vol. 18, pp. 157–162. In the first of these, Maupetit advised his friends to read *Qu'est-ce que le Tiers Etat?*, of which he had had a copy in Mayenne in February, in order to understand the plan to be followed. (Maupetit explained his vote on 17 June in a letter of 3 August 1789, vol. 19, p. 215.)

Mounier. It is possible to suspect Maupetit of inwardly preferring the ideas of Mounier or Thouret (whom he particularly admired) but being brought to recognize that in the circumstances in June the Bretons were right. Yet he did not explain the matter that way to his constituents. He judged that the consistency of the whole series of decisions appeared credible, as well as politically advantageous, and he believed that what the majority of the Third Estate had done represented a clear policy.

Most of the moderates in the Third Estate were undoubtedly as determined as Maupetit to secure individual voting in a single assembly. But a firm purpose did not dictate a timetable or arouse a feeling of urgency, nor did it engender hostility toward nobles. A high-ranking commoner from a provincial town, particularly a royal judge, was still able to enjoy social acceptance by nobles in the whirl of dinners and salons at Versailles: this is exemplified by passages in the letters of Ménard de la Groye to his wife.[23] Equally characteristic was uneasiness over the measures adopted by the Third Estate in June, vague fear of what the king or his ministers might do. The chief judge and deputy for the Third Estate of Sarrelouis, Lasalle de Berweiller, was a noble himself, but like Maupetit he thought that for the clergy and the nobility to divide the Estates General into separately voting orders was unreasonable precisely because "they hold the same principles we do as to the substantive matters."[24] He said some members of the Third Estate believed that the vote of 10 June had been too hasty, that answers from the clergy and the nobility should have been

23. Mss., A.D. Sarthe, 10 J 122. Ménard's letter of 26 May 1789 reported a busy social calendar. His letter of 29 May began: "Nous continuons d'être entièrement divisés d'avec la Noblesse, pendant que le Clergé nage entre deux eaux et n'ose prendre aucun parti. Cela ne m'empêche point de fréquenter un grand nombre de seigneurs et de gentilshommes avec lesquels je dispute, mais sans aigreur, et qui me donnent les marques d'estime les plus flatteuses."

24. Letter of 9 June 1789, p. 195.

awaited, and that he himself was "somewhat of that opinion." Then, although he announced the vote of 17 June to his constituents as "an act of justice and reason," Lasalle said it would be so strongly disapproved by some in Versailles that he could not help feeling "a little anxiety" over the possible consequences.[25] The social acquaintanceships with nobles, the hesitations, and the afterthoughts of these deputies altogether suggest that the firmness of the Third Estate was due in great part to the clarity and the obstinacy with which the majority of the nobles manifested their purpose. Such was in fact the opinion, retrospectively, of still another magistrate, the king's advocate from Guéret, Grellet de Beauregard. He wrote to his friend the marquis de La Celle that the nobles, if they had been able to bring themselves to join with the commoners in order to draw up a constitution and reform the existing abuses, could then have obtained separate voting for future sessions of the Estates General.[26]

The bailliage magistrates sitting as deputies disagreed, in May and June 1789, over the policies to be adopted toward the nobles and toward the crown, just as their colleagues in the Third Estate disagreed. This should not be taken to mean that there were no important differences between them and the other deputies. The professional experience of the magistrates prepared them particularly well to endure the tedious business of organizing a deliberative body. Few magistrates put themselves forward as leaders in the sessions of the Third Estate. But Creuzé de Latouche, Grellet de Beauregard, Lasalle de Berweiller, Maupetit, and Ménard de la Groye each manifested confidence as to the eventual outcome of the Estates General,

25. Letters of 12 and 18 June 1789, pp. 196–197, 199. Similarly, Ménard de la Groye noted, a week after the resolution of 10 June, that the king had not yet responded to it: "Nous ne sommes pas sans inquiétudes en attendant que ses intentions nous soient manifestées." (Letter of 17 June 1789, evidently written before the session of that day, ms., A.D. Sarthe, 10 J 122).

26. Letter of 10 July 1789, p. 65.

patience in the face of the clumsy machinery of deliberation and an expectation that his views would be taken seriously by other deputies. The magistrates' state of mind contrasts with the discouragement expressed by, for example, certain of the lawyers, and with the aggressiveness displayed by others.

The advocate Duquesnoy was pessimistic before the middle of May. He predicted that the Third Estate was going to declare that it really was the Nation, and on 22 May he observed that the purpose of the deputies from Brittany was the same as that of the English Levellers: "they would like to remove every inequality of condition." None of this was to Duquesnoy's liking. Although on 7 June he wrote that he was ready to see the Third Estate take the title of "National Assembly," it was because he could see no other possible action.[27] Conscious of his ability as a political analyst, Duquesnoy wrote voluminously during May and June, freely expressing his gloomy prognostications. Disappointment over his own small part in practical politics was only partly concealed by his sarcasm on the talkativeness of his colleagues from the bar.[28] The discouragement of another advocate, Poncet-Delpech, was manifested in a different way. His first observation, at the beginning of May, was that until the hotheads in the Third Estate calmed down it would be difficult to accomplish anything beneficial. He disapproved of current talk that the Third Estate might act alone if the clergy and the nobility should refuse to join in a single assembly. In early June, he was no longer following matters with much attention, and so failed to perceive the strategem behind the clergy's proposal for unity on 6 June, missed the significance of Sieyès's motion adopted on 10 June,

27. Duquesnoy, *Journal*, I, 18, 36, 78.
28. "Unfortunately, the assembly is composed of a mob of lawyers who, having enjoyed a little reputation as members of the little bar of their little towns, thought that they were going to play a considerable role here and cause themselves to be noticed. All are wildly eager to talk." (I, 57.)

and regarded as uninteresting the numerous pamphlets then being published. He expressed the wish to be back in his own province in peaceful obscurity.[29]

An altogether different mentality is conveyed by the letters of Gaultier de Biauzat, another advocate. Impersonal, unreflective, extremely well-informed, foresighted, and combative, he wrote as an emissary in an unfriendly territory aiming at well-defined objectives and setting about his task with skill and determination. Only once, on 25 May, did he yield to discouragement so far as to express it to his constituents. He was already beginning to make a mark as an orator, notably on matters of procedure and draftsmanship, and he did not hesitate to turn upon his constituents with an angry retort to some mild criticism of his letters.[30] He was emerging as a political leader.

While the Third Estate deputies aligned themselves on the political issues of May and early June and identified orators and organizers, leaders and followers, they also began to define a legislative procedure. As they denied that the nobles' separate assembly was legitimate, they maintained that they themselves were incapable of legally binding action. For this reason they hesitated to draw up any rules. Yet there were decisions to be made for which voting by acclamation was not a trustworthy method. There was also the classic difficulty, which the National Assembly was never able to resolve, of reconciling the right of each member to be heard and the right of the majority to obtain a decision. In May, the Third Estate employed two roll calls on each question, the first for contributions to debate and the second for votes.[31] This encouraged oratorical prolixity, especially on the part of the many speakers who depended on prepared texts, and prevented any real exchange of

29. Poncet-Delpech, *Bulletins,* pp. 21, 35, 36, 39, 40.
30. *Correspondance.* esp. pp. 83, 88.
31. Gaultier de Biauzat, *Correspondance,* pp. 42, 57.

opinions.[32] The need for preliminary discussions was shown also by the rudimentary arrangements for them that had already developed. Regional groupings of deputations from adjacent provinces met in the rooms next to the assembly hall once a week, more or less, and talked over the state of affairs.[33] Cafés in the center of Versailles were scenes of unofficial gatherings like the daily dinner table shared by most of the deputies from Maine.[34] Since the end of April, the deputies from Brittany had been meeting regularly in a hall they rented for the purpose, also admitting deputies from other provinces, and it was there, on 8 June, that Sieyès was first to present the motion which was adopted by the Third Estate two days later.[35] Personal canvassing was also used to prepare the way for motions and to obtain supporting speeches, in advance of presentation in the assembly.[36] All these practices enabled groups of deputies to act in concert but gave only sporadic and unequal enlightenment for the assembly of the Third Estate as a whole.

Opportunities for preliminary consideration were provided for all the Third Estate deputies through the procedural device adopted on 7 June. The deputies were distributed into twenty groups, each of thirty members. These groups were denominated bureaux, like the subdivisions in the Assembly of Notables in 1787 and 1788. In order to counteract local and

32. Maupetit, vol. 17, p. 135, described the session of 18 May: "One saw only everlasting papers at each name called chill the assembly with repetitions, endless restatements of the same reasons."

33. Gaultier de Biauzat, *Correspondance*, pp. 53, 70; Creuzé de Latouche, *Journal*, pp. 19–22.

34. Ménard de la Groye, in a letter of 2 June, wrote: "Cette table. où je me trouve toutes les fois que je n'ai point d'engagement particulier, est habituellement occupée par MM. Enjubault de la Roche, Lasnier, Maupetit, Guérin, Lalande, Gournay et [Chenon de] Beaumont, qui sont tous de braves et honnêtes gens." [Omitting Jouye des Roches, who was not then on good terms with the others from Maine.] (Ms., A.D. Sarthe, 10 J 122.)

35. Boullé, vol. 10, Documents, p. 163; vol. 12, Documents, p. 40.

36. Gaultier de Biauzat, *Correspondance*, p. 77.

provincial loyalties, the deputies from each electoral circumscription were assigned to different bureaux.[37] These arrangements suited particularly the magistrates, accustomed to the deliberative practices of the council chamber in a bailliage.[38] Indeed, magistrates of every shade of political opinion quickly acquired in the bureaux an importance they did not have in general debate.[39] From the outset, impatient or radical deputies in the Third Estate expressed disapproval of the bureaux and sought to prevent any matters other than routine business from being referred to them.[40] In early June, the inevitable confrontation with the nobility overrode whatever inclination most moderates might have had to delay or evade making decisions.[41] But the bureaux remained objects of suspicion in the minds of the determined antiaristocrats, some of whom were magistrates. By the end of June, disbelief in any good intentions on the part of the majority of nobles, impatience with any effort to temporize or compromise, faith in the opinions of the public which crowded the galleries of the assembly hall—in

37. On the list of deputies of the Third Estate, arranged in alphabetical order of electoral circumscriptions (Agen through Vitry-le-François), each deputy was assigned a number, consecutively. Deputies 1, 21, 41 . . . 581 were placed in Bureau 1; deputies 2, 22, 42 . . . 582 in Bureau 2; and so on. (Membership lists of 17 of the bureaux are conserved in A.N., C 28, plaquette 216.)

38. Maupetit, letter of 8 June 1789, vol. 18, p. 157; Grellet de Beauregard, letter of 12 June 1789, p. 60.

39. On 13 June, Bureaux 1, 2, 3, 8, 18, and 19 each chose a magistrate as its spokesman in the process of certifying the elections of deputies. On 19 June, Bureaux 2, 8, 19, and 20 each chose a magistrate as a member of the assembly's comité de rédaction, and Bureaux 2, 3, 4, 5, 10, 12, 15, and 20 each chose a magistrate as a member of the assembly's comité de règlement. (*AP*, VIII, 102–106, 137.)

40. Robespierre argued, on 5 June, that meetings of mere fractions of the assembly would strengthen the influence of certain personalities and would encourage intrigue. Creuzé de Latouche, *Journal*, p. 58.

41. Gaultier de Biauzat, *Correspondance*, p. 102; Boullé, vol. 12, Documents, p. 49, noted that on 9 June he was "not dissatisfied in general with the attitudes" of his fellow-members of Bureau 12 (in which there were 8 bailliage magistrates).

brief, experience in a new kind of politics—caused some of the most perspicacious deputies to reject the mode of proceedings for which their professional experience most suited them.[42] From this fact, and the impending union of nobles and commoners in a single assembly, the later purely formal function of the bureaux might have been foretold.[43]

In the third week of June, the Third Estate manifested unanimity, but this was momentary and superficial. Only one deputy signified opposition to the Tennis Court oath, although ninety had voted against the title, National Assembly, which was displayed in the oath over the signatures. Deputies who happened not to be in attendance when Mounier presented the oath, 20 June, hastened the next day to Paris, where the document had been taken to be printed, or sought out the secretaries of the Assembly on 22 June, in order to sign.[44] After the royal session in which the king quashed the resolutions of 10 and 17 June, the Third Estate reaffirmed them while its opposing minority sat silently acquiescent in this resistance to the royal will, a resistance to which the royal will yielded four days later. The royalist and aristocratic minority in the Third Estate was apparently swayed by fear of the consequences of popular disapproval and guided by a calculation that the bishops and the nobles, once present in the Assembly, would be sufficiently powerful to change the direction in which the

42. "Good principles and patriotic spirit, which acquire so much strength in a numerous assembly, weaken and decline in committees, where bad maxims are deployed more boldly. Proposals that no one would dare to bring forward in the general assembly, where we are so to speak visible to the Nation, are sometimes appreciated in these bureaux by misguided little minds and supported by bad citizens who believe themselves altogether beyond reach of censure." Creuzé de Latouche, *Journal,* pp. 175–176.

43. Cf. Oliver J. Frederiksen, "The Bureaus of the French Constituent Assembly of 1789. An Early Experiment in the Group-Conference Method," *Political Science Quarterly,* 51 (1936), 418–437, a convenient outline of the brief procedural development but a faulty interpretation of the political circumstances.

44. Maupetit, letter of 3 August 1789, vol. 19, p. 213.

Assembly was moving.[45] At the same time it was possible for the majority of the Third Estate to be guided by the opposite calculation, that bishops and nobles would be committed by their presence in an Assembly that would enact a constitutional program they disapproved and disliked. Yet this was illusory, and some of the commoners saw clearly that the millennial optimisim of the populace in Versailles during the last days of June was even less justified than it would have been earlier. In the reflections of the chief judge of Châtellerault, for instance, the tone of regret is as noteworthy as the anxiety.[46]

The transformation of the National Assembly effected by the formal union of the clergy and the nobility with the Third Estate did not at once conform to such somber expectations as those of Creuzé de Latouche. Political realignment within the Assembly, doubled in size, proved to be a slower and far more complicated process than he and other resolute patriots foresaw. The first few examples of nobles' oratory won the admiration of calm and methodical legislators among the commoners,[47] but eloquence was not enough to overcome organizational ability, determination, and voting strength. In the election of

45. Jean-François-César de Guilhermy, *Papiers d'un émigré, 1789–1829*, ed. Gustave de Guilhermy (Paris, 1886), p. 9.

46. "We do not believe that the nobles . . . are suddenly changed into zealous patriots full of good inclinations for the reform of abuses and the freedom of the Nation. Not without anxiety de we see them together with the least sound part of the clergy added to an assembly which, before their arrival, had reached so admirable a point of harmony and energy and was starting upon the most important operation . . . The National Assembly was stronger and offered greater hopes before the recent union than at present. The weak souls who are to be found among the commons' deputies, previously drawn along by the manly spirit which had become dominant in the assembly, will now be less fearful of siding with bad opinions when they see themselves supported by a number of votes. We must fear that the aristocratic and anti-citizenly maxims of so many members of the clergy and the nobility may divide the assembly and sometimes become dominant in it." Creuzé de Latouche, *Journal*, pp. 165–166.

47. Maupetit, letters of 3 and 8 July 1789, vol. 18, pp. 453, 454.

the Committee of Thirty to plan for constitutional reform, the Bretons and their allies were as successful as they had been in the debates three and four weeks previously. From a viewpoint other than that of factional politics, however, this committee election marks a turning point. The result signified that bailliage magistrates were to be largely effaced not only in debate but also, henceforth, in the proceedings of the bureaux. On 1 July these had been completely reorganized, increased in number from twenty to thirty bureaux and enlarged from thirty to forty members. On 6 July, each bureau chose one of its members to serve on the committee to prepare a preliminary plan for the constitution. Only two magistrates, Ulry, king's advocate from Bar-le-Duc, and Le Grand from Châteauroux, were selected (by Bureau 16 and Bureau 28, respectively.)[48]

In the deliberations of the bureaux during July few magistrates were able to win the respectful attention that was given to moderate and conciliatory nobles like the marquis de Ferrières.[49] After the members of each bureau had had an opportunity to become acquainted with one another, the political position of the magistrates within them was no more powerful. On 28 July, each bureau chose one of its members to serve on the committee to examine and report on incoming memoranda, complaints, and petitions. Two magistrates were selected, Alquier, king's advocate at La Rochelle, and Babey, king's advo-

48. *Procès-verbal de l'Assemblée Nationale*, 7 July (pp. 6–7). In the bureaux that elected Ulry and Le Grand, there were comparatively few magistrates: 2 in Bureau 16; 4 in Bureau 28. The Committee of Thirty was succeeded by the Committee of Eight on the constitution, elected on 14 July, which included no magistrates.

49. Ferrières, *Correspondance*, pp. 84, 97, 98, 106; he was in Bureau 9, whose most notable member was Clermont-Tonnerre. A member of Bureau 25, a commoner from Brittany wrote, on 29 July, "the work does not advance, and our firmness will inevitably weaken, the aristocrats having banished their former arrogance for which they pretend to substitute affability and politeness." Laurent-François Le Gendre, "Correspondance," ed. Corre and Delourmel, *Révolution Française*, 39 (1900), on p. 537.

cate at Orgelet (by Bureau 4 and Bureau 23, respectively).[50] Leadership in an Assembly beset by conflict did not devolve upon the magistrates, and it was easy for some of them to resent the energetic and disruptive performances of such politicians as Gaultier de Biauzat and Pétion.[51] From the first days of July, most magistrates withdrew, or were relegated, to the position of observers, commentators, and followers of one or another of the political tendencies at work in the Assembly.

The decline in the importance of the magistrates as legislative leaders was simultaneous with the atmosphere of rising alarm created by the movement of troops into Paris and Versailles. One of the magistrates made a point of asserting that the members of the Assembly were "impervious to fear."[52] But the statement is neither the truth nor its opposite. The deputies reacted variously to the prospect and the reality of violence. The magistrates, although professionally opposed to violence, evinced no single reaction any more than did other deputies. Throughout the period from Mirabeau's warning speech of 8 July to the king's appearance in the National Assembly on 15 July, the deputies considered violence in relation to its political causes and effects, and their attitudes fluctuated in accordance with their perceptions and expectations.

Some characteristic psychological processes are exemplified in Faulcon's journal, which contains entries made every four or five hours during the most critical days.[53] As an alternate

---

50. *Procès-verbal de l'Assemblée Nationale,* 30 July (p. 2). [The manuscript version of this list (A.N., C 28, plaquette 221, no. 11) shows that the committee members are named in order of bureaux, 1 through 30.] In the bureaux that elected Alquier and Babey, there were large concentrations of magistrates: 8 of them in Bureau 4 and 6 in Bureau 23.

51. Maupetit, letter of 8 July 1789, vol. 18, pp. 455, 457.

52. Grellet de Beauregard, letter of 10 July, p. 67.

53. "Semaine à jamais mémorable, ou Récit de ce qui s'est passé à Versailles et à Paris depuis le 11 jusqu'au 19 juillet 1789," *Correspondance,* II, 48–93, pp. 50, 54, 65 for the sentences quoted in this and the next paragraph.

deputy, he had accompanied the deputies from his province to the opening session and was still in the capital. In Paris, on 11 July, he noted rumors of the king's intention to dismiss the National Assembly, predicted that this would destroy the monarch's authority and plunge the country into bloodshed, and reflected that it was a good thing that the people finally felt the weight of the chains by which they were borne down but a great evil that they were seeking violent means to break them, "or rather, that the present agents of authority are constraining them to do so." After learning, on 12 July, of Necker's dismissal, he went to Versailles, and that night, in despair, he found it impossible to sleep. On 13 July, he went to the Assembly hall at dawn and there, manifesting his patriotism, seated amid the deputies, he noted four hours later: "I feel myself to be a different man. I fear no dangers." During the long day, Faulcon absorbed the oratory, the news that in Paris the shops were closed, the tocsin was ringing, and the angry populace intending to come to Versailles, and consciously shared the atmosphere of pessimism and heroism.

The same anxieties, persisting on 14 July, did not prevent Faulcon from observing attentively as the deputies established the Committee of Eight on the constitution and elected the members. About 8 o'clock in the evening, the vicomte de Noailles arrived from Paris and reported that a large crowd had forced its way into the Bastille, killing the governor of the prison, had also entered the Invalides and obtained arms, and that surprisingly good order was being maintained. Faulcon wrote: "I could not very well say with what sort of feeling I heard this news. Certainly I am apprehensive over the consequences of this popular insurrection, but on the other hand the courtiers' and the ministers' conduct is so horrible, so oppressive, that it is necessary to be delivered from it no matter what the price." Two hours later, further details became available. Like most people at the time, Faulcon believed the early accounts which asserted that the governor of the Bastille had flown a white flag, had permitted part of the crowd outside to enter, and then had raised a drawbridge and massacred those who had come inside.[54] He also believed that the *prévot des marchands* of Paris had betrayed the inhabitants by concluding an agreement with them and then entering into an understanding with "the oppressors of the State." Like many others, Faulcon appears to have judged that treachery of this kind was the reason, or even a justification, for the brutal murder of these two officials and the degradation of their corpses.[55] Underlying his reaction was the implicit belief that honorable adherence to a pledge could have protected them against the consequences of their false and untenable position. Thus it was at first not their fate that made him apprehensive. Indeed, he noted at 11 o'clock that night, "I will spend the rest of the night in the hall, even should we all be dismembered by the cruel henchmen of despotism."[56]

After a sleepless night interrupted by alarms, at dawn on 15 July, Faulcon reflected further on the state of affairs. Having received no news from Paris, he imagined the scene there inaccurately: "carnage, horror, desolation." His indignation again rose against those "few abominable personages" who had ordered troops into the city, thus making it necessary for "the most moderate citizens to take up arms" at a time when concord between the king and his subjects was so desirable.[57] He

54. The discourse prepared for delivery by Bancal des Issarts, spokesman for the *Comité permanent de la sûreté publique* of Paris, which appears in the *Procès-verbal de l'Assemblée Nationale,* 14 July (pp. 10–15), reprinted in *AP,* VIII, 233–234, spread very widely the story that the governor had violated a truce.

55. The chief judge of Châtellerault reacted in essentially the same way. Of the governor of the Bastille he wrote that death was due him, and of the prévôt des marchands that he deserved the punishment of a traitor; and he concluded, "However frightful these events were, it is thought that the ministry was preparing more horrible ones." Creuzé de Latouche, *Journal,* p. 231.

56. Faulcon, *Correspondance,* II, 67.

57. Faulcon, *Correspondance,* II, 70 for these phrases, and p. 76 for the statement quoted in my next sentence.

trusted the king, whose appearance in the Assembly hall that day prompted him to exclaim: "He is never better advised than when he follows the inspirations of his heart, naturally good, sensitive, and moved toward [his subjects'] well-being!" This idea received a different emphasis from the chief judge of Châtellerault, who reflected that if the Parisians had not been so well prepared, if the soldiers had not refused to march against the citizenry, "torrents of blood would have inundated the kingdom, thousands of citizens would have been massacred in the name of their chief before his good impulses had had time to take effect."[58] The thought of what might have happened was even more disturbing to the chief judge of Sarrelouis. Two days after the capture of the Bastille he was still overcome by horror and was incapable of giving a coherent account of what had happened or even of controlling his handwriting while attempting to do so.[59]

The minds of most deputies, magistrates as well as others, turned to efforts to comprehend the new state of affairs. On the day after the capture of the Bastille, the chief judge of Toul left the Assembly to go and observe Paris. There, on 16 July, he spent a melancholy day, deploring the fate of the king ("a good and decent man, but too weak not to be deceived"), fearing future scenes of violence, hiding his indignation at the "frightful network [of control] exercised by the present democracy."[60] Back in Paris on 20 July, Faulcon wondered what turn public affairs would take. "Are we going to fall into complete democracy, or rather remain in it? . . . License is not liberty, and certainly one can deplore the one without rendering oneself

58. Creuzé de Latouche, *Journal,* pp. 234–235.
59. Lasalle de Berweiller, letter of 16 July 1789, p. 208, and editor's note.
60. Claude-Pierre Maillot, letter of 18 July 1789 to Emmanuel-Maurice-Edme Desbroux, king's proctor in the bailliage of Toul, ed. Albert Denis, *Annales de l'Est,* 5 (1891), 549–555, reprinted by Pierre de Vaissière, *Lettres d'"aristocrates"* (Paris, Perrin & Cie., 1907), pp. 68–75.

unworthy of the other!"[61] On these pessimistic and uncertain minds, a powerful impact resulted from the murder of the councillor of state, Foullon, on 22 July, followed by that of his son-in-law, Bertier de Sauvigny, the intendant of Paris, the same evening, and the mutilation and public display of the corpses. Even assuming the justice of putting these officials to death, Faulcon felt inexpressible horror at the cruelty practiced against them.[62] Others, confident of the political stability of Paris, were less troubled by popular ferocity. The chief judge of Châtellerault had been impressed on 19 July by the orderly behavior of the Parisians, and on 23 July he noted: "To calm the people's fury in the present circumstances, the only need is for a tribunal in which they have confidence. They have none in the parlements as to these extraordinary matters."[63]

The events of July in Versailles and Paris, as well as those in the provinces, gave the night of 4 August its historic character. It was not until 16 July that all the ecclesiastical and noble deputies joined the sessions of the National Assembly. It is understandable, even if it was not a conscious purpose, that the new unity of the whole assembly be sanctified by an extraordinary collective gesture. This unity had been achieved in the face of the threat of force exercised by royal authority and was reinforced by the obvious need to prevent further popular violence. Like the unanimity of the Third Estate on 20 June, the unity of the National Assembly in late July left many unresolved issues and multiple disagreements.

61. Faulcon, *Correspondance*, II, 88–89.

62. *Ibid.*, pp. 90–91. Cf. Ferrières, *Correspondance*, p. 97: "I would never have believed that an amiable and good people would give itself over to such excesses."

63. Creuzé de Latouche, *Journal*, pp. 260, 270. Remarking upon "the impressive order that reigns in Paris," Maupetit wrote: "It is to be hoped that the constitution, so difficult to prepare, will be completed, will assure the happiness of France, and will effectuate, without bloodshed, without too violent commotions, the much desired regeneration of the kingdom." Letter of 16 July, vol. 18, p. 473.

Since 9 July it had been understood that the first constitutional questions to be taken up would be whether to draw up a declaration of rights and, if so, what to assert in it. Lafayette's draft of 11 July, resembling the preamble of the American Declaration of Independence,[64] had alarmed the conservative-minded by its equalitarianism. At the same time, it had failed to satisfy the radical patriots because (despite Jefferson's recommendation to the contrary) Lafayette included "the right of property" in his list of natural, inalienable, and imprescriptible rights. Among the patriots was the chief judge of Châtellerault, who commented that the right of property "is neither inalienable nor imprescriptible" except by particular, positive law.[65] The significance of the comment is not primarily the intellectual allegiance it reveals to a tradition reaching back through Montesquieu and Domat, as against the ideas of Locke and the physiocrats. Rather, it is that the right of property could supply a principled defense, for nobles and for commoners, against the abolition of seigneurial rights and the elimination of proprietary rights in public offices. In the three weeks following Lafayette's formulation, drafts of declarations had proliferated. The Committee of Eight on the constitution reported, on 27 July, principally on drafts by Sieyès and Mounier; the subject was then referred to the bureaux. One of these, Bureau 6, carried its discussions so far as to produce still another draft of a declaration of rights within the next three days.[66] The most prominent members of Bureau 6 were its president, the bishop of Nancy, de La Fare, the 23-year-old comte de Montmorency, and a *receveur général des finances,* Anson. In all, thirteen members were of the nobility, and of these six were generals holding the rank of *maréchal de camp.*

64. Gilbert Chinard, "La Déclaration des droits de l'homme et la Déclaration de l'indépendance," *Cahiers d'Histoire de la Révolution Française,* no. 1 (1946), pp. 66–90.

65. Creuzé de Latouche, *Journal,* p. 214.

66. Maupetit, letter of 31 July 1789, vol. 19, p. 210.

The other members included six parish priests and five lawyers but only three magistrates, Maillot, Maupetit, and Palasne de Champeaux.[67] Although only one bureau prepared a draft, "metaphysical declarations," as Barère put it, preoccupied all the deputies' minds.[68]

The National Assembly was reluctant, during the week after the capture of the Bastille, to set aside its work on the constitution in order to act on the disquieting reports of violence in the neighboring towns of Poissy, Saint-Germain-en-Laye, and Pontoise. After the murders of Foullon and Bertier de Sauvigny in Paris, and the letters received the next day reporting riots in ten other towns, the Assembly issued a proclamation calling on all citizens to keep the peace. This was followed by far more sinister information. An explosion had occurred at the château of Quincey late at night, and a number of inhabitants of nearby Vesoul and soldiers from the garrison there had been injured, and five killed. A preliminary investigation indicated that the seigneur, Jean-Antoine-Marie de Mesmay, had let it be known in the town that he would provide refreshments for all who came to his château to celebrate the capture of the Bastille; he had departed, saying that as a noble, a magistrate in the Parlement of Besançon, and one of those who had protested against the innovations favorable to the Third Estate in the electoral procedure for the Estates General, he might diminish the gaiety by his presence; and an explosive placed underground had been lighted while the celebration was in progress.[69] In Franche-Comté, this event was the signal for an agrarian re-

67. Only 2 of the nobles, a magistrate of the Parlement of Grenoble and 1 other, were from the robe. The other members were a canon of Notre Dame of Paris and 9 obscure commoners (2 notaries, 4 businessmen, and 3 men engaged in agriculture or estate management).

68. *Point du Jour*, II, 29.

69. The description here summarizes the report drawn up on 20 July by an officer of the maréchaussée, read aloud to the National Assembly on 25 July, and printed in *AP*, VIII, 276. The number killed was reported by Barère in the *Point du Jour*, I, 287.

volt, which gave rise to the panic that was later to spread through several eastern and southeastern provinces.[70] Before three days had elapsed, the municipality of Vesoul wrote to the National Assembly mentioning châteaux burned or pillaged, archives forcibly entered, rent-rolls and seigneurial court records removed, fearful threats, and extreme violence.[71]

In the National Assembly, deputies of the Third Estate commonly believed that the explosion at Quincey was a deliberate atrocity against the patriots.[72] The first president of the Parlement of Besançon, a deputy of the nobility, announced on 29 July that the Parlement had sent commissioners to investigate but they had been badly received by the inhabitants of Vesoul and had been unable even to obtain a meeting with the royal judges of the bailliage there.[73] The Parlement asked the National Assembly to take measures against the disorders in the province and declared that it desired nothing so much as the establishment of all the laws which the Assembly's wisdom would suggest. This admission of helplessness came from the parlement of the only province where serfdom was widespread (in the form of mortmain), the magistrates having done their utmost to preserve it. Not only that, the Parlement of Besançon had ruled in January 1789 that the Estates General must be convoked under the procedures of 1614 and could in no event diminish the immunities and privileges of Franche-Comté.[74]

70. Georges Lefebvre, *La Grande Peur de 1789* (Paris, Librairie Armand Colin, 1932), p. 111.

71. *AP*, VIII, 276.

72. Boullé, vol. 15, Documents, p. 16; Gallot, p. 98.

73. Creuzé de Latouche, *Journal,* p. 290.

74. Jean Egret, "La Révolution aristocratique en Franche-Comté et son échec (1788–1789)," *Revue d'Histoire Moderne et Contemporaine,* I (1954), 245–271, pointed out that the Parlement's ruling of 27 January, drawn up by a councillor whose father had been a commoner, was slightly less reactionary than the resolutions adopted by the chamber of the clergy and the chamber of the nobility in the provincial estates: the Parlement wanted to eliminate the prerequisite of 100 years' status as noble, needed to qualify for the chamber of the nobility in the provincial estates.

The latter point was seized upon immediately by two deputies from the province, a liberal noble and a bailliage judge, who called upon the Parlement to retract the maxims which were in principle opposed to the National Assembly. Another liberal noble asserted that the Parlement had forfeited public confidence, that it was intervening in the affair of Quincey illegally, and that the Parlement ought to be abolished.[75]

The political bearing of violence and disorder continued to dominate the reactions of the deputies. It was easy to perceive in such events the plots, or at least the advantage, of one's adversaries in the debates over constitutional principles. Most deputies were determined to proceed with those debates. The *comité des rapports* drew up a proclamation reaffirming this intention, but declaring also that meanwhile seigneurial dues, as well as royal taxes, must continue to be paid. On 3 August, the proclamation was turned over to the *comité de rédaction* to be amended and presented to the Assembly again the next day.[76] It was this interval of one day that gave the proclamation's critics, the Bretons and their allies, an opportunity to devise tactics which would turn the debate toward an attack on the seigneurial dues and the tax privileges of the nobility and the clergy. The Breton club included, as it had in June, some bailliage magistrates among its members. One of them, Corroller du Moustoir, wrote: "We convinced a few rich seigneurs at our meeting of the necessity that the privileged orders completely abandon their tax exemptions in order for the proclamation to have good results; they were ready to

75. The *Point du Jour*, I, 332, identifies the nobles as Bureaux de Pusy and the marquis de Toulongeon, and the third speaker as Gourdan, a judge from Gray. Creuzé de Latouche, *Journal,* pp. 290–291, identifies the nobles as Roux de Raze (the chief civil judge at Vesoul, he was in fact not a noble), and the vicomte de Toulongeon, but does not identify the third speaker.

76. The amended text is in the *Procès-verbal de l'Assemblée Nationale,* 4 August, afternoon [and evening] session (pp. 2–3).

follow us."[77] The first three speeches, at least, were planned: the vicomte de Noailles, the duc d'Aiguillon, and Le Guen de Kerangall brought prepared texts to the Assembly session.[78]

At some point in the evening session of 4 August, the Bretons' plan was superseded by the emotional atmosphere it had generated. The proceedings came to resemble an auction in which the bidding had become so competitive that prudence was set aside and calculation was redirected to objectives previously thought unattainable. Doubtless there were speeches that represented simple altruism. There were other speeches, however, offering to sacrifice privileges that were dearer to the speakers' political rivals or opponents than to the speakers themselves. It was the duc du Châtelet who called

77. Quoted by A. Bouchard, *Le Club breton* (Paris, Jouve, 1920), pp. 85–86.

78. The texts by Noailles and Aiguillon were copied by the secretary, Fréteau, into the *Procès-verbal*, pp. 3–11; that by Le Guen de Kerangall was published by Barère in the *Point du Jour*, II, 30–33. For the order of speakers, I follow these sources despite Patrick Kessel, *La Nuit du 4 août 1789* (Paris, Arthaud, 1969), who says (pp. 135–142) that Noailles and Aiguillon were followed by Le Grand and only thereafter by Le Guen de Kerangall.

Kessel emphasizes the differences between Noailles' and Aiguillon's proposals, and suggests that they may have emanated from 2 distinct caucus meetings the night before. But it still seems to me probable that the Breton club meeting referred to by Corroller du Moustoir was in fact the same meeting as that of about 100 deputies in a "special committee" mentioned by Parisot in a letter to his electors at Bar-sur-Seine, 4 A.M. on 5 August 1789, ed. R. Hennequin, *Révolution Française*, 80 (1927), 19–21.

As to the respective roles of the two noblemen, another deputy, François, whom Kessel does not mention and who was from the same electoral circumscription as Aiguillon, reported: "It was the vicomte de Noailles who made the motion, and it was at once supported by the duc d'Aiguillon . . . Nothing can stop him [Aiguillon] when it is a question of the public good . . . ; if he did not make the motion, it was a [complicated] story of an agreement between him and the vicomte de Noailles, his friend." *Correspondance des députés de la sénéchaussée d'Agen aux Etats Généraux et à l'Assemblée Nationale* (1789–1790), ed. Louis Desgraves (Nérac, 1967, as *Recueil des travaux de la Société Académique d'Agen*, 3rd ser., 1), p. 39.

for the right to convert the tithe from a permanent annual obligation into a capital sum to be paid once. It was the bishop of Chartres who called for abolition of the exclusive prerogative of hunting. There were also speeches offering to sacrifice minor privileges while omitting any mention of greater ones. This was the sort of speech made by some spokesmen for bailliage magistrates when they finally managed to obtain the floor late in the night. They offered to abandon the privileges attached to their offices, saying that they aspired only to perform service agreeable to themselves and useful to the nation.[79] In other words, they would give up not only their exemption from the taille but also their fees and other payments from litigants. This speech was followed by that of a deputy from Vesoul proposing a far more radical step, the abolition of proprietary rights in offices.[80] Nothing needed to be said about the explosion at Quincey or the effort of the Parlement of Besançon to investigate it. The National Assembly joyfully voted to abolish proprietary rights in offices. Several other deputies from Franche-Comté carried the attack further and called for abolition of the Parlement of Besançon or, according to one source,[81] all the parlements. At this, Fréteau, who was a councillor in the Parlement of Paris, left the secretary's table and spoke, suggesting instead the elimination of important privileges: inheritability of the offices, ennoblement by holding office, and tax exemptions. He succeeded in damming the

79. This phrasing is substantially that of Fréteau in the *Procès-verbal*, p. 36. One of these judges was Lasalle de Berweiller, who reported it in a letter written immediately afterward, p. 218.

80. The *Procès-verbal* says "un député de Franche-Comté, d'accord avec ceux de Provence," perhaps a misprint for "ceux de la Province." The *Point du Jour*, II, 43, says "un député d'Amont," i.e., the bailliage at Vesoul, where the first deputy of the Third Estate was the chief civil judge, Roux de Raze.

Reform in the judiciary had been urged earlier in the evening, but the sources disagree on what was said and by whom: *Procès-verbal*, p. 18; *Point du Jour*, II, 35; Lombard de Taradeau, p. 237.

81. *Point du Jour*, II, 43.

flood, and the parlements were left in existence for the time being. The meaning of abolition of proprietary rights in the offices was not yet fully clear; it depended on the provisions concerning property in the declaration of rights, still to be adopted.

In formulating the principles adopted on 4 August, few bailliage magistrates were actively involved. Many attended the session as enthusiastic spectators.[82] A week later, when the final version of the decree was being drafted, they manifested unanimous support for the article on abolition of property rights in judicial offices.[83] The next day, the National Assembly voted to establish three committees to work out applications of the decree: on seigneurial rights, on ecclesiastical affairs, and on the liquidation of judicial offices.[84] Each of the latter two committees was to have fifteen members; the two committees were elected simultaneously under a novel and elaborate procedure, designed to make them representative without giving free play to factional influences.[85] The process was finally

82. Lasalle de Berweiller, pp. 217–218; Lombard de Taradeau, pp. 234–242; Maupetit, vol. 19, pp. 216–220; Ménard de la Groye, letter of 5 August: "Cette journeé d'hier fut signalée par les événements les plus heureux, et la mémoire s'en transmettra glorieusement aux siècles à venir . . . Dans la séance du soir, l'enthousiasme du patriotisme se manifesta de la manière la plus heureuse et la moins prévue . . . tel qu'une flamme rapide, il embrasa subitement tous les coeurs . . . Jamais les citoyens de tous les ordres ne montrèrent tant d'amour pour le bien public, tant de générosité et de désintéressement . . ." (Ms., A.D. Sarthe, 10 J 122.)

83. *Point du Jour,* II, 104.

84. *Procès-verbal de l'Assemblée Nationale,* 12 August (p. 2).

85. The initial selection occurred in the bureaux, each of which nominated 3 of its members to form a list of 90 nominees in all. (Bureau 2, Bureau 4, and Bureau 5 each nominated one clergyman, one noble, and one of the Third Estate; some other bureaux nominated only commoners.) The nominees chose, among themselves, 30 committee members, who then assigned (by ballot) half their number to ecclesiastical affairs and half to judicial offices. *Procès-verbal de l'Assemblée Na-*

complete on 19 August. Five clergymen became members of the committee on ecclesiastical affairs, and two clergymen became members of the committee on the liquidation of judicial offices.[86] Only three magistrates became members of the committee on ecclesiastical affairs.[87] Nine magistrates became members of the committee on the liquidation of judicial offices.[88] Having accepted the principle that the rights of property in judicial offices were to be extinguished, these magistrates were given majority control of the committee to draw up the terms on which their own offices, as well as those of the parlements, would be liquidated.[89]

For many deputies, the decree of 4 August, rather than the Declaration of the Rights of Man and Citizens, was the "death certificate of the old régime."[90] A declaration of rights seemed to them an invitation to perpetual uncertainty and instability in politics. At the beginning of August, some bailliage magistrates were inclined to this opinion. Grellet de Beauregard, for example, was distinctly unenthusiastic. He took seriously the objections which emanated from such traditional spokesmen for authority as royal administrators and bishops: that a declaration of rights would suggest ideas of equality and inde-

---

tionale, 13 August (p. 8); *Liste de MM. les députés, par bureaux* (B.N., 4° Le²⁶.9, first list).

86. *Procès-verbal de l'Assemblée Nationale,* 20 August (p. 2).

87. Despatys de Courteille, chief civil judge at Melun; Le Grand, of Châteauroux; Sallé de Chou, king's advocate at Bourges.

88. Dufraisse Duchey, chief civil judge at Riom; Giraud Duplessix, king's advocate at Nantes; Gossin, chief judge at Bar-le-Duc; Henry de Longuêve, king's advocate at Orléans; Jouye Desroches, chief judge at Le Mans; Lofficial, chief judge at La Châtaigneraie; Meusnier Dubreuil, chief judge at Mantes; Milscent, acting chief judge at Angers; Tellier, king's advocate at Melun.

89. The work of this committee will be analyzed in the next chapter.

90. The well-known phrase of Aulard, *Histoire politique de la Révolution française,* 5th ed. (Paris, Librairie Armand Colin, 1913), p. 45, has since been quoted by several commentators who recognize (as he did) that the Declaration also looked forward to an ideal society.

pendence which might obscure the right of property and the laws of subordination; and that metaphysical propositions might entail unforeseen consequences.[91] More definitely, Lasalle de Berweiller wrote that a declaration of "rights which can belong only to savages" was needless for Frenchmen and possibly dangerous for uneducated men, "whose emotions or bad character will lead them to interpret literally those maxims which flatter their vices and desires."[92] Four days after writing these phrases, Lasalle de Berweiller hailed the decrees of 4 August with admiration. But he persisted in his opposition to anything that could be described as a declaration of rights and hoped that if one were adopted it would be short.[93]

After the National Assembly began to debate the wording of the declaration of rights, on 19 August, such deputies as Grellet and Lasalle wished principally to get the business disposed of.[94] Their desire for a prudent enactment did not lead them to manifest opposition to majority sentiment.

The most resolute of the reform-minded deputies favored a strong declaration of rights. This group, too, included some bailliage magistrates. In the mind of the chief judge of Saint-Brieuc, the declaration of rights was a matter of the highest interest because it set forth the fundamental principles of the future constitution. For this reason, he wrote, "we are examin-

91. Letter of 3 August, p. 71.
92. Letter of 1 August, p. 215.
93. On 18 August, he wrote (pp. 221–222) that he intended to present his own draft of a declaration saying simply "that the only right of man in society is that of making laws, under which and from which he can live protected and act without fear of being troubled in any of his actions when they are not contrary to the law." This declaration had been adopted that evening by the bureau of which he was a member. (Lasalle was in Bureau 7; of its 40 members, 21 represented the Third Estate and 6 of these were magistrates, Bonet de Treiches, Dumesnil Desplanques, Giraud Duplessix, Gontier de Biran, Lasalle, and Vyau de Baudreuille.)
94. Grellet de Beauregard, letter of 21 August, p. 75; Lasalle de Berweiller, letter of 27 August, p. 223.

ing with the most scrupulous attention all the articles in the declaration, and each word is weighed so that nothing can later be inferred which might impair the rights we want to establish for the people's happiness."[95] The drafting of the declaration was certainly not the judicious affair that Palasne's letter suggests. It was a political battle, whose heat and vigor can be sensed in the letters of the chief judge of Draguignan. When the National Assembly began by adopting as the basis of discussion the draft declaration prepared by Bureau 6 in July, he was indignant at this success of "la cabale" of aristocrats. That night he wrote: "We'll have our turn tomorrow, and we'll sweep it away so that not a trace remains."[96] The adoption of the preamble and the first six articles, a process which appears relatively calm and orderly in the minutes of proceedings and the newspaper accounts, entailed ceaseless "obstruction, disagreement and struggle from the privileged classes and even from a multitude of commoners." The sessions could not have been stormier: "everything had to be carried at sword's point."[97] On a less combative personality, Ménard de la Groye, the debates had a different effect, producing a pensive mood and a particular awareness of the tranquillity that had to be sacrificed in order to achieve the revolution.[98] If any single

95. Palasne de Champeaux, letter of 21 August, p. 252.
96. Lombard de Taradeau, letter of 19 August, p. 258.
97. Lombard de Taradeau, letter of 21 August, pp. 259, 261.
98. Letter of 21 August 1789; "Il est 11 heures du soir, et je sors à l'instant de notre assemblée. C'est, ma chère amie, une grande et pénible entreprise que de réformer les antiques lois d'un grand empire et de changer presque entièrement sa constitution. Il faut combattre une multitude d'intérêts particuliers, et faire céder à la raison des préjugés consacrés par une suite de siècles et qui avaient acquis l'autorité la plus imposante . . . La sublime qualité de législateurs, qui nous est confiée, doit nous faire porter nos regards vers un avenir éloigné; et nous devons préparer aux races futures le bonheur dont il nous sera peut-être impossible de faire jouir le génération présente. Car, je l'avoue, ma chère amie, une secousse violente est donnée au corps politique, et tous les membres qui le composent s'en trouveront longtemps affectés. Si l'on

state of mind could be represented as typical of most magistrates in the Assembly at the time, it would be this mingling of nostalgia and steady determination.

The most tumultuous of the sessions devoted to the Declaration of Rights was the one in which the National Assembly decided, by a considerable majority, to impose a vague limitation upon freedom of religious worship. In Article 10, the Declaration states that a person must not be troubled "for his opinions, even religious [opinions], provided that their manifestation does not disturb the public order established by law." One of the opponents of this limitation noted that the word "even" weakens the idea of liberty and asked what might be meant by the concluding phrase: "Would Mendelssohn be a criminal for having written in favor of his religion?"[99] The article aroused the fury of the chief judge of Draguignan, who wrote: "This is a declaration of rights intended for all men, for all peoples. Will posterity believe that such a maxim was established in the eighteenth century?"[100] By no means all the magistrates shared these feelings. The moderate Maupetit, in an embarrassed justification, explained that he would have preferred to omit both of the qualifying clauses and especially the second one. But, he said, more than half the commoners in the Assembly favored the qualifying clauses.

Is it prudent at this moment, is it politic, to alarm all the timorous souls? . . . The clergy, discontented over the tithe, still has a strong influence on the people . . . The *philosophes* will blame the Assembly; prudent men will say that ideas have not yet been suffi-

---

ne considerait que les hommes qui existent présentement, il eût donc mieux valu peut-être les laisser tranquilles sous un gouvernement vicieux que de les faire parvenir, au travers de troubles et de désordres inévitables, à un régime sage et bien ordonné. Nous sommes occupés depuis plusieurs jours à faire et rédiger une déclaration des droits de l'homme et du citoyen. C'est ce qui formera la base de la constitution." (ms., A.D. Sarthe, 10 J 122); *cf.* Duquesnoy, *Journal*, I, 311.

99. Duquesnoy, *Journal*, I, 310.

100. Lombard de Taradeau, letter of 23 August, p. 263.

ciently matured by the passage of time . . . There are virtues which can be displayed only with moderation, and this is one of them.[101]

The last article of the Declaration, which describes the right of property as "inviolable and sacred" occasioned long and tedious debate over the terms on which property could be legally confiscated. Nothing like this article had been included in the draft declaration of Bureau 6 in July. The article originated with Du Port, a councillor in the Parlement of Paris. His draft specified that, in virtue of a clear law, a person possessing a property duly judged harmful to the public could be constrained to surrender it and receive an indemnity immediately.[102] Debate revolved around the description of the indemnity as "just," "equivalent," and "previous" to the deprivation of the property. The identity of the speakers indicates whose property was actually envisaged. Des Monstiers, bishop of Dijon, found the proposed article destructive of property rights in that it would permit confiscation. Lambert de Frondeville, a president in the Parlement of Rouen, wanted to specify that the indemnity must be both "just" and "equivalent." On the other side, the duc de Mortemart, who was a maréchal de camp and a member of the newly elected committee on the liquidation of the judicial offices, sought to eliminate the requirement of a "previous" indemnity.[103] In this debate, so far as the records reveal, no bailliage magistrates took part. The only one whose reaction at the time can be determined is Lombard de Taradeau, the impatient Provençal patriot. He agreed with the duc de Mortemart, and he reported:

101. Letter of 23 August, vol. 19, pp. 235–236. The parish priest of Prouvy, who was a deputy from Hainaut, wrote that the qualifying clauses "occasioned many disorders, speeches, even threats from those *philosophes* who have neither faith nor law and who, on the pretext of liberty, want only anarchy." Emmanuel Barbotin, *Lettres,* ed. Alphonse Aulard (Paris, Société de l'Histoire de la Révolution Française, 1910), p. 57.
102. Michon, *Adrien Duport,* p. 103.
103. *Ibid.,* p. 109; *Point du Jour,* II, 220.

"With the word 'previous' inserted in this article, we will not be able to abolish the offices without previous compensation. That is the danger, and all our efforts could not succeed in getting it eliminated."[104]

The debates of August covered a wide range of fundamental issues, and resulted in the formation of new alignments. At the end of July, the clergy and the nobility still sat as two blocs of deputies; by the middle of August, deputies no longer appeared to be spokesmen for one of the three Estates but instead for a broader principle or a narrower interest; and before the end of August, there had begun to emerge a crude outline of a new pattern in which many deputies could be identified as radical, liberal, moderate, conservative, or reactionary.[105]

Groups of deputies hitherto unorganized began to prepare effectively to win elections within the Assembly. There had already been a concerted attempt by the Bretons, on the last day of July, to defeat Thouret for the presidency.[106] Election management required either a political organization which met elsewhere, such as the Bretons had, or at least some means of systematic communication among members of different bureaux in the Assembly. The regular balloting for Assembly offices and committees occurred in separate meetings of the thirty bureaux, without any formal nominating process. The new assignments of deputies to bureaux on 3 August had led to many a new acquaintanceship or recognition of shared opinions. Conservative deputies were able to take advantage of this, partly because the Breton Club dissolved at the end of August, its agreed objectives having been achieved.[107] On 29

104. Letter of 27 August, p. 265.

105. Duquesnoy, *Journal*, I, 239, 294, 311–312.

106. *Ibid.*, I, 260; Maupetit, letter of 3 August, vol. 19, p. 216.

107. The Bretons were divided over the desirability of a royal veto of any kind. (Boullé, letter of 8 September, vol. 15, Documents, p. 117; Le Gendre, letter of 13 September, p. 540.) The chief judge of Saint-Brieuc wrote: "Aristocracy is winning partisans for itself even among the mem-

August, the conservatives secured the election of La Luzerne, the bishop of Langres, as president, and Deschamps, Redon, and Henry de Longuêve as secretaries; and a few days later they placed several conservative deputies on the *comité des recherches*, important because its duty was to receive and report on information about plots against the safety of the state and of citizens.[108] Animating force and organizing activity in these elections came partly from associates of Pierre-Victor Malouet, a Third Estate deputy from Riom who had had a 25-year career in the royal naval administration. In 1790, he described his group as "fifteen or twenty deputies living in a close association . . . partisans of royal authority in a [sound] relationship with the constitution and with public liberty"; and in his recollections, written in 1808, he said "our central committee was composed of fifteen deputies, who corresponded through subdivisions with more than three hundred."[109] His inner group included two bailliage magistrates from Riom, one from Orléans, one from Chalon-sur-Saône, and one from the smaller town of Martel in Quercy. Such groups of deputies could not, however, be called political parties. On another kind of issue, confidence in Necker's financial plan at the end of September, it was possible to discern seven different attitudes.[110] These were related very indirectly, if at all, to the affinities and preferences that had emerged in August over constitutional questions.

In voting enactments whose historic importance everyone

---

bers of the commons." (Palasne de Champeaux, letter of 31 August, p. 257.)

108. *Procès-verbal de l'Assemblée Nationale*, 31 August (p. 1), and 3 September (p. 6); Duquesnoy, *Journal*, I, 335.

109. See his testimony and that of Tailhardat de la Maisonneuve in the *Procédure criminelle instruite au Châtelet de Paris sur la dénonciation des faits arrivés à Versailles dans la journée du 6 octobre 1789* (Paris, 1790), Depositions 111 and 126; and Malouet's *Mémoires*, ed. Victor-Pierre Malouet, 2nd ed., 2 vols. (Paris, 1874), I, 303.

110. Duquesnoy, *Journal*, I, 368–369.

recognized, in beginning to debate on new institutions for the constitutional monarchy, in forming groups of deputies united by opinion rather than status, the National Assembly as a whole developed its own esprit de corps. This was tested by threatening manifestations of crowds of Parisians on 30 August and 5 October, and it proved sufficiently cohesive to cause most deputies to remain in the Assembly, or to return after a brief absence, even many who disapproved its entire previous course of action.[111] In the two years of the National Assembly's ensuing existence, it acted as both a regular legislature and a constitutional convention. Its debates and enactments in that period fill twenty-three volumes in the very incomplete edition provided by the *Archives Parlementaires* in 1877–1889. A narrative account of all this activity would exhaust the reader and the historian, without casting much light on the part played in it by the bailliage magistrates sitting (most of them silently) as deputies. The vast majority of these magistrates were not only honored to be members, they believed they were performing an important duty by being present. In order to explain how mere attendance could seem useful, it is necessary to characterize the way in which the National Assembly carried on its business.

Critics of the National Assembly blamed some of its worst faults on the deputies who were judges and, especially, lawyers. This idea was commonplace a year before Edmund Burke presented it to English readers.[112] At the end of October 1789, the lawyer Duquesnoy observed that the Assembly was

filled with men of the robe, advocates, petty and wretched formalists . . . reckless destroyers, cowardly builders . . . How could wretched lawyers, who have spent their lives arguing wretched little lawsuits before wretched little tribunals, be legislators . . .? The

111. On the roll call of 11 September, there were 998 deputies voting; on the roll call of 2 November, there were 914 voting, and 40 present but abstaining. Duquesnoy, *Journal,* I, 331; II, 17.

112. *Reflections on the Revolution in France,* ed. William B. Todd (New York, Holt, Rhinehart and Winston, 1959), p. 49.

men of the robe have ruined France, and they can ruin it again through their loquacity, their ignorance, their self-importance.[113]

Admirers of the National Assembly's work, from Rabaut de Saint-Etienne[114] to Sagnac,[115] have been primarily concerned with describing its accomplishments, and most have simply asserted that its membership was broadly representative of the politically articulate. They seem never to have contended that the Assembly accomplished as much as it did because many of its members were familiar with orderly methods for deciding disputed questions. The procedures employed by the National Assembly are, however, reminiscent of those used by the parlements, even if there was no conscious transfer of familiar methods. The Assembly had no steering committee after October 1789 and obtained practically no positive leadership from the executive side of government. Like a parlement, it made its decision-making services available to those who might wish to present proposals to be acted on; most of these, naturally, emanated from deputies, any one of whom could offer a motion. In acting on a motion, the National Assembly first heard argument on whether it was proper to be considered; a negative decision on this was the equivalent of the judicial *non-lieu*. The first stage of consideration might be oral argument (rather than referral to a committee, as would be routine in a twentieth-century legislature). As an alternative or a sequel, there might be referral to a committee for fact-finding, appointment of a *rapporteur,* and drafting of a proposed decree. Finally, there would be further oral argument and a disposition. No decided question or enacted law could be debated anew.[116]

113. Duquesnoy, *Journal,* I, 490–491.
114. *Almanach historique de la Révolution française* (Paris, 1792), p. 66.
115. "La Composition des Etats Généraux et de l'Assemblée Nationale (1789). Etude statistique et sociale," *Revue Historique,* 206 (1951), 8–28.
116. The rules of the National Assembly, reprinted in *AP,* VIII, 300–302, specify the preliminary consideration, "s'il y a lieu ou non à délibérer," and the finality of a vote (amounting to "chose jugée"). The

There was a definite tendency for deputies to become specialists. A few were orators, whose energies were devoted to setting forth the principles that ought to guide the National Assembly's decision. These were the men whom critics like Duquesnoy regarded as the only real statesmen, and whose performances they subjected to aesthetic as well as political evaluation, much as they had responded to the advocates' *plaidoiries* before the parlements. Other deputies served primarily as committee members, the most important of these being the ones often chosen as rapporteurs. The great majority of the deputies, forming something like a grand' chambre full of councillers, prized their independence and impartiality above all and sat as if in judgment deciding on legal principles and applications to facts; this was the part played by most of the magistrates from the bailliages. These functional specializations among the deputies interacted with differences of another kind, alignments according to opinion.

The conservative and reactionary minority in the National Assembly drew up and published a series of declarations protesting against its most important decisions. The tactic resembled that of the parlements before 1789 in issuing remonstrances against royal legislation. The declaration of 19 April 1790 protested against the Assembly's refusal to declare Catholicism the state religion.[117] It was signed by 297 deputies, of whom 13 were bailliage magistrates. In March 1791, there appeared a reckless wholesale attack on the Assembly majority, including all shades of moderates in its total of 624 deputies and thereby characterizing primarily the deputies whose names were deliberately omitted from the list.[118] Of more than 400

intervening stages were determined by customary practice, not by rule; the Assembly as a whole insisted on control of its agenda and the order of proceedings.

117. *Déclaration d'une partie de l'Assemblée Nationale, sur le décret rendu le 13 avril 1790, concernant la religion* (Paris, 1790).

118. *Liste par ordre alphabétique de bailliage et sénéchaussée de MM. les députés de la majorité de l'Assemblée Nationale, vulgairement*

right-wing deputies thus omitted, 32 were bailliage magistrates. The declaration of 29 June 1791, after the king's departure and enforced return, protested against the suspension of royal authority.[119] It was signed by 290 deputies, of whom 17 were former magistrates in bailliages. The declaration of 31 August 1791 protested against the completed constitution, against all the enactments since 16 June 1789 as null and most as inherently unjust.[120] It was signed unreservedly by 126 deputies, of whom 7 were former magistrates, and with additions or restrictions by 70 others, of whom 8 were former magistrates.

In the conservative minority of the National Assembly, a few bailliage magistrates made themselves highly visible. Thirteen magistrates signed both the declaration of April 1790, favoring Catholicism as the state religion, and the declaration of June 1791, supporting royal authority.[121] Four other magis-

---

appelés le côté gauche ou les enragés (Paris, 1791) (B.N., Lb³⁰.4582). This was apparently based on a list of deputies published late in 1789. A feeble effort was made to bring it up to date: the names of 15 *suppléants,* mostly clergymen, were substituted for those of deputies who died or resigned before December 1790. But the names of 19 other deputies no longer in the Assembly remained on the list. The compiler then removed, apparently, the names of the deputies who voted with the "côté droit" on some occasion(s) in early 1791. (He also removed, seemingly by mistake, all mention of 9 electoral circumscriptions.) The list thus appears to be a mere residual; hence my utilization of it is the inverse of that of Palmer, who considered it as a gross measure of the revolutionary zeal of various social categories, and who was challenged on this by Cobban: *Annales Historiques de la Révolution Française,* 31 (1959), 154–156, 387–391.

119. *Déclarations de 290 députés sur les décrets qui suspendent l'exercice de l'autorité royale, et qui portent atteinte à l'inviolabilité de la personne du Roi* (Paris, 1791), reprinted in *AP,* XXVIII, 91–98.

120. *Déclaration d'une partie des députés aux Etats-Généraux, touchant l'Acte constitutionnel et l'état du Royaume* (Paris, 1791).

121. Three of these were from Riom (Chabrol, Dufraisse Duchey, and Tailhardat de la Maisonneuve), two were from Orléans (Henry de Longuêve and Seurrat de Laboulaye); the other localities represented were Meaux (Houdet), Bourges (Sallé de Chou), Poiters (Irland de Bazôges), La Rochelle (Griffon), Nîmes (Ricard), and three small towns

trates,[122] who had not signed the declaration of April 1790, joined in the declaration of June 1791. All of these seventeen participated in the National Assembly as active counter-revolutionaries, and they constituted 6 percent of the deputies who did so.

Silent support for the conservative cause came from a still smaller number of bailliage magistrates. A list of 466 right-wing deputies, published at the time the National Assembly adjourned, included 200 who had been elected by the clergy, 180 elected by the nobility, and 86 elected by the Third Estate[123] Again, 6 percent of those listed were magistrates: the 17 deputies who had signed one or both of the declarations of April 1790 and June 1791, and 13 others.[124] All except one of these magistrates had been omitted from the pamphlet of March 1791 which attacked the "enragés" of the left.[125]

The liberal and radical minority in the National Assembly wielded its influence in a very different way. It did not publish declarations intended to persuade readers in provincial towns far from the National Assembly or addressed to posterity. It organized the Jacobin club, and discussed major issues in ad-

---

in the southwest, Bergerac (Gontier de Biran), Castelnaudary (Guilhermy), and Martel (Lachèse).

122. From Mantes (Meusnier Dubreuil), Chalon-sur-Saône (Bernigaud de Grange), Le Buis, in Dauphiné (Bertrand de Montfort), and Béziers (Gleises de Lablanque).

123. *Liste par lettres alphabétiques des députés du côté droit, aux Etats-Généraux, au mois de septembre 1791* (Paris, 1791) (B.N., Lb[39]. 10185).

124. The majority of the 13 were from towns in the West; Mamers, in Maine (Pélisson de Gennes), Fougères, in Brittany (Fournier de la Pommeraye), Blois (Turpin), Tours (Gaultier), Châtellerault (Dubois), Saint-Jean-d'Angély (Bonnegens), Limoges (Roulhac), and Uzerche (Delort de Puymalie); the rest were from Bailleul, in Flanders (Kytspotter), Sarrelouis (Lasalle de Berweiller), Bourg-en-Bresse (Picquet), and two localities in the southeast, Mende (Rivière) and Sisteron (Burle).

125. The exception, listed with the "côté gauche" in March 1791 and with the "côté droit" in September 1791, was Kytspotter, former chief criminal judge at Bailleul.

vance of debate in the National Assembly.[126] Not until about
a year after its establishment did the Jacobin club prepare the
membership list that Aulard discovered.[127] It includes the
names of 180 deputies, of whom 24 were former magistrates
in bailliages.[128] As had been true in 1789, magistrates constituted about the same proportion of the liberal and radical
minority, at the end of 1790, as of the National Assembly as a
whole.

Many deputies maintained their independence, never joined
the Jacobin club, but nonetheless voted consistently in agreement with most of its members. Magistrates were especially
inclined to reconcile in this way their idea of their own function in the National Assembly and their convictions on political
issues. The active minority of liberals and radicals therefore
had a large silent following among the independents. It could
rely confidently on some of them, as is shown by one of those
booklets, common at the time, which sketched the characters

126. The club was established in December 1789. From the beginning
it included members who were not deputies. Among the founders were
liberal nobles like the duc d'Aiguillon, the vicomte de Rochambeau,
Alexandre de Lameth, the marquis de La Tour Maubourg, and Du Port,
as well as prominent commoners like Barnave and Emmery. Charles Le
Téo, "Le Club breton et les origines du club des Jacobins," *Révolution
Française*, 36 (1899), 385–392; H. Lemoine, "L'Origine du club des
Jacobins d'après un document nouveau," *Révolution Française*, 87
(1934), 17–28.

127. *La Société des Jacobins. Recueil de documents pour l'histoire du
Club des Jacobins de Paris*, ed. Alphonse Aulard, 6 vols. (Paris, 1889–
1897), I, xxxiii-lxxvi.

128. They were principally from the west—Brittany (Corroller du
Moustoir, Legoazre de Kervelegan, Palasne de Champeaux), La Rochelle
(Alquier), Poitou (Agier, Cochon de Lapparent, Creuzé de Latouche,
Lofficial), Anjou (Brevet de Beaujour), Maine (Ménard de la Groye)—
and the east—Lorraine (Anthoine, Petitmengin), Franche-Comté (Babey,
Gourdan, Muguet de Nanthou), Burgundy (Petiot). Four towns in the
southwest were repesented, Périgueux (Fournier de Lacharmie), Saint-
Sever (Basquiat de Mugriet), Pamiers (Vadier), and Tarbes (Barère);
and four other widely separated localities, Sens (Leblanc), Châteauroux
(Le Grand), Péronne (Prevost), Aix-en-Provence (Audier-Massillon).

Table 13. Occupations in 1789 of the Deputies in the
"Patriot" Minority in 1791

Occupation	Number of deputies
Lawyers	77
professors of law, 2 (Bouvier, Lanjuinais)	
avocats, villes de parlement, 10	
avocats, villes de bailliage, 38	
avocats, smaller localities, 27	
Judges	54
conseiller au parlement, 1 (Roederer)	
magistrates, bailliages, 43	
judges, lesser royal jurisdictions, 4	
judges, seigneurial jurisdictions, 6	
Catholic clergy	39
bishops, 2 (Gobel, Talleyrand)	
curés, 29	
others, 8	
Agriculturalists and proprietors	38
titled nobles, 4	
écuyers, 2, other seigneurs, 4	
laboureurs and *cultivateurs*, 21	
fermiers, 5, others, 2	
Businessmen	26
from cities, 8 (Paris, 3, Lyon, 3, Marseille, 1, Nantes, 1)	
from towns, 18	
Physicians	7
Officeholders (finance)	6
in élections, 4, grenier à sel, 1	
traites, 1	
Army officers	5
maréchal de camp, 1 (duc de Biron)	
lieutenant-colonel, 1 (Prez de Crassier)	
captains, 2	
mestre de camp général, cavalerie, 1	
Others	35
(including the duc d'Orléans and his chancellor, comte de La Touche; 6 mayors, 9 "bourgeois," 3 *maîtres de forges;* 8 various and 7 unspecified)	

Sources: Le Véritable Portrait de nos législateurs, ou Galerie des tableaux exposés à la vue du public depuis le 5 mai 1789 jusqu'au 1ᵉʳ octobre 1791 (Paris, 1792); *Recueil de documents relatifs à la convocation des Etats Généraux de 1789,* ed. Armand Brette, 4 vols. (Paris, 1894–1915), II, 35–333, and III, 743–753.

of leading deputies. This publication was written in December 1791, probably by Alquier, former king's advocate in the sénéchausée of La Rochelle and a Jacobin. It evaluated, on the basis of their "cabalistic conduct" and "secret motives," the 75 most important deputies on "the left, consisting of patriots and ministerials." It recommended a few of them (especially Alquier) for election to public office in the new institutions established in 1790 and 1791. At the end, it provided a list of "patriots who have not varied," including 37 of those characterized in earlier pages and 250 other deputies. The list ended with the thought: "This combative minority, which has done such great things, is not the least astonishing monument of our revolution: it leaves a fine lesson to its successors."[129]

Among the 37 important patriots, 6 were former magistrates: Alquier, Anthoine, Babey, Barère, and Buzot. The characterizations make it clear that the author regarded none of these as leaders comparable to Pétion and Robespierre. An occupational classification of the 287 deputies listed as unwavering patriots shows, however, that former magistrates were one of the most numerous occupational groups in the patriot minority. They outnumbered the parish priests and the businessmen. By a greater margin, they outnumbered the advocates engaged in practice before the parlements, the physicians, the financial officials, and the army officers. Within the patriot minority, the former magistrates were matched in numbers only by the advocates practicing before bailliages and

129. *Le Véritable Portrait de nos législateurs, ou Galerie des tableaux exposés à la vue du public depuis le 5 mai 1789 jusequ'au 1ᵉʳ octobre 1791* (Paris, 1792), pp. 2, 163, 165, 176. The date of writing is fixed by references to elections in Paris (pp. 106, 120) and by the fact that Alquier had not yet been elected presiding judge of the criminal court at Versailles. The work was attributed to Dubois de Crancé (by Barbier, with no comment by Tourneux who listed it in his bibiography as no. 431). But Alquier had a liking for this sort of catalogue: in 1795 he published a *Liste des principaux agens et moteurs de la Révolution française* (B.N., 8° Lbⁿ.4275), which he claimed to have found in the Stadholder's desk in The Hague.

by the landed proprietors engaged in no occupation other than agriculture or estate management.

The distinction between the law-trained and the landowning groups should doubtless not be drawn very sharply. Many lawyers and judges were landed proprietors, and many proprietors occupied only with their lands had received some training in law. The liberal and radical deputies came predominantly from landed families and from the traditional professions of intellectuals, the judiciary, the law, and the church.[130] They came particularly from the practice of these occupations in towns and villages. In that environment, an important share of social distinction and political leadership had ordinarily devolved upon the king's judges and king's counsel in the bailliages. It was of outstanding importance in the achievements of the National Assembly that many of these magistrates lent silent but steady support to revolutionary change.

130. Cf. Cobban's description of the revolutionary bourgeoisie: "primarily the [officeholders] and the lawyers and other professional men, and not the businessmen of commerce and industry." *The Social Interpretation of the French Revolution* (Cambridge, Eng., Cambridge University Press, 1964), p. 67. This should be amended to note the considerable number of parish priests and the small numbers of such professional men as physicians and army officers; on the other hand, it is correct as to men engaged in industry.

VI

The Liquidation of the Bailliage Offices and the Opportunity to Buy Nationalized Land

The bailliage magistrates in general remained on the bench until the autumn of 1790. Their political and economic position was then profoundly affected by the reform of the judiciary. The National Assembly acted to place the judiciary on a new constitutional basis and to extinguish the proprietary rights in judicial offices while safeguarding, as much as possible, the nation's fiscal and monetary situation. The existence of the bailliages formally ceased, and new courts were established instead. The former magistrates were permitted to continue their judicial careers only if chosen by the electors. The property rights in the old judicial offices were converted into capital sums for actual reimbursement by the state, and the holders of the old offices were encouraged to spend these sums in purchasing nationalized land.

Each phase of this complex process had different effects on various localities and particular magistrates. Before considering some of these effects, we should note the importance of the total result, which for the judicial profession was the principal revolutionary event. Thereafter, governmental authorities, journalists, and political associations took no notice of nearly one-third of former magistrates, whose participation in the life of their times deposited in accessible documents little but the records of property owned, wealth evaluated, taxes assessed, sons and daughters born or married, and death. Such men remained merely a part, although a considerable one, of the class of well-to-do landowners and rentiers which has been named, as aptly from a political as from an economic standpoint, the *bourgeoisie passive*.[1]

The reform of the judiciary involved several issues, of which some had already been decided on the night of 4 August 1789 and others were subjected to full debate during the next year. On 4 August, the Assembly laid down the principle that the administration of justice was public business from which every private privilege ought to be excluded. Seigneurial courts were to be eliminated, sale and ownership of royal judgeships ended, and judges' fees abolished.[2] The abolition of épices suited the reforming mood of many judges in the bailliages, and some judicial companies effected it voluntarily at once.[3] But the

1. The term has been employed to characterize economic behavior, for example by Michel Vovelle, "Structure et répartition de la fortune foncière et de la fortune mobilière d'un ensemble urbain: Chartres, de la fin de l'ancien régime à la Restauration," *Revue d'Histoire Economique et Sociale,* 36 (1958), 385–398.

2. Arts. 4 and 7 of the decree of 4–11 August 1789, reprinted in *French Revolution Documents,* ed. John M. Roberts and Richard Cobb (Oxford, Basil Blackwell, 1966–   , in progress), I, 151–154.

3. The judges of the bailliage of Troyes decided on 15 August that thenceforth they would collect no fees for judgments. Their order was read aloud and applauded in the National Assembly four days later. (The

more important changes indicated by the decree of 4 August required reorganization of the judiciary. The legislation that accomplished this was prepared mainly by Duport, a judge in the Parlement of Paris, and Thouret, a lawyer from Rouen, both leading political figures in the National Assembly. Their competing proposals were discussed at length and eventually amalgamated, primarily in accordance with constitutional principles and political objectives rather than the professional interests of judges or lawyers.

The law adopted on 16 August 1790, providing for a new system of courts to decide civil disputes, manifested a fundamental hostility to professional judges and their characteristic activities in the eighteenth century.[4] It sought to discourage the whole business of adversary litigation and appellate proceedings, and it prohibited judicial interpretation of law, judicial review of legislative acts, and judicial interference in administrative processes. Its first article declared that arbitration is "the most reasonable means of ending disputes between citizens," and settlement by this means was made available at any stage of any dispute. As a whole, the law revealed the reformers' preference for a type of proceeding in which the judge could be expected to possess special concern and knowledge about the welfare of the persons involved and would be inclined to exercise common sense. A justice of the peace, who was not required to be a lawyer, was to be elected in each of the approximately 6,500 cantons. He was given primary juris-

---

text has been reprinted in *AP*, VIII, 456.) Similar decisions were reported by the judges in Provins, Montélimar, and Loudun and mentioned in the *Procès-verbal* of 15, 18, and 22 September. During these and ensuing weeks, twelve magistrates in various bailliages renounced their claim for reimbursement of the capital value of their offices, thereby making substantial gifts to the treasury which are recorded in the *Extrait du registre des dons patriotiques,* nos. 19, 93, 127, 166, 178, 196, 198, 315, 725, 965, 1566, and 2233.

4. The text is in *AP*, XVIII, 104–110; the phrase quoted below is on p. 104.

diction over small claims (less than 100 livres) and over all cases of damage to fields and harvests, recent usurpations of land, claims for repairs to leased houses and farms, disputes between masters and workmen, and insults and brawls. Family arbiters and family tribunals were to be selected by the disputants in any family quarrel. Municipalities were assigned judicial authority to enforce ordinances for the safety of streets, the orderliness of large gatherings, the honesty of retail sales, and security from fires, epidemics, insane persons and wild animals. Commercial courts, each consisting of five businessmen, were to be elected by businessmen to hear commercial cases, as had been done since the sixteenth century. All these institutions were intended to divert many potential lawsuits from the ordinary courts of law. And, even to be heard by a judge, a lawsuit had to be accompanied by a certification that an effort to mediate had been unsuccessful. For residents of one canton, this was the responsibility of the conciliation service headed by the local justice of the peace; for residents of diverse cantons, it devolved upon a larger conciliation office located in one of the 543 administrative districts that had been created in February 1790.

In each of these districts, and six subdivisions of Paris, a court was to be established with five judges chosen by the electors and a commissioner appointed by the king. The judges were to hear appeals from decisions of the justices of the peace, the municipalities, and the commercial courts. In cases of other kinds, they were to decide in first instance. An appeal from a district court decision was permitted only if a substantial sum was involved (more than 1,000 livres in capital or 50 livres in annual income). The appeal would be heard by one of the seven neighboring district courts, and procedures were specified by which the contending parties would select the appellate tribunal for their case. Further appeal would be possible, under a law adopted on 27 November 1790, to the tribunal of cassation.[5] But it was empowered only to quash the judgment and remand the case to a district court and could do so only for serious procedural defects or clear judicial contravention of a law. The judges in the district courts, like those in the bailliages previously, were to conduct trials and appeals of important cases. The importance of a case was newly defined, by the criteria of economic value and probable legal complexity, without reference to the status of the persons involved. The effective power of judges in provincial towns was greatly increased by the elimination of the parlements, the office of chancellor, and the privy council. As for the king's commissioner in a district court, he was not to be a prosecutor but an enforcement official for civil judgments and a spokesman for the public interest where it was affected by a civil dispute.

A subsequent law, finally adopted on 16 September 1791, provided for the administration of justice and the institution of juries in criminal cases.[6] In each of the eighty-three departments, a criminal court was to be established with a presiding judge chosen by the electors, three judges from the district courts assigned by turns every three months, a public prosecutor chosen by the electors, and a commissioner appointed by the king. The initial reception of complaints and the process of indictment were placed in the hands of the district court, where each judge in turn would serve for six months as director of the presentment jury. When this jury discovered grounds for an indictment, the matter would be turned over to the public prosecutor for proceedings before a trial jury under the direction of the presiding judge of the criminal court.

These laws had several effects on the judicial profession. The first was a great decrease in the number of professional judges. The abolition of the parlements alone eliminated approximately 1,050 judges and was followed by the establishment of

5. *AP,* XXI, 38–41.
6. *AP,* XXX, 696–712.

only one very partial substitute, the tribunal of cassation, with 42 judges. The abolition of the seigneurial courts eliminated an unknown but certainly large number of minor judgeships and some more powerful courts, such as the peerage duchies. It was followed by the establishment of the justices of the peace, who were expected to be chosen simply for their trustworthiness and local prominence.

The disappearance of the seigneurial courts also left many blank areas in the map of jurisdictions. Another result, therefore, was a redistribution of royal courts. The redistribution was affected by the rivalry of localities for honorific distinctions and economic benefits, which was especially intense in 1790 because it involved simultaneously the geographic assignment of administrative entities and the redistribution of lawcourts.[7] The National Assembly did what it could to satisfy most localities, by establishing a large number of districts, by selecting the districts rather than the departments as jurisdictional territories, and, in some districts, by locating the administration in one town and the district court in another. Nonetheless, it preserved the status of three-fourths of the towns where there had been royal bailliages. There were 373 of these, and to 282 of them district courts were assigned.[8] In Lorraine, the environs of Paris, Normandy, and Brittany, altogether 64 percent of the former bailliage towns were assigned district courts; for the rest of the country, the proportion was 82 percent. The National Assembly assigned district courts to 261 other towns (including nine in Corsica, seven in Alsace, and three in Roussillon) where previously there had been no royal bailliage.

A further consequence for the judicial profession followed from the geographic definition of the districts, which were intended to be similar in territorial extent rather than population.

7. The competition is well described by Jean Soulas, "Rivalités urbaines en France, 1789–1790," *Information Historique,* 18 (1956), 138–143.

8. See Appendix, infra, for the details.

The old ideal of obtaining justice after no more than one day's journey was put into effect in 1790 with a thoroughness never approached by reforming chancellors from Olivier to d'Aguesseau. The number of judges in a locality no longer depended even in part, as it had done, on the volume of litigation. A large town, where there had been a dozen or a score of judges, would have only the five judges of the district court and the presiding judge of a criminal court.[9] The nationwide total of judges, king's commissioners, and public prosecutors was to be approximately 3,550, which exceeded by about 850 the total number of magistrates in the bailliages. More important, opportunities for a judicial career were sharply reduced in many localities and greatly enlarged in many others.

Many of the men who had held office in the bailliages disappeared from the judiciary as a result of hundreds of local political contests. Personal rivalries and allegiances played a part in them that is almost beyond the reach of historical analysis. But other forces, of broader scope, were also at work, and can be examined by comparison of the results in different areas. In Burgundy, the eighteen royal bailliages comprised 118 magistrates who, being more than 30 years of age and having more than five years' experience as lawyers or judges in 1790, were eligible for election. The district courts would require a total of 80 judges. Because of the disparity in numbers between the old and the new judiciary, nearly one-third of the former officeholders would necessarily be excluded from the new positions. In the event, the electors rejected many more. They chose only 27 bailliage magistrates to be judges in district courts; not quite one-fourth of the membership of the old bailliages and about one-third of the membership of the new courts.

The regional figures conceal local variation in the bailliage magistrates' fortunes ranging from almost total defeat to com-

9. Only Paris, with 6 courts, and Lyon, with 1 court for the city and 1 for the surrounding area, were accorded exceptional treatment.

Table 14. Results of Elections to District Courts, Northern Burgundy, 1790.

District and bailliage[a]	Number of eligible magistrates in bailliage	Number of judgeships in district court	Number of former magistrates elected	Proportion of former magistrates elected (percent)	Proportion of new judges drawn from bailliages (percent)
Auxerre	15	5	5	33	100
Avallon	5	5	3	60	60
Semur-en-Auxois		5		9	20
Semur	5		1		
Saulieu	6		0		
Arnay-le-Duc	3	5	2	67	40
Châtillon-sur-Seine	8	5	3	37.5	60
Is-sur-Tille	0	5	0	[inapplicable]	0
Dijon	12	5	1	8	20
Saint-Jean-de-Losne		5		60	60
Auxonne	3		3		
Saint-Jean	2		0		
Beaune		5		10	20
Beaune	8		1		
Nuits	2		0		
Totals	69	45	19	27.5	42

Source: Procès-verbaux d'élections de juges, 1790 (A.D. Yonne, L 647; A.D. Côte-d'Or, L 215–221).

[a] In the districts of Semur-en-Auxois, Saint-Jean-de-Losne, and Beaune, there were two bailliages, as indicated under the district name.

Table 15. Results of Elections to District Courts, Southern Burgundy, 1790.

District and bailliage[a]	Number of eligible magistrates in bailliage	Number of judgeships in district court	Number of former magistrates elected	Proportion of former magistrates elected (percent)	Proportion of new judges drawn from bailliages (percent)
Autun					40
Autun	7	5	1	14	
Montcenis	5		1	20	
Bourbon-Lancy	4	5	1	25	20
Chalon-sur-Saône	11	5	1	9	20
Louhans	0	5	0	[inapplicable]	0
Charolles	7	5	1	14	20
Marcigny					20
Semur-en-Brionnais	2	5	1	50	
Mâcon	13	5	2	15	40
Totals	49	35	8	16	23

Sources: Procès-verbal d'élection de juges, Chalon-sur-Saône, 1790 (A.D. Saône-et-Loire, 2 L 314); Léonce Lex and P. Siraud, Le Conseil général et les conseillers généraux de-Saône-et-Loire (Mâcon, 1888), pp. 190, 239–242; Tableau des juges. Saône-et-Loire (A.N., D III 225).
[a] In the district of Autun, there were two bailliages, indicated under the district name. In the district of Marcigny, the bailliage was located at Semur-en-Brionnais and so was the district court.

plete triumph. Where there had been no royal bailliage, only a seigneurial court, as at Is-sur-Tille, the electors did not bring in former royal judges from elsewhere but chose local lawyers for the district court. Where there had been two royal bailliages, and there was henceforth to be only one district court, the election turned into a contest between the two towns. In the district of Semur-en-Auxois, none of the six magistrates from the bailliage of Saulieu was elected to the district court, which was to sit in the principal town. In the district of Saint-Jean-de-Losne, the men of Saint-Jean had won the elections to the district administration in June, but the electors from Auxonne succeeded in placing all three of the magistrates from their bailliage in the district court in October.

For individual candidates, it was highly advantageous to possess the prestige derived from a distinguished family, wealth, or personal reputation. In Beaune, it was Bachey, the chief civil judge, whose father had held an ennobling office and whose wife was a daughter of a noble in the Mâconnais, who was elected to the district court, while two other ex-judges in the bailliage were defeated.[10] In Châtillon-sur-Seine, the three principal judges of the bailliage, led by Debruère—Trésorier de France and father of a magistrate in the Parlement of Burgundy—were elected to the district court.[11]

Rivalry between towns evoked contests for control of the institutions they shared. The desire to follow the leadership of a notable personage suggested the choice of wealthy scions of distinguished families. Allegiance to one's local community and loyalty to its leading families were old tendencies in French public life, and they continued to influence elections in

10. Bachey had married Marie-Charlotte Peltrat de Borde; his father had held office in the cour des comptes, aides et finances at Dôle. (Parish register, Saint-Pierre de Mâcon, 31 March 1783.)

11. Debruère's son is mentioned by Albert Colombet, *Les Parlementaires bourguignons à la fin du XVIIIe siècle* (Dijon, chez l'auteur, 1937), pp. 46, 72, 86, and 100, as a newcomer whose wealth and style of life resembled those of the established families.

1790. But new forces were also at work. Politics had been translated into a new framework, in which change was envisaged as possible and in which, therefore, political ideas counted heavily. Acceptance of the reforms of 1789 and 1790 enabled a former officeholder to obtain the support of an electioneering group. Elections of judges were not sharply distinguished from elections of local administrative officials or legislative representatives; all were affected by the new atmosphere. This gave a new meaning to the idea of judicial independence. It had been secured, in theory, by the emphasis which venality of office naturally laid upon wealth and family position as prerequisites for a judicial career. Where the former magistrates in a bailliage combined wealth and family distinction with reforming attitudes, they were able to sweep up all the new judgeships. At Auxerre, the assembly of electors adopted a resolution expressing regret that they could not retain all nineteen members of the bailliage as district judges; the five elected were prominent for wealth and lineage as much as for their liberal views. Heading the list was Marie d'Avigneau, former chief civil judge in the bailliage, whose family had been noble for four generations. In some elections, ideological and factional criteria were decisive. The election of Guényot as presiding judge in Semur-en-Auxois is to be explained by his political sympathies and civic participation more than by his wealth.[12] At Saint-Jean-de-Losne, the former magistrates of Auxonne were elected to the district court for similar reasons, not because of widespread admiration for their lineage or wealth. One of these magistrates was Chaudot, whose father had been a master cobbler; another was Gremeret, whose

12. Guényot later came under attack for his opinions and active participation: "Le premier à Semur qui se soit élancé dans la carrière révolutionnaire . . . Quelles honteuses manœuvres n'a t'il pas employés pour arriver aux places . . . commandant de la garde nationale, président du tribunal du district." Rapport fait aux sections de la commune de Semur [1795] (A.N., D III 55, 103[1]), ff. 67–73.

fortune at marriage consisted of a couple of thousand livres in cash, his books, and his bailliage office.[13]

In eastern Poitou, the election results were statistically very similar to those in northern Burgundy. In each region, 28 percent of the bailliage magistrates were elected to the new district courts, and a few others were appointed as king's commissioners. In eastern Poitou, with fewer district courts than northern Burgundy, this meant that a larger proportion of the new elected judiciary came from the old sénéchaussées: 53 percent, as against 42 percent from the old bailliages in northern Burgundy. But in central and western Poitou (the departments of Deux-Sèvres and Vendée), the statistical results were very different, principally because there district courts were established in seven towns or *bourgs* that had formerly possessed no royal tribunal. (The prévôté of Melle and the bailliage at La Châtaigneraie were royal tribunals of the lesser type from which all appellate cases went to the sénéchausée of Poitiers.) In the districts where there were no ex-magistrates, local men were elected, not former officeholders from Niort, Saint-Maixent, nor Fontenay-le-Comte. In Poitou as a whole, despite the continuation of the popularity that magistrates had enjoyed in 1789, they were eliminated from the judiciary in even larger proportions than in Burgundy.

At the same time, politics in Poitou had a complexion different from that in Burgundy. The largest sénéchaussée, and the one most distinguished by the lineage and wealth of its members, was in Poitiers. The leading magistrates there disapproved of various measures adopted in 1789 and 1790, including the judicial reform. One of them was elected a judge in the district court but declined to serve. Two other former magistrates, Rampillon and Nicolas, were elected. Younger, lower in rank, distinctly of bourgeois origin, they were candidates of

13. Chaudot's father signed the record of his baptism. (Parish register, Auxonne, 26 January 1733.) Gremeret's wealth was evaluated in his marriage contract, registered 17 July 1786 (A.D. Côte-d'Or, C 8000).

Table 16. Results of Elections to District Courts, Poitou, 1790.

District and sénéchaussée[a]	Number of eligible magistrates in sénéchaussée[a]	Number of judgeships in district court	Number of former magistrates elected	Proportion of former magistrates elected (percent)	Proportion of new judges drawn from sénéchaussées (percent)
Châtellerault	6	5	4	67	80
Civray	10	5	2	20	40
Loudun	10	5	3	30	60
Lusignan[b]	3	5	1	33	40
Montmorillon	10	5	2	20	40
Poitiers[b]	18	5	4	22	60
Bressuire	0	5	0	[inapplicable]	0
Melle	0	5	0	[inapplicable]	0
Niort	11	5	2	18	40
Parthenay	0	5	0	[inapplicable]	0
Saint-Maixent	8	5	1	12.5	20
Thouars	0	5	0	[inapplicable]	0
Challans	0	5	0	[inapplicable]	0
Fontenay-le-Comte	14	5	3	21	60
La Châtaigneraie	0	5	0	[inapplicable]	0
La Roche-sur-Yon	0	5	0	[inapplicable]	0
Les Sables d'Olonne	0	5	0	[inapplicable]	0
Montaigu	0	5	0	[inapplicable]	0
Totals	90	90	22	24	24

Sources: Marie de Roux, La Révolution à Poitiers et dans la Vienne (Poitiers, 1910, as Mémoires de la Société de Antiquaires de l'Ouest, 3rd ser., 4) pp. 319–321; Charles-L. Chassin, La Préparation de la guerre de Vendée, 3 vols. (Paris, 1892), III, 48; A.N., F¹ᶜ III Deux-Sèvres 1 and D III 294.

[a] The 3 magistrates of the prévôté of Melle and the 5 magistrates of the bailliage of Vouvant at La Châtaigneraie are not counted in col. 2. (See the text.)

[b] Babinet, a councillor in the sénéchaussée of Poitiers, was elected to the district court at Lusignan; here he is counted at Poitiers in col. 5, and at Lusignan in col. 6.

an antiaristocratic faction. The district in Poitou where former magistrates were most popular was that of Châtellerault. There, four of them were elected to the district court and a fifth was elected an alternate judge; only one former officeholder in the sénéchaussée of Châtellerault was not elected to the new bench.[14]

Former magistrates were politically strong in a few places, exemplified by Auxerre, Saint-Jean-de-Losne, and Châtellerault, and notably weak in others, such as Mâcon, Saulieu, and Poitiers. No simple explanation applies to all these situations. Wealth and social standing, or their absence, were not decisive in themselves. The electors' view of these attributes was important, to be sure, as was their attitude toward whatever seemed distinctive in the former magistrates' political style, whether it was procedural caution, dignity, or moderate social attitudes. The electoral strength of the former magistrates was more decisively affected by the nature and intensity of political disagreement around them. They were typically readier to fill representative positions where a consensus existed, with which they agreed, than to engage directly in factional strife. At one extreme, exemplified in Mâcon and Poitiers, political contests were already in progress in 1790 in which some of the magistrates were associated with unpopular views. At the other extreme, exemplified in Auxerre and Châtellerault, serious resistance to change did not appear so early, and the electors could easily choose the men who had had the greatest local prestige under the old establishment to help achieve the construction of the new. Everywhere, however, the magistrates encountered competition. A class of small-town attorneys sought to move up from the private practice of law to the

14. Roux, *La Révolution à Poitiers et dans la Vienne,* pp. 319–321.
The state of affairs at Châtellerault seems to have resembled that at Agen, where there had been 15 royal magistrates in the sénéchaussée, of whom 4 were elected to the district court: Aristide Douarche, "Notes sur la justice et les tribunaux à Agen pendant la Révolution," *Révolution Française,* 22 (1892)–24 (1893), vol. 23, p. 208.

exercise of those judicial functions which were still especially honorable, and such men displaced many bourgeois holders of royal offices: this was, among other things, what the bourgeois revolution meant. The usual result was the local political prominence of one or two former magistrates in a bailliage and the retirement of the others into the comfortable private life of the town dweller sustained by the income from rural property, a style of life soon to be enhanced by the reimbursement of capital which had been locked in the judicial offices.

The liquidation of the judicial offices was planned by men who themselves owned offices in bailliages and who had been serving as judges or king's counsel until their election as deputies to the Estates General. After the decree of 4 August 1789, the task of preparing the necessary detailed legislation on the venal offices was assigned to the committee on the judiciary. The committee was elected in a peculiar way, which had as one result that its fifteen members included nine magistrates.[15] The committee's work consisted mainly of collecting information from the chancellery and from the branch of the financial administration which had sold the offices, the *bureau des parties casuelles*. After compiling forty boxes full of lists and documents, the committee announced its readiness to report at the end of 1789. But until September 1790, the Assembly was not prepared to consider the procedure for compensating the officeholders. The committee's first report was by Gossin, chief civil judge and deputy from the bailliage of Bar-le-Duc.[16] He explained that reimbursement could be based on any of three

15. The National Assembly divided into bureaux, each of which nominated 3 members; the 90 nominees chose, among them, 30 who in turn assigned half their own number to the committee on ecclesiastical affairs and half to the committee on the judiciary. The latter committee included 5 chief civil judges, from Bar-le-Duc, Le Mans, Mantes, Riom, and La Châtaigneraie (in Poitou); 3 king's advocates, from Melun, Nantes, and Orléans; and the acting chief judge of Angers; as a whole, a well-to-do and prudent group.

16. The text is in *AP*, XVIII, 494–501.

measures of the value of the offices: the original price at the time when each office was created; the price at the most recent sale; or the evaluation made by the officeholder himself in accordance with the edict of February 1771. The committee recommended the last of these, because it was the easiest to obtain. The original price of many offices would have had to be sought in seventeenth- or sixteenth-century documents. The most recent sale price might date back two or three generations for perhaps a quarter of the offices, which had been inherited by the current holders. The evaluations of 1771 had been adopted by vote of each corps of officeholders and were supposed to be recorded in their minutes. They had been required as the basis for a reformed version of the annual tax on the inheritability of the offices. For this reason, some officeholders in 1771 had deliberately undervalued their offices.[17] In some localities, the market value of offices in the bailliages had risen since 1771 to a figure considerably above the recorded evaluation.[18] The officeholders serving on the committee on the judiciary proposed to inflict financial losses on some of their colleagues in the bailliages.

If the offices were to be liquidated rapidly, there was no other practical choice. Pamphlets, in the spring of 1790, urging the National Assembly to provide for quick reimbursement, had also favored the evaluations of 1771 as the basis for it.[19] In the autumn of 1790, speed was desirable for two reasons. In

17. Eight officeholders in Rouen asserted that in buying offices after 1771 they paid prices higher than the recorded evaluations of 1771 and that some of them paid 50 or 75 percent more; their letter is in *AP*, XVIII, 632.

18. For a documented example, see my note, "Sur le prix des offices judiciaires à la fin de l'ancien régime," *Revue d'Histoire Economique et Sociale*, 42 (1964), 390–392.

19. Boutaric, president in the élection of Figeac, in Quercy, and a member of the National Assembly, was one of those who urged that offices evaluated in 1771 should be liquidated on that basis, in his *Réflexions d'un député sur les moyens à prendre pour liquider* (B.N., Lf⁴. 34).

the first place, the parlements were attempting to stir up resistance to the National Assembly. (They were soon to take the pretentious step of quashing the constitution.) Owners of judicial offices who accepted reimbursement would imply their acceptance of the National Assembly's right to carry out the judicial reforms and of the reforms themselves. The essential point had been seen by Maupeou in 1771. It was one reason why he was careful to arrange for compensation to the evicted members of the parlements.[20] This policy was no less prudent in 1790, and Gossin's report emphasized in particular the need for generous compensation for the parlements.

Secondly, the nationalized property which had belonged to the church or the royal domain was being put up for sale. If the liquid capital which would be turned over to the former office-holders became available in time to be largely absorbed in purchases of these lands, there would be reason to hope that monetary instability might be prevented. Political disaffection of the ex-magistrates in the lower courts, also, would be minimized.[21] The emphasis on speed and practicality, conveyed in Gossin's report, was shared by the National Assembly as a whole in acting on the committee's draft decree. The Assembly refused to consider an amendment which would have permitted additional compensation for those offices which had reached a market value more than twice the recorded evaluation.[22] It then adopted the decree without debate.[23]

20. Robert Villers, *L'Organisation du Parlement de Paris et des conseils supérieurs d'après la réforme de Maupeou* (Paris, Sirey, 1937).

21. A pamphlet, *Mémoire sur le remboursement par une société de magistrats,* in the summer of 1790, advocated plans closely resembling those adopted in September. It concluded that they would have a great effect: "De 10,000 antagonistes de la Révolution actuelle, dans l'ordre des magistrats, l'Assemblée Nationale en fait 10,000 partisans." (B.N., Lf[23]. 89).

22. The proposed amendment referred to a situation that actually existed in some bailliages: how many, it is impossible to determine. In Mâcon, for example, the transfer taxes paid for the office of conseiller permit the calculation that its recorded value was 1,500 livres and the

The decree required each corps of officeholders to send to the committee on the judiciary a list of all offices, occupied and vacant, and a statement of debts owed by and to the corps. A mass of documentation was thus to be produced, on which the National Assembly had no means of securing reports. The payments to holders of liquidated offices were to be made by a special treasury, the *caisse de l'extraordinaire;* plans for this had been under desultory consideration by the finance committee for six months.[24] In December 1790, the Assembly adopted a plan of organization for the special treasury and established another executive agency, the General Directory of Liquidation, charged with examining and reporting on the claims to be submitted by the officeholders.[25] Together, these two agencies were to carry out as rapidly as possible an immense transfer of property.

The two agencies operated with reasonable speed. In their first four months, more than one hundred million livres in assignats were actually paid to former holders of judicial and municipal offices, and in the second four months an even larger additional sum was paid.[26] But the payments were not

reimbursement (including taxes) slightly more than 2,200 livres. But two conseillers had stated, in marriage contracts in 1782 and 1783, that the market value of the office was 10,000 livres. The transfer taxes are noted in A.N., V¹ 507 and V¹ 511. The marriage contracts are registered in A.D. Saône-et-Loire, C 3049 (7 October 1782) and C 3050 (17 January 1783). A similar comparison, involving slightly larger sums, can be made for the office of avocat du roi at Mâcon: A.N., V¹ 524, and A.D. Saône-et-Loire, C 3053 (12 October 1784).

23. *Procès-verbal de l'Assemblée Nationale,* 6 September, 1790.

24. *Procès-verbaux du comité des finances de l'Assemblée Constituante,* ed. Camille Bloch (Rennes, Imprimerie Oberthur, 1922), pp. 216, 406.

25. The proposals and discussion are in *AP,* XXI, 459 and 508. The administrative context in which all this occurred is explained by John F. Bosher, *French Finances, 1770–1795. From Business to Bureaucracy* (Cambridge, Eng., Cambridge University Press, 1970), pp. 239 and 270–273.

26. The precise amounts were 102,222,847 livres and 129,284,528 livres, reported in *Compte de la caisse de l'extraordinaire au 31 mai*

issued as rapidly as some former officeholders wished, especially at first, during the winter of 1791. Letters expressing their anxiety and impatience accumulated in the files of the committee on the judiciary.[27] Members of the National Assembly, too, desired greater speed. They secured the enactment of several decrees intended to simplify the procedure for liquidating offices.[28] The essential steps in the procedure thereafter were the submission of a claim and proof by a corps of officeholders or by one or more members, the preliminary report by the General Directory of Liquidation of the sum claimed for each office, the routine legislative sanction by the National Assembly, the verification by the General Directory of the amount, and finally the issuance to the officeholder of a certificate, which could be and ordinarily was exchanged for assignats. The General Directory of Liquidation and the officeholders themselves discovered many small errors and a few important omissions in the sums initially claimed, inaccuracies attributable to the complexity of calculations which sometimes involved a variety of taxes and fees to be reimbursed. The investigation of these details caused a considerable delay between the legislative sanction and the issuance of a certificate. During the first eight months of operations, the National Assembly approved the liquidation of offices totalling nearly 319 million livres in value while subsequent certificates and assignats were issued totalling about three-fourths of that amount.[29]

In the mass of offices to be liquidated, those in the bailliages constituted only one category. The General Directory of Liqui-

---

1791 and *Compte de la caisse de l'extraordinaire au 30 septembre 1791* (A.N., AD IX 496).

27. A.N., D XVII, cartons 6–8.

28. *Procès-verbal de l'Assemblée Nationale,* 9 February 1791.

29. The liquidation decrees totalled 318,877,656 livres. Assignats amounting to 231,507,375 livres and certificates (*reconnaissances*) amounting to 2,738,504 livres were issued: Ms. "Résumé des opérations de la Direction Générale de la Liquidation jusques et compris le 27 septembre 1791" (A.N., D XI 1). By December 1791, the agency had paid out five-sixths of the total decreed: *AP*, XXXV, 683.

dation had sixty-six clerks working on the judicial and municipal offices in 1791, of whom nine were assigned to the bailliages.[30] The categories of offices were not separately reported in the accounts prepared for the National Assembly, which was merely informed of the total compensation to be paid for all the offices in each company.[31] But some of the preliminary reports of the General Directory of Liquidation exist, and they specify the amounts to be paid to each judicial officeholder in 100 bailliages.[32] The decrees enacted by the National Assembly indicate approximately the date when the officeholders complied with the procedure and the period when they probably received payment. The documentation, although incomplete, shows that the officeholders in the bailliages were much quicker than those in the parlements to send in their claims for compensation.[33] More than half of all the former magistrates in the bailliages received payment before the end of 1791. In some provinces, the proportion was considerably greater: two-thirds

30. Ms. "Etat de la division des travaux de la Direction Générale de la Liquidation" (A.N., D XI 1).

31. These accounts, as well as the decrees based on them, were reprinted in *AP*, XXII, 769–770; XXIII, 502; XXIV, 140–141; XXV, 64–67 and 662–665; XXVII, 60–63; XXVIII, 106–109; XXIX, 78–80 and 606–608; XXX, 566–573; and XXXI, 600–608. They include 218 bailliages, 58 percent of the number existing in 1789.

32. The preliminary reports were addressed to the committee on the judiciary, which provided the summary accounts for the National Assembly. The preliminary reports underlying the first four liquidation decrees (5 February, 24 February, 17 March, and 14 April) and the sixth liquidation decree (8 June) are in A.N., D XVII 9 (nos. 123–127). The preliminary reports underlying the liquidation decrees of 8 May, 10 July, 31 July, 21 August, 12 September, and 29 September are not in subseries D XI or D XVII. It is presumed that most of the liquidation agency's papers were turned over to the Ministry of Finance after 1810 and were destroyed by fire in 1871.

33. The parlements of Toulouse, Besançon, Rennes, and Rouen, and for a shorter period, Paris and Dijon, held out against accepting compensation for their offices. Henri Carré, *La Fin des parlements (1788–1790)* (Paris, Hachette, 1912), pp. 255–258.

in Burgundy; three-fourths in Poitou. There had been scattered resistance in some bailliages in the autumn of 1790, but the irrevocability of the judicial reform and the desire to reinvest the capital sums that were involved made the futility of delay increasingly apparent even to the members of the parlements.

At first, early in 1791, the magistrates' compliance with the liquidation procedures was delayed in some places by the complexity of the claims and by political reluctance but was hastened elsewhere by a desire to manifest support for the National Assembly and its reforms. Simultaneously, political as well as financial motives were influencing the officeholders' decisions on a related matter, the opportunity to purchase nationalized property formerly held by the church or the royal domain. Financially, these decisions were not simple. The alternatives were multiple, and the prospective losses imponderable. Refined accuracy cannot be claimed for any attempt to distinguish, in the motives of an individual, the political gesture from the prudent investment. What can be determined is whether the National Assembly's purposes were matched in the aggregate by the decisions of former officeholders in the bailliages. The Assembly intended the assignats to be absorbed by investment in landed property that was not already in private hands but had belonged to the church or the royal domain. To retire the state debt most conveniently, the ideal result would have been a mere transfer of property rights, through the temporary medium constituted by the assignats, from a state-created asset to a state-appropriated one. The former officeholders in the bailliages, in disposing of the compensation for their extinct offices, accomplished something very different.

Most former magistrates in the bailliages reserved the sums derived from their offices for investments other than the purchase of nationalized property or for current expenditures. More than half of them purchased no nationalized property at all. Many of these had borrowed in order to acquire their offices and when the offices were liquidated merely used the proceeds to liquidate their own debts. Thoughts probably typical of many such magistrates were expressed by Ménard de la Groye, former councillor in the sénéchaussée of Le Mans and member of the National Assembly, in letters to his wife.[34] He expected the price of land to rise considerably within a few years, and he much regretted his decision not to acquire nationalized land that he would have liked to acquire. But his primary desire was to repay a loan he had obtained from a noblewoman, Mlle de Saint-Simon. She died in the autumn of 1790, leaving as the probable heir her brother, the marquis de Saint-Simon, a member of the National Assembly representing the nobility of Angoulême. Ménard de la Groye became even more determined to extinguish the rente, which was now "fort désagréable" because the creditor was "un des principaux suppôts de l'aristocratie"; but above all, "ma principale ambition est de n'avoir aucunes dettes." Underlying his statements were some old-fashioned attitudes. He viewed the debt as a personal relationship, not simply a business transaction, and he wanted personal independence. The more antagonistic the creditor, the more undesirable the debt. There was in his letters no suggestion that he might incur the risk of making a new investment while a previous debt remained unpaid.

But, in contrast, a considerable minority of former magistrates invested heavily in nationalized property, spending substantially larger sums than they obtained for their offices. In Burgundy, this minority constituted nearly one-fifth of the former magistrates in the province. Twelve of them spent on nationalized property sums which ranged from two to ten times the amounts they received for their offices. Eight others spent sums which ranged from thirteen to eighteen times as much as they received. In all, these twenty men received about 92,000 livres for their bailliage offices, and invested 695,000 livres in

34. Letters dated 10 September, 1 and 22 October, and 19 November 1790; 18 January and 15 February 1791 (mss., A.D. Sarthe, 10 J 122).

Table 17. Expenditures on Nationalized Property, in Relation to Sums Received in Liquidation of Offices, by Former Bailliage Magistrates in Burgundy, 1790–1792.

| Bailliage | Total expenditure ÷ Sum reimbursed for office (one ratio for each purchaser) | | |
	Ratio ≥ 2:1 (1)	2:1 > Ratio ≥ 1:1 (2)	Ratio < 1:1 (3)
Arnay-le-Duc	[none]	1:1	[none]
Autun	13:1, 3:1	1:1	[none]
Auxerre	18:1, 13:1, 4:1, 4:1, 3:1	1½:1, 1:1	1:3, 1:4, 1:4
Auxonne	[none]	1:1	1:3
Avallon	13:1	1:1	5:8
Beaune	8:1, 6:1, 3:1, 2:1	1½:1, 1:1	1:90
Bourbon-Lancy	[none]	1⅓:1, 1:1	1:6
Chalon-sur-Saône	[none]	1:1	1:10
Charolles	[none]	1:1	1:11
Châtillon-sur-Seine	45:1, 35:1, 2:1	[none]	1:2
Dijon	15:1, 3½:1	[none]	[none]
Mâcon	13:1	1½:1, 1:1	[none]
Montcenis	[none]	[none]	3:5
Nuits	[none]	1½:1	[none]
Saint-Jean-de-Losne	[none]	[none]	1:22
Saulieu	14:1	[none]	[none]
Semur-en-Auxois	17:1, 10:1, 5:1	[none]	[none]

Sources: The actual expenditures are summarized in Table 20, infra. For the sums reimbursed, the sources are indicated in notes 35 and 36; the sources for col. (2) are indicated in note 37; the sources for col. (3) are A.N., D XVII 9, nos. 123 and 127 (for Martineau, Seurrat, and the king's advocate Marie, all of Auxerre, Malot of Avallon, and Bachey of Beaune), and V¹ 486, 489, 491, 508, 511, 513, and 516 (for, respectively, Buvée of Auxonne, the elder Darentiere of Châtillon-sur-Seine, Lazare Garchery of Montcenis, Lavaivre de Rigny of Bourbon-Lancy, the younger Aubery of Charolles, Hernoux of Saint-Jean-de-Losne, and Journet of Chalon-sur-Saône).

nationalized property.[35] A dramatic disparity between the value of the liquidated office and the amount invested in nationalized property was to be seen in the purchases made by two former magistrates in Châtillon-sur-Seine, Debruère and Humbert. They invested, respectively, thirty-five and forty-five times the value of their offices, undertaking to pay a combined total in excess of 400,000 livres.[36]

A smaller minority of former magistrates followed the course that the National Assembly had planned and invested in nationalized property approximately as much as the sums they received for their offices. In Burgundy, this minority constituted one-eighth of all the former magistrates in the province. They received a total of about 86,000 livres for their offices and spent a combined total of 103,500 livres on nationalized property.[37]

35. The sums received from the liquidation are recorded in A.N., D XVII 9, nos. 123 and 127, for 12 former magistrates (Robinet de Pontagny, Soufflot, Housset, Marie de La Forge, and Choppin, all of Auxerre; Richerolle, of Avallon; Bitouzet, Boucheron, Terrand, and Virely, all of Beaune; Louet and Narjollet, both of Dijon). The sums received by 6 others can be calculated approximately, because they entered office after 1771 and therefore paid the reformed transfer tax of 4.58333 percent of the capital value of the office (the 24e *denier plus les deux sols pour livre*), the amount of which is noted on the minutes of the lettres de provisions (A.N., series V[1]). This calculation has to be adjusted upward by about 5 percent, because the fees paid for issuance of the documents are not mentioned. Such calculations were possible for Nuguet, of Autun (V[1] 503); Mariotte, of Châtillon-sur-Seine (V[1] 513); Monin, of Mâcon (V[1] 495); Reuillon de Brain (V[1] 526); Guényot (V[1] 496); and Creusot (V[1] 427); all of Semur-en-Auxois. Estimates of the sums received by Abord of Autun and Dupré of Saulieu derive from comparison with similar offices.

36. The sums received are essentially indicated on the minutes of the lettres de provisions: Debruère (V[1] 418), capital value of office, 3,960 livres, plus various taxes; Humbert (V[1] 516), capital value of office, 5,000 livres, plus various taxes.

37. The sums received from the liquidation are recorded in A.N., D XVII 9, nos. 123 and 127, for 6 former magistrates (Hay and Raffin, of Auxerre; Gaudot, of Avallon; Décologne and Maufoux, of Beaune; Durand, of Nuits). The sums received by 7 others have been calculated from the *finance* or the transfer tax noted on the minutes of lettres de

The Liquidation of the Bailliage Offices

The sales of nationalized property to former bailliage magistrates could nevertheless be regarded, in the aggregate, as a financial success. In Burgundy, for instance, the special treasury received from them about 200,000 livres more than it disbursed for all their offices. This aggregate balance was, however, the effect of investment decisions by 17 former magistrates. Each of them spent more than 20,000 livres for nationalized property, amounting to a total of a million livres; against this could be set the sum, likewise amounting to approximately a million livres, received by all 125 surviving former magistrates in Burgundy for their bailliage offices. What occurred was thus not simply a transfer of ownership from extinguished offices to newly available state lands. The effect of the liquidation of the offices and the sales of nationalized property, considered without reference to other economic facts, was to distribute paper money and real estate very unevenly among the former magistrates. The whole pattern of investment and noninvestment by former bailliage magistrates shows that the liquidation of the offices did not determine most of their decisions concerning nationalized property. More important, most of them took a course of action quite different from that desired by the patriotic majority of the National Assembly. In this sense, their motives were financial. The decision to invest or not to invest in nationalized property resulted from the total economic position of each individual.

The published records of purchases of nationalized property tend to suggest that in the smaller bailliages (like Epinal) a large percentage of former magistrates made some purchases,

---

provisions: A.N., V^1 440, 484, 478, 496, 505, and 515 (two documents), for Pinot and Guillemain, of Bourbon-Lancy; Batault, of Chalon-sur-Saône; Godard, of Arnay-le-Duc; Lagrange and Viard, of Mâcon; and Gremeret, of Auxonne, respectively. The sums received by Serpillon of Autun and Saulnier of Charolles could only be estimated by comparison with similar offices.

Table 18. Purchases of Nationalized Property
by Former Magistrates in Diverse Bailliages, 1790–1792.

	Purchasers		Total expenditure by each purchaser (in livres)		
Locality	Number	Percent of magistrates in locality	Lowest	Median	Highest
Lyon	5	22	3,250	44,700	115,100
Marseille	2	22	14,395	—	15,100
Sens	2	12	4,100	—	22,225
Epinal	3	43	2,725	4,075	8,580

Sources: Appendix, infra, and *Documents relatifs à la vente des biens nationaux dans le département du Rhône,* ed. Sébastien Charléty (Lyon, Imprimerie R. Schneider, 1906), pp. 189, 232, 234, 236, 251, 266, 273; *Documents relatifs à la vente des biens nationaux dans le département des Bouches-du-Rhône,* ed. Paul Moulin, 4 vols. (Marseille, Barlatier, 1908–1911), II, 195, III, 130; *Documents relatifs à la vente des biens nationaux dans le district de Sens,* ed. Charles Porée, 2 vols. (Auxerre, Imprimerie l'Universelle, 1912–1913), I, 260, 315, 354, 463, II, 57, 232, 400; *Documents relatifs à la vente des biens nationaux dans le district d'Epinal,* ed. Léon Schwab (Epinal, Imprimerie Nouvelle, 1911), pp. 87, 166, 214.

and that in the larger bailliages (like Lyon) a few magistrates made very large investments in nationalized property.

The smaller bailliages were far more numerous than the large ones. In their response to the opportunity to buy nationalized property, the magistrates of Epinal were typical and those of Lyon were exceptional. Manuscript sources in eastern Poitou, for instance, show that in a locality there it was common for two or three magistrates to buy some nationalized property. In only two towns was the number of purchasers larger: Poitiers and Loudun. In Poitiers, also, the median total expenditure was large, 8,750 livres, as compared with the median of 4,050 livres for all six localities.

In Burgundy, too, it was common for one, two, or three magistrates in a locality to buy some nationalized property. The

| Locality | Purchasers | | Total expenditure by each purchaser (in livres) | | |
	Number	Percent of magistrates in locality	Lowest	Median	Highest
Châtellerault	2	29	3,100	—	36,600
Civray	3	30	3,500	3,525	9,250
Loudun	6	55	170	(3,000 & 3,838)	21,500
Lusignan	3	75	770	2,650	7,000
Montmorillon	3	30	1,001	10,100	11,000
Poitiers	9	47	800	8,750	88,000
Total	26	43	170	4,050	88,000

Sources: A.D. Vienne, Q² 16 arts. 32 and 70 (Châtellerault); Q² 26 arts. 11, 14, 68, and 84 (Civray); Q² 30 arts. 31, 74, 81, 101, 104, 112, 126, 138, 200, 201, and 244 (Loudun); Q² 3 art. 275, Q² 33 arts. 1 and 79 (Lusignan); Q² 9 art. 826, Q² 37 arts. 8 and 58 (Montmorillon); Q² 1 art. 2, Q² 2 art. 152, Q² 5 arts. 405 and 457, Q² 6 arts. 508 and 589, Q² 7 art. 679, Q² 8 arts. 732 bis, 742, and 773, Q² 33 art. 12, and Q² 37 art. 6 (Poitiers).

number of purchasers was notably larger only in Auxerre and Beaune. In the wooded areas of northern Burgundy, the median total expenditure greatly exceeded the median for the province as a whole. Speculation in rising land values may have been involved in the purchases at Châtillon-sur-Seine and Semur-en-Auxois, as well as at Lyon.

The economic position of the heaviest investors in nationalized property is of particular interest. Concerning the ten former magistrates in Burgundy who invested most heavily in nationalized property, there is other information. For six of them, marriage contracts indicate roughly their economic level at about the time they entered office. Eight were assessed in the Côte-d'Or department for the forced loan of 1799. For five, the

Table 20. Purchases of Nationalized Property
by Former Magistrates in Bailliages in Burgundy, 1790–1792.

| Locality | Purchasers | | Total expenditure by each purchaser (in livres) | | |
	Number[a]	Percent of magistrates in locality	Lowest	Median(s)	Highest
Arnay-le-Duc	1	33	—	3,550	—
Autun	3	33	8,100	10,750	35,400
Auxerre	10	55	1,075	(5,500 & 11,225)	57,325
Auxonne	2	67	2,425	—	5,600
Avallon	3	60	2,000	9,725	24,665
Beaune	7	88	300	11,100	25,675
Bourbon-Lancy	3	75	800	1,000	3,150
Chalon-sur Saône	2	17	1,150	—	10,000
Charolles	2	28	850	—	6,000
Châtillon-sur-Seine	4	44	6,000	(7,600 & 150,000)	267,000
Dijon	2	17	28,570	—	60,400
Mâcon	3	21	3,350	4,200	30,150
Montcenis	1	20	—	600	—
Nuits	1	50	—	33,500	—
Saint-Jean-de-Losne	1	50	—	450	—
Saulieu	1	17	—	64,300	—
Semur-en-Auxois	3	42	57,825	84,675	91,305
Semur-en-Brionnais	1	50	—	2,000	—
Totals	50	40	300	8,100	267,000

Sources: A.D. Côte-d'Or, series Q, registers 11–14, 16, and 17; A.D. Saône-et-Loire, series Q, registers 215, 218, 226, 236, and 239; A.D. Yonne, Q 226 and Q 235.

[a] Where there is only 1 purchaser, his total expenditure is indicated in the "Median(s)" column. Where there are only 2 purchasers, their total expenditures are indicated, respectively, in the "Lowest" and "Highest" columns.

Table 21. Total Assets of the Ten Largest Purchasers of
Nationalized Property among Former Magistrates in Burgundy,
1759–1826.

Purchaser and locality	Expenditures for nationalized property	Total assets		
		At marriage (*Dot du futur*)	In 1799	At death
Iumbert Châtillon	267,000	40,800 (1784)	94,078	—
)ebruère Châtillon	150,000	30,000 (1759)	173,473	87,082 (1806)
;uényot Semur-en-Auxois	91,300	32,000 (1783)	67,292	—
teuillon de Brain Semur-en-Auxois	84,675	—	54,130	—
)upré Saulieu	64,300	33,000 (1763)	59,050	123,237 (1806)
√arjollet Dijon	60,400	—	105,662	—
;reusot Semur-en-Auxois	57,825	—	31,058	28,293 (1807)
tobinet Auxerre	57,325	35,000 (1774)	—	144,000 (1826)
ιbord Autun	35,400	11,000 (1768)	—	175,041 (1822)
)urand Nuits	33,500	—	53,417	—

Sources: As to expenditures, same sources as in Table 20. As to assets, sources ιdicated in footnote 38, this chapter.

declared value of an estate at death is available. The figures
rest essentially on estimates of annual income from property
as reported by the recipient or his heirs.[38] The practice of

38. Marriage contracts: summaries registered 18 July 1763, 19 January 1783, 31 October 1784 (A.D. Côte-d'Or, C 10492, C 8788, C 8441,
respectively), and 16 February 1768 (A.D. Saône-et-Loire, C 972);
notary's minute, 29 December 1774 (A.D. Yonne, étude Guimard, no.
283). Forced loan, Year VII (A.D. Côte-d'Or, L 875). Successions declared 13 January 1807 (Debruère), 24 June 1806 (Dupré), 1 November
1807 (Creusot) (A.D. Côte-d'Or, 8 Q 4/13, 29 Q 4/7, and 31 Q 4/12,
respectively), 18 July 1826 (A.D. Yonne, série Q, enregistrement, bureau
d'Auxerre), and 5 June 1822 (A.D. Saône-et-Loire, série Q, enregistrement, bureau d'Autun).

notaries and tax-collecting authorities was to multiply such estimates by twenty in order to obtain a figure for total assets. It is appropriate to reverse their procedure, and to interpret these figures, divided by twenty, as annual incomes.

As one would surmise, these heavy investors were well-to-do or wealthy. The two youngest, Guényot and Humbert, had married in 1783 and 1784, and had then been promised incomes from landed property of 1,600 and 2,040 livres, respectively; and each income was approximately matched by that contributed to the marriage on behalf of the bride. (Those who married a decade or more earlier had probably experienced some improvement of their incomes, particularly through inheritances.) Forty-two other magistrates in Burgundy, who did not invest heavily in nationalized property, had married during the 1780's, but I have been able to find comparable data for only fourteen of these. Six were provided with larger incomes from rentes and landed property, ranging from 2,500 to 4,250 livres; two were provided with incomes of 1,600 livres; and six were provided with smaller incomes, ranging from 375 to 1,250 livres.[39] The data are too incomplete to reveal whether the two large purchasers of nationalized property, Humbert and Guényot, had incomes very close to average for a bailliage magistrate. It is certain, however, that they were neither the wealthiest nor the poorest among the bailliage magistrates of about their age.

Eight of the former magistrates in Burgundy who invested heavily in nationalized church property were residents of what became the Côte-d'Or department and were assessed there in

39. A.D. Côte-d'Or, C 8000 (17 July 1786), C 8442 (2 October 1785), C 8782 (19 December 1780), C 8788 (11 February 1783), C 8798 (15 February 1787), E 868 (Fyot marriage contract, 6 December 1784); A.D. Saône-et-Loire, C 1000 (14 June 1784), C 1001 (17 September 1784), C 1003 (19 April 1787), C 3049 (7 October 1782), C 3050 (17 January 1783), C 3053 (12 October 1784); A.D. Yonne, C 736 (3 April 1780), C 743 (6 May 1788).

the summer of 1799 for the forced loan of Year VII.[40] Their average income from landed property was 3,219 livres, nearly twice the 1,800 livres that one of them would have received as salary had he been a judge in the department civil court. But there were notable inequalities among these eight heavy investors. Creusot, with an income from landed property of 1,853 livres, declining slightly to 1,723 livres at his death eight years later, was distinctly less well-to-do than any of the others. Debruère's income from landed property, 8,674 livres, was the largest of any former bailliage magistrate in the Côte-d'Or. (He was in a class with Robinet de Pontagny and Abord, who were, in 1810, among the 600 largest taxpayers in their respective departments.[41] Besides the heavy investors in church property, there were thirty-two other former bailliage magistrates living in the Côte-d'Or in 1799: twenty-one of them were not assessed for the forced loan; four were assessed on the basis of incomes between 1,500 and 1,800 livres, and seven were assessed on the basis of incomes over 1,800 livres. According to these assessments, the eight heavy investors in nationalized property in the Côte-d'Or had higher incomes in 1799 than three-fourths of the other former bailliage magistrates still living in the department at that date.[42] The data are insufficient to determine whether these heavy investors improved their relative economic position. It is possible that they did so. But in either case, it seems clear that in 1791 and 1792 the wealthiest

40. This was a surtax on individuals who paid more than 300 francs tax on landed property or paid *contribution mobilière* on property presumed to be worth 100 francs (= 100 livres) or more. Doubtless the assessments reflect some income increases resulting from investments in former church property; but the alternative investments that were not made might have been equally profitable, so these income estimates are best considered as a general index of economic position.

41. A.D. Yonne, III M¹ 9; A.N., F¹ᶜ II 35 (Saône-et-Loire).

42. Of the 7 other former magistrates with comparably high incomes, 5 had purchased no nationalized church property; 1 had invested a sum equivalent to the amount reimbursed for his former office; and 1 had invested triple the value of his office.

former magistrates chose, in approximately equal numbers, one or the other of two contrasting investment decisions: to purchase no nationalized church property at all; or to purchase a large amount, greatly exceeding the liquidated value of a bailliage office.

The large-scale purchasers were evidently engaged in major rearrangements of their landed investment. Narjollet, who had been living in Dijon for twenty years as a judge in the bailliage there, bought the former abbey of Saint-Jean-le-Grand and its lands, at Cirey-lès-Nolay.[43] Humbert's large outlay was partly for wooded hills southwest of Châtillon. He took the opportunity to establish himself in the wholesale fuel business supplying Paris. In September 1794, his importance as a wood-dealer was particularly emphasized by his wife in her plea for his release from prison, where he was being held as a suspect.[44]

In such large investments in nationalized property, it is difficult to perceive a political motive. But there remains the likelihood that former magistrates who spent small sums for nationalized property were actuated in part by a desire to conform to patriotic expectations. In Table 17, we saw that twelve former magistrates in Burgundy spent in this way sums that were notably less than they received for their bailliage offices. A few of these purchases involved very small expenditures. Bachey, the chief judge in Beaune who had been elected to the new district court, received 27,000 livres for his bailliage office and spent 300 livres to purchase a garden that had been nationalized in Beaune. Hernoux, the chief judge in Saint-Jean-de-Losne, who had been selected as a member of the administrative directory of the Côte-d'Or department, received 10,000 livres for his bailliage office and spent 450 livres to purchase a tenant-occupied house in the town. Similarly in Poitou, Faulcon, who should have received about 10,000 livres in the liqui-

43. Sixty kilometers southwest of Dijon. The purchase is recorded in A.D. Côte-d'Or, Q 69[4].
44. A.N., F[7] 4746[2].

dation of his office, spent 800 livres for a meadow and a wooded tract adjacent to his small estate of La Fenêtre; his biographer remarked that the purchase could have been intended to some extent as an example to others.[45]

Rapid completion of the process of liquidating a judicial office was a patriotic action, and so, too, was even a token purchase of nationalized property. But in the liquidation of an office, self-interest and patriotism both pointed toward compliance with the National Assembly's plans. In the expenditure of the proceeds, self-interest and patriotism much more commonly diverged.

Even so, if we compare bailliage magistrates with other occupational categories and social groups, the striking fact is the large proportion of bailliage magistrates who bought at least some nationalized property. Of the tens of thousands of noblemen and the millions of peasants in France, the proportion making some such investment could not have attained the 22 percent that we found among the magistrates of the sénéchaussée of Marseille, still less the 40 percent or more that we found among the magistrates in Burgundy and eastern Poitou.

In all, 1790 and 1791 were years of political and economic revolution for the bailliage magistrates, revolution that most accepted readily and many welcomed. The majority were retired from the judicial profession. Those who continued as judges, or who held other offices, did so as a result not of proprietary right but of elections in which their personal reputations and political attitudes were important assets, but they remained prominent in politics chiefly where sharp conflict between revolutionaries and counterrevolutionaries had not developed. The bailliage magistrates who formulated the National Assembly's policy concerning the liquidation of the offices did not aim primarily to serve their own economic in-

45. Gabriel Debien, "Vie de F. Faulcon," introduction to Faulcon's *Correspondance*, 2 vols. (Poitiers, 1939–1953, as *Archives Historiques du Poitou*, 51 and 55), I, i–xxxiv, on p. xix.

terests and those of their judicial colleagues. Instead, they kept in the foreground considerations of practicality and the larger political objective of disposing of the parlements. The result was a system which inflicted financial losses on some bailliage magistrates but enabled them to liquidate their offices rapidly. The timing of the compensation for the liquidated offices and the sudden availability of capital sums had some influence on their decisions to purchase or not to purchase nationalized property of the church and the royal domain. The desire to cooperate in the transfer of property in order to contribute to monetary and fiscal stability also had some influence on those decisions. But the strongest factor was the desirability of a major change in the composition of an individual's total investment. In 1791, the process of dissolving the judicial companies of the bailliages was completed, eliminating their tendency toward corporate action, and leaving the former magistrates to act henceforth simply as individual property-owners.

VII

Careers of Former Bailliage
Magistrates in Public Life, 1790–1795

The former bailliage magistrates disappeared from public life after 1790 with varying rapidity and completeness in different provinces and localities. Those who continued to participate in politics displayed attitudes and convictions that were extremely various. The extent of political change at each stage of the revolutionary process determined the degree to which they might adapt to new circumstances and occupy newly defined positions of power or, alternatively, might come to appear or to act as counter revolutionaries. As they had held an important place in the bourgeoisie, their destinies reflect some of the ways in which revolutionary political change favored the bourgeoisie and how or when it ceased to do so.

The relationships between individual experiences and social changes are not easy to elucidate. Biographies added together are not history, for they include both too much and too little.[1] On the one hand, some biographical events, when seen in a large perspective, appear inconsequential: the wife of the associate chief judge, Pigenat, sang in concerts at social gatherings in Autun; in his later years the former chief judge of the bailliage of Dijon prepared a very bad translation of the *Aeneid*.[2] On the other hand, not all the potentialities created by a changing social system are revealed in the collective experience of even a great number of men in one occupational category. We should search in vain among the 2,700 former bailliage magistrates for a bishop in the constitutional church or a leader of a crowd fighting in the streets. The most instructive events, therefore, are those that were possible for most but occurred in the biographies of only some former magistrates.

In ordinary times, biographical possibilities are clearly defined by the social order already functioning. Various opportunities were closed, and others opened, as we have seen, for the bailliage magistrates in 1788–1790. A new structure of possibilities was rapidly created by revolutionary processes, and it was transformed more than once during the years after 1790. A career necessarily took on a new social meaning as it was continuously invented. Yet men confronted with threats to the predictability of experience attempt to discover or create it anew. Particularly was this true of those who had recently

1. Lawrence Stone, "Prosopography," *Daedalus, Journal of the American Academy of Arts and Sciences*, 100, no. 1 (Winter 1971), pp. 46–79, presents a judicious discussion of the origins, limitations, and achievements of this mode of inquiry, but refrains from examining the special difficulties resulting from rapid and drastic change.

2. Isaac-Mathieu Crommelin, "Mémoires," ed. Harold de Fontenay, *Mémoires de la Société Eduenne*, 6 (1873), 395–473, mentions Mme Pigenat's performances on p. 418. The translation by Frécot is described by Léon de La Sicotière, "Deux poètes excentriques, l'abbé Gérard des Rivières et Frécot Saint-Edme," *Bulletin de la Société Historique et Archéologique de l'Orne*, 12 (1893), 449–475.

acceded to improved situations in life. To a certain extent, the attempt at mental reordering was successful, and it is possible, in retrospect, to discern and classify turning points in political careers during the years of revolutionary change.

The magistrates in the bailliages, in commencing judicial careers before 1789, had undertaken a responsible and honorable kind of service to the king and his subjects. After 1790, the pivotal question for them was the nature of the new political community to be created and, especially, the extent of their participation in it. The elections to the Estates General had offered an opportunity to enter a new kind of political activity, for which many, having been victorious in elections, voluntarily interrupted their judicial careers. Thereafter, membership in the national legislative body continued to be the preeminent form of participation in politics. It became the ordinary occupation of some politicians, beginning with the elections of August 1792, when former deputies to the National Assembly of 1789–1791 and the Legislative Assembly of 1791–1792 were all eligible for election.

A few former magistrates achieved long legislative careers. In Poitou, fourteen (14.7 percent of the number in office in 1789) served in one legislative body or another during the decade.[3] Seven of these won more than one election. Creuzé de Latouche, Bion, Dutrou de Bornier, and Cochon de Lapparent, who were ineligible for reelection in 1791, emerged thereafter as professional politicians in a sense that would have been recognizable a hundred years afterward. The same

3. *Recueil de documents relatifs à la convocation des Etats Généraux de 1789,* ed. Armand Brette, 4 vols. (Paris, 1894–1915), II; *Les Députés à l'Assemblée législative de 1791,* ed. Auguste Kuscinski (Paris, 1900); Auguste Kuscinski, *Dictionnaire des Conventionnels* (Paris, 1916–1919); *Les Députés au Corps législatif, Conseil des Cinq-Cents, Conseil des Anciens, de l'an IV à l'an VIII,* ed. Auguste Kuscinski (Paris, 1905).

In 1789, Irland de Bazôges was elected a suppléant for the nobility, Faulcon and Cochon de Lapparent suppléants for the Third Estate. Their service as legislators began some months after the opening session, that of Faulcon, the latest to be seated, in April 1790.

Table 22. Legislative Careers of Former Magistrates
in the Sénéchaussées in Poitou, 1789–1799.

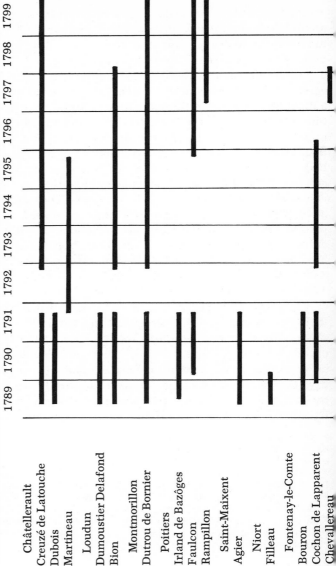

Location of
sénéchaussée;
name of
ex-magistrate

Membership in national legislative body

was true, in a lesser degree, of Rampillon, and of Faulcon (who presided over the legislative body which, early in 1814, voted to depose Napoleon). These six men made the sort of transition that Cobban referred to when he said "a class of officials and professional men moved up from the minor to the major posts in government."[4] But, in making careers in the national legislature, they were exceptional even in a province where former magistrates enjoyed exceptionally widespread popularity.[5]

A different political situation is visible in Burgundy, where ten former magistrates (7.7 percent of the number in office in 1789) served in a legislature.[6] None was subsequently reelected. Eight of those elected came from either Chalon-sur-Saône or Auxerre. The success that former magistrates in Burgundy enjoyed in the legislative elections was thus episodic and local. In this respect, Burgundy typified most of France.

In the nation as a whole, the decisive downturn in the popularity of former bailliage magistrates as legislative candidates was manifest in the first general election under the constitutional monarchy, in late August and early September 1791. They won fewer than 7 percent of the seats. Two years before, bailliage magistrates had won 21 percent of the seats representing the Third Estate; these, like all other members

4. "The Myth of the French Revolution," reprinted in *Aspects of the French Revolution* (London, Jonathan Cape, 1968), on p. 106.
5. In 1789, the Vosges was the other region where bailliage magistrates enjoyed unusual electoral popularity. But it did not persist there in legislative elections as it did in Poitou. Only 3 magistrates (Cherrier and Couhey of Neufchâteau and Fricot of Remiremont) won more than 1 election, and only Cherrier was a legislator for more than 6 years.
6. *Recueil de documents relatifs à la convocation des Etats Généraux*, II; *Les Députés à l'Assemblée législative; Kuscinski, Dictionnaire des Conventionnels; Les Députés au Corps législatif*; Paul Montarlot, *Les Députés de Saône-et-Loire aux assemblées de la Révolution, 1789–1799*, 3 vols. (Autun, 1902–1911, appearing first in installments in the *Mémoires de la Société Eduenne*).
In 1789, Sancy was elected suppléant for his father, who resigned in October of that year. In 1792, Millard was elected a suppléant, and in October 1793 he was called upon to sit as a deputy.

Table 23. Legislative Careers of Former Magistrates
in the Bailliages in Burgundy, 1789–1799.

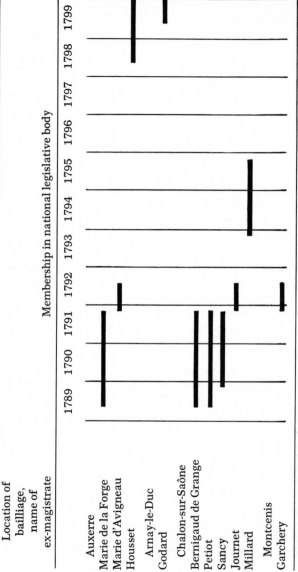

of the National Assembly of 1789–1791, were ineligible for re-election. The electoral circumscriptions in 1791 were no longer the bailliages but new and larger territorial units, the départements. Within a département, electors of one district were commonly unacquainted with candidates and electors from other districts, and on early ballots voted only for men from their own districts. The electoral assemblies were interrupted by visitations and speeches of administrative officials of departments, districts, and municipalities, judges in district courts, officers of the national guard—implicit candidacies were thereby forwarded. The majority of former bailliage magistrates had no such opportunities, since they had not been elected to local administrative or judicial offices in 1790. Historians have tended to assume, perhaps because of the property qualifications for voters and the more stringent ones for persons elected, that the members of the Legislative Assembly were drawn from the same social groups as the deputies in 1789 for the Third Estate. With respect to the relative importance of bailliage magistrates, however, the legislative elections of 1791 were the logical sequel of the administrative and judicial elections the preceding year.[7]

7. Alphonse Méry, "Les Elections à l'assemblée législative de 1791," *Révolution Française*, 67 (1914), 101–124, 247–264; 68 (1915), 15–23, 121–127, presents a general impression, leaving much unexplored; see, however, vol. 67, pp. 115, 123.

The members of this assembly, despite its historic role in voting to declare war and to depose the king, have never been adequately studied, but simply listed by Kuscinski. There were initially 745, including 44 former bailliage magistrates (plus perhaps a half dozen who eluded my researches), not counting men who had resigned bailliage offices before 1789 (the most notable being François, of Neufchâteau, chief judge at Mirecourt from 1776 to 1783) and not counting alternate deputies, a few of whom had been bailliage magistrates.

Dictionnaire de biographie française, ed. Michel Prévost, Jean-Charles Roman d'Amat, et al. (Paris, Letouzey & Ané, 1933–   , in progress), II, 743; V, 421, 361, 1012; VI, 1367; VII, 370, 1162; VIII, 1263; IX, 708, 1124, 1228, 1377; *Dictionnaire des parlementaires français*, ed. Adolphe Robert, Edgar Bourloton, and Gaston Cougny, 5 vols. (Paris, 1891), I,

The next legislative elections, in August and September 1792 for the National Convention, revealed practically no change in the popularity of former bailliage magistrates. They won 5.5 percent of the seats.[8] Almost half of those elected had been deputies for the Third Estate in 1789. One-fourth had been members of the Legislative Assembly. Only eleven former magistrates came directly from local politics to sit in the National Convention when it first met.

The legislative body was incomparably the most important new national institution in both power and size. The executive was limited by it until 1792, then more or less dependent on it until 1799. It was not the sole new institution comprising posts attractive to former bailliage magistrates. But the court of cassation's narrowly circumscribed powers were exercised by only forty-two members. Only a small minority at any time were former bailliage magistrates.[9] For ambitious judges

194; III, 472; IV, 33, 143, 273; V, 74, 135, 204, 309/310, 466; Kuscinski, *Dictionnaire des Conventionnels,* pp. 357, 399, 425, 438/439, 500; Montarlot, *Les Députés de Saône-et-Loire,* I, 20–25, 246–258; Brette, *Recueil,* III, 366, 695, and IV, 566, 603 (Juéry, Chirat, Frécine, Dalibourg); *Almanach de Normandie,* 1790 (Demées, Le Conte de Betz); *Almanach général de la province de Dauphiné,* 1789 (Gaillard); A.N., V¹ 465, 478, 490, 500, 505, 511, 515, 533 (Granet at Toulon, 1773, Lolivier at Saint-Mihiel, 1776, Dehaussy de Robécourt at Péronne, 1778, Rubat at Belley, 1780, Haudouart at Bapaume, 1781, Gosselin de Sancerre at Castres, 1783, Bruley at Tours, 1784, and Pierron at Briey, 1788, respectively).

8. Kuscinski, *Dictionnaire des Conventionnels,* pp. 4, 7, 16, 23, 42, 53, 58, 93, 96, 99, 118, 138, 143/144, 155, 156, 161, 163, 189, 236, 272, 295, 304, 320, 340, 356, 357, 397, 399, 425, 438/439, 442, 453, 475, 500, 504, 518, 524, 552, 581, 593, 597.

9. Six of the 42 elected in early 1791 were former bailliage magistrates. Two years later, there were 8 vacancies; of the 34 judges, 4 were former bailliage magistrates. This includes Albarel, whose position as associate chief judge in the sénéchaussée of Limoux from 1780 to 1790 was not mentioned by Louis-Hector Chaudru de Raynal and Augustin-Charles Renouard, *Le Tribunal et la Cour de cassation. Notices sur le personnel (1791–1879)* (Paris, 1879), pp. 7, 9, 10, 16, 24, 29.

in the lower tribunals, the court offered a career opportunity probably less desirable and less attainable than that which had been presented by the parlements.

Far more than under the old monarchy, careers in the judiciary and in administrative politics developed in a geographically limited context and were controlled by a local constituency. This circumstance gave a new importance to the difference between national and provincial offices, because they involved differing degrees of responsiveness and vulnerability to local factional struggles. In order to examine the careers of the former bailliage magistrates who remained active in public life, it is essential to follow them, as closely as the documentation permits, in the towns where they had sat in the bailliages and in the villages where their landed property was situated.

The administration and the judiciary were organized, in accordance with the political geography adopted in 1789, in a coherent and logical order. Each department consisted of three to nine districts. Each district consisted of a number of cantons, which were, in 1790–1795, electoral circumscriptions but not administrative areas. In the principal locality of the canton, the citizens having the right to vote assembled to choose electors: they also chose a justice of the peace for the non-urban part of the canton. In the principal town of the district, all its electors assembled to choose administrators and judges, and in the principal town of the department all its electors assembled to choose administrators and a chief judge and a prosecutor for the criminal court. In a village or town, all citizens having the right to vote could participate in direct elections of municipal officials. In a commune where the population was sufficiently large, they also elected one or several justices of the peace.

The administration and the judiciary can be visualized as parallel hierarchies. Not all distinctions in the accompanying

Administration	Judiciary

Department

Administration	Judiciary
President (a member of the department council, chosen by it), position abolished in December 1793.	Chief judge of the criminal court (chosen by the electors).
Executive officer (*procureur général syndic,* chosen by the electors), position abolished in December 1793.	Public prosecutor (chosen by the electors).
Directory members (eight, members of the department council; chosen by it in 1790, by the electors in 1792).	
Council members (thirty-six, chosen by the electors), institution abolished in December 1793.	

District

Administration	Judiciary
President (a member of the district council, chosen by it).	Judges of the civil court (five, chosen by the electors).
Executive officer (*procureur syndic,* chosen by the electors), retitled national agent in December 1793 and appointed.	State's attorney (*commissaire du roi,* appointed in 1790; *commissaire national,* chosen by the electors in 1792).
Directory members (four, members of the district council; chosen by it in 1790, by the electors in 1792).	Conciliation service members (five, chosen by the electors).
Council members (twelve, chosen by the electors).	

Commune

Administration	Judiciary
Mayor (one of the municipal officers, chosen by the voters).	
Executive officer (*procureur de la commune,* chosen by the voters) retitled national agent in December 1793 and appointed.	
Municipal officers (number varies: six for a town with 500 to 3,000 in-	Justice(s) of the peace (chosen by the voters).

Administration (continued)
habitants; nine for a town with 3,000
to 10,000 inhabitants; twelve for a
town with 10,000 to 25,000 inhabitants; and so on; chosen by the
voters).

Notables (number varies, fixed as
twice the number of municipal officers; chosen by the voters).

---

presentation make much difference in political reality. Importance rapidly accrued to the distinction between municipal
and higher ranking offices, for, in the municipalities, direct
elections involved a comparatively large fraction of the citizenry. The distinction between districts and departments was
less important. In a district, a geographically concentrated
minority of the department's electors voted and, as a result,
local affiliations and antagonisms could have greater effect.
Politically, the distinction between administrative and judicial
offices did not have nearly the importance attributed to it by
the constitution-makers. Men who had been lawyers or judges
for five years were eligible for election to judicial as well as
administrative posts. Some served in the unpaid administrative
posts (as council members or municipal notables) and judicial
posts simultaneously. Some were elected to one kind of office
and then to the other.

The formal list of offices can be regarded as a scale indicating approximately the extent and the kind of political influence exercised directly or indirectly by an official elected
in 1790 or 1792. In 1793 and thereafter, the intervention of
representatives on mission, the activities of political clubs and
surveillance committees, and the legislative sanction given by
the National Convention especially in the law of 4 December
1793, combined to change radically the methods of selecting
the officials and even, at some points, the list of offices. An
official title could have one political meaning in 1791 and

quite another in 1794. But, for the purpose of mere description, what matters most is a man's ability or inability to make himself politically acceptable, in whatever way this might be accomplished, and his willingness or unwillingness to enter or remain in office.

Description of a career in local politics during the revolutionary period is difficult partly because the number of offices was large and there was no regular progression forming a common pattern. The career that would have been normal, for former bailliage magistrates, was that of judge in a district civil court. For such a career, it was necessary to be elected to the office in the autumn of 1790 and reelected in the autumn of 1792, and to refrain from manifestations of moderatism during 1793–1794 or radicalism during 1794–1795. This kind of career was achieved by six of the fifty-two former magistrates in the Côte-d'Or department,[10] and by two of the sixty-one former magistrates in the Vienne department.[11] Except in a judicial career, a former magistrate active in politics in his department occupied a succession of posts not precisely the same as those held by any other former magistrate. The principal common characteristic of these careers, whether parallel or divergent, was the timing of the critical moments or turning points in them.

The elections of 1790 marked the terminal point in the careers of the majority of bailliage magistrates, and a new beginning for a substantial minority of them. In the Côte-d'Or

10. Guényot, of Semur-en-Auxois; Godard and Cattin, of Arnay-le-Duc; Dromard, of Dijon; Buvée and Gremeret, of Auxonne. The latter 3 continued as judges in the department civil court from 1795 to 1800 and then in judgeships under the Consulate. (A.D. Côte-d'Or, L 215–221; A.N., D III 52, 55 and BB⁵ 43).

11. Pontenier, of Civray; Durand, of Loudun. [Marie de Roux, *La Révolution à Poitiers et dans la Vienne* (Poitiers, 1910, as *Mémoires de la Société des Antiquaires de l'Ouest,* 3rd ser., IV), pp. 319–321, 473; A.N., D III 295–297.]

and Saône-et-Loire departments, nineteen were elected to judgeships in district courts.[12] In the Auxerre and Avallon districts (in the Yonne department), eight were elected to judgeships.[13] Others were elected to administrative posts in the same or the following year, and still others received royal appointments as state's attorneys in district courts.

The next common turning point in the local careers of former bailliage magistrates occurred with the elections of 1792, the first to be held under the Republic and universal male suffrage in the primary assemblies which chose electors. The general effect can be discerned in statistics for Burgundy. Of about one hundred former bailliage magistrates in Côte-d'Or and Saône-et-Loire, thirty-nine occupied administrative or judicial offices in a department, district, or municipality at the beginning of 1792, and twenty-three occupied such offices after the elections at the end of that year. Of the twenty-one former magistrates in the Auxerre and Avallon districts, fifteen occupied the same kinds of offices at the beginning of 1792, and eleven at the end of the year. The former magistrates' position in local politics declined more notably in central and southern than in northern Burgundy. But nowhere was the total result as negative as it had been two years earlier. In the department and district elections for the whole province, taking into account the numbers of former magistrates and of

12. Chaudot, former king's proctor in the bailliage of Auxonne, was elected a judge in the district court at Saint-Jean-de-Losne in October 1790, but never took office. He moved to Saint-Hippolyte (Doubs) early in 1791 and was elected state's attorney in the district court there in November 1792. His absence from Auxonne caused him to be listed as an émigré in February 1794, and correspondence extending through the year was required to clear his name. (A.D. Côte-d'Or, Q 933[9]; A.N., F[7] 5009.) He is among the 19 men referred to here but is not included in Table 24.

13. Villetard, former councillor in the bailliage of Auxerre, was elected a judge in the district court in September 1790. He died a year later, hence is not included in Table 24.

Table 24. Former Bailliage Magistrates in Burgundy in Offices in
Yonne, Côte-d'Or, and Saône-et-Loire, January 1792.

Offices	Administrative			Offices	Judicial			Totals
	Yonne	Côte-d'Or	Saône-et-Loire		Yonne	Côte-d'Or	Saône-et-Loire	
Department directory members		Hernoux	L.-M. Fricaud	Department criminal court	Martineau			3
District executive officers	Soufflot	C.-B. Reuillon	Abord	District court judges	Housset de Champton, Thierriat, Robinet de Pontagny, Marie de La Forge, Letors, Gaudot, Richerolles	Debruère, Chamon, Humbert, Guényot, Godard, Bachey, Dromard, Buvée, Gremeret	Pigenat, L. Garchery, D. Guillemain, P. Aubery, L.-C. Aubery, Perret, Delaye, Monin, Petiot	40
District directory members		Gault						
District council members	Malot		Curé, Lagrange					

				Totals
Mayors	Mariotte, Terrand			7
Commune executive officers	Housset de Fortbois			3
Municipal officers	J.-A. Darentière, Maufoux			4
State's attorneys	Rémond	J. Darentière, Frécot, Cattin, Popelard	L.-A. Fricaud, Pinot, Millard	
Conciliation service members		Simon		11
Justices of the peace	Seurrat, Hay, Arthault	Bitouzet	Saclier	
Totals	12	15	13	54

Sources: A.D. Côte-d'Or, L 210, 215–220; Almanach du département de la Côte-d'Or pour l'an 3e de la liberté (Dijon, 1792); A.D. Saône-et-Loire, 1 L 8/37; A.N., F 1c III Saône-et-Loire 1; Léonce Lex and P. Siraud, Le Conseil général et les conseillers généraux de Saône-et-Loire (1789–1889) (Mâcon, 1888).

Table 25. Former Bailliage Magistrates in Burgundy in Offices in
Yonne, Côte-d'Or, and Saône-et-Loire, January 1793.

	Administrative				Judicial			
Offices	Yonne	Côte-d'Or	Saône-et-Loire	Offices	Yonne	Côte-d'Or	Saône-et-Loire	Totals
Department directory members	Housset de Fortbois		Millard	Department criminal court	Martineau			3
District directory members			Lavaivre	District court judges	Marie de La Forge, Arthault	Petitot, Guényot, Godard, Terrand, Dromard, Buvée, Gremeret, Hernoux	P. Aubery	23
				State's attorneys	Malot	Frécot, Cattin, Boucheron, Gault	Saulnier	
				Conciliation service members	Seurrat, Hay	J. Reuillon, Bruzard, Bitouzet		
Mayors	Robinet de Pontagny, Thierriat		Lagrange, P. Garchery	Justices of the peace	Gaudot	Simon		8
Municipal officers	Housset de Champton	Bruzard						
Totals	4	1	4		7	16	2	34

Sources: A.D. Côte-d'Or, L 210, 215–220; A.D. Saône-et-Loire, 1 L 8/37, 1 L 8/38[2]; A.N., D III 225[9], F[1c] III Saône-et-Loire 1; Léonce

posts to be filled, their electoral popularity was higher than in 1789 or in any other legislative elections.[14]

Yet totals and averages give a deceptive appearance of stability. Of the former magistrates in office at the beginning of 1792, most were not reelected to the same offices at the end of the year. In Burgundy, none of those occupying administrative posts was reelected; only eight of twenty-six judges were reelected; only two of eight state's attorneys were reelected. On the other hand, new careers commenced for a number of former magistrates who had not been elected in 1790. For example, Saulnier of Charolles and Boucheron of Beaune were elected state's attorneys; and Lavaivre de Rigny, older brother of a leading Jacobin in Bourbon-Lancy, was elected to the administrative directory of that district. A few other former magistrates were promoted by the electors to more important positions: Housset de Fortbois, who had been executive officer of the municipality of Auxerre, and Millard, who had been state's attorney in the district court of Chalon-sur-Saône, are the most significant examples; each was elected to the administrative directory of a department. Finally it is noteworthy that after November 1792 none of the district executive officers in Burgundy was a former bailliage magistrate. The administrative position which was to become the key to the revolutionary government of 1793–1794 had already

---

14. The index of their electoral popularity was 1.34 in these elections. This index is the product of two fractions: (the number of former magistrates elected ÷ the total number of former magistrates) × (the number of former magistrates elected ÷ the number of positions to be filled), multiplied, for convenience, by 100. In the elections to the Estates General in 1789, the bailliage magistrates' index of electoral popularity, calculated in the same way, was 0.36 in Burgundy and 0.98 in the nation as a whole.

In a department there were 37 administrative and 2 judicial positions. In a district there were 13 administrative and 11 judicial positions. The departments of Côte-d'Or and Saône-et-Loire and the 14 districts comprised in them totalled 414 positions. (Positions in municipalities could not realistically be included in these calculations.)

been assigned to men from other occupational and social groups.

In Poitou, the administrative and judicial elections of 1792 reveal a more marked decline than in Burgundy in the local political position of former magistrates. At the beginning of the year, there were about sixty former magistrates in sénéchaussées in the Vienne department, of whom fourteen were judges in district courts, four were state's attorneys, one was a department directory member, one was a district directory member, and three were executive officers of districts. Only three of the district court judges were reelected; another, Rampillon (cofounder and first president of the Jacobin club of Poitiers), was elected public prosecutor in the department criminal court. Butaud was reelected to the administrative directory of the department. None of the three district executive officers was reelected.[15]

Still another state of affairs is to be seen in the elections in the Vendée[16] At the beginning of 1792, there were fourteen

15. Roux, *La Révolution à Poitiers et dans la Vienne*, pp. 275, 291, 299, 321, 473–475, and his *Histoire religieuse de la Révolution à Poitiers et dans la Vienne* (Lyon, Librairie Lardanchet, 1952).

For all department and district offices, the former magistrates' index of electoral popularity in the Vienne in 1792 was 0.33, only one-fourth of that in Burgundy.

In the Vosges, the decline in their electoral popularity was not as extensive because the electors of the Mirecourt district elected 2 former magistrates to the district directory and 2 others to the district court, and reelected N.-Fr. Delpierre district executive officer. In other districts, altogether, 6 were elected judges and 1 a member of a district directory. For department and district offices, their index of electoral popularity in the Vosges was 0.92, slightly below that in Burgundy. *Almanach civique du départment des Vôges, pour l'année 1793, seconde de la République française* (Epinal, 1793), pp. 96–119; Jean Kastener, "Tableaux des administrations que se sont succédé dans les Vosges de 1790 à l'an VIII," *Révolution dans les Vosges*, 12 (1923–1924), 142–153, 193–203; 13 (1924–1925), 41–52, 154–166, 222–233; 14 (1925–1926), 26–35, 78–89, 136–147, 219–232; 15 (1926–1927), 16–26, 87–96, 123–135, 189–195, esp. vols. 14 and 15.

16. Charles-L. Chassin, *La Préparation de la guerre de Vendée*, 3 vols. (Paris, 1892), III, 48, 50, 60, 70, 135, 136, 144.

former magistrates in the sénéchaussée of Fontenay-le-Comte, of whom one was chief judge of the department criminal court, two were district court judges, and one was a justice of the peace (Bouron, who had been a deputy in the Estates-General and National Assembly of 1789–1791). All four of these men were chosen by the department electors in 1792. Bouron, "a veritable citizen [who] sometimes warmed up his civic virtue . . . with excellent wine,"[17] was elected executive officer of the department. Raison was reelected chief judge of the criminal court. Three former magistrates were elected to the department council (Desaivre des Guerches, Godet de la Riboullerie, and Beurrey de Châteauroux, the latter two having been district court judges in 1790–1792). At the district level, the absence of former magistrates from administrative offices was complete. Only one judgeship in the Fontenay district court went to a former magistrate, Daudeteau.[18] The elections

17. The description is by Mercier du Rocher, in his memoirs quoted by Chassin, III, 149. He had been defeated by Bouron in the election for the post.

18. In February 1793 he joined the Jacobin club; Bouron, Godet de la Riboullerie, and Beurrey de Châteauroux had been among the founders, in 1791, of the Société ambulante des Amis de la Constitution, as it was then known. (A.D. Vendée, L 1367).

Family ties helped supply cohesiveness to little groups of reform-minded, well-to-do bourgeois in and around Poitou. Daudeteau's relations illustrate this. His brother, the curé of Saint-Nicolas in Fontenay, was the only one of the 3 parish priests who took the oath indicating acceptance of the civil constitution of the clergy. His first wife was a first cousin of Beurrey de Châteauroux (marriage contract, 23 January 1780, ms. minute, A.D. Vendée, III E, étude 8); the date of her death is not known exactly. Before 1789, Daudeteau married M.-A.-Th.-L.-Charlotte Bonnamy de Bellefontaine and thus became part of the Bonnamy-Alquier connection, which was important in both Fontenay and La Rochelle.

It had originated with the marriage of Jean-René Alquier and M.-Fr.-Thérèse Bonnamy de Bellefontaine. Their son was Charles-Jean Alquier, king's advocate in the sénéchaussée of La Rochelle and mayor (his marriage contract, 30 January 1781, ms. minute, Daviaud, notaire, A.D. Charente-Maritime); he became an active revolutionary politician. Their daughter, Marie-Anne Alquier, was married to Mme. Alquier's younger brother, Ch.-A.-J.-Louis Bonnamy de Bellefontaine, *maître particulier des*

of 1792 eliminated none of those previously in office and marked the reentry into politics of only two former magistrates. Half the membership of the sénéchaussée remained in obscurity. The abstentions appear voluntary, for there was plenty of civic work to be done and responsibility to be taken in that troubled area, and no oversupply of men with relevant experience and independent means.

The judges and especially the administrators elected at the end of 1792 were confronted at one point or another in early 1793 with a critical moment in their political careers. They were increasingly troubled during the winter and spring by the intensifying factional strife in the Convention. Letters from some of the deputies opposed to Marat, Robespierre, and the political power of Paris tended to stir up conflict in the provincial towns and contributed to grim expectations. Sooner or later every political participant realized that the factions in the Convention were not going to compose their differences without an appeal to outside forces. This realization became universal with the news that on 2 June the Convention had voted to place twenty-nine of its members and two ministers under house arrest: thereby legality was redefined in a revolutionary fashion under threat of force by the militants of Paris. In response to this event or the antecedent conflict in the Convention, politically active bourgeois made choices whose precise character and determinants are for the most part difficult to ascertain. The difficulties are enhanced by the fact that the next political phase was the revolutionary government of Year II of the Republic. This government punished many who

---

eaux et forêts of Fontenay-le-Comte and a social notable [cf. Leo Desaivre, "Les Salons du maître des eaux et forêts en 1786," *Bulletin de la Société de Statistique, Sciences, Lettres et Arts du Département des Deux-Sèvres,* 6 (1885–1887), 239–249]. These were the parents of Daudeteau's second wife; her sister, Marie-Adelaïde, was married to another magistrate, Parenteau du Beugnon (by contract of 24 November 1789, ms. minute, A.D. Vendée, III E, étude 8), with Bonnamy, then a widower, and Daudeteau and his wife among those present.

had made imprudent choices in early 1793, and has since been itself the subject of extremely divergent retrospective judgments by men who lived through the period and of equally divergent historical interpretations. But the difficulties in knowing what the provincial bourgeois officials thought they were doing are inherent in the political activity of 1793 when the outcome was unforeseeable and ambiguity was safer than clarity.

The choice that officials and political participants had to make was whether to continue as part of an audience subservient to the drama in the Convention or to begin acting independently without waiting for the outcome there. Early in 1793, several department directories proposed to raise troops and send them to Paris to guard the Convention. In May, many believed that the Convention was not free to exercise sovereignty responsibly. They concluded that the departmental administrations throughout France ought to form a federal organization temporarily in order to establish an alternate convention at Bourges. Both these ideas emanated originally from the Brissotin minority within the Convention.[19] Only in planning to act through a league of department administrations were the adherents of the movement "federalists," as they were called by their opponents and are referred to by historians. They rejected a federal republic as an ideal or eventual goal. The movement is most accurately described as a "departmentalist" response to Brissotin leadership from within the Convention. A response organized in this way entailed two presuppositions: that representative authority, if

19. Buzot's report, 8 October 1792, proposing a departmental guard, is in *AP*, LII, 399–400. Guadet's motion, 18 May 1793, that the municipal authorities of Paris be removed and that the alternate deputies be summoned from their home departments to meet in Bourges, is in *AP*, LXV, 46. On 24 May, the directory of Jura ordered the alternate deputies from that department to go to Bourges, accompanied by a detachment of cavalry and a company of grenadiers. From Lons-le-Saunier, this proposal was transmitted to Dijon, Limoges, Poitiers, Rennes, and elsewhere.

its exercise was impaired at the highest level of government, devolved upon lower levels of government; and that this version of the doctrine of popular sovereignty could appropriately be invoked to control the militants in the city of Paris and the Montagnard minority in the Convention, notwithstanding their claims to represent popular well-being. The coalition of Breton and Norman federalists planned to establish a departmental guard for the Convention, dismantle the municipality of Paris and replace it with six municipalities, reduce the power of the Comité de Salut Public and expand that of the council of ministers, recall the Convention members who had been sent on missions in the provinces, abolish the special tribunal for the trial of counterrevolutionary offenders, and closely supervise the future activities of the Jacobin and Cordelier clubs.[20]

Neither the doctrine nor the program of the federalist movement suffices to explain its adherents' motives, which seem a varying mixture of diverse components. Property interests and personal autonomy were menaced by requisitions and conscription; provincial independence was infringed by a centralized government of national defense; provincial self-esteem was injured by the domination of the populace of Paris and its exceptional political and economic claims. Within many provincial towns there was antagonism toward leading Jacobin patriots. There was hatred for some members of the Convention, notably Marat, and allegiance to others. The king's execution had evoked feelings of regret which merged with inchoate plans to restore the monarchy. Of all this, much was concealed by the federalists themselves.[21]

20. Resolutions adopted at Rennes and modified at Caen in June 1793, as analyzed by Albert Goodwin, "The Federalist Movement in Caen during the French Revolution," *Bulletin of the John Rylands Library*, 42 (1959–60), 313–344, on pp. 339–340.

21. Elucidation of their motives is a task for local specialists, one of whom has put the matter excellently: "From beginning to end, federal-

Among the former bailliage magistrates in posts of political responsibility in 1793, the federalists obtained few leaders. Within the Convention, there was Buzot, a former councillor in the bailliage of Evreux, who appears to have been unusually rich compared with other magistrates.[22] In Brittany, there was Roujoux, of Landerneau, who became president of the "central assembly of resistance to oppression" of the insurrectionary administrations of the six Breton departments and the Calvados. In Lyon, the "republican popular commission of public safety," elected by the voters of Rhône-et-Loire in June, assigned important positions to four former magistrates.[23] In Toulouse, the most prominent if not the most influential

---

ism is ambiguity. In a study of this kind, it is especially appropriate to investigate in depth. It is necessary to become acquainted with the individuals themselves, to explore their social milieu, to grasp their relationships with family members and friends, to discern their ambitions, their hopes. The slightest detail can be useful." Paul Nicolle, "Le Mouvement fédéraliste dans l'Orne en 1793," *Annales Historiques de la Révolution Française*, 13 (1936), 481–512; 14 (1937), 215–233; 15 (1938), 12–53, 289–313, 385–410, in vol. 13, p. 483.

22. His widow sent in a claim 30 September 1794 for 152,920 francs in compensation for the destruction of their house and its contents in July 1793; of this sum, 22,000 francs was for the house, 60,000 francs was for Buzot's books, and the rest was for household furnishings (including almost 900 bottles of wine) and personal effects. Their landed property is of course not represented at all in this claim. Albert Soboul, "Sur la fortune de Buzot," *Annales Historiques de la Révolution Française*, 23 (1951), 181–183.

23. Clerjon du Carry, of Villefranche, was elected vice-president at the commission's first meeting 30 June; Laurent-Ponthus Loyer, of Lyon, was elected secretary the next day, and later served as a municipal officer of Lyon during the siege, 8 August–9 October 1793. Faure de Montaland, former chief criminal judge in the sénéchaussée of Lyon, was one of the 8 members of the commission's committee of general security, and Rambaud de la Vernouse, associate chief civil judge from 1772 to 1787, was president of the commission from 16 to 24 July: these 2 were noblemen and royalists. Camille Riffaterre, *Le Mouvement antijacobin et antiparisien à Lyon et dans le Rhône-et-Loire en 1793 (29 mai–15 août)*, 2 vols. (Lyon, 1912–1928, as *Annales de l'Université de Lyon*, n.s. Droit, Lettres, fascs. 24 and 41), II, 25, 26, 113, 538.

federalist was the mayor, Derrey de Belbèze.[24] Ennobled, and very wealthy, he had been a councillor in the sénéchaussée and the syndic of the magistrates before 1790, then a municipal officer and a member of the local Jacobin club.[25] With four municipal officers he set off for Paris in June 1793 to present an address from Toulouse to the Convention, which forestalled this by voting on 24 June to remove him from the mayoralty and order his arrest; he was guillotined a year later. An address actually presented in behalf of the citizens of Angers to the Convention led similarly to the execution of three former magistrates in the sénéchaussée there. It is not clear that all

24. Madeleine Albert, *Le Fédéralisme dans la Haute-Garonne* (Paris, Librairie Universitaire J. Gamber, 1932), p. 74.

Similarly, Nicolas-Remi Lesure, former chief judge in the bailliage of Sainte-Menehould, justice of the peace there, was sent to represent his district in a federalist assembly in Châlons-sur-Marne on 14 June 1793; and Pierre-Jean Sourdille de Lavalette, former king's advocate in the sénéchaussée of Château-Gontier, executive officer of the Laval district, played an important part in the federalist movement in the Mayenne department. They were guillotined in December 1793 and March 1794, respectively. Henri Wallon, *Histoire du tribunal révolutionnaire de Paris,* 6 vols. (Paris, 1880–1882), II, 250, 452.

25. He was 6 years old when his father was ennobled as a *capitoul* in 1754. His older brother, Derrey de Roqueville, chevalier, became advocate general in the *requêtes de l'hôtel du roi* in Paris in 1771 and the next year agreed to pay 64,000 livres for the fief and seigneurie at Belbèze-lès-Toulouse which passed to him after a litigated settlement of their father's inheritance. This estate and land nearby at Rouffiac contained 273 arpents, more than average for a nobleman at Toulouse, and after Derrey's execution (29 June 1794) were evaluated at 122,606 francs.

Abel and Froidefont, *Tableau chronologique des noms de messieurs les capitouls de la ville de Toulouse* (Toulouse, 1786); marriage, Derrey de Roqueville, 5 November 1771 (A.M. Toulouse, GG 348); Derrey family papers (A.D. Haute-Garonne, E 93–96); Robert Forster, *The Nobility of Toulouse in the Eighteenth Century: A Social and Economic Study* (Baltimore, Johns Hopkins Press, 1960); Jean Sentou, *Fortunes et groupes sociaux à Toulouse sous la Révolution (1789–1799). Essai d'histoire statistique* (Toulouse, Edouard Privat, 1969), p. 264.

were leaders, however, in that city's manifestation of resistance
to the Convention.[26]

Leadership in local federalist activity was punished less

26. The department council had shown its antipathy to the Montagnards
in January [texts edited by Canon François Uzureau, *Anjou Historique,*
39 (1939), 212, and 44 (1944), 107]. Four deputies from Maine-et-Loire
(La Revellière-Lépeaux, Leclerc, Le Maignan, and Pilastre) shared the
council's viewpoint.

On 29 May 1793, the 9 sections of the city held meetings and approved
an address drawn up by an ex-Oratorian, Mévolhon, criticizing the Convention for its failure to prepare a constitution, exclaiming over its
"impious session" of 17 May, denouncing the municipality and the
Jacobin club of Paris, demanding the recall of all deputies on mission
[Choudieu, who was a native of Angers and former assistant king's
counsel in the sénéchaussée, was then in Angers seconded by Richard],
and threatening that "the people will go, en masse, to dictate their will"
to the Convention. This was signed by various officials including J.-B.-
Louis La Revellière (older brother of the deputy), Couraudin de la Noue,
and Brevet de Beaujour, former magistrates in the sénéchaussée cur-
rently holding administrative as well as judicial posts. Couraudin, accompanied by a member of the Angers surveillance committee, Des-
pugeols, read the address to the Convention on 6 June and was greeted
by interruptions and protests from the Montagnards (*AP,* LXVI, 93–96).
Three days later he reported to the citizens of Angers concluding that
they should now "exercise their right of sovereignty" [text edited by
Uzureau, *Anjou Historique,* 38 (1938), 163–169].

The "catholic and royal army" of the Vendée entered Angers on 17
June and occupied the city for a week, leaving to besiege Nantes. In
July, the republicans formed a new revolutionary committee in Angers,
and in August and September it instigated the arrests of 20 men for
federalism and related offenses, including the entire directories of the
department and the district. Seven were interrogated by the military
commission of Angers. [The exculpations of La Revellière and Brevet de
Beaujour were edited by Uzureau, *Anjou Historique,* 36 (1936), 198–203,
and 46 (1946), 110–115, respectively; that of Couraudin, in A.N., W
346, denied having anything to do with writing the address of 29 May
and stated that delivering it to the Convention was simply a mistake.]
They were tried by the revolutionary tribunal in Paris: 2 were acquitted
and 5, including the 3 former magistrates, executed on 15 April 1794.

The summary by Uzureau, "Arrestation des fédéralistes angevins,"
Révolution Française, 67 (1914), 230–246, leaves unexplained the political processes that may have generated the offending address to the
Convention and those that may have contributed to selective prosecution:
in particular, the civil war's effects on politics in Angers, the food supply

severely in towns more distant from civil war. For instance, Malot and his sister's husband, Arthault, wrote and circulated a federalist address from citizens of Avallon to the Convention on 10 June 1793. Retribution at the end of the summer consisted of removal from their respective positions in the district court as state's attorney and chief judge, ejection from the Jacobin club which they had organized in 1791, and detention in the local collège for ten months. This ended a couple of promising careers in republican politics.[27]

More commonly, former bailliage magistrates were not political leaders, federalist or otherwise, even where they oc-

---

problem, and the motives of the president of the revolutionary committee, Vial, who had signed the address to the Convention, and Choudieu, who had been a political associate of Couraudin and Brevet de Beaujour.

27. In 1789, Malot drew up the final list of grievances for the Third Estate of Avallon but was defeated in the election of deputies to the Estates General, 94 to 63. He was the first president of the Jacobin club of Avallon in 1791, and he wrote the poem declaimed the following year at the unveiling of a memorial to Mirabeau.

Malot taught rhetoric in the college from 1805 to 1810. In 1811 he was appointed state's attorney (*procureur impérial*). The sub-prefect commented that he was "skilled in the art of guiding the hearts and minds of the young," and in this respect the appointment was "a great loss for many families." He estimated Malot's annual income from property at 4,000 francs. In his seventies, in 1822–1825, Malot conducted an archeological investigation of a Roman site near Vézelay.

Arthault was assistant state's attorney in the correctional court of Avallon under the Directory, then judge in the tribunal of first instance, 1800–1810. In 1807, the state's attorney in the criminal court of the Yonne department said of him: "adequately trained, intelligent, good morals, only much too opinionated"; the chief judge of the court of appeal in Paris said: "excessively partial, especially toward former Jacobins, limited ability, no morality, sordid avarice."

Marriage contract, Arthault, 6 May 1788 (A.D. Yonne, C 743); elections, 1789 (A.N., Bᵃ 78, nos. 56, 57); Pierre Tartat, *Avallon au XVIIIᵉ siècle*, 2 vols. (Avallon, Imprimerie l'Universelle, 1951–1953); statistique personnelle, 1811 (A.D. Yonne, III M¹ 12); Henri Forestier, *L'Yonne au XIXᵉ siècle, 1ᵉ partie (1800–1830)*, 2 vols. (Auxerre, Imprimerie l'Universelle, 1959), II, 619; Jean Bourdon, "Magistrats du Premier Empire. L'épuration de 1807–1808 en Bourgogne," *Annales de Bourgogne*, 18 (1946), 16–36.

cupied prominent positions. In Semur-en-Auxois, the chief judge of the district court and one of the secretaries of the Jacobin club was Guényot. His contribution to the federalist question was a remark to fellow club members that Marat, Robespierre, Danton, and Legendre "are four scoundrels." He was purged from the Jacobin club 9 March 1794, but continued to occupy the judgeship.[28] In Poitiers, as a member of the Vienne department directory, Butaud voted on 27 May 1793 for an anti-Montagnard address to the Convention and on 14 June for the project of an alternate convention in Bourges; but it was not Butaud who was selected to forward the idea to other departments. He was denounced by the Jacobin club and removed from office. He tried thereafter to curry favor with the dominant revolutionary personality in the department, Piorry, and partly perhaps for this reason was not punished further.[29]

Former bailliage magistrates, if still in politics under the Republic, were typically sympathetic to federalist ideas. Such men were also typically no more inclined to take risks in 1793 than they had been in 1788. A noteworthy exception was the former associate chief judge in the sénéchaussée of Toulouse who became the president of the revolutionary tribunal: Montané de La Roque. His origins and conduct resembled those of many former magistrates, in most respects. His career differed primarily in his incautious acceptance of a prestigious but dangerous post.

Jacques-Bernard Montané de La Roque came from a small town (Grenade, in Gascony) where his great-grandfather and his grandfather had been known as bourgeois and his father

28. Marcel Henriot, *Le Club des Jacobins de Semur, 1790–1795* (Dijon, 1933, as *La Révolution en Côte-d'Or*, n.s., fasc. 9), p. 351.
29. Roux, *Histoire religieuse de la Révolution à Poitiers et dans la Vienne*, pp. 115–116, 222; Pierre Massé, *Pierre-François Piorry, Conventionnel et magistrat (1758–1847)* (Poitiers, 1965, as *Mémoires de la Société des Antiquaires de l'Ouest*, 4th ser., 9), p. 47.

was president of the royal administrative-judicial body in charge of direct taxes (the élection).[30] In 1774, at the age of 23, he acquired his judicial office for 14,300 livres.[31] His determination to secure all the honorific and pecuniary rights of the office led to a vigorously contested lawsuit against most of the other magistrates in the sénéchaussée. Harsh statements were made on both sides.[32] But three years later, in May 1788, he had somehow gained an influential position among his col-

30. Jules Villain, *La France moderne. Grand dictionnaire généalogique, historique et biographique.* (*Haute-Garonne et Ariège*), 2 vols. (Montpellier, 1911–1913), I, 552. A descendant, Professor Pierre Montané de La Roque of the faculty of law of Toulouse, has given me supplementary information: Jacques-Bernard Montané's grandfather and father had been ennobled, but the nobility of Toulouse refused to recognize him as a noble in 1789.

31. He mentioned the price in the course of argumentation in a lawsuit (see n. 32). Montané was wealthy, and in 1803 was one of the 550 most heavily taxed residents of the department (A.D. Haute-Garonne, 2 M 7).

32. The chief judge and the councillors, relying on an *arrêt de règlement* of the parlement of 24 July 1777, arranged the assignments of judges to the sénéchaussée's 3 sessions in such a way as to prevent the lieutenants particuliers from presiding in any criminal cases, thereby depriving them of honor and fees. J.-B.-Dominique-Eloy Demont and Jacques-Bernard-Marie Montané de La Roque, *Récapitulation pour Mes Demont et Montané de La Roque, lieutenants-particuliers en la sénéchaussée de Toulouse, contre le juge-mage et les conseillers au même siège, réunis* (Toulouse, 1785); the *Réponse sur soit-montré pour le syndic des officiers de la sénéchaussée de Toulouse contre Mes Demont et Montané, lieutenans-particuliers du même siège* (Toulouse, 1785), p. 1, said of Montané: "Quels regrets pour une compagnie de le compter au nombre de ses membres! . . . Ses confrères out beau lui donner l'example de la modération et de la concorde . . . Sa tête s'échauffe, son coeur s'altère, sa raison l'abandonne; il invoque les lois, il publie leur inexécution, il crie sans cesse que tout est confondu, bouleversé, qu'on n'en veut qu'à ses privilèges"; the *Observations contenant replique, pour Mes Demont et Montané de La Roque, lieutenans-particuliers en la sénéchaussée de Toulouse, contre Me de Lartigue, juge-mage, et contre les conseillers au même siège, et non le syndic des officiers* (Toulouse, 1785), p. 5, replied: "Que les adversaires cessent de diffamer Me Montané, soit dans l'esprit de Nosseigneurs de la cour, soit dans le public, en faisant passer cet officier pour litigieux et tracassier . . ." The

leagues and was a leading figure in their acceptance of the reforms promulgated by Lamoignon. These reforms assigned most of the parlement's duties to the sénéchaussée and permitted it to insist on precedence over its old rival, the law faculty, in public ceremonies.[33] The sénéchaussée's cooperation with Lamoignon was extremely unpopular in Toulouse. As a result, in 1789, in the struggle against the aristocratic provincial estates, lawyers and masters of artisan trades dominated the interim commission of the Third Estate (the essential instrument in the struggle). Yet Montané was again able to move with the tide of opinion. He was the only member of the sénéchaussée elected to the interim commission.[34] But in the election of deputies to the Estates-General, it was the chief judge, Lartigue, who was chosen by the Third Estate.

Montané was elected justice of the peace in Grenade at the end of 1790. Before going there to take up his new duties, he obtained membership in the Jacobin club of Toulouse.[35] Until 1793, his career resembled those of scores if not hundreds of bailliage magistrates and lawyers. He had shown a desire for public recognition, an ability to compete with other aspirants, and a certain flexibility amidst changing circumstances. In the obscurity of his position in Grenade, these qualities were by no means sufficient to make him an obvious candidate for

---

issue was finally settled in favor of Demont and Montané: Extrait des registres du conseil d'état privé du Roy, 20 mars 1786 (ms., property of Pierre Montané de La Roque, to whom I am very grateful for the opportunity to consult these and other documents).

33. Pierre-Henri Thore, "Le Tiers-Etat de Toulouse à la veille des élections de 1789. Querelles intestines et requêtes partisanes (mai–décembre 1788)," *Annales du Midi*, 65 (1953), 181–191.

34. Pierre-Henri Thore, "Le Tiers-Etat de Toulouse à la veille des élections de 1789. L'union dans la lutte contre les Etats de Languedoc (janvier–février 1789)," 8e Congrès de la Fédération des Sociétés Académiques et Savantes de Languedoc-Pyrénées-Gascogne et 26e Congrès de la Fédération Historique du Languedoc Méditerranéen et du Roussillon, Carcassonne, 24–26 mai 1952, [*Actes*], pp. 225–242.

35. 2 January 1791 (A.D. Haute-Garonne, L 4542, fol. 144).

the judgeship in the revolutionary tribunal to which the Convention elected him on 13 March 1793.

The special criminal court in Paris, established under a decree voted on 10 March 1793, later became the major tribunal implementing the policy of Terror. In twenty-five months it sent more than 2,700 men and women to the guillotine.[36] Its primary revolutionary characteristic was the nature of the accusations on which it was to render judgment: "every counter-revolutionary enterprise, every attempt against the liberty, the equality, the unity, the indivisibility of the Republic, the internal and external security of the State, and all plots tending toward the reestablishment of royalty or the establishment of any other authority injurious to the liberty, the equality, and the sovereignty of the people."[37] Much depended on how these phrases were interpreted. The task of interpreting them was initially assigned to Montané de La Roque through a political maneuver.

Montané himself wrote, more than twenty years afterward, that "the right wing in the National Convention, not having been able to prevent the creation of the tribunal . . . wanted the tribunal to be composed of well-known magistrates."[38] He remembered learning this after his arrival in Paris at the end of March 1793; he also learned that his nomination on the secret ballot had resulted from private canvassing by several deputies, including Brulart de Sillery, Estadens, Pémartin, Pérès de Lagesse, Rouzet, and Villar.[39] (It would seem that

36. James L. Godfrey, *Revolutionary Justice, a Study of the Organization, Personnel, and Procedure of the Paris Tribunal, 1793-1795* (Chapel Hill, University of North Carolina Press, 1951), p. 136.

37. *AP*, LX, 95. Procedurally, it is true, there were 2 innovations: the jurors were to vote in public, and no appeal was allowed to the tribunal of cassation.

38. Montané de La Roque to Louis XVIII, 23 August 1814 (ms., property of Professor Pierre Montané de La Roque).

39. Brulart de Sillery was a deputy from Somme; presumably he knew Rouzet through their mutual connection with the loose association of friends of the Orléans family. Villar was bishop of and deputy from

they put Montané forward because he was in fact not a well-known magistrate and because they knew he shared their political views.) Whatever their reasoning, he remembered their telling him "that it was absolutely necessary that he accept the presidency in order to prevent greater misfortunes."[40]

During the four months when Montané was presiding (April–July 1793), the revolutionary tribunal heard accusations against 178 persons. A large majority were set free: 53 percent after interrogatory, simply by a judge's order (*arrêt de non-lieu*), and 17 percent after trial, through acquittal by the jury. Sentences of death were imposed on 25 percent; of deportation or imprisonment, on 5 percent.[41] At the end of July, the prosecutor, Fouquier-Tinville, accused Montané of deleting significant phrases from the minutes of two judgments before turning them over to the printer. Two of the other three judges then serving stated that Montané had lost their confidence. The

---

Mayenne, but a native of Toulouse. Pémartin was from Basses-Pyrénées; Estadens, Pérès de Lagesse, and Rouzet were from Haute-Garonne. (Kuscinski, *Dictionnaire des Conventionnels*, p. 247, 479, 482, 540, 568, 606).

Estadens, Pémartin, and Villar were among those who voted, on 13 April 1793, to impeach Marat for trial by the revolutionary tribunal. Rouzet, a personal antagonist of Marat, abstained; Pérès de Lagesse and Brulart de Sillery were absent, the latter having been put in prison a week before the roll call (*AP*, LXII, 70–75). Pémartin, Pérès de Lagesse, Rouzet, and Villar all voted, on 28 May 1793, to reinstate the Commission des 12; Estadens and Brulart de Sillery did not vote (*AP*, LXV, 534–538). Cf. Alison Patrick, "Political Divisions in the French National Convention, 1792–93," *Journal of Modern History*, 41 (1969), 421–474.

In electing the 5 judges, 12 jurors, prosecutor and other officials of the revolutionary tribunal, each member of the Convention was to cast a single ballot naming all his choices. (*AP*, LX, 113). The number of ballots cast was 377, and each of 10 candidates for judge received 160 to 173 votes. (*AP*, LX, 176.) This concentration in favor of a few candidates indicates that efforts had been made to organize the voting.

40. Montané de La Roque to Louis XVIII, 23 August 1814, as cited in n. 38. (The first 2 men elected judges on 13 March 1793 declined to serve, thereby leaving the presidency open to Montané.)

41. Wallon, I, 433–442; Godfrey, pp. 137, 142.

Comité de Salut Public recommended, and the Convention voted, that Montané be removed from office and imprisoned to await trial by the revolutionary tribunal.[42] During the next eleven months, the numbers accused increased very greatly and the judges left many more decisions to the jury. As a result there were more acquittals, more sentences of deportation or imprisonment and, especially, more death sentences.[43] There can scarcely be doubt that Montané tried to exercise discretionary power both generally in favor of dismissing accusations

42. *AP*, LXX, 32–34. One of the deleted phrases ordered (as required by the law of 10 March 1793) the confiscation of the property of 9 men sentenced to death for attacking the deputy Léonard Bourdon in Orléans on the evening of 16 March. The other phrase attributed counterrevolutionary intentions to Charlotte Corday's act of fatally stabbing Marat on 13 July.

In reporting the matter to the Convention, Prieur (of Marne) said that among the would-be assassins of Bourdon "there were several millionaires" and that, in the second case, the deletion implied "that assassination of a representative of the people was not a crime of lèse-nation. I shall not extend my observations further, the character of Montané's crime is well enough known."

Montané remained in prison for more than a year. He was acquitted on 14 September 1794 and elected by the Convention to a judgeship in Paris on 25 September 1794. Later he served as mayor of Grenade, justice of the peace in Grenade, and, from 1800 to 1811, judge in the criminal court at Toulouse. In 1805, in a request to the Minister of Justice for nomination to the Legion of Honor, Montané said that his real offense in the revolutionary tribunal "was to have opposed openly the death of the nine unfortunate Orléanais, alleged assassins of Léonard Bourdon, victims of anarchy, and the ruin of their families." [Joseph Durieux, "Recherches biographiques. Le président Montané-La Roque," *Révolution Française*, 86 (1933), 353–356, on p. 354.] He was pensioned by the imperial government in 1811 and decorated with the order of the Lys by Louis XVIII 2 months before his death on 17 November 1814.

43. After the election of a new presiding judge and the resumption of judicial activity, the tribunal heard accusations during September–December 1793 against 446 persons, of whom 43 percent were set free (17 percent by arrêt de non-lieu and 26 percent through acquittal), 44 percent were guillotined, and 13 percent were either deported, imprisoned, or held in preventive detention after acquittal. (Wallon, I, 434–443, and II, 479–495, 522–525, 529–533, 542–547; Godfrey, pp. 137, 142, and on p. 149 graph comparing monthly numbers of death sentences and other dispositions of cases.)

and specifically in opposition to the political objectives of dictatorial and popular democrats like Bourdon and Marat. He apparently did not perceive, when he accepted the judgeship in the revolutionary tribunal, that his political attitudes would make the position untenable. The forbearance of Fouquier-Tinville, who did not bring him to trial, prevented it from being fatal.

The experience of Montané de La Roque is significant but parenthetical in an analysis of careers of former bailliage magistrates under the Republic. Many doubtless agreed privately with the opponents of the Montagnards in the prolonged crisis of the first half of 1793. Clearly the few who committed themselves publicly were taught to refrain from doing so; in the aftermath, this lesson was emphasized by the fate of former colleagues whose confidence or self-importance had exceeded the bounds of realism and discretion. The republican electorate at the end of 1792 had largely eliminated former bailliage magistrates from administrative positions that called for initiative and individual responsibility, notably the position of department or district executive officer. Those who had been elected to office had been relegated to judicial posts for the most part. The meaning of this was then modified and underlined by the political events we have just cursorily reviewed.

As a judge, one could secure some degree of immunity from political consequences by avoiding political partisanship. That this was actually possible is illustrated by the career of Louis Dromard, who served as a judge in Dijon continuously from January 1782 when he acquired his bailliage office until December 1803 when he resigned.[44] An element in such a career

44. Elections, A.D. Côte-d'Or, L 218 (for 1790 and 1792), L 211 (for October 1795); reappointments by representatives on mission, L 1114; resignation, A.N., BB[5] 43.

Dromard was an early member of the Jacobin club of Dijon and remained a member though never a leader. He was among those, numbering more than 400, who signed the address 25 August 1794 (a month after Robespierre's execution) urging "measures to be taken to maintain

was the good citizenship implied by continuing as a member of the local Jacobin club without trying to become one of the leaders or influential speakers. Like Dromard in Dijon, four former magistrates occupying office in the nearby small town of Saint-Jean-de-Losne remained club members throughout the revolutionary years.[45] This sort of civic participation was not confined to those former bailliage magistrates who themselves occupied office under the Republic. In Niort, Chauvin (older brother of the Convention member), the Delaroi brothers, and the Palustre brothers—half the former sénéchaussée—were club members.[46] More commonly, however, an official post and club membership were two aspects of one situation.

Another possibility was participation simply in municipal politics. In Auxerre, Robinet de Pontagny was unusually successful in this. A councillor in the bailliage and the intendant's subdelegate, he was from the first a member of the continuing committee (*comité permanent*) which in August 1789 displaced the mayor and council in the municipal revolution in Auxerre. He nearly commenced a career of wider scope, as a candidate for executive officer of the Yonne department in April 1790 losing by 254 to 205 votes; five months later he was elected judge in the Auxerre district court but was not reelected in 1792. His electoral strength within his town was unabated,

---

all the force and energy of the revolutionary government." La Société populaire et régénerée de Dijon à la Convention nationale (ms., A.N., D III 53, dossier 36[5]). It had a momentary national significance. Cf. Louis Hugueney, *Les Clubs dijonnais sous la Révolution* (Dijon, Nourry, 1905), pp. 197–202; Albert Mathiez, *After Robespierre. The Thermidorian Reaction* translated by Catherine Alison Phillips (New York, Alfred A. Knopf, 1931), p. 46.

45. Liste générale des membres composant la société populaire de la commune de Belledéfense, 10 ventose an III [28 February 1795] (A.D. Côte-d'Or, L 2025 [1]): Buvée, Gault, Gremeret, founding members on 23 March 1791, and Hernoux, a member since 8 July 1791, among more than 300 members.

46. Liste des membres, 2 nivose an III [23 December 1794] (A.D. Deux-Sèvres, L 174).

and at the end of 1792 he was elected mayor, a post he still occupied two years later.[47]

The smaller the town, the greater the likelihood that a former bailliage magistrate might continue as an influential personage or even occupy office. A considerable number, difficult to determine precisely, were municipal officials in towns or villages where they were important landowners.[48] Such positions afforded the esteem of the inhabitants, the opportunity to perform public service, and, ordinarily, the possibility of avoiding factional conflict which might require decisive action at great risk. In large towns, these advantages were less reliable.[49] In

47. "Les procès-verbaux de l'administration municipale de la ville d'Auxerre pendant la Révolution," ed. Charles Demay, *Bulletin de la Société des Sciences Historiques et Naturelles de l'Yonne*, 45 (1891), 377–521; 46 (1892), 291–454; 47 (1893), 59–244 and 335–501 (the lacunae, all of 1793 and the first half of 1794 as well as the first 5 months of 1795, are unfortunate); A.N., F $^{1 \, c}$ III Yonne 1; A.D. Yonne, L 647.

Robinet de Pontagny was mayor again from 1800 to 1805. In 1806, the prefect noted: "he is very well educated. He has long enjoyed well-deserved esteem. The positions he has always occupied, his social rank, and his wealth render him widely and honorably known . . . During the Revolution, he showed himself in a prudent way to be a supporter of the new order." (A.D. Yonne, III M^1 12.)

48. Thierriat, former judge in Auxerre, was mayor of Crain in 1793; Lanot, former judge in Poitiers, was executive officer of Bapteresse; Mallet de Fois, another former judge in Poitiers, was mayor of Ceaux. A.D. Yonne, Q 558; A.N., D III 296.

49. In Mâcon, 29 April 1793, a number of wagons loaded with wheat were stopped by a crowd. Municipal officials issued a warning against violation of the law that prohibited interference with movement of grain and went off to obtain an armed force. On returning to the scene they found the crowd gone and they entrusted the grain to a café keeper in the neighborhood. The next day, an armed crowd of men and women moved through the streets shouting opposition to the local authorities. The mayor, Lagrange, former judge in the bailliage of Mâcon, tried to disperse the crowd. He was attacked by women armed with pikes, and people threw stones at him. He fled to the college. His house was surrounded by the crowd, entered, and searched. It took an official proclamation, organized patrols, and the passage of 3 days to end the demonstrations. Soon afterward, Lagrange departed for Montpellier, whence he sent in his resignation on 18 June. Gabriel Badet, "Une Émeute à Macon

areas of civil war, they vanished. Vexiau, former councillor in the sénéchaussée of Fontenay-le-Comte, was mayor of the village of Réaumur in 1793 when a Vendéan force arrived there. He was later accused of having served on their municipal committee, and so was called upon to explain his activities:

When the revolt occurred in your canton, where were you?

Replied that he was at Réaumur in continuing session in the municipality, of which he was a member, and not until the brigands were threatening Réaumur did he withdraw to La Châtaigneraie, remained there until 7 May, at which time, with a pass issued by the commune of La Châtaigneraie he went to Fontenay and remained there until 21 May, at which time he followed the republican troops back to La Châtaigneraie, where he remained until the troops redeployed and did not leave there until 25 May, date of the capture, in order to go to Marans, where he remained eight days, and afterward went to Niort, where he remained another eight days, at the end of which time, at the request of a relative who had lost her husband in the battle of 25 May, he returned to Fontenay, where he remained fifteen days, at the end of which time he returned to Réaumur in accordance with the requests of his wife, whose life was constantly threatened particularly because of his absence.

... Since 5 November, where have you been?

Replied that he has been at Réaumur, Niort, Saint-Maixent, and Poitiers until 20 November, at which time he returned to Réaumur, where he hid until Charette's army returned to Pouzauges, when he withdrew to Saint-Maurice-des-Nouhès, in the canton of la Fougereuse, where he remained until the time when he surrendered and became a prisoner.[50]

The breathlessness of the narrative doubtless owes something to the haste of the clerk for the military commission of Fontenay-le-Peuple, which ordered Vexiau set at liberty.[51] But the short dashes from one beleaguered town to another form a

---

en l'an II" [in reality, "an I"] *Annales de l'Académie de Mâcon*, 3rd ser., 44 (1958–1959), 85–91.

50. Interrogatoire de Jean-Charles Vexiau, maire de Réaumur, 27 nivose an II [16 January 1794], A.D. Vendée, L 1589.

51. A.D. Vendée, L 1586, no. 129.

succession which conveys a state of mind shared to some degree at least by a number of former bailliage magistrates caught between warring factions.

Internal migration, to a village where one's family or landed property was situated or to a city, was probably not very common among former bailliage magistrates in 1793 and the first half of Year II. It is true that many cannot now be easily traced in public documents of that period but reappear as voters, candidates for office, and taxpayers in 1795–1799 or as decedents a few years later. In Burgundy, for example, of 110 former magistrates known to have been alive in 1795, the whereabouts of 38 in early 1794 cannot be positively specified. Doubtless most of these remained quietly in their town houses. Prolonged absence of well-to-do former royal officeholders attracted the attention of revolutionary surveillance committees. In Saulieu (not a very revolutionary community), on orders of the surveillance committee, seals were placed on the property of the former chief civil judge, Laligant, on 7 November 1793. His wife, interrogated, said he was in Paris. Arrested there four days later, Laligant explained that he had been living in Paris since 22 April 1793 and had come back to the Morvan, where he owned property in three different departments, only for the summer.[52] Similarly, seals were placed on the property of the former chief criminal judge, Dupré, on 17 March 1794, and he explained that two months before he had gone to live in Pierrepointe, nearby.[53] It was not difficult, for those who remained in their towns, to keep out of the public eye. In Avallon, Richerolles served as librarian.[54] In Montcenis, Garchery

52. A.D. Côte-d'Or, Q 1031; A.N., F 7 4760 dossier 1 and D III 55 dossier 99.

53. A.D. Côte-d'Or, Q 969.

54. The fact is mentioned in a list of notables drawn up in 1811 by the sub-prefect. Richerolles, whose income was estimated as 6,000 francs, is described as a "landowner and man of letters . . . None of his works is well known." (A.D. Yonne, III M 1 12.)

whiled away his days inventorying the archives of the bailliage.[55]

Few former bailliage magistrates emigrated from revolutionary France. For the country as a whole, 6 percent is a
likely maximum proportion. In Poitou, five former magistrates
in the sénéchaussée of Poitiers and one from Montmorillon
emigrated.[56] Four of these were noblemen. The total amounts
to 6 percent of the number of magistrates in office in 1790 in
the province, which was generally an area of moderately heavy
emigration.[57] On the eastern frontier, the Moselle department
was one where emigration was exceptionally heavy. The total
number of émigrés exceeded 3,800. Among them were nine
former bailliage magistrates, 14 percent of the number in office
in 1790 in the department. Five were from the bailliage of
Metz and seem to have followed the example of twenty members of the Parlement of Metz.[58] Emigration in general was

55. After one year as a legislator, 1791–1792, Garchery had a long
career in local political offices ending with the expiration of a two-year
term as justice of the peace, February 1804. During the next two years he
wrote a half dozen letters to the Minister of Justice and the Minister of
the Interior asking for an appointment ("toutes les places un peu riche-
ment dotées me conviendraient," he observed in his letter of 20 March
1804). In the letter dated 10 October 1806 he mentioned his service as
an archivist. (A.N., F $^{1\ d}$ II G².)

56. From Poitiers, Irland de Bazôges, chief civil judge, Filleau, king's
proctor, and Dutillet, his brother-in-law Dansays, and de Cressac, councillors, departed in late 1791 or early 1792. Roux, *La Révolution à Poitiers
et dans la Vienne,* p. 457. The first 3 mentioned were noblemen, as was
Goudon de la Lande, of Montmorillon, who left at the same time (A.D.
Vienne, Q ¹ 65/1).

No former magistrates were included in the Liste des émigrés du
département des Deux-Sèvres, 8 ventôse an II (A.D. Deux-Sèvres, 5 F 37),
or the Liste générale des émigrés (A.D. Vendée, L 202).

57. Donald Greer, *The Incidence of the Emigration during the French
Revolution* (Cambridge, Mass., Harvard University Press, 1951), pp.
124–125.

58. André Gain, *Liste des émigrés, déportés et condamnés pour cause
révolutionnaire du département de la Moselle,* 2 vols. (Metz, Les Arts
Graphiques, 1925–1932), I, 116, 197, 234, 382, 400; II, 42, 121, 122,
268, 395, 748.

almost negligible in Yonne, moderately heavy in Côte-d'Or, and comparatively light in Saône-et-Loire. Only one former bailliage magistrate in Burgundy is known to have emigrated: Denamps, chief civil judge in Mâcon, whose absence was officially recorded late in 1792 after the fall of the monarchy.[59] He amounted to 0.8 percent of the bailliage judiciary in the province.

The number of bailliage magistrates executed was in general much smaller than the number who emigrated. A proportion less than half of one percent is a probable estimate of the total. None was executed in Burgundy or Poitou. An exceptional concatenation of circumstances could, however, send to the guillotine a substantial proportion of the former magistrates of a particular locality. Of the sixteen magistrates in the sénéchaussée of Angers at the end of 1789, four were executed; one, fighting for the Vendéans in the civil war, was killed in battle.[60] Of the twenty-two magistrates in office in Moulins in 1789, four were among the "counterrevolutionaries" of the Allier department who were transported to Lyon at the end of

59. Charles Porée, alphabetical table, series Q, A.D. Yonne; E. Nolin, alphabetical table, series Q, A.D. Côte-d'Or; Paul Montarlot, "Les Emigrés de Saône-et-Loire," *Mémoires de la Société Eduenne*, n.s., 41 (1913), 75–139; 42 (1914), 149–242; 43 (1919), 17–132; 44 (1920–1923), 9–100, 129–198, 313–328, 343–370; 45 (1924–1927), 5–64, 113–158, 231–296, 347–398; 46 (1928–1931), 7–46, 105–158, 217–268.

60. Besides the 3 accused federalists, Berthelot was executed. His son had joined the Vendéan forces. He was then arrested as the parent of an émigré. The Vendéans took the town of La Flèche, where he lived, and freed him. He received them in his house and was denounced to the military commission of Angers.

Bodard de la Jacopière expressed opposition to the nationalization of ecclesiastical property in May 1790. He went to England in April 1791, returned on a mission to the Vendéan leader Charette, and was killed in April 1796.

Célestin Port, *Dictionnaire historique, géographique et biographique de Maine & Loire et de l'ancienne province d'Anjou*, 2nd ed. rev. by Jacques Levron and Pierre d'Herbécourt, 3 vols. (Angers, H. Siraudeau et Cie, 1965– , in progress), I, 354, 390.

1793, condemned by the Revolutionary Commission presided over by Parein, and executed.[61]

Political processes in Angers and Moulins were alike in two respects. In 1789, the magistrates were accustomed to an important share in local power in these placid, traditional towns far from Paris and Versailles, as is indicated for example by the fact that they drew up corporate cahiers de doléances. In 1793, the situation had been transformed. Each town was near but not in an area of civil war. The political forces operative in the town merely represented, with little clarity or predictability, larger struggles elsewhere. Participation in local politics remained comparatively accessible to former magistrates; the consequences of participation rapidly became incalculable. In detail, however, the fate of the guillotined magistrates was differently determined in the two localities.

In Angers, two to three months after the outbreak of the insurrection to the south and west, neither its effects on the Convention's attitude nor the outcome of the simultaneous struggle within the Convention were obvious. The federalist critique of factionalism in the Convention was clearly pertinent, but the ambiguity and folly of the federalist program had not yet been revealed. The punitive reaction to federalism locally and regionally was likewise difficult to foresee.

In Moulins, the weight of poverty, customary usages, private self-interest, and civic indifference constituted a heavy burden for the little minority of active republicans.[62] But at the end of

61. Jacques Imbert de Balorre, age 65; his wife's brother, Jacques Heulhard de Certilly, age 50, mayor of Moulins from 1786 through 1790; André Dumont, age 33; and Louis Barbara, age 40. The first three were councillors and legally ennobled through other offices held by themselves or their fathers; Barbara was a king's advocate, as his father had been, and a commoner. All except Heulhard de Certilly had signed the reform-minded cahier de doléances of the Moulins magistrates in 1789. (Maurice-Gilbert-Bon Perrot des Gozis, notes, nos. 3253, 3210, and 362, mss., A.D. Allier; and, for Dumont, marriage, 9 June 1789, A.M. Moulins, 490.)

62. This conclusion is conveyed with much illustrative detail in a series of contemporary reports by Antoine Diannyére, a native of Moulins,

the summer of 1793, they found a powerful ally at their side when Fouché, representative on mission for the Convention, arrived. He mobilized them to act against the high cost of food, the misery of the populace, the "egoism" of the rich, the symbols of religious observance, and canonical celibacy which shielded priests from economic responsibility for the welfare of women, children, and old people.[63] The fifteen-member revolutionary committee appointed by Fouché implemented his order to establish a welfare fund. The committee issued a list of eighty-five rich men ordered to pay a capital levy. Among them were Imbert de Balorre, to pay 80,000 francs; Heulhard de Certilly, 50,000 francs; and Barbara, 25,000 francs.[64] Imbert de Balorre, Heulhard de Certilly, and two others protested that it was an illegal tax and declined to pay.[65] In retrospect, the

---

trained in medicine, devoted to economic and social improvement, and Jean Garnier, a priest originally from Brittany, a deputy in 1789–1791 in the Estates General and National Assembly where he had become friendly with Garat, who was Minister of the Interior in the spring and summer of 1793. They depict a province which, compared with some other parts of central France, was dominated by poverty and tradition. *Rapports des agents du Ministre de l'Intérieur dans les départements (1793–an II)*, ed. Pierre Caron, 2 vols. (Paris, Imprimerie Nationale, 1913–1951), I, 253–298, 404–482.

63. *Rapports*, I, 295–297, 439–443. Fouché was in Moulins from 25 September to 1 October. Since April he had relied on Jean-Charles Boissay, *commissaire des guerres* there appointed by the Minister of War, Pache. [Richard Cobb, *Les Armées révolutionnaires. Instrument de la Terreur dans les départements, avril 1793-floréal an II*, 2 vols. (The Hague, Mouton & Co., 1961–1963), I, 141.] Neither Diannyére nor Garnier mentions Boissay; both attribute signal importance to Fouché's authoritative actions.

64. Joseph Cornillon, *Le Bourbonnais sous la Révolution française*, 5 vols. (Vichy, 1888, and Riom, 1889–1895), III, 35. Payment would have necessitated borrowing and perhaps selling land. Some months after the execution of these men, rural property of Heulhard de Certilly was sold to a large number of buyers for a total of about 330,000 francs, and rural property of Imbert de Balorre was sold to a dozen buyers for a total of about 273,000 francs. Cornillon, IV, 213, 216.

65. They were put in the pillory for several hours, with a nearby sign saying: "Mauvais riches, qui n'ont rien donné à la caisse de

unwisdom of the protest is evident. Each of these former magistrates was already incarcerated as a relative of an illegal émigré, having protested to no avail against that measure on 18 June, and Heulhard had been arrested in the first place for sending money to his wife's brother in Freiburg.[66] On the other hand, the chief judge of the department criminal court was their former colleague, Vernin, a moderate.

Between the republicans in the revolutionary committee and the wealthy former magistrates protesting against the tax, the conflict was fundamental because it involved entirely different conceptions of legality and morality. It was also immediate, because of the proximity of Lyon. The capture of the rebel city in October, and the assignment there of Fouché and Collot d'Herbois, led to the creation of repressive and punitive machinery unimaginable in Moulins. The revolutionary committee in Moulins ignored the department criminal court and dispatched to Lyon thirty-two of the many suspects incarcerated in Moulins for trial and execution.[67] From the viewpoint of the four former magistrates among them, this outcome was unforeseeable.

---

bienfaisance." Henry Faure, *Histoire de Moulins* (X^e *siecle-1830*), 2 vols. (Moulins, 1900), I, 263. On 4 December, Garnier reported that for 2 weeks the guillotine had been constantly situated in a central place, with a sign: "Aristocrates, riches, égoïstes, affameurs du peuple, tremblez! Je suis en permanence." Two of the imprisoned rich men had spent 4 hours on the scaffold the previous day; 2 others were there at the time he wrote. *Rapports*, I, 465.

66. Cornillon, III, 10, 104. A fourth former magistrate, Dumont, had been incarcerated since March; he had had a dozen or more horses in the vicinity of Moulins, was suspected of buying them for a nefarious purpose, and was the brother-in-law of Gibon, émigré member of a very wealthy local family (Perrot des Gozis, notes, no. 2302).

67. Cornillon, III, 111–112, describes their petition to Fouché and Collot on 12 December 1793 stating that they intended to arrange a loan obligating themselves severally and jointly in order to pay the sums required by the revolutionary committee in Moulins, and the refusal of the revolutionary committee to agree to their return to Moulins. All were executed on 31 December 1793.

A sequence of events like those in Angers and Moulins resulting in the execution of several former members of one bailliage was rare, but preventive detention as suspects was a common experience for them. It was much more common than for the general population, of which apparently 0.5 to 1.4 percent was actually incarcerated during part or all of Year II of the Republic.[68] In the district of Dijon, 390 suspects were incarcerated at some time in that year, more than three-fourths

68. Methodological difficulties surround any such estimate.

Louis Jacob, *Les Suspects pendant la Révolution, 1789–1794* (Paris, Hachette, 1952), pp. 165–171, attempted to derive conclusions from statements made in debate in the Convention and thereby convinced me that its members did not know how many suspects were imprisoned elsewhere than in Paris.

Other historians have determined the percentage arrested in a local population and then applied the same percentage nationwide. But the fraction arrested was so small that it was practically independent of the size of the total population, locally or nationally.

The number of suspects incarcerated can only be investigated district by district. My estimate here is derived from local studies of 5 comparatively untroubled districts in the southwest and of the Gironde department, a scene of vigorous repression.

Antoine Richard, "Le Comité de surveillance et les suspects de Dax," *Annales Historiques de la Révolution Française*, 7 (1930), 24–40, enumerated 253 prisoners (p. 34). In the 78ᵉ Congrès des Sociétés Savantes, Toulouse, 1953, *Actes*, pp. 185–230, Mme Septe, "Les Suspects dans le district d'Auch," enumerated 334 prisoners (p. 190); René Descadeillas, "Les Suspects pendant la Terreur dans le district de Castelnaudary (Aude)," 147 prisoners (pp. 201, 204); Daniel Ligou, "Les Suspects dans le district de Montauban," 355 prisoners (p. 223). Marcel Rufas, "Le Comité de surveillance et les suspects de Carcassonne," *Annales Historiques de la Révolution Française*, 26 (1954), 232–253, enumerated 120 prisoners. (The totals I selected do not count persons arrested before September 1793 or after August 1794, nor those merely confined to their own residences.)

Pierre Bécamps, "Les Suspects à Bordeaux et dans le département de la Gironde," 78ᵉ Congrès, *Actes*, pp. 167–179, enumerated 5,037 suspects arrested and discovered the dates of 3,846 of the arrests. About three-fourths of the dated arrests occurred from October 1793 through July 1794. This suggests a total of about 4,680 arrests in that period in the 7 districts of the Gironde; doubtless most of the arrests were in Bordeaux.

of them from the city of Dijon.[69] This total was probably slightly lower than the median of all districts, and the concen-

Table 26. Number of Former Bailliage Magistrates in Burgundy Imprisoned as Suspects in Year II, by Districts.

District	Number known to be alive, beginning of Year II[a]	Number imprisoned as suspects for a month or more	Percentage imprisoned
Auxerre	15	3	20
Avallon	5	4	80
Semur-en-Auxois	12	3	25
Arnay-sur-Arroux [Arnay-le-Duc]	3	0	0
Châtillon-sur-Seine	8	5	62.5
Dijon	10	2	20
Belledéfense [Saint-Jean-de-Losne]	5	0	0
Beaune	8	1	12.5
Autun	13	5	38.4
Bellevue-les-Bains [Bourbon-Lancy]	3	2	66.7
Chalon-sur-Saône	10	1	10
Charolles	7	2	28.6
Marcigny	1	0	0
Mâcon	10	5	50
Total	110	33	30

Sources: A.D. Yonne, L 204, L 1404 (f. 334), L 1118; A.D. Côte-d'Or, L 428/30, L 435/5, L 2231/12, L 1638, Q 969; A.D. Saône-et-Loire, 1 L 8/38[2], 2 L 135, 2 L 4/682; A.N., F[7] 4567, 4569[3], 4575, 4712, 4745, 4746[2], 4760[1], 4774[35].

[a] This column omits 9 men of whom I found no trace after 1790 and no record of death, viz. (ages on 22 September 1793 in parentheses): Marie (70), king's advocate, Auxerre; Marlot (58), Châtillon-sur-Seine; Villard (33), Louet (41), and Guyot (48), Dijon; Nuguet (32), Autun; Petit (46), Chalon-sur-Saône; Bouthier (35), Semur-en-Brionnais; Barjaud (64), Mâcon. But it includes Siraudin, of Mâcon, who died in prison in December 1793.

69. Nelly Bazin, "Les Suspects dans le district de Dijon," *Annales de Bourgogne,* 41 (1969), 63–74.

tration of arrests in the city may have been unusual in degree. But the indication is that generally Burgundy was not very far from typical.

In Burgundy, the former bailliage magistrates incarcerated as suspects were 28 to 30 percent of those still living there in September 1793. There were extreme local differences for which no single explanation suffices. On the one hand, continued participation in republican politics involved the possibility of a choice condemned by later events, particularly in connection with the federalist movement as at Avallon. This factor accounts for a minority of the imprisonments of former magistrates. Of those arrested as suspects in Burgundy, only 18 percent had been elected to any kind of public office in 1792. On the other hand, notoriously conservative sentiments, especially if a relative had emigrated, were very likely to attract the attention of a surveillance committee, as in Châtillon-sur-Seine and Mâcon (as well as Moulins). Associated with these factors were the intensity of political conflict in the town, the degree to which the bailliage magistrates had been predominant in the prerevolutionary local elite, and prominence in local politics under the constitutional monarchy. (Of the former magistrates arrested as suspects in Burgundy, 45 percent had been elected to a public office in 1790.) Uncertainty cannot be eliminated from any explanation, because even where a surveillance committee set down a fairly long justification for an arrest the predominant motive of detention is not always clear. The account given by the surveillance committee of Nuits, for the incarceration of the former chief judge of the bailliage, said:

Joseph Durand-Locquin, widower having two daughters aged 12 and 9, arrested in Nuits on 3 brumaire [24 October 1793] on warrant of the surveillance committee dated 11 October, known as a suspect by public notoriety and by a deliberation of the general council of the commune on 29 May 1793, for having loaned money to Charpy, émigré, and for having been violently suspected of hav-

319

ing correspondence with other émigrés. Former lieutenant civil; since, living from his income, 2,000 livres before the Revolution, and since, 3,500 livres according to the declaration he made to the municipality on 1 frimaire [21 November 1793] in the matter of the forced loan. He has had at all times an opinion opposed to the Revolution, has disdained to come to the assemblies of primary voters as well as of the patriots, [is] very despotic in character.[70]

This was drawn up in answer to a questionnaire asking for identity, income, associations, and political opinions of incarcerated suspects. If the questionnaire had not asked about his opinions but had asked for an inventory of his wine cellar,[71] or the names of his personal enemies in Nuits, perhaps a different picture would have emerged. In any event, the gravamen of his alleged offense was friendly communication with émigrés. In this respect he was typical of one large category of suspect former magistrates.

In Poitou, the number of former magistrates incarcerated as suspects was much smaller than in Burgundy and amounted to about 10 percent of those alive on 22 September 1793. Three of the suspects were from Poitiers, two from Civray, and one each from Lusignan, Niort, and Fontenay.[72] If the six émigré magistrates from Poitou had been apprehended in France in Year II, they would have been imprisoned, certainly, and executed, possibly. But even the total number of suspects and émigrés among the former magistrates was less than 18 percent of those in the province. This comparatively small propor-

70. Tableau à remplir par le comité de surveillance de Nuits, 13 germinal an II [2 April 1794] (A.D. Côte-d'Or, L 1638).

71. Such an inventory was made later: "one *pièce* [= 60 gallons] of Vosne red wine of 1793 . . . can be kept several years; two pièces and three *feuillettes* [total, 210 gallons] of Messanges wine, one pièce, of 1786, ready to drink and would not keep for the year . . . the rest can last the year; 79 bottles of *vin extraordinaire* of different years and qualities . . . can be kept for the year." Etat sommaire des vins trouvés chez Joseph Durand-Locquin, 7 vendémiaire an III [28 September 1794] (A.D. Côte-d'Or, Q 969[15]).

72. A.D. Vienne, L 466bis, L 467; A.D. Deux-Sèvres, L 188; A.D. Vendée, L 862, L 1268, L 1273, L 1280.

tion is doubtless to be explained by the regional political history. Many former magistrates harbored more or less royalist sentiments which eliminated them from positions of political responsibility in 1792. Those active in politics were mostly members of the Convention and beyond reach of local surveillance committees. In central and western Poitou, the civil war had a terrifying effect. That struggle, however, remained one for the control of territory in the name of the Republic or the insurgents and did not take on the economic and social aspects that were so important in many other places, notably the Lyon region. In short, the political situation in Poitou was comparatively simple and unambiguous, and for well-to-do men who kept out of the way of the armies it was relatively easy to avoid imprisonment as a suspect.

In both Burgundy and Poitou, former magistrates were designated as suspects and incarcerated more commonly in large than in small towns. In Languedoc, the sénéchaussées had nearly all been located in large towns, where, it appears, similar tendencies were operative. Besides Derrey de Belbeze and Montané de La Roque, fifteen to eighteen former magistrates in Toulouse were still alive at the beginning of Year II (not all in Toulouse). Four were imprisoned as suspects.[73] In Montpellier, of the sixteen to nineteen former magistrates in the sénéchaussée, five were imprisoned; and in Béziers, of thirteen former magistrates, six were imprisoned.[74]

Imprisonment as a suspect is the last of the turning points in

73. Jean-François-Rose Duroux, a former capitoul's son, king's advocate from 1786 in the office previously held by his father-in-law, Loubeau (A.N., V¹ 524, and A.D. Haute-Garonne, 3 E 10790, marriage 27 July 1777); Antoine-J.B. Delaporte-Marignac, also a former capitoul's son, king's advocate from 1765; Pierre-Paul Baric, councillor from 1776; and Jean-François-Madeleine Corail, councillor from 1785, brother of the advocate and law professor Corail de Sainte-Foy. Raymond de Bouglon, *Les Reclus de Toulouse sous la Terreur. Registres officiels concernant les citoyens emprisonnés comme suspects*, 2 vols. (Toulouse, 1895), I, 59, 96, 163; II, 59.

74. A.D. Hérault, L 4168, L 3202.

former magistrates' careers to be examined here. To a considerable degree, in Burgundy, these episodes of political choice on the part of former magistrates or their fellow citizens involved the same former magistrates who had sought election in 1790 or had purchased nationalized property. At the beginning of the Revolution, 44 percent of the bailliage magistrates in Burgundy withdrew into private life with the liquidation of the bailliages; 17 percent purchased some nationalized property but were not elected to office; 16 percent were elected to office but purchased no nationalized property; and 23 percent were elected to office and purchased some nationalized property. Those involved in public life later on, as elected officials or as imprisoned suspects, came almost entirely from among the victors in elections and buyers of land in 1790 and 1791.

The Republic, especially after the outbreak of civil war, marked a new phase that appears in the statistics. In Burgundy, of the former magistrates who had purchased nationalized property in 1790–1791 but had not been elected to office, 18 percent were elected to office in 1792; of the others, who continued in private life, 33 percent were arrested as suspects. Of those who had been elected in 1790 but had bought no nationalized property, 38 percent were elected to office in 1792; of the rest, who returned to private life, half were arrested as suspects and most reappeared in politics under the Directory. Of those who had been elected in 1790 and had purchased some nationalized property, 52 percent were elected to office in 1792 and 24 percent (distributed equally between officials and private citizens) were later imprisoned as suspects; again, most continued in politics under the Directory, although recent experience could not have failed to chill the ardent desires for reform and political participation that were common among them in 1790 and 1791.

The careers of the former bailliage magistrates traced a complex pattern in which psychological as well as sociological factors were involved. Bailliage magistrates before the Revolution were not an absolutely homogeneous social category. In particular, they exhibited differences in wealth and family status.

Those elected under the Republic were in a variety of economic positions ranging from affluent to precarious. In Burgundy, of the thirty-three elected to offices in 1792, eleven marriage contracts are available for scrutiny. The wealthiest, Joly, elected chief judge of the district court of Châtillon-sur-Seine, declined the office. At his marriage in 1785, income-producing assets valued at 83,000 livres had been bestowed on him and his bride, indicating an income in excess of 4,000 francs in 1792. This total does not include his bailliage office, which he donated to the treasury in 1789 as a patriotic gift.[75] The least well-to-do of the eleven men whose position can be determined was Gremeret, reelected a judge in the district court of Saint-Jean-de-Losne. At his marriage in 1786, he received 2,000 livres in cash and his bride received assets valued at 11,800 livres. These figures would suggest an income of about 700 francs in 1792. In addition, in the liquidation of his bailliage office Gremeret had received about 2,500 livres and he had invested 2,425 livres in nationalized land. Even so, a judge's salary of 1,800 francs must have been important to him.[76] Of the other nine marriage contracts, six bestowed total assets between 37,000 and 63,000 livres in value, indicating annual incomes between 1,800 and 3,200 francs from property owned.[77] If

75. Joly was a candidate in 1792 for state's attorney, the post that resembled his bailliage office, but was defeated 36 to 30. (A.D. Côte-d'Or, L 217.) A summary of his marriage contract was registered 3 October 1785 (A.D. Côte-d'Or, C 8442). His patriotic gift was recorded in the *Extrait du registre des dons patriotiques* as no. 2233. At his death, he left a house and 2 domaines valued at a total of 41,250 francs (succession declared 6 July 1807, A.D. Côte-d'Or, 8 Q 4/13, fol. 139 verso).

76. Marriage contract summary registered 17 July 1786 (A.D. Côte-d'Or, C 8000); capital value of office and transfer taxes (A.N., V¹ 515); biens nationaux (A.D. Côte-d'Or, Q 16).

77. Marriage contracts registered 3 April 1780 (A.D. Yonne, C 736), 19 December 1780 (A.D. Côte-d'Or, C 8782), 19 January 1783 (A.D.

these marriage contracts are a fair sample, then for about one-third of the former bailliage magistrates in Burgundy elected to remunerative offices in 1792 the salary would double or more than double their incomes, but for about two-thirds of them the salary would supplement an already comfortable income.

Ten of the eleven men whose marriage contracts indicate to us their economic position had been elected to offices in 1790 as well as in 1792. Forty other former bailliage magistrates in Burgundy were also elected to offices in 1790, but for only four of them has it been possible to locate marriage contracts or comparable evidence. Thirty-three former bailliage magistrates were imprisoned as suspects in 1793–1794, but for only five of them has it been possible to locate such documents. Accordingly, no answer can be given to the question whether the former magistrates elected in 1792 were, on the average, less well to do than those elected two years earlier or those imprisoned as suspects later. It is clear, however, that the range of incomes had been as wide among those elected in 1790 as it was among those elected in 1792.

Before the Revolution, the principal status differentiation among the bailliage magistrates in Burgundy had been indicated by one's father's occupation. A minority of upper bourgeois families was established in the bailliage judiciary. Magistrates from these families were generally sons of bailliage magistrates or of holders of ennobling offices in a chambre des comptes or a chancellery. Of the magistrates in office in 1789 in Burgundy, 26 percent were sons of bailliage magistrates and 9 percent were sons of ennobling officeholders. Similar proportions were maintained among those elected in 1790 to new offices: 26 percent were sons of bailliage magistrates, 12 per-

Côte-d'Or, C 8788); notary's minute, 6 November 1774 (A.D. Yonne, étude Guimard); registration 17 September 1784 (A.D. Saône-et-Loire, C 1001).

cent were sons of holders of ennobling offices. In the elections
of 1792, there was a noticeable change: 22 percent of those
elected were sons of bailliage magistrates, 6 percent were sons
of holders of ennobling offices. Thus in Burgundy there was a
slight shift favoring former magistrates who had been, before
the Revolution, rising within the bourgeoisie by holding bailliage offices. On the other hand, it is noteworthy that in 1793–
1794, of the former magistrates imprisoned as suspects, 24
percent were sons of bailliage magistrates and 9 percent were
sons of holders of ennobling offices. Established high status
within the bourgeoisie did not systematically affect the likelihood of arrest as a suspect in Burgundy as a whole, although it
may have done so in some localities.

The experiences that were fairly typical for former bailliage
magistrates during the revolutionary years were the conduct
of affairs as landed proprietors, local public careers with
limited responsibility and limited risk, and the possibility of
arrest and imprisonment for incautious actions. There were a
few active opponents of constitutional monarchy, some of
whom fought in royalist armies against the republic: the handful of émigrés from Poitou, for example. Finally, a very small
number of former bailliage magistrates were uncompromising,
revolutionary republicans. Their careers are of interest because
they were so exceptional.

In the elections of 1792, which relegated many former bailliage magistrates to the judiciary, the municipalities, or private
life, a few were promoted to important new responsibilities.
One of these was Housset, a physician's son, then twenty-seven
years old. He had been king's advocate in the bailliage of
Auxerre since 1785, then, in 1790, municipal officer, in 1791
executive officer of the town of Auxerre. He was elected a
member of the administrative directory of the Yonne department. He held this post throughout Year II, and in the anti-
Jacobin reaction which followed was ordered, as a "terrorist,"

to surrender any arms he might have in his possession.[78]

Of more than a hundred former bailliage magistrates in Burgundy, only one other had a rising career parallel to Housset's. This was Millard, son of a vintner and merchant in Chalon-sur-Saône, associate chief criminal judge in the bailliage there from 1787. A municipal officer in 1790 and 1791, he was elected an alternate deputy to the Convention in September 1792 and a member of the administrative directory of Saône-et-Loire two months later. He was called to take a seat in the Convention in October 1793, and was one of only a dozen former bailliage magistrates who came to the Convention straight from local politics without prior legislative experience in 1789–1791 or 1791–1792.

Millard followed the Montagnard leadership. He developed the ferocity that was common in the spring of Year II, and a sans-culotte attitude which condemned his former professional colleagues and social acquaintances. On 24 March 1794, he wrote to the Jacobin club in Chalon-sur-Saône:

Do you want to know why your administrative bodies and your tribunals have been so affected with gangrene . . . You named as electors lawyers, practitioners, judges, big merchants, in short, statesmen. *Eh parbleu!* They have filled the tribunals and the administrative bodies only with themselves and their ilk . . .

Read and re-read the two reports of Saint-Just.[79]

78. "Les Procès-verbaux de l'administration municipale," ed. Demay; A.D. Yonne, L 326; *Département de l'Yonne. Procès-verbaux de l'administration départementale* [1790–1795], ed. Françis Molard, Charles Schmidt, Charles Porée et al., 7 vols. (Auxerre, 1889–1913), V–VII, passim.

The disarmament order, issued by the representative Mailhe on 12 May 1795, was rescinded 3 months later. Housset was appointed state's attorney in the department civil and criminal courts and, in 1798, elected to the Corps législatif, where he opposed Bonaparte's coup d'état the following year. His name does not appear on the lists of most heavily taxed residents and wealthy notable persons in Auxerre under the Consulate and Empire.

79. Millard aux sans-culottes de Chalon, 4 germinal an II (A.N., D III 225²). The reports of Saint-Just are those of 8 ventôse [26 February

And a month later:

> Nothing new to tell you for the moment. The revolutionary tribunal is charging forward more than ever. They are being dispatched in twenties and thirties at present. Three days ago it sent the members of the Parlement of Paris as well as those of Toulouse to sit in the other world.[80]

What differentiated Millard from most other bailliage magistrates was apparently an unusual combination of personal qualities. A fellow member of the Convention, also from Saône-et-Loire, described him with some sympathy:

> Millard does not have a fortune and having spent his time and efforts for the revolution he needs a position whose salary suffices for his needs . . .
>
> Millard is a man of probity, very hard work, mediocre intelligence, an ardent patriot. Not at all amicable, he has made himself many enemies in his home area through an inordinate liking for denunciations. What would suit him would be a position in Paris which would require much writing and assiduousness, in which contacts with the public would be few. He has an uncommon aptitude for continuous work.[81]

Some of the same qualities are discernible in Perrotin de Chevagnes, a former councillor in the sénéchaussée of Moulins

---

1794] and 23 ventôse [13 March 1794] (*AP*, LXXXV, 516–520, and LXXXVI, 434–441).

This, with 4 other extracts from Millard's letters, was enclosed in a denunciation of him drawn up in June 1795 during the anti-Jacobin reaction and transmitted to the Convention. Quotations from 2 of the other letters are given by Montarlot, *Les Députés de Saône-et-Loire*, II, 256, 260.

80. A.N., D III 225².

81. Observations de J.-B. Chamborre sur le tableau des commissaires du Directoire nommés provisoirement dans le département de Saône-et-Loire, 8 frimaire an IV [29 November 1795] (A.N., AF III 301); the phrase translated here as "not at all amicable" is, in the original, "nullement liant."

Addressed to Reubell, these remarks apparently contributed to Millard's appointment as commissioner for the Directory in the correctional court of the Paris suburb of Saint-Denis (renamed Françiade), a post he held until 1800.

who had an exemplary career in local revolutionary politics.[82] In November 1793 he was selected as vice president of the temporary commission organized in Lyon by Fouché and Collot d'Herbois. As such he signed the Instruction which it addressed to the department administrators, the rural municipalities, and the revolutionary committees on 16 November and which constitutes a remarkable statement of a particular variety of revolutionary radicalism.[83] At the end of November, he wrote the surveillance committee in Moulins a letter notable for its political inflexibility and its contrast between the corrupt guilt in Lyon and the public spirit and punitive legality to be developed by the commission.[84] He exemplifies the puritanical and moralizing tendency that Richard Cobb found among the men from Bourbonnais who were members.[85] Two

82. Gabriel-François Perrotin de Chevagnes was born about 1752, son of J.-B. Perrotin, king's proctor in the bureau des finances (who died when his son was less than 12 years old) and Marie-Elisabeth Petitjean, daughter of a collector of tailles. In 1776 he became a councillor in the sénéchaussée. In 1783 he became a Trésorier de France in the bureau des finances as well, and married Marie Burin, daughter of a proctor practicing before the sénéchaussée; their son, Charles, died 4 years later. (Under prerevolutionary law, Perrotin could expect to be legally ennobled in 1803.) In mid-1787, he was one of the founders of the Société de Moulins, the forerunner of the local Jacobin club. Two of his colleagues, elected to the society later in the year, Barbara and Dumont, were to be among those executed on the last day of 1793.

Perrotin was elected executive officer of the district of Moulins in June 1790. In the sales of former ecclesiastical property, he bought an estate with a vineyard in Bresnay, a short distance south of Moulins, for 30,900 livres. Elected a judge in the district court in November 1792, he still occupied that office in late 1793 while continuing actively in the Jacobin club.

A.D. Allier, D 39, B 855; A.M. Moulins, 496; Perrot des Gozis, notes, no. 4602, mss., A.D. Allier; Faure, I, 169, 248; Cornillon, I, 270.

83. The text is in *Die Sansculotten von Paris. Dokumente zur Geschichte der Volksbewegung, 1793–1794*, ed. Walter Markov and Albert Soboul (Berlin, Akademie-Verlag, 1957), pp. 218–236.

84. Quoted by Cornillon, II, 124.

85. "La Commission temporaire de Commune-Affranchie (brumaire-germinal an II)," *Cahiers d'Histoire*, 2 (1947), reprinted in Cobb's

days after the execution of the thirty-two wealthy counter-revolutionaries from the Allier department, among whom were four of his former colleagues, he wrote: "Aristocracy is a gangrene that does not heal; it has to be amputated, otherwise it reaches the sound and little enlightened part of the people."[86] This expresses concisely a philosophy that very few former bailliage magistrates could fully share even at that critical moment. Yet it was not Perrotin who appeared out of touch with political realities and popular needs. After the temporary commission was dissolved, he was imprisoned briefly but then from 1795 to 1799 occupied a succession of elective and appointive posts.[87]

The majority of bailliage magistrates revealed, during the revolutionary years, inaptitude for democratic politics, reluctance to engage in factional controversy, and inability to set aside their commitment to some familiar conception of legality. Ambiguity and lack of clarity nurture political disagreement. Once the administrative monarchy's constitutional status, indefinite as it was in 1788, had fundamentally disintegrated, the remainder of existing legality was questionable. A whole array of issues emerged on which the former bailliage magistrates disagreed. Their disagreements appear in every political context, even what had previously been the corporate group of judicial colleagues. In Chalon-sur-Saône, for an extreme instance, the chief judge, Bernigaud de Granges, was a royalist who regarded all the major changes after 17 June 1789 as fun-

---

Terreur et subsistances, 1793–1795 (Paris, Librairie Clavreuil, 1965), where this observation appears on p. 87.

86. Quoted by Cornillon, II, 125.

87. Perrotin, together with other members of the Commission temporaire, was imprisoned in Grenoble in September 1795. The Comité de Sûreté Générale ordered his release on 25 October 1795. A week later he was elected municipal officer in Moulins; in February 1797 he was appointed commissioner for the Directory in the municipality; and in April 1798 he was elected chief judge of the criminal court of the Allier department, but he was not reelected the following year. Cobb, p. 86 (note); Faure, I, 329; Cornillon, V, 280.

damentally wrong; Journet accepted the constitutional monarchy with satisfaction and the Republic with reluctance, although he held local office under the Directory; Sancy was active for a time in republican politics, as a member of the local surveillance committee in September 1792 and executive officer of the municipality in Year II, but was unwilling to serve in the department directory in 1795; and Millard had been a colleague of all these men. The Revolution did undoubtedly proceed through class conflict, but it also generated disagreements over principle and hatred between persons among the bourgeois magistrates.

In one sense, revolutions are not made by majorities. It is important that a few former bailliage magistrates were able and willing to participate in a new and conflict-ridden kind of political life, even after the execution of the king in whose name they had previously rendered judgments and after the suspension of any constitutional legality resembling that for which their training and experience suited them. With this important fact the historian is obliged to consider the social value of endurance, the survival of the majority which sustains continuity and permits change while limiting its pace. It was of some value to Napoleon that many former bailliage magistrates reappeared, after 1800, on those lists of heavily taxed residents and local notables from which he sought to organize a new polity embodying consensus.[88]

88. In Poitou, more than half the magistrates in office in 1790 were among the most heavily taxed or the notable residents in 1802–1805. Many of the rest had died in the intervening years.

In the Vienne, of 59 magistrates, 32 were listed as notables of the department on 24 April 1805 and 25 of them had been among the 550 most heavily taxed residents on 28 February 1803. In Deux-Sèvres, there had been 10 magistrates at Saint-Maixent of whom 5 were listed as notables of the arrondissement of Niort in 1802, and 10 magistrates at Niort of whom 8 were among the town's 100 most heavily taxed residents on 25 February 1803. (A.D. Vienne, 3 M 2³; A.D. Deux-Sèvres, 3 M¹¹ 1.)

In Burgundy, the continuity of the population of former magistrates was less steady, the willingness to cooperate actively with the Napoleonic

The men who had begun their careers in the service of Louis XVI as judges and king's counsel diverged, in the early nineteenth century, in their appreciations of the recent past. Some were reluctant to discuss it in public. A legal scholar, amateur scientist, and philosophe, Juge de Saint-Martin, published a slender volume in 1817 on the social history of Limoges during the previous half century. Concerning the revolutionary years he said:

Two events that could not be foreseen principally contributed to upsetting our style of existence. I mean the fire of 6 September 1790, which consumed one-third of the town, and the revolution which overturned all received ideas, all ranks, all fortunes. The damage caused by the fire was soon repaired. Help of every kind was provided for the unfortunates who had lost, in a moment, all they had in the world . . .

Effects of the revolution. I remember it only as like a river for long in flood which finally subsided into its course.[89]

There was much that he might have remembered. As a councillor in the sénéchaussée, he had signed the cahier de doléances in which the magistrates of Limoges called for abolition of their own and other judicial offices and for election of judges. His brother-in-law, Pétiniaud de Beaupeyrat, was chosen mayor in the municipal revolution of August 1789. Juge was elected a judge in the district court the following year. A cofounder of the Jacobin club of Limoges, he was its president in May 1791. The federalist agitation led to the trial and acquittal of his brother-in-law on charges of aristocratic and uncivic conduct

---

regime more common among those who remained in place. A considerable number of letters from former magistrates asking for appointments came to the ministries. An extreme example was from Humbert, former associate chief judge at Châtillon-sur-Seine, to Bonaparte himself two months after the coup d'état of brumaire, asking for "une fonction publique honorable" and saying "Mes principes sont les vôtres, Citoyen Consul" (A.N., F^{1d} II H^5).

89. Jacques-Joseph Juge, *Changemens survenus dans les moeurs des habitans de Limoges, depuis une cinquantaine d'années* (Limoges, 1817), pp. 87–88.

in 1793. His older brother, a director in the seminary and canon of the cathedral of Limoges, declined to take the required oath to the constitution, was deported to Rochefort, and died of illness there in 1794. His younger brother was appointed the Directory's commissioner in the municipality in late 1795 at the same time he was elected a judge in the department civil court.[90] The old man, aged 74, who looked back with such extreme discretion may have had in mind present political circumstances or personal considerations.

Others thought that they had experienced an unparalleled cataclysm. Coutineau, who had overcome troublesome difficulties in obtaining his judgeship in Poitiers in 1780, noted in his journal in 1802:

I had interrupted writing in this register because of the revolution which supervened, which covered France with mourning through the blood it spilled, which destroyed everything, despoiled us of our positions, of our fortunes, and made us languish in prisons with which France was filled. I shall not undertake to set down the details of all the horrors and atrocities that were committed through the overturning of the altars, the destruction of religion. I leave it to history to set down the details, my pen refuses to sketch such horrors here. Posterity will have difficulty believing them.[91]

Still others were ready to amalgamate the diverse elements of the past, diminishing their symbolic value so as to form a more comfortable present. Brochot du Breuil, former chief judge at Arnay-le-Duc, had become presiding judge of the tribunal of first instance at Autun in 1801 when he inquired of the Minister of Justice:

I am charged by the tribunal to consult you as to the rank which belongs to judicial bodies in public ceremonies. Under the old re-

90. Alfred Leroux, "J.-J. Juge Saint-Martin (1743–1824)," *Bulletin de la Société Archéologique et Historique du Limousin*, 30 (1882), 41–42; L.-Barthélemy Breton, Les activités judiciaires et politiques à Limoges et dans la Haute-Vienne sous la première Révolution, 2 vols. (typewritten, deposited in A.D. Haute-Vienne), I, 75, 389, 390.

91. Simon-Pierre Coutineau, ms. journal (on loan to A.D. Vienne).

gime, the judges had precedence; but the Constituent Assembly took it from them to give it to the administrative bodies and even to the municipal officers. Should this rule still be followed? I think not . . . I beg you to send your decision to me before the festival of 14 July. [92]

To us it must seem absurd to recommence the antiquated contest for ceremonial precedence on the occasion when the capture of the Bastille was to be commemorated. Certainly it was an exaggeration for Coutineau, remembering tranquillity with emotion, to imply that intervening events had despoiled him of his fortune: before five years had passed, he bequeathed to his nieces 3,800 francs in rentes, two houses in Poitiers, and a farm nearby, evaluated altogether at 18,000 francs.[93]

Historical change, transmitting a divisive past and making possible anachronism and nostalgia, affected Juge de Saint-Martin, Brochot du Breuil, and Coutineau, and their former colleagues, in ways that are immeasurable.

92. A.N., BB[5] 163.
93. Succession declared 10 November 1807 (A.D. Vienne, Q registre 4422, fol. 9). It was almost as exaggerated to say that he "languished in prison" during the year he spent locked in the convent of La Trinité in Poitiers (A.D. Vienne, L 467).

VIII

Conclusion

A revolution presents in acute form that classic dilemma of historical thought, the need to understand both structure and process. Indeed, the problem here is more complex than a dilemma, for the revolutionary process itself is multiple. The finest perception of a reality of revolutionary change is necessarily partial and inevitably depends on an assumption that other aspects of the process are understood. Hence the urge to explain everything all at once. Hence also those schematic narratives, which began to originate in 1789 as efforts to comprehend the French Revolution in a totality. These provide themes to which a monographic study such as the present one can be related and on which it may have some effect. For my purposes,

334

the most useful themes are to be found in the writings of Georges Lefebvre and Alfred Cobban.

In Lefebvre's view, the French Revolution was the principal point in European history where four social elements, each with its special conception of society and its own aspirations, came into a series of conflicts from which they emerged in a new relationship.[1] The first element was kingship, with the complementary doctrine of royal absolutism. This character-ized what has since been called the ancien régime. Political power was concentrated in the king's person, and the doctrine that he was God's lieutenant had become predominant over natural-law and contract theories of society. The second ele-ment was the nobility, which retained social primacy but had not forgiven the monarchy for having deprived it of political power, and which longed for liberty as an attribute of dignity. Thus the conflict between kingship and nobility was a survival of the past. The third element was the bourgeoisie, which de-rived its wealth from trade, industry, and finance much more than from land, and which placed learning and rationality as well as economic power in the king's service. Like the nobility, the bourgeoisie wanted to share political power and to obtain personal liberty; unlike the nobility, the bourgeoisie wanted abolition of the exclusive rights of nobles to hold the highest ranks, and establishment of equal opportunity for all property-owners. In this sense, the aspirations for liberty and equality entailed future developments, not traditional conflicts. The fourth element was the working people, artisans and peasants, for whom liberty meant freedom from social subordination and equality meant economic independence for every man. These required the destruction of all the privileges of the nobility and the limitation of the exploitative freedom of the wealthy.

1. "La Révolution française dans l'histoire du monde," *Annales: Economies, Sociétés, Civilisations*, 3 (1948), reprinted in Lefebvre's *Etudes sur la Révolution française* (Paris, Presses Universitaires de France, 1954), pp. 317–326.

The interaction of these four social elements did not occur in a series of simple collisions. The nobility and the bourgeoisie were connected, Lefebvre thought, by an intermediary social category: the *noblesse de robe*. It had formed as a result of the sale of property rights in royal offices that conferred nobility on the possessors and their descendants. Even while it developed closer relations with the *noblesse d'épée*, it remained comparatively bourgeois in its economic behavior and still associated with other officeholders who were commoners and, still lower in the social scale, with lawyers. This "intermediary class, nobles at the top, office-holders in the middle, commoners at the bottom,"[2] was attached as a whole, through its occupation, to notions of law, of the legal order, and of a monarchy limited by the prerogatives of the parlements.

Yet, for Lefebvre, the nobility, the bourgeoisie, and the working people constituted social classes with a more profound reality. The professional ideal shared by members of parlements, lesser magistrates, and lawyers, attaching them to law and to limited monarchy, was important in 1788 and 1789 because it permitted them to make common cause against absolute kingship. But almost at once this unity was broken. Many members of the parlements took the side of aristocracy, and many lawyers were included in that part of the bourgeoisie which cooperated with the popular classes to destroy aristocracy. All this is implied by Lefebvre in the passages where he analyzes the civil war between aristocratic and democratic forces, which he respectively associates in a general way with the nobility and the populace.

Cobban never attempted explicitly to summarize the significance of the French Revolution, and it might appear that he would have rejected any summary as inadequate. He repeatedly used metaphors emphasizing the formlessness of the revolutionary process: "the confluence of a host of contributory

2. *Etudes*, p. 322.

currents, small and great, flowing together to swell suddenly into a mighty flood," which soon became "a destructive torrent" or, in another book, "a great ocean" that "defies generalization."[3] But elsewhere Cobban made clear his conviction that it was "primarily a political revolution, a struggle for the possession of power and over the conditions in which power was to be exercised. Essentially the revolution was the overthrow of the old political system of the monarchy and the creation of a new one in the shape of the Napoleonic state."[4] In the face of criticism, while conceding that "a very strong social element" was involved, Cobban affirmed that with respect to political development "the Revolution was a cataclysm."[5]

The contestants in the revolutionary struggle over power were not, Cobban believed, social classes that could be clearly designated in a word or a simple phrase. Thus he said that in 1788 the combined forces of the noblesse d'épée, the parlements and the upper clergy resisted the royal administration. Then "a class of officials, lawyers, financiers, rentiers, landowners was able to acquire the leadership of a popular movement constituted mainly of peasants and craftsmen." And the popular movement in turn was directed against "all those who might be described as belonging to the privileged classes." The result of the struggle was that officeholders, lawyers, professional men, proprietors, "with a few financiers and merchants," won the opportunity to obtain "some of the lands and more of

3. *A History of Modern France,* 3rd ed., 3 vols. (Harmondsworth, Penguin Books, 1963), I, 137, 138; *In Search of Humanity: The Role of the Enlightenment in Modern History* (New York, George Braziller, 1960), p. 185.

4. *The Social Interpretation of the French Revolution* (Cambridge, Eng., Cambridge University Press, 1964), p. 162; cf. explanatory comments in Cobban's *Aspects of the French Revolution* (London, Jonathan Cape, 1968), p. 283, and other statements of the same idea in *A History of Modern France,* 3rd ed., I, 259, and II, 21.

5. *Problèmes de stratification sociale. Actes du Colloque international (1966),* ed. Roland Mousnier (Paris, Presses Universitaires de France, 1968), p. 225.

the offices of the privileged classes and to complete the process of rising to become the ruling class in France . . . In their way of life they were the heirs of the obsolescent *noblesse,* and if they were bourgeois their aim was to be *bourgeois vivant noblement . . .* Their eyes remained turned to the past in which their ideal had been set."[6]

Differing conceptions of society and aspirations were not, in Cobban's mind, distinctively associated with particular groups. Ideas "cannot be identified with social forces; for once an idea has been let loose on the world, no one knows where it will settle or what new movement it will start."[7] In the revolutionary period, ideas were not only symbols in the name of which the power struggle was waged, they were "living forces which developed and even changed sides as the Revolution progressed."[8]

Cobban regarded the noblesse de robe not as an intermediary social group but as a plutocracy covering its own interests with a cloud of liberal propaganda. The parlements had come to conceive of themselves as an intermediary power between the king and the nation, had then begun to assert the rights of the nation, of which they regarded themselves as the representative, and had at last demanded the convocation of the Estates General. But they were in a false position because there was a "fundamental opposition of interests" between themselves and the Third Estate.[9] This was revealed when the Parlement of Paris ruled that the Estates General of 1789 should be conducted under the procedures of 1614 (which had provided a

6. *A History of Modern France,* 3rd ed., I, 263–265.

7. "The Enlightenment and the French Revolution," in *Aspects of the Eighteenth Century,* ed. Earl R. Wasserman (Baltimore, The Johns Hopkins Press, 1965), reprinted in *Aspects of the French Revolution* where the passage quoted appears on p. 20.

8. *A History of Modern France,* 3rd ed., I, 233.

9. "The Parlements of France in the Eighteenth Century," *History,* 35 (1950), reprinted in *Aspects of the French Revolution* where the phrase quoted appears on p. 81.

veto power for each of the three Estates). Then occurred "the most revolutionary change of all" in political attitudes: "the Third Estate, which had been faithfully seconding the struggle of the privileged classes against royal despotism, suddenly discovered that its supposed allies were its enemies."[10]

Lefebvre's interpretive outline is remarkable for clarity and for the tidiness of the explanatory connections that hold it together. In any outline drawn from Cobban's works, one notices the very imperfect rationality of revolutionary politics, the prominence of clashing selfish interests unconnected with either distinct economic functions or characteristic social doctrines, and the loosely articulated explanations of revolutionary behavior. In another respect, Lefebvre's and Cobban's interpretations are similar. They attribute great political importance to the parlements, and in one way or another they allow some ambiguity as to the parlements' position at the beginning of the revolution.

The parlements' position was in fact ambiguous in more than one way. In Lefebvre's terms, the parlements were appropriate to the ancien régime because they were royal institutions, extending the power of the crown; but they also limited the action of its ministers. Besides, they defended aristocratic privilege but also proclaimed the impersonal rule of law from which the bourgeoisie would benefit as much as the nobility. It is understandable that Lefebvre departed from his straightforward outline of class conflict in order to characterize the parlements and their adherents as intermediaries between classes. In Cobban's terms, too, the parlements were in an ambiguous position. Their members were among the privileged classes but were at the same time officeholders trained in law; and they asserted the rights of the nation but denied those of the Third Estate which formed the largest part of the nation. Cobban did not apply the word "hypocrites" to them, but he offered no other explanation of their conduct.

10. *A History of Modern France*, 3rd ed., I, 135.

The magistrates of the bailliages, too, were enmeshed in ambiguities, and in the last decade before the Revolution this was the most important fact determining their position. As royal judges, they maintained loyalty to the leaders of their profession, the parlements. As corporate groups in a distinctly subordinate position, they readily perceived divergences between their own interests and those of the parlements. As notable residents of their respective towns, they supported the particular interests of those localities; yet at the same time they were engaged in vigorous contests for authority and prestige with competing local groups, especially the municipal officials and other royal officeholders. Finally, as individuals who had reached the social pinnacle of the bourgeoisie, recently for the most part, the bailliage magistrates had benefited from existing career opportunities; but for the great majority of them any further ascent would be on the arduous path leading to legal status as a noble.

It should not be thought that the magistrates, in the parlements or in the bailliages, were peculiar in being held in the social web by multiple strands, some of which led in opposite directions. Such a position would be characteristic of any group with relatively high status in a stable or slowly changing society. What was unusual in the position of the royal magistrates was that the impending transformation of the state made them into both upholders and critics of the legitimacy of the whole political regime. It thus forced them, more than most groups of Frenchmen, to choose among their own most cherished ideals. The ambiguous political and social position they had occupied rapidly became untenable, as institutions and individuals were forced to one side or the other of a conflict over those ideals. Then the members of parlements became, in general, counterrevolutionaries. The members of the bailliages in general, supported reform and accepted, at least by declining to oppose, a republican revolution.

The contrast between the political behavior of the magistrates in the bailliages and that of the members of the parlements could be measured, more precisely than has so far been done, in the election results of 1790, 1792, and later years, the numbers who emigrated from France or were guillotined, the memberships in Jacobin clubs, and other statistics. But the contrast cannot so readily be explained. In the present state of knowledge, it is easier to reject possible explanations than to affirm them. Political divergence between the parlements and the bailliages was not based on a difference in economic function, since all magistrates were officeholders and practically all were landed proprietors. If it was a case of the rich against the merely well-to-do, this remains to be proven through laborious collection of data and statistical analysis; initially, it does not seem very probable, since the range of wealth among the members of parlements overlapped the range of wealth in the bailliages to a considerable extent. Cobban suggested that, in contrast to the members of the parlements, the bourgeois officeholders were in general experiencing a decline in relative wealth and social status. The scattered indications I have found suggest that on the contrary the prices of offices in the bailliages were tending to rise and so were the family fortunes of the magistrates.[11]

We are left with the fact that the divergence between the parlements and the bailliages was part of the broader conflict between nobles and commoners and may be explained by the difference in class membership and allegiance. More than 80 percent of the members of parlements were nobles before becoming magistrates; more than 90 percent of the members of bailliages were commoners, and few had prospects of ennoblement.[12] The difference in status was defined in law, but it also involved informal aspects of association and group mem-

11. "Sur le prix des offices judiciaires à la fin de l'ancien régime," *Revue d'Histoire Economique et Sociale*, 42 (1964), 390–392, and above, p. 88.

12. Above, pp. 71–73.

bership, notably attitudes and expectations concerning the nature of the state. Lefebvre was right to suggest that the idea of liberty, for example, had one set of meanings in the context of nobles' beliefs and another set of meanings in the context of commoners' beliefs. There was some overlap between the two systems of beliefs in the minds of nobles and commoners in the royal judiciary. This permitted the bailliage magistrates to accept and even at times to disseminate some of the constitutional and political ideas that emanated from the parlements and became operative in the Revolution. In thus characterizing the positive relations between the parlements and the bailliages we should not exaggerate their unity or overstate the initiative of the magistrates in the lower courts. It is not helpful but confusing to consider the parlements, lesser magistrates, and lawyers together as an "intermediary class," for they were not one class either legally or ideologically. It is misleading to attribute to the bailliages a distinctive part in intellectual innovation or ideological formulation, for they were characteristically not originators but observers, before and after the Revolution.

During a period of two and a half years, from the spring of 1788 to the autumn of 1790, magistrates in the bailliages appeared intermittently in large numbers on the political stage. At the beginning of that period, Lamoignon's reforms brought them, unwillingly, from the audience to a prominent role. At the end of the period, the liquidation of the old judicial offices and the establishment of elected judges permitted them to retire once again to the position of spectators, and that is what most of them did. In the period 1788–1790 itself, most bailliage magistrates participated in politics by responding to circumstances and to the initiative of other groups rather than by attempting to exercise independent influence, collectively or individually. Their antipathy to the parlements, for example, did not arise in a few weeks' time after a sudden revelation that the parlements held aristocratic sentiments. Before 1788, the magistrates in the bailliages had ample reason to fear and dislike the parlements. In the winter of 1789, they still disagreed among themselves over the constitutional and political part that should be assigned to the parlements. Their cahiers de doléances demonstrate the fact. The turning point came later, during the summer of 1789, with the development of the counterrevolutionary movement and the political polarization leading to the decree of 4 August. By the end of the summer, most magistrates in the bailliages accepted revolutionary change because alternative courses of action had been made more unacceptable to them. They were not the leaders of the revolutionary bourgeoisie. Before 1789, they had been in the highest rank of the bourgeoisie and they remained a notable part of it, but most of them had come to support revolution hesitantly, cautiously, with moderation and many a backward glance.

Acceptance of sudden, far-reaching change in the political order was the contribution to the revolutionary process that was typical of the bailliage magistrates. This contribution was not heroic, but it was important because it helped to make the process possible. Such acceptance was not primarily determined by the expectation of immediate personal gain. In the event, a minority received direct substantial gain from the revolutionary changes that actually occurred, in landed property or new public careers. The political transformation they supported had, however, important symbolic value for them. They had hoped for a polity different from the administrative monarchy they had known. They secured one that, except at times in 1793 and 1794, appeared to most of them more open and responsive, and more lawful, with a wider range and a greater degree of predictability of opportunities, not only for men like themselves but, indeed, for all their countrymen.

Appendix
Sources and Bibliography
Glossary
Index

Appendix

The Bailliages and the Number
of Judicial Officeholders in 1789

Enumerating the lawcourts and the judges of the ancien régime is a task complicated by problems of definition, by changes from time to time in the number of jurisdictions and the number of offices legally in existence, and by the fluctuating number of vacant offices. The following list includes only the courts which were empowered to decide cas royaux subject to appeal directly to a parlement, as of 1788–1790. Such courts are listed under the name of the parlement to which they were subordinate. For the territories of the parlements of Paris, Toulouse, Bordeaux, and Nancy, the list is subdivided by provinces or pays. Présidial jurisdiction is indicated, with the date when it was attributed if this was later than 1552. In the last column are noted the district courts and departmental criminal courts which were assigned (by legislation of 23 August 1790 and 11 February 1791) to towns where there had been bailliages.

Excluded, because they did not have cognizance of cas royaux, are the prévôtés, *châtellenies* and equivalent royal jurisdictions, the seigneurial courts, and the tribunals for the salt monopoly, the property taxes, the customs dues, and the waters and forests. Also excluded are the courts from which all decisions were appealed to a bailliage, not directly to a parlement.

This list is shorter than the list of electoral circumscriptions drawn up in 1789. The elections to the Estates General were ordinarily conducted by bailliages, but parts of France had no bailliages in the sense used here. Lower royal jurisdictions and seigneurial jurisdictions served as electoral districts in Alsace, Nivernais, parts of Gascony, and elsewhere. Nonetheless, this list is partly based on the *Recueil de documents relatifs à la convocation des Etats Généraux* edited by Armand Brette, 4 vols. (Paris, Imprimerie Nationale, 1894–1915). That collection was left incomplete at the editor's death. It can be supplemented by reference to almanacs published, in imitation of the *Almanach royal,* in various provincial towns in the years 1786 to 1790.

Not all holders of offices connected with the bailliages were judges or king's counsel. In the numbers recorded here, ceremonial officials are excluded: *bailli d'épée* or *sénéchal d'épée, lieutenant-général d'épée,* and *conseiller d'honneur.* Nonjudicial functionaries are also excluded: clerks (*greffiers*), commissioners in charge of preliminary investigations (*commissaires enquêteurs et examinateurs*), collectors (*receveurs*) and comptrollers (*contrôleurs*).

On the other hand, the procureur du roi and his assistants (*substituts*), and the *avocat(s) du roi,* are included because they were necessarily trained in law and were considered to be members of the judicial company.

A former judge, if entitled *honoraire* or *vétéran*, retained the right to vote in judicial proceedings although he no longer held office. The number of such semiretired magistrates is recorded below for those localities where it could be ascertained.

The number of judicial officeholders in 1788–1790 is recorded in two kinds of official sources. First, there are lists, preserved in the archives of the respective départements (series C), of officeholders paying the capitation tax in a locality, an élection, or a généralité. Second, there are reports, preserved in the Archives Nationales (D XVII 9, nos. 123–127), of the sums to be paid as compensation for offices liquidated in 1791. Neither type of official documentation has been preserved in its entirety or even for the majority of the offices in the bailliages.

The provincial almanacs contain lists of judicial officeholders. Their errors appear to be few, and random, where the almanacs can be compared with surviving official records (Normandy and Burgundy, for example). Locating provincial almanacs has been greatly facilitated by the careful work of Gaston Saffroy, *Bibliographie des almanachs et annuaires administratifs, ecclésiastiques et militaires français de l'ancien régime* (Paris, Librairie Gaston Saffroy, 1959).

In the *Etat de la magistrature en France*, by Duhamel, almost all the présidial courts but none of the ordinary bailliages except that of Versailles are included. This work exists in a manuscript dated 1784 (A.N., MM 849) and two editions, for 1788 and for 1789 (B.N., 8° Lc^{25}. 127). The 1788 edition contains short historical notes on the présidial courts at Angers, Aurillac, Auxerre, Chaumont-en-Bassigny, Lyon, Mâcon, and Poitiers. The 1789 edition contains similar notes on the présidial court at Abbeville and the bailliage of Versailles. For a few présidial courts, there appear to be no membership lists other than the ones in this publication.

Table A1. Jurisdiction of the Parlement of Paris.[a]

Province, city, or town	Number of magistrates in office, 1789	Number of semiretired magistrates, 1789	District court (D) and criminal court (C), 1790–1795
ANGOUMOIS[b]			
Angoulême, présidial	18	4	D, C
Cognac	—	—	D
ANJOU[c]			
Angers, présidial	17	0	D, C
Baugé	6	1	D
Beaufort	7	0	
Château-Gontier, présidial (1639)	8	2	D
La Flèche, présidial (1595)	7	1	D
Saumur	12	0	D
AUNIS[d]			
La Rochelle, présidial	10	4	D
Rochefort	—	—	D
AUVERGNE[e]			
Aurillac, présidial	16	2	D, C
Clermont-Ferrand, présidial (1582)	18	—	D
Cusset	5	—	D
Montaigut-en-Combrailles	3	—	
Riom, présidial	26	4	D, C
Saint-Flour	7	—	D
Vic-en-Carladès	4	—	
BERRY[f]			
Bourges, présidial	18	2	D, C
Châteauroux	8	2	D, C
Concressault	2	0	
Dun-le-Roi	2	0	D
Issoudun	8	1	D
Mehun-sur-Yèvre	3	0	
Vierzon	3	0	D
BOURBONNAIS[g]			
Moulins, présidial	22	5	D, C
BOURGOGNE[h]			
Auxerre, présidial	16	1	D, C
Bar-sur-Seine	5	1	D

Province, city, or town	Number of magistrates in office, 1789	Number of semiretired magistrates, 1789	District court (D) and criminal court (C), 1790–1795
Mâcon, présidial (1639)	14	5	D
CHAMPAGNE & BARROIS[i]			
Bar-le-Duc	11	—	D
Châlons-sur-Marne, présidial (1637)	10	—	D, C
Château-Thierry, présidial	9	—	D
Châtillon-sur-Marne	2	—	
Chaumont-en-Bassigny, présidial	12	2	D, C
Clermont-en-Argonne	2	—	
Epernay	5	0	D
Fismes	4	1	
La Marche-en-Bassigny-Barrois	5	—	D
Langres, présidial (1641)	15	1	D
Méry-sur-Seine	2	0	
Nogent-sur-Seine	2	0	D
Reims, présidial	8	1	D
Saint-Dizier	6	—	
Sainte-Menehould	11	—	D
Sens, présidial	17	0	D
Sézanne	8	—	D
Troyes, présidial	15	2	D, C
Villeneuve-le-Roi	3	—	
Vitry-le-François, présidial	13	1	D
ILE-DE-FRANCE & BRIE[j]			
Beaumont-sur-Oise	2	—	
Chambly	1	—	
Chaumont-en-Vexin	1	—	D
Choisy-le-Roi	2	—	
Compiègne	3	—	D
Creil	2	—	
Dourdan	3	—	
Etampes	2	—	D

Province, city, or town	Number of magistrates in office, 1789	Number of semiretired magistrates, 1789	District court (D) and criminal court (C), 1790–1795
Magny-en-Vexin	2	—	
Mantes, présidial	—	—	D
Meaux, présidial	11	—	D
Melun, présidial	10	—	D, C
Meudon	3	—	
Meulan	3	—	
Montereau	—	—	
Montfort-l'Amaury	2	—	D
Moret	2	—	
Nemours	—	—	D
Paris, Châtelet; présidial	75	13	8 D, 1 C
Pontoise	3	—	D
Provins, présidial	8	—	D
Senlis, présidial	11	—	D
Versailles	3	—	D, C
Vincennes	2	—	
LYONNAIS, FOREZ, & BEAUJOLAIS[k]			
Bourg-Argental	5	—	
Lyon, présidial	22	1	2 D, 1 C
Montbrison	19	3	D
Villefranche-de-Beaujolais	11	1	D
MAINE & PERCHE[l]			
Beaumont-le-Vicomte	—	—	
Bellême	—	—	D
Château-du-Loir	5	—	D
Châteauneuf-en-Thymerais	—	—	D
Fresnay-le-Vicomte	—	—	D
Laval	—	—	D, C
Le Mans, présidial	14	—	D, C
Mamers (baill. of Sonnois)	4	—	D
Mortagne	—	—	D
Sainte-Suzanne	—	—	D
MARCHE[m]			
Bellac	5	—	D

Province, city, or town	Number of magistrates in office, 1789	Number of semiretired magistrates, 1789	District court (D) and criminal court (C), 1790–1795
Guéret, présidial (1635)	18	—	D, C
Le Dorat	6	—	D
NIVERNAIS[n]			
Saint-Pierre-le-Moutier, présidial	13	—	D
ORLEANAIS & BLESOIS[o]			
Beaugency	3	0	D
Blois, présidial	9	—	D, C
Boiscommun	1	0	D
Chartres, présidial	17	3	D, C
Gien	5	0	D
Lorris	2	—	
Mondoubleau	2	—	D
Montargis, présidial (1638)	10	2	D
Neuville-aux-Bois	2	—	D
Orléans, présidial	16	2	D, C
Romorantin	3	0	D
Saint-Calais	2	—	D
Vendôme	8	1	D
Vitry-aux-Loges	1	—	
Yenville	3	0	D
Yèvre-le-Châtel	2	—	
PICARDIE[p]			
Abbeville (sén. of Ponthieu), présidial	10	2	D
Amiens, présidial	14	1	D, C
Beauvais, présidial (1581)	13	1	D, C
Boulogne-sur-Mer	4	—	D
Calais	5	—	D
Clermont-en-Beauvaisis	6	—	D
Montdidier	6	—	D
Montreuil-sur-Mer	4	—	
Péronne	7	—	D

Province, city, or town	Number of magistrates in office, 1789	Number of semiretired magistrates, 1789	District court (D) and criminal court (C), 1790–1795
Roye	6	—	
POITOU[q]			
Châtellerault	7	0	D
Civray	9	0	D
Fontenay-le-Comte	14	1	D, C
Loudun	11	0	D
Lusignan	4	0	D
Montmorillon	10	1	D
Niort	10	0	D, C
Poitiers, présidial	20	5	D, C
Saint-Maixent	10	0	D
TOURAINE[r]			
Châtillon-sur-Indre, présidial (1639)	—	—	D
Chinon	10	—	D
Langeais	2	—	
Loches	8	3	D
Montrichard	2	—	D
Tours, présidial	13	—	D, C
VERMANDOIS[s]			
Chauny	2	—	
Coucy	2	—	D
Crépy-en-Valois	4	—	D
Guise	2	—	D
Ham	1	—	
La Fère	2	—	
Laon, présidial	14	—	D, C
Marle	1	—	
Noyon	5	—	D
Saint-Quentin	8	—	D
Soissons, présidial (1595)	11	—	D
Villers-Cotterets	3	—	

[a] The principal source is the "Liste alphabétique des bailliages, sénéchaussées, et autres jurisdictions royales ressortissans nuement au Parlement," in the *Dictionnaire des paroisses du ressort du Parlement de Paris* (Paris, chez Pierre-Guillaume Simon, Imprimeur du Parlement,

Appendix

1776), pp. vi-xi, which lists 171 jurisdictions. In the present list, 31 of those are omitted and 3 others added.

The additions are the *châtellenie* of Chambly (in accordance with the *Almanach historique de la ville et du diocèse de Senlis,* 1788) and the bailliages of Mondoubleau and Saint-Calais (see Brette, *Recueil . . . ,* III, 362, 464, 466).

The omissions are of 3 kinds: 6 jurisdictions subordinate to the Conseil provincial of Artois (the *gouvernance* of Arras and the bailliages of Aire, Bapaume, Béthune, Hesdin, and Saint-Omer); 18 jurisdictions omitted, in 1789, from the list of electoral circumscriptions (Bar-sur-Aube, Bonneval, Brie-Comte-Robert, Charlieu, Corbeil, Crécy-en-Brie, Dunkerque, Fontainebleau, Gannat, La Ferté Alais, La Ferté Milon, the sénéchaussée of Bourgnouvel sitting at Mayenne, Monlignon, Montluçon, Neuilly-Saint-Front, Pont-sur-Seine, Saint-Ferréol, and Saint-Germain-en-Laye); finally, 7 jurisdictions which, although included in the list of electoral circumscriptions in 1789, were either not competent in cas royaux or not immediately subordinate to the Parlement, as indicated by Brette, *Recueil . . . ,* III, 112 (Ardres), 388 (Dreux), 455 (Château-Renard), 642 (Usson), 649 (Salers), and 685 (the bailliage of Andelat, sitting at Murat), and IV, 504 (the bailliage of Vouvant, sitting at La Châtaigneraie).

[b] Rapports de liquidation (D XVII 9): Angoulême (in no. 126).

[c] Rapports de liquidation (D XVII 9): Angers (in no. 123); *Almanach de la province d'Anjou, apanage de Monsieur,* 1790.

[d] *Calendrier ou Etrennes rochelloises,* 1790.

[e] Capitation, officiers de judicature, généralité de Riom, 1787 (A.D. Puy-de-Dôme, 1 C 3142); Rapports de liquidation (D XVII 9): Aurillac (in no. 124), Saint-Flour (in no. 123), Riom (in nos. 123 and 126); Edouard Evérat, *La Sénéchaussée d'Auvergne et siège présidial de Riom au XVIIIe siècle* (Paris, 1885), pp. 331, 380.

[f] Rapports de liquidation (D XVII 9): Bourges (in no. 125), Châteauroux (in no. 127); *Etrennes curieuses et utiles de la province de Berri,* 1790.

[g] *Etrennes nouvelles à l'usage de la généralité de Moulins,* 1789, 1790.

[h] Rapports de liquidation (D XVII 9): Auxerre (in no. 127), Bar-sur-Seine (in no. 125); *Almanach chorographique et topographique du pays et comté de Mâconnois,* 1786; Parish register, burials, Mâcon (Saint-Pierre), 6 February 1787. See also Francis Molard, "Le Bailliage d'Auxerre," *Annuaire historique du département de l'Yonne,* (1891), 94–138."

[i] Capitation, officiers de judicature, généralité de Châlons, 1788 (A.D. Marne, C 968); Capitation, officiers de judicature, généralité de Soissons, 1787, élection de Château-Thierry (A.D. Aisne, C 272); Rapports de liquidation (D XVII 9): Bar-le-Duc (in no. 123), Château-Thierry (in no. 127), La Marche (in no. 126), Sainte-Menehould (in no. 125), Vitry-le-François (in no. 124); *Almanach historique, civil, ecclésiastique et topographique de la ville et du diocèse de Reims,* 1788; *Almanach historique de la ville, diocèse et bailliage de Sens,* 1790; *Almanach de la ville et du diocèse de Troyes, capitale de la Champagne,* 1789, 1790.

Appendix

[j] Capitation, officiers de judicature, généralité de Rouen, 1789, élection de Chaumont et Magny (A.D. Seine-Maritime, C 2129); Rapports de liquidation (D XVII 9): Melun (in no. 124), Meulan (in no. 124), Paris Châtelet (in nos. 125 and 126), Provins (in nos. 124, 126, 127); *Almanach royal*, 1788–1790; *Almanach de la ville et du diocèse de Meaux*, 1789; *Almanach historique de la ville et du diocèse de Senlis*, 1788; *Calendrier historique de l'Orléanais*, 1788, 1790; Ernest Aubergé, "De la justice dans le bailliage de Melun, spécialement à l'époque immédiatement antérieure à 1789," *Bulletin de la Société d'Archéologie, Sciences, Lettres et Arts du Département de Seine-et-Marne*, 6 (1869–1872), 157–166; Brette, *Recueil . . .* , III, 279, 280, 283, 380, 384, 387, 398.

[k] *Almanach astronomique et historique de la ville de Lyon*, 1789, 1790.

[l] Etat des décharges et modérations de la capitation, 1789, officiers de judicature, élection de Château-du-Loir (A.D. Indre-et-Loire, C 696); Rapports de liquidation (D XVII 9): Le Mans (in no. 125), Sonnois [at Mamers] (in no. 123); *Almanach ou Calendrier du Maine*, 1789, 1790.

[m] Louis Laroche, "Le Présidial de Guéret," *Mémoires de la Société des Sciences Naturelles et Archéologiques de la Creuse*, (1895–1896), 392–401; Camille Rosier, *Les Institutions judiciaires de la Basse-Marche* (Limoges, Ducourtieux, 1921).

[n] Edmond Duminy and Paul Meunier, "Bailliage royal et présidial de Saint-Pierre-le-Moutier; état de cette juridiction en 1789," *Bulletin de la Société Nivernaise des Lettres, Sciences et Arts*, 15 (1893), 337–402.

[o] Rapports de liquidation (D XVII 9): Montargis (incomplete, in no. 126), Orléans (in no. 123); *Calendrier historique de l'Orléanais*, 1788, 1790; Brette, *Recueil . . .* , III, 413, 415, 416, 419, 456, 464, 466.

[p] Capitation, officiers de judicature, généralité de Soissons, 1787, élection de Clermont-en-Beauvaisis (A.D. Aisne, C 272); Rapports de liquidation (D XVII 9): Beauvais (in no. 124), Montreuil-sur-Mer (in no. 127); *Almanach historique et géographique de Picardie*, 1789.

[q] Rapports de liquidation (D XVII 9): Chatellerault (in no. 123), Fontenay-le-Comte (in no. 125), Niort (in nos. 126 and 127), Saint-Maixent (in nos. 125 and 126); *Almanach provincial et historique du Poitou*, 1790; Henri Beauchet-Filleau, Paul Beauchet-Filleau and Joseph Beauchet-Filleau, *Dictionnaire historique et généalogique des familles du Poitou*, 2nd ed. (Poitiers, Oudin & Cie., 1891–1915, and Fontenay-le-Comte, Lussaud frères, 1963–   , in progress), III, 53, 311; IV, 475. See also Charles Babinet, "Le Présidial de Poitiers; son personnel de 1551 à 1790," *Mémoires de la Société des Antiquaires de l'Ouest*, 2nd ser., 25 (1901), 151–341.

[r] *Almanach historique de Touraine*, 1790.

[s] Capitation, officiers de judicature, généralité de Soissons, 1787 (A.D. Aisne, C 272); Rapports de liquidation (D XVII 9): Crépy-en-Valois (in no. 124), Saint-Quentin (in no. 124), Soissons (in no. 127); *Almanach historique de la ville et du diocèse de Senlis*, 1788; *Almanach historique et géographique de Picardie*, 1789.

Table A2. Jurisdiction of the Parlement of Toulouse.[a]

Province, city, or town	Number of magistrates in office, 1789	Number of semiretired magistrates, 1789	District court (D) and criminal court (C), 1790–1795
ARMAGNAC			
Auch, présidial (1639)	19	—	D, C
Isle-Jourdain	2	—	(none)
Lectoure, présidial (1621)	14	—	D
BIGORRE			
Tarbes	10	—	D, C
FOIX			
Pamiers, présidial (1646)	11	—	D
LANGUEDOC			
Béziers, présidial	14	0	D
Carcassonne, présidial	10	0	D, C
Castelnaudary, présidial	10	0	D
Castres	6	0	D, C
Limoux, présidial (1642)	8	1	D
Montpellier, présidial	19	2	D, C
Nîmes, présidial	20	0	D, C
Toulouse, présidial	22	1	D, C
QUERCY			
Cahors, présidial	13	—	D, C
Figeac	12	—	D
Gourdon	7	—	D
Lauzerte	6	—	(none)
Martel	5	—	(none)
Montauban, présidial (1630)	9	—	D
ROUERGUE			
Rodez, présidial (1635)	18	0	D, C
Villefranche-de-Rouergue, présidial	14	1	D
VELAY			
Le Puy, présidial (1635)	11	—	D, C

Appendix

Table A2. *continued*

Province, city, or town	Number of magistrates in office, 1789	Number of semiretired magistrates, 1789	District court (D) and criminal court (C), 1790–1795
VIVARAIS			
Annonay	10	—	(none)
Villeneuve-de-Berg	12	—	(none)

[a] Rapports de liquidation (D XVII 9): Auch (in no. 126), Limoux (in nos. 124 and 126), Martel (in no. 123), Villefranche-de-Rouergue (in no. 127), Annonay (in no. 127); *Almanach historique de la province de Languedoc*, 1789; *Calendrier historique de la généralité de Montauban*, 1789; *Calendrier de la ville de Nîmes et de sa sénéchaussée*, 1789. See also Albert Boudon, *La Sénéchaussée présidiale du Puy* (Valence, Imprimerie C. Legrand, 1908).

Table A3. Jurisdiction of the Parlement of Grenoble.[a]

Province, city, or town	Number of magistrates in office, 1789	Number of semiretired magistrates, 1789	District court (D) and criminal court (C), 1790–1795
DAUPHINE			
Briançon	5	—	D
Crest	4	—	D
Die	3	—	D
Embrun	4	—	D
Gap	4	—	D, C
Grenoble	6	—	D, C
Le-Buis-lès-Baronnies	3	—	D
Montélimar	6	—	D
Saint-Marcellin	6	—	D
Saint-Paul-Trois-Châteaux	2	—	(none)
Valence, présidial (1636)	11	—	D, C
Vienne	6	—	D

[a] Rapports de liquidation (D XVII): Montélimar (in no. 127); *Almanach général de la province de Dauphiné*, 1789.

Table A4. Jurisdiction of the Parlement of Bordeaux.[a]

Province, city or town	Number of magistrates in office, 1789	Number of semiretired magistrates, 1789	District court (D) and criminal court (C), 1790–1795
AGENAIS & CONDOMOIS			
Agen, présidial	18	—	D, C
Condom, présidial	11	—	D
ALBRET			
Casteljaloux	—	—	D
Castelmoron	—	—	(none)
Nérac, présidial (1629)	5	—	D
Tartas	—	—	D
GUIENNE & BAZADOIS			
Bazas, présidial	8	—	D
Bordeaux, présidial	11	—	D, C
Libourne, présidial (1639)	10	—	D
LANDES & LABOURD			
Bayonne	—	—	(none)
Dax, présidial	9	1	D, C
Mont-de-Marsan	—	—	D
Saint-Sever	—	—	D
Ustaritz	—	—	(none)
LIMOUSIN			
Brive, présidial	13	—	D
Limoges, présidial	15	—	D, C
Saint-Yrieix	7	—	D
Tulle, présidial (1635)	15	—	D, C
Uzerche	7	—	D
PERIGORD			
Bergerac	6	—	D
Périgueux, présidial	16	—	D, C
Sarlat, présidial (1641)	9	—	D

Appendix

Table A4. *continued*

Province, city, or town	Number of magistrates in office, 1789	Number of semiretired magistrates, 1789	District court (D) and criminal court (C), 1790–1795
SAINTONGE			
Brouage	—	—	(none)
Saintes, présidial	11	—	D, C
Saint-Jean-d'Angély	—	—	D

[a] *Etrennes bordelaises, ou Calendrier raisonné du Palais,* 1789, pp. 89 and 91, lists the thirty sénéchaussées from which appeals were brought to Bordeaux. The present list omits seven of these and adds two others: omitted, the jurisdictions at Aiguillon, Coutras, Fronsac, Rohan-Rohan, Ussel, and Ventadour, which were not called upon to serve as electoral circumscriptions in 1789, and the sénéchaussée of Martel, in Quercy, from which apparently some appeals went to Bordeaux and others to the Parlement of Toulouse (*q.v.*); added, the jurisdictions at Ustaritz in the Basque country and Brouage in Saintonge (see Brette, *Recueil . . . ,* IV, 378, 447).

For lists of judicial officeholders: Rapports de liquidation (D XVII 9): Agen (in no. 125), Bazas (in no. 126), Bordeaux (in nos. 125 and 126), Brive (in no. 125), Limoges (in no. 123), Tulle (in no. 126), Uzerche (in no. 123), Saintes (in nos. 124 and 126); *Etrennes bordelaises,* 1789, pp. 134, 137 (Bordeaux and Libourne), *Calendrier du Limousin,* 1790; *Etat de la magistrature en France,* 1788, 1789 (Condom, Nérac, Dax, Périgueux, Sarlat, Saintes). See also Jules Serret, *Les Magistrats du présidial sénéchal, des tribunaux révolutionnaires et de la cour d'appel d'Agen (1551–1900)* (Agen, 1900); Aymar d'Arlot, comte de Saint-Saud, *Magistrats des sénéchaussées, présidiaux et élections, fonctionnaires des vice-sénéchaussées et maréchaussées du Périgord* (Bergerac, Imprimerie Castanet, 1931).

Appendix

Table A5. Jurisdiction of the Parlement of Dijon[a]

Province, city, or town	Number of magistrates in office, 1789	Number of semiretired magistrates, 1789	District court (D) and criminal court (C), 1790–1795
BOURGOGNE			
Arnay-le-Duc	3	0	D
Autun, présidial (1696)	9	1	D
Auxonne	3	0	(none)
Avallon	5	0	D
Beaune	8	1	D
Bourbon-Lancy	4	1	D
Chalon-sur-Saône, présidial (1696)	12	4	D, C
Charolles	7	0	D
Châtillon-sur-Seine, présidial (1696)	9	1	D
Dijon, présidial (1696)	12	1	D, C
Montcenis	5	1	(none)
Nuits	2	0	(none)
Saint-Jean-de-Losne	2	0	D
Saulieu	6	1	(none)
Semur-en-Auxois, présidial (1696)	7	1	D
Semur-en-Brionnais	2	0	D
PAYS ADJACENTS			
Belley (baill. of Bugey)	6	0	D
Bourg-en-Bresse, présidial (1601)	18	3	D, C
Gex	4	1	D
Trévoux (sén. of Dombes)	8	0	D

[a] Capitation, officiers de judicature, généralité de Dijon, 1789 (A.D. Côte-d'Or, C 5687); Rapports de liquidation (D XVII 9): Avallon (in no. 127), Beaune (in no. 127), Bourg-en-Bresse (in no. 125), Dijon (in no. 125), Nuits (in no. 123); *Almanach du Parlement de Bourgogne*, 1789, 1790.

Table A6. Jurisdiction of the Parlement of Rouen[a]

Province, city, or town	Number of magistrates in office, 1789	Number of semiretired magistrates, 1789	District Court (D) and criminal court (C), 1790–1795
NORMANDIE			
Alençon, présidial	11	1	D, C
Argentan	8	3	D
Avranches	10	3	D
Bayeux	13	2	D
Beaumont-le-Roger	5	0	(none)
Bernay and Orbec	8	3	D
Breteuil	5	1	(none)
Caen, présidial	20	5	D, C
Cany	4	0	D
Carentan	3	1	D
Caudebec (baill. of Caux), présidial	6	0	D
Charleval	1	0	(none)
Conches	6	0	(none)
Coutances (baill. of Cotentin), présidial	22	0	D, C
Dieppe (baill. of Arques)	6	0	D
Domfront	5	0	D
Evreux, présidial	7	0	D, C
Exmes	7	0	(none)
Falaise	13	3	D
Honfleur	3	0	(none)
Le Havre	3	0	(none)
Montivilliers	4	0	D
Mortain	7	0	D
Neufchâtel-en-Bray	3	0	D
Nonancourt and Ezy	1	0	(none)
Périers and Cérences (baill. of Saint-Sauveur-Lendelin)	9	1	(none)
Pont-Audemer	7	0	D
Pont-de-l'Arche	4	0	(none)
Pont-l'Evêque	6	0	D

Table A6. *continued*

Province, city, or town	Number of magistrates in office, 1789	Number of semiretired magistrates, 1789	District court (D) and criminal court (C), 1790–1795
Rouen, présidial	13	1	D, C
Saint-Lô	12	2	D
Saint-Sauveur-le-Vicomte	3	1	(none)
Tinchebray	4	1	(none)
Torigni	8	1	(none)
Valognes	11	3	D
Verneuil	3	0	D
Vire	12	0	D

[a] Capitation, officiers de judicature; généralité de Caen, 1789 (A.D. Calvados, C 4645), généralité de Rouen, 1789 (A.D. Seine-Maritime, C 2129); Rapports de liquidation (D XVII 9): Avranches (in nos. 125 and 126), Caen (in no. 123), Coutances (in no. 127), Domfront (in no. 123), Falaise (in nos. 125 and 127), Bernay and Orbec (in no. 125), Saint-Lô (in nos. 124 and 125), Thorigny (in no. 125); *Almanach de Normandie,* 1787, 1790. See also Pierre Carel, "Note sur les magistrats du bailliage et siège présidial de Caen," *Bulletin de la Société des Antiquaires de Normandie,* 20 (1898), 583–647.

Table A7. Jurisdiction of the Parlement of Aix.[a]

Province, city, or town	Number of Magistrates in office, 1789	District court (D) and criminal court (C), 1790–1795
PROVENCE		
Aix	10	D, C
Arles	7	D
Brignoles	—	D
Castellane	4	D
Draguignan	6	D
Digne	—	D, C
Forcalquier	2	D
Grasse	—	D
Hyères	—	D
Marseille	9	D
Sisteron	7	D
Toulon	—	D, C

[a] Rapports de liquidation (D XVII 9): Aix (in nos. 123 and 126), Arles (in no. 123), Draguignan (in no. 125); *Almanach de Marseille, 1789; Les Bouches-du-Rhône, encyclopédie départementale,* ed. Paul Masson et al., 16 vols. (Paris, Champion, and Marseille, Les Archives Départementales, 1913–1937), III, 397–400; Frédéric Mireur, "Notice historique sur la sénéchaussée de Draguignan," in *Inventaire sommaire des archives départementales antérieures à 1790, Var, séries A et B* (Draguignan, imprimerie de Olivier-Joulian, 1895), pp. ix–cxxiv; Marie-Zéphirin Isnard, "La Sénéchaussée de Forcalquier," in *Inventaire sommaire des archives départementales antérieures à 1790, Basses-Alpes, série B,* 2 vols. (Digne, imprimerie de Chaspoul, Constans et veuve Barbaroux, 1892–1908), II, iii–lxvi; N.-F.-Saint-Marcel Eysseric, *Les Tribunaux de Sisteron, leur personnel de1790 à 1900* (Sisteron, Allemand fils, 1900).

Table A8. Jurisdiction of the Parlement of Rennes.[a]

Province, city, or town	Number of Magistrates in office, 1789	District Court (D) and criminal court, (C), 1790–1795
BRETAGNE		
Auray	2	D
Antrain	2	(none)
Bazouges-la-Pérouse	2	(none)
Brest	4	D
Carhaix	2	D
Châteaulin	2	D
Châteauneuf-du-Faou	2	(none)
Concarneau (sén. of Conq)	2	(none)
Dinan	2	D
Fougères	3	D
Gourin	2	(none)
Guérande	4	D
Hédé	2	(none)
Hennebont	3	D
Jugon	1	(none)
Lannion	2	D
Lesneven	4	D
Morlaix	4	D
Nantes, présidial	17	D, C
Ploërmel	4	D
Quimper, présidial	12	D, C
Quimperlé	2	D
Rennes, présidial	16	D, C
Rhuys	2	(none)
Saint-Aubin-du-Cormier	2	(none)
Saint-Brieuc	4	D, C
Vannes, présidial	9	D, C

[a] Rapports de liquidation (D XVII 9): Brest (in no. 126), Concarneau (in no. 126), Fougères (in no. 123), Nantes (in no. 124), Ploërmel (in no. 124), Quimperlé (in no. 123), Rennes (in nos. 124 and 126); *Almanach de Bretagne,* 1790; *Etrennes bretonnes,* 1790; Julien Trévédy, "Organisation judiciaire de la Bretagne avant 1790," *Nouvelle Revue Historique de Droit Français et Etranger,* 17 (1893), 192–257, 376–381.

Table A9. Jurisdiction of the Parlement of Pau.[a]

Province, city, or town	Number of Magistrates in office, 1789	District court (D) and criminal court (C), 1790–1795
NAVARRE & BEARN		
Licharre	2	(none)
Morlaas	2	(none)
Oloron	2	D
Orthez	2	D
Pau	2	D, C
Saint-Palais	2	D
Sauveterre	2	(none)

[a] *Tableau annuel, historique et géographique du Béarn,* 1784.

Table A10. Jurisdiction of the Parlement of Metz.[a]

Province, city, or town	Number of Magistrates in office, 1789	District Court (D) and criminal court (C), 1790–1795
TROIS EVÊCHES		
Château-Regnault	3	(none)
Longwy	3	(none)
Marville	3	(none)
Metz, présidial (1685)	21	D, C
Mohon	1	(none)
Montmédy	3	(none)
Mouzon	2	(none)
Phalsbourg	3	(none)
Sarrebourg	2	D
Sarrelouis, présidial (1685)	2	(none)
Sedan, présidial (1661)	4	D
Thionville	4	D
Toul, présidial (1685)	13	D
Verdun, présidial (1685)	12	D
Yvoi-Carignan	2	(none)

[a] Rapports de liquidation (D XVII 9): Metz (in no. 125), Mohon (in no. 123), Thionville (in no. 125), Toul (in no. 127); *Almanach des Trois Evêchés,* 1789.

Table A11. Jurisdiction of the Parlement of Besançon.[a]

Province, city, or town	Number of Magistrates in office, 1789	District court (D) and criminal court (C), 1790–1795
FRANCHE-COMTE		
Arbois	4	D
Baume-les-Dames	8	D
Besançon, présidial (1696)	15	D, C
Dôle, présidial (1771)	7	D, C
Gray, présidial (1696)	15	D
Lons-le-Saunier, présidial (1696)	14	D
Orgelet	8	D
Ornans	9	D
Poligny	7	D
Pontarlier	8	D
Quingey	4	D
Salins, présidial, (1696)	13	(none)
Vesoul, présidial (1696)	12	D, C

[a] Rapports de liquidation (D XVII 9): Besançon (in nos. 123 and 125), Ornans (in no. 124), Poligny (in no. 127), Pontarlier (in no. 123), Salins (in no. 125); *Almanach historique de Besançon et de la Franche-Comté,* 1786.

Table A12. Jurisdiction of the Parlement of Douai.[a]

Province, city, or town	Number of Magistrates in office, 1789	District court (D) and criminal court (C), 1790–1795
FLANDRE & HAINAUT		
Avesnes	4	D
Bailleul, présidial (1704)	11	D
Douai	8	D, C
Le Quesnoy	9	D
Lille	14	D
Maubeuge (prévôté)	2	(none)

[a] Rapports de liquidation (D XVII 9): Avesnes (in no. 127); *Calendrier général du gouvernement de la Flandre, du Hainaut et du Cambrésis,* 1789.

Table A13. Jurisdiction of the Parlement of Nancy.[a]

Province, city, or town	Number of Magistrates in office, 1789	District court (D) and criminal court (C), 1790–1795
BARROIS		
Bourmont	5	D
Briey	10	D
Etain	7	D
Longuyon	3	(none)
Pont-à-Mousson	11	D
Saint-Mihiel	8	D, C
Thiaucourt	5	(none)
Villers-la-Montagne	3	(none)
GERMAN LORRAINE		
Bitche	3	D
Boulay	5	D
Bouzonville	7	(none)
Château-Salins	2	D
Dieuze, présidial (1772)	10	D
Fenestrange	2	(none)
Lixheim	2	(none)
Sarreguemines	3	D
LORRAINE PROPER		
Blamont	4	D
Commercy	7	D
Lunéville	11	D
Nancy, présidial (1772)	11	D, C
Nomény	4	(none)
Rozieres-aux-Salines	4	(none)
Vezelise	8	D
PAYS DES VOSGES		
Bruyères	4	D
Charmes-sur-Moselle	5	(none)
Châtel-sur-Moselle	5	(none)
Darney	5	D
Epinal	7	D
Mirecourt, présidial (1772)	11	D, C
Neufchâteau	8	D
Remiremont	5	D
Saint-Dié, présidial (1772)	8	D

ᵃ Rapports de liquidation (D XVII 9): Bourmont (in no. 126), Briey (in no. 124), Bruyères (in no. 126), Charmes (in no. 123), Château-Salins (in nos. 125 and 126), Châtel (in no. 123), Commercy (in no. 124), Fenestrange (in no. 124), Lunéville (in no. 123), Mirecourt (in no. 127), Nancy (in nos. 124 and 127), Rozieres (in no. 127), Saint-Dié (in no. 123), Saint-Mihiel (in no. 125), Sarreguemines (in no. 124), Thiaucourt (in no. 124); *Almanach de Lorraine et Barrois*, 1789, 1790.

Sources and Bibliography

The lists that follow are selective, omitting many manuscripts, books, and articles that were consulted with little or no direct benefit, and omitting a number of items already cited in footnotes. My purpose here is to indicate the major types of materials used.

Much of this study is based on biographical information, especially about the magistrates who were in office on 1 May 1789 in the bailliages in Burgundy (97 judges and 30 king's counsel) and the sénéchaussées in Poitou (77 judges and 17 king's counsel).

An expert investigator of obscure biographical information from the revolutionary period, Pierre Caron, remarked on the

371

complexity of the methods entailed.* With respect to former magistrates, I gradually worked out a few ways in which the inquiry could be standardized. When my research was fairly well advanced, I was systematically looking for:

1. Names of all magistrates in office in 1789. The sources are of three types: provincial almanachs, lists of judicial office-holders paying the capitation tax (departmental archives, series C), and lists of officeholders reimbursed in the liquidation of the offices in 1791 (Archives Nationales, carton D XVII 9). Sources used have been specified above, in the notes of the Appendix.

2. Letters of appointment to office (*lettres patentes de provisions*). Occasionally an *expédition* on parchment is amongst family papers. Copies were registered by the parlement and the bailliage. By far the most convenient collection, however, consists of second minutes from the chancellery (Archives Nationales, series V¹). This was a routine document. It includes name of appointee, title of office, date of appointment, name of previous proprietor, name of previous incumbent (if other than proprietor), and date of baptism of appointee; in addition, the copy in series V¹ notes the amount of transfer tax or, alternatively, capital value of office, and certain fees paid. For bailliage magistrates in Burgundy and Poitou after about 1735, series V¹ is more than 90 percent complete. For Lorraine, Picardy, Anjou, and Languedoc, soundings after about 1750 indicate a similar degree of completeness. I obtained information from more than two hundred cartons, V¹ 314–539.

3. Record of baptism. This indicates father's name and occupation, mother's name, and, through the identity of the godfather and godmother, other family ties. With the date of baptism (obtained from letters of appointment), examination of parish registers is much facilitated. Where the latter were readily available and nearly complete, as in Côte-d'Or, it appeared that about half the magistrates had been born in the towns where they served in bailliages. For those born else-

* "Recherches biographiques sur la période révolutionnaire," in his *Manuel pratique pour l'étude de la Révolution française*, 2nd ed. (Paris, A. et J. Picard, 1947), pp. 272–277.

where, records of marriage or death sometimes indicated place of birth. Hence I found, for magistrates in Côte-d'Or, baptismal records in parish registers of Argilly, Géanges (Saint-Loup-de-la-Salle), Cussey-les-Forges, Pierre, Seurre, and Chissey-en-Morvan, as well as the bailliage towns, Châtillon-sur-Seine, Semur-en-Auxois, Saulieu, Arnay-le-Duc, Dijon (Saint-Jean, Saint-Michel, Saint-Pierre, and Notre-Dame), Auxonne, and Saint-Jean-de-Losne; the proportion of baptismal records found was 63 percent in Côte-d'Or, and less in other departments.

4. Records of marriage. Both the contract and the ecclesiastical record are useful, but especially the former. In Burgundy and in Poitou, marriage contracts were regularly drawn up by notaries and, for persons in the upper bourgeoisie, appear as elaborate treaties defining property settlements and involving long lists of "relatives and friends," the social milieu of the bride and the groom. Marriage contracts were taxed. A record of the tax payment was kept by the *contrôle des actes des notaires*, which also prepared, for its own use, alphabetical and chronological tables of contracting parties (departmental archives, series C). The record of the tax payment summarizes the property clauses and provides the two details needed to locate the contract itself: the name of the principal notary and the date of the contract, which may then be found if it has been deposited (departmental archives, series E). This chain of research has two weak links: if one does not know approximately where the marriage was contracted, it may be necessary to search the records of many bureaux of the *contrôle des actes* (about fifty bureaux for an area the size of a department); secondly, either the registers of the *contrôle des actes* or, rather commonly, the notary's minute of the contract may be lost or may never have been deposited in the archives. In Burgundy, I found summaries of marriage contracts registered in the contrôle des actes for 30 percent of the magistrates; most were sufficiently detailed for my purposes. In Poitou, the records of the contrôle des actes were not as detailed, so I used them chiefly in a search for marriage contracts themselves, with uneven results (in Poitiers, 19 magistrates, 7 marriage contracts found; in Fontenay-le-Comte, 14 magistrates, 5 marriage

contracts found; in other towns, a number of summaries registered by the contrôle but no more than one or two actual contracts).

5. Habitual signature. This is sometimes the only means of distinguishing brothers, cousins, or homonyms. The necessity to secure as many means of identification as possible was borne in upon me by reading the registration of the death of Hubert-François Le Tors, reported by his first cousin, Hubert-François Le Tors (*état civil*, Avallon, 22 June 1812).

6. Records of death. The registration in the état civil identifies the decedent's wife and often mentions his parents, birthplace, or age. The declaration of succession was recorded several months later by the *bureau de l'enregistrement et des domaines*, which also prepared tables of decedents leaving successions (departmental archives, series Q). The succession indicates a minimum estimate of the estate remaining after the establishment of sons and the dowering of daughters. In Burgundy, I found declarations of successions of 28 percent of the magistrates; in Poitiers, 40 percent; elsewhere in Poitou, less than 5 percent because of the difficulty of discovering where the former magistrates died.

7. Inclusion in lists of departmental notables and heavily taxed residents. This often served for my purposes as the practical equivalent of a declaration of succession, in that it indicates an approximate economic level late in life. There were several types of such lists drawn up in the Napoleonic period (departmental archives, series M).

In working out the application of the above scheme in the archival collections, I depended primarily on the following research guides:

Chaume, Maurice. "L'Histoire des familles dans un grand dépôt provincial," *Annales de Bourgogne*, 15 (1943), 71–80.
Meurgey de Tupigny, Jacques, and Vaux de Foletier, François de. *Guide des recherches généalogiques aux Archives Nationales avec une étude sur les recherches biographiques aux Archives de la Seine*. Paris, Imprimerie Nationale, 1956.
Clémencet, Suzanne; Langlois, Monique; Lanhers, Yvonne; et

al. *Guide des recherches dans les fonds judiciares de l'ancien régime.* Paris, Imprimerie Nationale, 1958. [Archives Nationales, series V, X, Y, and Z.]

Vilar-Berrogain, Gabrielle. *Guide des recherches dans les fonds d'enregistrement sous l'ancien régime.* Paris, Imprimerie Nationale, 1958. [Archives Nationales and archives départementales.]

Tracing a former bailliage magistrate through the revolutionary years was essentially a task of searching for his name in various lists and documentary collections. These were indicated by the fundamental guides to the archives. For the Archives Nationales:

Etat sommaire par séries des documents conservés aux Archives Nationales. Paris, Imprimerie Nationale, 1891.

Etat sommaire des versements faits aux Archives Nationales par les ministères et les administrations qui en dépendent. 4 vols. Paris, Imprimerie Nationale, 1924–1957. In particular, vol. I (Intérieur) and vol. IV (Justice).

For the departmental archives, printed and manuscript inventories are described by:

Etat des inventaires des Archives Nationales, départementales, communales, et hospitalières au 1er janvier 1937. Paris, Imprimerie Nationale, 1938; followed by a *Supplément.* Paris, Imprimerie Nationale, 1955.

As a foreigner with a limited time for archival research, I was especially aided by the copious summaries compiled by the archivists of the Yonne:

Porée, Charles. *Inventaire sommaire des archives départementales postérieures à 1790. Yonne, archives de la Révolution, série L.* Auxerre, Imprimerie de l'Indépendant Auxerrois, 1911.

―――― *Sources manuscrites de l'histoire de la Révolution dans l'Yonne. Archives Nationales.* 2 vols. Auxerre, Imprimerie l'Universelle, 1918–1927. [Vol. I: series B, C, and D. Vol. II: series F.]

Forestier, Henri. *L'Yonne au XIXe siècle, 1e partie (1800–1830).* 2 vols. Auxerre, Imprimerie l'Universelle, 1959. [Not a complete list, but a selection from departmental series M, P, R, S, T, and V, relating to general administration, public health, industry and commerce, agriculture, military affairs, education, religion, finance, and transportation.]

The principal manuscript materials examined systematically were as follows:

Archives Nationales

B^a 16, 31, 37, 49, 53, 78. Elections, 1789, bailliages of Autun (secondary bailliages Montcenis, Bourbon-Lancy, Semur-en-Brionnais), Auxerre; Chalon-sur-Saône, Charolles; Dijon (secondary bailliages Auxonne, Saint-Jean-de-Losne, Beaune); Mâcon; Châtillon-sur-Seine; Semur-en-Auxois (secondary bailliages Avallon, Saulieu, Arnay-le-Duc).

D III 51–55, 224–227, 295–297, 304. Correspondence addressed or referred to the Comité de Législation, Convention Nationale, concerning Côte-d'Or, Saône-et-Loire, Deux-Sèvres, Vienne, Yonne; mostly dating from Year III and providing much retrospective information on 1793 and Year II.

D XI 1. Comité de Liquidation, Assemblée nationale constituante; Direction générale de la liquidation.

D XVII 1–9 and D* XVII 1, 2. Comité de Judicature, Assemblée nationale constituante; most of these papers pertain to the liquidation of the old offices, not elections or appointments to new ones.

F^{1c} III. Côte-d'Or 1 and 2; Saône-et-Loire 1; Deux-Sèvres 1; Vendée 1; Vienne 1; Yonne 1. Esprit public, elections.

F^{1d} II. Diverse requests addressed or referred to the Minister of the Interior by individuals, in alphabetical order.

F^7 4577–4775^{53}. Information transmitted to the Comité de Sûrete Générale concerning arrested or suspected persons, in alphabetical order, some 340 cartons indexed in a card file by Pierre Caron.

BB^5 43, 44, 163, 164, 215, 216. Appointments and personnel, judiciary, Côte-d'Or, Saône-et-Loire, Yonne.

BB^6 1–4. Information concerning magistrates.

BB^{30} 30. Composition of tribunals, 1793–Year II.

BB³⁰ 66, 67. Correspondence of bailliages, 1789–1790.
AD IX 82, 431, 438–439, 451–453, 496–497. Legislative and administrative texts concerning royal finances, in particular (respectively): capitation and 100ᵉ denier, gages, marc d'or, offices, and caisse de l'extraordinaire.

Archives Départementales, Côte-d'Or, Saône-et-Loire, Yonne, Vienne, Deux-Sèvres, Vendée.

Series L. Cartons concerning elections, persons arrested, and *sociétés populaires.*
Series Q. Tables of purchasers and records of purchases of *biens nationaux,* except in Deux-Sèvres and Vendée.

Principal Published Sources

1. GEOGRAPHY

Atlas des bailliages ou juridictions assimilées ayant formé unité électorale en 1789, ed. Armand Brette. Paris, Imprimerie Nationale, 1904.
Courtépée, Claude, abbé. *Description générale et particulière du duché de Bourgogne.* 6 vols., Dijon, 1774–1785. 2nd ed., 4 vols., Dijon, 1847–1848.
Expilly, Jean-Joseph, abbé d'. *Dictionnaire géographique, historique et politique des Gaules et de la France.* 6 vols. Paris, 1762–1770. [Never completed; covers geographic names with initials A through S.]
Young, Arthur, *Travels during the Years 1787, 1788, and 1789, Undertaken More Particularly with a View of Ascertaining the Cultivation, Wealth, Resources, and National Prosperity of the Kingdom of France.* 2nd ed., 2 vols. London, 1794; French trans. and critical ed. by Henri Sée, 3 vols. Paris, Librairie Armand Colin, 1931.

2. ROYAL LEGISLATION

Recueil général des anciennes lois françaises, depuis l'an 420 jusqu'à la révolution de 1789, ed. Francois-André Isambert, N. Decrusy, Alphonse-Henri Taillandier, and Athanase-Jean-

Léger Jourdan. 29 vols. Paris, 1821–1833. [Volumes XXI and XXII, règne de Louis XV, ed. Decrusy and Taillandier, comprise excerpts from about 5 percent of the printed *actes royaux* of that period catalogued at the Bibliothèque Nationale. In volumes XXIII–XXVIII, règne de Louis XVI, ed. Jourdan (after his death, completed by Armet), the proportion is somewhat larger, but still few edicts are printed in full.]

3. REMONSTRANCES OF PARLEMENTS

Many are in print, but the only ones I consulted extensively are those of Paris:

Remontrances du Parlement de Paris au XVIIIe siècle, ed. Jules Flammermont. 3 vols. Paris, Imprimerie Nationale, 1888–1898.

4. REFERENCE WORKS ON LAW AND JUDICIAL ADMINISTRATION

Ferrière, Claude-Joseph de. *Dictionnaire de droit et de pratique.* Paris, 1734. [The author was professor of law in Paris from 1703 until his death in 1748, after which the dictionary was revised by Antoine-Gaspard Boucher d'Argis and republished several times; the 8th edition, 1787, was the one I consulted.]

Guyot, Joseph-Nicolas, ed. *Répertoire universel et raisonné de jurisprudence.* 2nd edition, 17 vols. Paris, 1784–1785.

———— and Merlin, Philippe-Antoine, ed. *Traité des droits, fonctions, franchises, exemptions, prérogatives et privilèges annexés en France à chaque dignité, à chaque office et à chaque état.* 4 vols. Paris, 1786–1788. [Covers the royal households, the judiciary in general, and some appellate courts; chapters were planned but never published on bailliages, municipalities, and financial administration.]

Jousse, Daniel. *Traité de l'administration de la justice.* 2 vols. Paris, 1771. [The author, a councillor in the bailliage of Orléans, also produced several commentaries and lesser treatises.]

Lerasle, N., ed. *Encyclopédie méthodique: Jurisprudence.* 8 vols., Paris, 1782–1789.

5. LETTERS TO AND FROM A BAILLIAGE MAGISTRATE

Faulcon, Félix. *Correspondance.* ed. Gabriel Debien. 2 vols.
Poitiers, 1939–1953, as *Archives Historiques du Poitou,* 51
and 55. [These letters, written in 1770–1791, are of the
greatest interest. Private papers of bailliage magistrates are
not commonly accessible. Faulcon was better educated and
probably more intelligent than many. In his social status,
economic position, and political attitudes, however, he typi-
fies an occupation and a milieu.]

6. THE ELECTIONS OF 1789

*Recueil de documents relatifs à la convocation des Etats Géné-
raux de 1789,* ed. Armand Brette, 4 vols. Paris, Imprimerie
Nationale, 1894–1915. [Vol. I: regulations, lists of intendants, military commandants, bishops. Vol. II: lists of deputies and alternates elected. Vols. III and IV: summary of
the electoral proceedings in sixteen généralités in northern,
central, western, and southwestern France; provinces not
covered, Normandy, Flanders, Artois, Hainaut, Cambrésis,
Lorraine, Trois Evêchés, Burgundy, Franche-Comté, Provence, Languedoc, Roussillon, Brittany, were intended to be
studied in additional volumes that were never published.
The collection was basic in my research.]

7. CAHIERS DE DOLEANCES. (Listed by geographic names alphabetically)

*Cahiers de doléances des corps et corporations de la ville d'Alen-
çon pour les Etats Généraux de 1789,* ed. René Jouanne.
Alençon, Imprimerie Alençonnaise, 1929. [Important introduction by the editor.]

*Cahiers de doléances des corporations de la ville d'Angers et
des paroisses de la sénéchaussée particulière d'Angers pour
les Etats Généraux de 1789,* ed. Arthur Le Moy. 2 vols.
Angers, A. Burdin & Cie, 1915–1916. [Important introduction
by the editor.]

"Cahiers des paroisses et communautés du bailliage d'Autun
pour les Etats Généraux de 1789," ed. Anatole Desplaces
de Charmasse, *Mémoires de la Société Eduenne,* n.s., 3

(1874), 219–297; 4 (1875), 283–344; 5 (1876), 65–153; 6 (1877), 153–216; 7 (1878), 315–380; 14 (1885), 115–139; reprinted separately, Autun, 1895.

"Cahiers des paroisses du bailliage d'Auxerre pour les Etats Généraux de 1789," ed. Charles Demay, *Bulletin de la Société des Sciences Historiques et Naturelles de l'Yonne,* 38 (1884), 65–405; 39 (1885), 5–150.

Cahiers de doléances du bailliage de Bourges et des bailliages secondaires de Vierzon et d'Henrichemont pour les Etats Généraux de 1789, ed. Alfred Gandilhon. Bourges, Imprimerie Tardy-Pigelet, 1910.

Cahiers de doléances pour les Etats Généraux de 1789, [bailliages de Châlons-sur-Marne, Sézanne and Châtillon-sur-Marne], ed. Gustave Laurent. 3 vols. Epernay, Imprimerie Henri Villers, 1906–1911. [Constituting vols. I–III of the cahiers in the department of the Marne; for the rest, see below, Reims.]

Cahiers de doléances de la sénéchaussée de Civray pour les Etats Généraux de 1789, ed. Prosper Boissonnade and Léonce Cathelineau. Niort, Imprimerie Saint-Denis, 1925.

"Doléances des corporations et corps constitués de Limoges, 1789," ed. Alfred Leroux, *Archives Historiques de la Marche et du Limousin,* 1 (1887), 1–126.

Cahiers de doléances des sénéchaussées de Niort et de Saint-Maixent et des communautés et corporations de Niort et Saint-Maixent pour les Etats Généraux de 1789, ed. Léonce Cathelineau. Niort, G. Clouzot, 1912.

Cahiers de doléances du bailliage d'Orléans pour les Etats Généraux de 1789, ed. Camille Bloch. 2 vols. Orléans. Imprimerie Orléanaise, 1906–1907.

Cahiers de doléances pour les Etats Généraux de 1789, [bailliage de Reims], ed. Gustave Laurent. 2 vols. Reims, Imprimerie Matot-Braine, 1930. [Constituting vols. IV and V of the cahiers in the department of the Marne. The texts are in vol. IV; the editor's extremely valuable introduction, in vol. V.]

Cahiers de doléances du tiers état du bailliage de Rouen pour les Etats Généraux de 1789, ed. Marc Bouloiseau. 2 vols.

Paris, Presses Universitaires de France, 1957, and Rouen, Imprimerie administrative de la Seine-Maritime, 1960. [Important introduction by the editor.]

Cahiers de doléances du bailliage de Troyes (principal et secondaires) et du bailliage de Bar-sur-Seine pour les Etats Généraux de 1789, ed. Jules-Joseph Vernier, 3 vols. Troyes, Imprimerie P. Nouel, 1909–1911.

8. NEWSPAPERS

Gazette nationale, ou le Moniteur universel, Paris, 24 November 1789–1795. [The second reprint edition (Paris, 1852–1870) and also a summary: *Révolution française, ou Analyse complette et impartiale du Moniteur.* 3 vols. Paris, Girardin, 1801–1802 (followed by 3 vols. of indexes).]

Point du Jour, ou Résultat de ce qui s'est passé la veille à l'Assemblée Nationale, Paris, 19 June 1789–1791. [By Barère.]

9. REVOLUTIONARY LEGISLATION

Collection des décrets de l'Assemblée nationale constituante, rédigés suivant l'ordre des matières, edited by Charles-André-Rèmy Arnoult. 6 vols. Dijon, 1792.

Archives Parlementaires de 1787 à 1860, recueil complet des débats legislatifs et politiques des chambres françaises, 1ᵉ série (1787 à 1799) edited by Jérôme Mavidal and Emile Laurent, et al., 82 vols., Paris, Librairie Paul Dupont, 1867–1913, and by Marcel Reinhard and Marc Bouloiseau, Paris, Centre National de la Recherche Scientifique, 1961– , in progress [presently reaching vol. LXXXVIII extending through 28 germinal an II (17 April 1794)].

10. NATIONALIZED PROPERTY

The basic collection of laws and regulations:

Recueil des textes législatifs et administratifs concernant les biens nationaux, ed. Pierre Caron and Eugène Desprez. 3 vols. Paris, Imprimerie Nationale, 1926–1944. [Texts dated from 23 September 1789 to 6 March 1796.]

Records of sales, listed by departements alphabetically:

Documents relatifs à la vente des biens nationaux dans le département des Bouches-du-Rhône, ed. Paul Moulin. 4 vols. Marseille, Barlatier, 1908–1911.

Documents relatifs à la vente des biens nationaux dans le départment de la Gironde, ed. Marcel Marion et al. 2 vols. Bordeaux, Imprimerie Cadoret, 1911–1912.

Haute-Garonne: *Documents relatifs à la vente des biens nationaux. District de Toulouse,* ed. Henri Martin. Toulouse, Edouard Privat, 1916.

Documents relatifs à la vente des biens nationaux dans le département du Rhône, ed. Sébastien Charléty. Lyon, Imprimerie R. Schneider, 1906.

Vosges: *Documents relatifs à la vente des biens nationaux. District d'Epinal,* ed. Léon Schwab. Epinal, Imprimerie Nouvelle, 1911.

——— *Documents relatifs à la vente des biens nationaux. District de Remiremont,* ed. Léon Schwab. Epinal, Imprimerie Vosgienne, 1913.

Yonne: *Documents relatifs à la vente des biens nationaux. District de Sens,* ed. Charles Porée, 2 vols. Auxerre, Imprimerie l'Universelle, 1912–1913.

11. Provincial politics, spring through autumn 1793

Rapports des agents du ministre de l'Intérieur dans les départements (1793–an II), ed. Pierre Caron. 2 vols. Paris, Imprimerie Nationale, 1913–1951. [The geographic coverage is uneven, and the reports vary in quality and credibility, but these documents report various degrees of moderation and unwillingness as well as republican zeal at the end of the first year of the Republic.]

Secondary Works

1. Library catalogues

Catalogue de l'histoire de France. 17 vols. Paris, Bibliothèque Impériale, 1855–1870, and Bibliothèque Nationale, 1879–1895.

Catalogue général des livres imprimés de la Bibliothèque Na-

tionale: Actes royaux. 7 vols. Paris, Bibliothèque Nationale, 1910–1960. [Vols. V and VI: Louis XV, Louis XVI, ed. Suzanne Honoré. Reference to the Rondonneau collection is necessary as well: A.N., AD + and AD I to AD XVIII.]

Catalogue de l'histoire de la Révolution française. Ecrits de la période révolutionnaire, 1789–1799. 5 vols. in 6, Paris, Bibliothèque Nationale, 1936–1957. [By André Martin and Gérard Walter. Especially valuable for: vol. IV, part II, anonymous writings; and vol. V, newspapers and almanacs.]

2. GENERAL HISTORICAL BIBLIOGRAPHIES

For works published in 1866–1897:

Caron, Pierre. *Bibliographie des travaux publiés de 1866 à 1897 sur l'histoire de la France depuis 1789.* Paris. Edouard Cornély & Cᵢₑ, 1912.

Saulnier, Eugène, and Martin, André. *Bibliographie des travaux publiés de 1866 à 1897 sur l'histoire de la France de 1500 à 1789.* 2 vols. Paris. Presses Universitaires de France, 1932–1938.

For works published in 1898–1913;

Caron, Pierre; Brière, Gaston; Burnand, Robert; et al. *Répertoire méthodique de l'histoire moderne et contemporaine de la France.* 11 vols. Paris. I–VI and IX–XI, *Revue d'Histoire Moderne et Contemporaine,* 1899–1914; VII, F. Rieder, 1914–1918; VIII, Centre National de la Recherche Scientifique, 1965.

For works published in 1920–1931:

Caron, Pierre, and Stein, Henri. *Répertoire bibliographique de l'histoire de France.* 6 vols. Paris. Rieder, Picard, 1923–1938.

For works published in and after 1953:

Albert-Samuel, Colette. *Bibliographie annuelle de l'histoire de France du Vᵉ siecle à 1939.* Paris. Centre National de la Recherche Scientifique, 1956– , in progress. [Presently extends through publications of 1969.]

3. SPECIALIZED BIBLIOGRAPHIES (see also later sections)

Caron, Pierre. *Manuel pratique pour l'étude de la Révolution française.* 2nd edition. Paris, A. & J. Picard & Cᵢₑ, 1947.

Dehergne, Joseph. "Bibliographie du Bas-Poitou à la veille de la Revolution. Principaux mémoires, ouvrages et travaux concernant le XVIIIᵉ siècle," *Mémoires de la Société des Antiquaires de l'Ouest,* 4th ser., 7 (1963), 65–197, and separately published, Paris, A. & J. Picard & Cⁱᵉ, 1965.

Lasteyrie du Saillant, Robert de, assisted by Vidier, Alexandre; continued for publications of 1910–1940 by Gandilhon, René. *Bibliographie générale des travaux historiques et archéologiques publiés par les sociétés savantes de la France.* 14 vols. Paris, Imprimerie Nationale, 1888–1961.

Milsand, Philibert. *Bibliographie bourguignonne, ou Catalogue méthodique d'ouvrages relatifs à la Bourgogne.* Dijon, 1885.

———— *Bibliographie bourguignonne. Supplément.* Dijon, 1888.

———— *Etudes bibliographiques sur les périodiques publiés à Dijon.* Dijon, 1861.

Monceaux, Henri. *La Révolution dans le département de l'Yonne, 1788–1800. Essai bibliographique.* Paris, 1890.

Saffroy, Gaston. *Bibliographie des almanachs et annuaires administratifs, ecclésiastiques et militaires français de l'ancien régime et des almanachs et annuaires généalogiques et nobiliaires du XVIᵉ siècle à nos jours.* Paris, Librairie Gaston Saffroy, 1959.

———— *Bibliographie généalogique héraldique et nobiliaire de la France des origines à nos jours, Imprimés et manuscrits.* Paris, Librairie Gaston Saffroy, 1968–   , in progress. [Seems destined to be the premier bibliography for studies of status and family histories in the nobility and the bourgeoisie. Vols. III and IV are still to be published.]

Walter, Gérard. *Répertoire de l'histoire de la Révolution française. Travaux publiés de 1800 à 1940. I. Personnes. II. Lieux.* 2 vols. Paris, Bibliothèque Nationale, 1941–1951. [A severe review by Anne Terroine, in *Annales Historiques de la Révolution Française,* 20 (1948), 1–26, warns of the incompleteness of this select list of works in the Bibliothèque Nationale. For a more equable judgment, see Caron, *Manuel,* p. 227.]

4. NOBILITY AND BOURGEOISIE

Aynard, Joseph. *La Bourgeoisie française. Essai de psychologie.* Paris, Perrin, 1934.

Babeau, Albert. *Les Bourgeois d'autrefois.* Paris, 1886. [Based on conscientious research in local history by a member of an old bourgeois family, which was represented in the eighteenth century by a councillor in the bailliage of Troyes.]

Barber, Elinor G. *The Bourgeoisie in Eighteenth Century France.* Princeton, Princeton University Press, 1955. [Explicit reference to theory of social stratification. Emphasis on ambivalent attitude of bourgeoisie toward social mobility.]

Bluche, François, and Durye, Pierre. *L'Anoblissement par charges avant 1789.* 2 vols. Paris, 1962, as *Les cahiers nobles,* 23 and 24. [A study of royal legislation and a catalogue of ennobling offices.]

Bois, Paul. "Structure socio-professionnelle du Mans à la fin du XVIIIᵉ siècle," 87ᵉ Congrès National des Sociétés Savantes, Poitiers, 1962. *Actes,* pp. 679–709. [Stratification based on tax assessments for the *taille.*]

Commission de recherche et de publication des documents relatifs à la vie économique de la Révolution. Assemblée générale de la Commission centrale et des comités départementaux, 1939, [*Communications*]. 2 vols. Besançon, Jacques et Demontrond, 1942, and Paris, Tepac, 1945. [Notably: Georges Lefebvre, "Circulaire adressée aux comités départementaux et aux sociétés savantes" and "Extrait du rapport général présenté à la séance de cloture" (I, 9–29); and studies of Albi (by Pierre Bayaud, I, 33–45), Marseille (by Alfred Chabaud, I, 47–143), Pontivy (by Eugène Corgne, I, 145–169), Grenoble (by G. Letonnelier, I, 209–220), and Evreux (by Jean Vidalenc, I, 221–248).]

Daumard, Adeline, and Furet, François. *Structures et relations sociales à Paris au XVIIIᵉ siècle.* Paris, Librairie Armand Colin, 1961. [Stratification based on the marriage contracts of 1749.]

Du Puy de Clinchamps, Philippe. *La Noblesse.* Paris, Presses

Universitaires de France, 1959. [A helpful introduction, in the *Que sais-je?* series.]

Garden, Maurice. "Niveaux de fortune à Dijon au milieu du XVIIIᵉ siècle," *Cahiers d'Histoire,* 9 (1964), 217–260. [Stratification based on the marriage contracts of 1748.]

Goblot, Edmond. *La Barrière et le niveau. Etude sociologique sur la bourgeoisie française moderne.* Paris, Félix Alcan, 1925.

Goubert, Pierre. *Familles marchandes sous l'ancien régime; les Danse et les Motte, de Beauvais.* Paris. S.E.V.P.E.N., 1959. [Two types of family history, sixteenth-nineteenth centuries.]

Hufton, Olwen H. *Bayeux in the Late Eighteenth Century. A Social Study.* Oxford, Oxford University Press, 1967.

Johannet, René. *Eloge du bourgeois français.* Paris, Bernard Grasset, 1924.

Kaplow, Jeffry. *Elbeuf during the Revolutionary Period: History and Social Structure.* Baltimore, The Johns Hopkins Press, 1964.

Labrousse, Camille-Ernest. "Voies nouvelles vers une histoire de la bourgeoisie occidentale aux XVIIIᵉ et XIXᵉ siècles (1700–1850)," X Congresso Internazionale di Scienze Storiche, Roma, 1955, *Relazioni,* IV, 365–396.

Lefebvre, Georges. *Cherbourg à la fin de l'ancien régime et au début de la Révolution.* Caen, 1965, as *Cahiers des Annales de Normandie,* 4. [Written in 1898–1903.]

———— "Urban Society in the Orléanais in the Late Eighteenth Century," *Past and Present,* no. 19 (1961), pp. 46–75. [Some passages are translated from his *Etudes orléanaises,* I, 228–230 (q.v.).]

———— *Etudes orléanaises.* I. *Contribution à l'étude des structures sociales à la fin du XVIIIᵉ siècle.* II. *Subsistances et maximum (1789-an IV).* 2 vols. Paris, 1962–1963, Commission d'Histoire Economique et Sociale de la Révolution, *Mémoires et documents,* 15.

Léon, Pierre. "Recherches sur la bourgeoisie française de province au XVIIIᵉ siècle," *Information Historique,* 20

(1958), 101–105. [A report presented at Rome in 1955: see above, Labrousse.]

Leuilliot, Paul. "Réflexions sur l'histoire économique et sociale à propos de la bourgeoisie en 1789," *Revue d'Histoire Moderne et Contemporaine*, 1 (1954), 131–144.

Meyer, Jean. *La Noblesse bretonne au XVIIIe siècle*. 2 vols. (continuous pagination). Paris, S.E.V.P.E.N., 1966. [A masterpiece.]

Morazé, Charles. *La France bourgeoise, XVIIIe–XXe siècles*. 2nd edition, Paris, Armand Colin, 1947.

Pariset, Georges. "La Bourgeoisie française depuis la Révolution," a lecture reprinted in his *Etudes d'histoire révolutionnaire et contemporaine*. Paris, Les Belles Lettres, 1929.

Reinhard, Marcel. "Elite et noblesse dans la seconde moitié du XVIIIe siècle," *Revue d'Histoire Moderne et Contemporaine*, 3 (1956), 5–37. [A study of efforts to redefine the criteria for membership in the elite in France.]

Roupnel, Gaston. *La Ville et la campagne au XVIIe siècle. Etude sur les populations du pays dijonnais*. Paris, Leroux, 1922, reprinted, Paris, S.E.V.P.E.N., 1955, with a foreword by Pierre de Saint Jacob. [A classic of urban-rural history.]

Saint Jacob, Pierre de. "Recherches sur la structure sociale de Chalon à la fin de l'ancien régime," *Mémoires de la Société d'Histoire et d'Archéologie de Chalon-sur-Saône*, 34 (1956–1957), 108–114.

———— "Le Tiers état châtillonais à la veille de la Révolution," 28e Congrès de l'Association Bourguignonne de Sociétés Savantes, Châtillon-sur-Seine, 1957, [*Communications*], pp. 99–102.

Taylor, George V. "Types of Capitalism in Eighteenth-Century France," *English Historical Review*, 79 (1964), 478–497.

———— "Noncapitalist Wealth and the Origins of the French Revolution," *American Historical Review*, 72 (1967), 469–496.

Thore, Pierre-Henri. "Essai de classification des catégories sociales à l'intérieur du tiers état de Toulouse," 78e Congrès National des Sociétés Savantes, Toulouse, 1953, *Actes*, pp.

149–165. [Stratification based on precedence in the proceedings of commissions and special councils, 1788–1790.]

Tudesq, André-Jean. "L'Etude des notables. Inventaire des sources et projets d'enquête," *Bulletin d'Histoire Moderne et Contemporaine (depuis 1715) du Comité des Travaux Historiques et Scientifiques*, 1 (1956), 25–52.

Vovelle, Michel. "Structure et répartition de la fortune foncière et de la fortune mobilière d'un ensemble urbain: Chartres, de la fin de l'ancien régime à la Restauration," *Revue d'Histoire Economique et Sociale*, 36 (1958), 385–398.

———— "Formes de dépendance d'un milieu urbain, Chartres, à l'égard du monde rural, de la fin de l'ancien régime à la Restauration," 83e Congrès National des Sociétés Savantes, Aix-Marseille, 1958, *Actes*, 483–512.

———— and Roche, Daniel. "Bourgeois, rentiers, propriétaires. Eléments pour la définition d'une catégorie sociale à la fin du XVIIIe siècle," 84e Congrès National des Sociétés Savantes, Dijon, 1959, *Actes*, pp. 419–452.

5. Laws, institutions, officeholders

(a) Bibliographies

Grandin, A. *Bibliographie générale des sciences juridiques, politiques, économiques et sociales de 1800 à 1925.* 3 vols. Paris. Recueil Sirey, 1926, followed by nineteen annual *Suppléments*, 1927–1951. [Lists only books in French.]

Lepointe, Gabriel, and Vandenbossche, André. *Eléments de bibliographie sur l'histoire des institutions et des faits sociaux, 987–1875.* Paris. Editions Montchrestien, 1958. [Lists books and articles in French published in 1926–1956.] Continued by Boulet-Sautel, Marguerite; Sautel, Gérard; and Vandenbossche, André. *Bibliographie en langue française d'histoire du droit, 987–1875.* Paris. Editions Montchrestien, 1961– , in progress. [Presently extends through publications of 1966.]

Portejoie, Paulette. "Bibliographie de droit poitevin," *Mémoires de la Société des Antiquaires de l'Ouest*, 4th ser., 3 (1958), part II, pp. 1–50.

(b) General works, on the period before 1789

Sources and Bibliography

Chénon, Emile. *Histoire générale du droit français public et privé, des origines à 1815*, tome II, fasc. 1, publié par les soins de François Olivier-Martin. Paris, Recueil Sirey, 1929. [Excellent on public law to 1789.]

Dawson, John P. *A History of Lay Judges*. Cambridge, Mass., Harvard University Press, 1960. [Pp. 39–94: "Popular Courts and their Displacement... France."]

———— *The Oracles of the Law*. Ann Arbor, University of Michigan Law School, 1968. [Pp. 263–431: "The French Deviation" and "The Modern French Reaction."]

Marion, Marcel. *Dictionnaire des institutions de la France aux XVIIᵉ et XVIIIᵉ siècles*. Paris, Editions A. & J. Picard & Cⁱᵉ, 1923.

Meynial, Edmond. "Remarques sur les traits originaux de l'ancien droit privé français," *Tijdschrift voor Rechtsgeschiedenis*, 4 (1923), 401–421. [Suggestive concerning the relations between law and the social system.]

Olivier-Martin, François. *Histoire du droit français des origines à la Révolution*. Paris, Domat-Montchrestien, 1948.

(c) Public offices as private property

Göhring, Martin. *Die Ämterkäuflichkeit im ancien régime*. Berlin, Verlag Dr. Emil Ebering, 1938, *Historische Studien*, 346.

Mousnier, Roland. *La Vénalité des offices sous Henri IV et Louis XIII*. Rouen, Editions Maugard, [1945].

Pagès, Georges. "La Vénalité des offices dans l'ancienne France," *Revue Historique*, 169 (1932), 477–495.

(d) Parlements

The mass of scholarly (and unscholarly) writings is considerable. A few are outstanding:

Bluche, François. *Les Magistrats du Parlement de Paris au XVIIIᵉ siècle (1715–1771)*. Paris, Les Belles Lettres, 1960.

Colombet, Albert. *Les Parlementaires bourguignons à la fin du XVIIIᵉ siècle*. [1774–1788.] 2nd edition. Dijon, chez l'auteur, 1937.

Egret, Jean. *Le Parlement de Dauphiné et les affaires publiques dans la seconde moitié du XVIIIᵉ siècle*. 2 vols. Grenoble and Paris, Arthaud, 1942.

———— "L'aristocratie parlementaire française à la fin de

l'ancien régime," *Revue Historique*, 208 (1952), 1–14.

———— *Louis XV et l'opposition parlementaire, 1715–1774.* Paris, Librairie Armand Colin, 1970.

Ford, Franklin L. *Robe and Sword. The Regrouping of the French Aristocracy after Louis XIV.* [1715–1748.] Cambridge, Mass., Harvard University Press, 1953.

Le Moy, Arthur. *Le Parlement de Bretagne et le pouvoir royal au XVIIIᵉ siècle.* Angers, Burdin & Cⁱᵉ, 1909.

On the judiciary reforms of 1771–1774 and 1788, there are many special studies, of which the following are most important:

Babinet, Charles. "Notice sur le conseil supérieur de Poitiers (1771–1774)," *Bulletin de la Société des Antiquaires de l'Ouest*, 7 (1895), 199–209.

Carabie, Robert. "L'Enregistrement au bailliage de Caen des édits de mai 1788," *Annales de Normandie*, 9 (1959), 301–314.

Carré, Henri. *La Fin des parlements (1788–1790).* Paris, Hachette, 1912.

Doyle, William O. "The Parlements of France and the Breakdown of the Old Regime, 1771–1788," *French Historical Studies*, 6 (1969–1970), 415–458.

Duboul, Axel. *La Fin du Parlement de Toulouse.* Toulouse, 1890.

Flammermont, Jules. *Le Chancelier Maupeou et les parlements.* Paris, 1883.

Georges, Etienne. "Résistance du bailliage de Troyes aux réformes judiciaires en 1788," *Annuaire de la Société Académique du Département de l'Aube*, 64 (1890), 3–25.

Huguenin, Anatole. "La Cour plénière et les édits de mai 1788, Les avocats de Dijon à Versailles," *Mémoires de l'Académie des Sciences, Arts et Belles-Lettres de Dijon*, 4th ser., 10 (1905–1906), 47–81.

Le Griel, Jacques. *Le Chancelier Maupeou et la magistrature française à la fin de l'ancien régime. Le conseil supérieur de Clermont-Ferrand, 1771–1774.* Paris, Champion, 1909.

Marion, Marcel. *Le Garde des sceaux Lamoignon et la réforme judiciaire de 1788.* Paris, Hachette, 1905.

Maupeou d'Ableiges, Jacques, vicomte de. *Le Chancelier Maupeou.* Paris, Editions de Champrosay, 1942.

Metzger, Paul. *Le Conseil supérieur et le grand bailliage de Lyon (1771–1774, 1788). Contribution à l'étude de deux réformes judiciaires au XVIIIe siècle.* Lyon, A. Rey, 1913, *Annales de l'Université de Lyon,* n.s., Droit, Lettres, 27. [The best local study.]

Pfister, Christian. "Les Préliminaires de la Révolution à Nancy. L'agitation parlementaire de 1788," *Mémoires de l'Académie de Stanislas,* 6th ser., 7 (1909–1910), 88–161.

Ramsey, John F. "The Judicial Reform of 1788 and the French Revolution," *Studies in Modern European History in Honor of Franklin Charles Palm* (New York, Bookman Associates, 1956), pp. 217–238.

Séeger, Charles-E. *Essai sur les grands bailliages établis en 1788 en Normandie.* Caen, E. Domin, 1911. [Thesis for the doctorate in law.]

Villers, Robert. *L'Organisation du Parlement de Paris et des conseils supérieurs d'après la réforme de Maupeou (1771–1774).* Paris, Recueil Sirey, 1937. [Thesis for the doctorate in law; the most trustworthy study of the reform in its institutional aspects. Brief but sensible concerning the political issues.]

(e) Bureaux des finances

Bonvallet, Adrien. "Le Bureau des finances de la généralité de Poitiers," *Mémoires de la Société des Antiquaires de l'Ouest,* 2nd ser., 6 (1883), 137–424.

Charmeil, Jean-Paul. *Les Trésoriers de France à l'époque de la Fronde. Contribution à l'histoire de l'administration financière sous l'ancien régime.* Paris. A. & J. Picard & Cie, 1964. [Substantial and precise. A thesis for the doctorate in law.]

Dumont, François. *Le Bureau des finances de la généralité de Moulins.* Moulins, Imprimerie du Progres de l'Allier, 1923. [Thesis for the doctorate in law.]

Thomas-Collignon, Jean. [Four articles:] "L'Organisation intérieure du bureau des finances de Dijon: la direction;" "Le 'Monde du Tresor' en Bourgogne;" "Monde du Parlement et monde du Tresor. Des influences locales sur le recrutement de certaines compagnies: les bureaux des finances;" "L'Échec d'une institution: les Trésoriers généraux de France," *Mémoires de la Société pour l'Histoire du Droit et des Institutions des Anciens Pays Bourguignons, Comtois et Romands*, 7 (1940–1941), 177–187; 9 (1943), 131–179; 11 (1946–1947), 125–133; 23 (1962), 83–135, respectively.

(f) Bailliages, before 1600

Dupont-Ferrier, Gustave. *Les Officiers royaux des bailliages et sénéchaussées et les institutions monarchiques locales en France à la fin du moyen âge*. Paris, Bouillon, 1903, *Bibliothèque de l'Ecole des Hautes Etudes*, 145.

Guenée, Bernard. *Tribunaux et gens de justice dans le bailliage de Senlis à la fin du moyen âge (vers 1380–vers 1550)*. Paris, Les Belles Lettres, 1963.

(g) Bailliages, primarily after 1600

The following list includes the best historical writing on the bailliage courts. Its length should not lead anyone to believe that they have been adequately studied. Rarely has series B of the departmental archives been seriously examined, although it contains the formal records of judicial activity and in many places has been well inventoried. (No attempt was made, in chapter II above, to commence such research, which would have been time-consuming and appeared not to be central in my study.)

Of the pertinent theses for the doctorate in law, only the more competent are listed here. They are usually brief essays based on slender documentation (essentially, royal legislation and eighteenth-century treatises and law dictionaries, with some sampling in series B). Most titles indicate the perspective adopted: rivalry between jurisdictions or among magistrates; progress of royal at the expense of seigneurial justice; assimilation of institutions in provinces acquired by the French crown.

Scholarly attempts to reconstruct lists of officeholders or lists of parishes within the jurisdiction of a bailliage are omitted from this section. Some lists of officeholders are mentioned above in the Appendix, notes.

Babinet, Charles. "Le Présidial de Poitiers, 65 années de sa vie publique et privée (1724–1790)," *Mémoires de la Société des Antiquaires de l'Ouest*, 2nd ser., 8 (1885), 381–497.

Boudon, Albert. *La Sénéchaussée présidiale du Puy*. Valence, C. Legrand, 1908. [Thesis for the doctorate in law.]

Cacheux, Albert. *Le Bailliage royal d'Avesnes*. Avesnes-sur-Helpe, Editions de l'Observateur, 1954, as *Mémoires de la Société d'Histoire du Droit des Pays Flamands, Picards et Wallons*, 25.

Chenal, André. *Etude sur le présidial d'Orléans (1551–1790)*. Orleans, Gout, 1908. [Thesis for the doctorate in law.]

Combes, Louis de. *Le Présidial de Bourg et le bailliage de Bresse*. Bourg-en-Bresse, 1874.

Combier, Amédée. *Etude sur le bailliage de Vermandois et siège présidial de Laon*. Paris, 1874.

Coron, André. *Essai sur la sénéchaussée de Saint-Etienne dans ses rapports avec le bailliage de Forez*. Lyon, Bosc frères, 1936. [Thesis for the doctorate in law. The royal court at Saint-Etienne was created in the seventeenth century. It encountered opposition from the magistrates of nearby Montbrison and at times from the seigneur of Saint-Etienne. The author retraces the long and involved struggle.]

Delaporte, Raymond. *La Sénéchaussée de Châteauneuf-du-Faou, Huelgoat et Landelau et les juridictions seigneuriales du ressort*. Paris, Pedone, 1905. [Thesis for the doctorate in law.]

Evérat, Edouard. *La Sénéchaussée d'Auvergne et siège présidial de Riom au XVIIIᵉ siècle, étude historique d'après les papiers et documents inédits de MM. Jacques Chabrol, Guillaume-Michel de Chabrol et Gaspard-Claude-François de Chabrol, avocats du roi et lieutenant-général-criminel audit siège. Paris*, Thorin, 1886. [Still the best local monograph, deriving much of its value from the Chabrol family papers.]

Fauchon, Maxime. *Etude juridique et historique sur le bailliage de Mortain*. Avranches, Imprimerie de l'Avranchin, 1923. [Thesis for the doctorate in law.]

Foucart, Jacques. *Une Institution baillivale française en Flan-*

dre: Le gouvernance du souverain bailliage de Lille-Douai-Orchies (1326–1790). Lille, Raoust, 1937. [Thesis for the doctorate in law.]

Goubert, Pierre. "Les Officiers royaux des présidiaux, bailliages et élections dans la société française du XVIIᵉ siècle," *XVIIᵉ Siècle*, nos. 42–43 (1959), pp. 54–75. [An attempt to situate the magistrates in local society; based on research in northern France only, but with the discernment and imagination characteristic of the author.]

La Bussière, P. de. *Le Bailliage de Mâcon; étude sur l'organisation judiciaire du Mâconnais sous l'ancien régime*. Dijon, Nourry, 1914. [Thesis for the doctorate in law.]

Laroche, Leon. "Le Bailliage comtal et le bailliage des cas royaux de Charolais," *Annales de Bourgogne,* 5 (1933), 129–161, 217–256.

Laurain, Ernest. *Essai sur les présidiaux.* Paris, 1896, first published in *Nouvelle Revue Historique de Droit Français et Etranger,* 19 (1895) and 20 (1896). [The origins, character, and aftermath of the principal reform measure for the judiciary of the sixteenth century, analyzed mainly from a political and jurisdictional viewpoint relying on royal legislation, the Joly de Fleury papers, and correspondence among bailliage magistrates. An excellent work.]

Lepointe, Gabriel. "L'Acquisition d'un office de magistrature judiciaire, au Mans, à la fin de l'ancien régime," *Province du Maine,* 2nd ser., 33 (1953), 196–209.

———— "Un Recueil de sentences de la sénéchaussé du Maine à la fin de l'ancien régime," *Etudes d'histoire du droit privé offertes à Pierre Petot* (Paris, Librairie Générale de Droit et de Jurisprudence, 1959), pp. 363–369. [A small first attempt to examine a large and entirely unexplored topic: the jurisprudence developed and applied in the bailliage courts. This and the preceding article are based on the papers of Ménard de la Groye, councillor in the sénéchaussée at Le Mans.]

Malmezat, Jean. *Le Bailli des Montagnes d'Auvergne et le présidial d'Aurillac comme agents de l'administration royale.* Paris, Recueil Sirey, 1941. [Thesis for the doctorate in law.]

Meyzonnade, Henry. *La Lieutenance-générale de police à Moulins au XVIIIᵉ siècle.* Mimeographed. Paris, 1953. [Thesis for the doctorate in law. A copy is in the Bibliothéque Municipale of Moulins.]

Musset, Georges. "Un Parlement au petit pied. Le présidial de La Rochelle," *Archives Historiques de la Saintonge et de l'Aunis,* 4 (1878), 312–369.

Pagart d'Hermansart, Emile. *Histoire du bailliage de Saint-Omer.* 2 vols. Saint-Omer, 1898. [An extensive, solid work.]

Perraud-Charmantier, André. *Le Sénéchal de Nantes dans ses rapports avec les conseillers au présidial (1551–1789). Contribution à l'histoire des juridictions nantaises.* Rennes, Plihon & Hommay, 1925. [Thesis for the doctorate in law. In Brittany, a senechal was a chief civil judge. At Nantes, his relations with the councillors were often antagonistic.]

Ricommard, Julien. *La Lieutenance-générale de police de Troyes au XVIIIᵉ siècle.* Paris, Hachette, 1934. [The basic work on this institution, heavily documented and carefully analytical. Does not attempt to examine all the regulatory activity of the chief police magistrate.]

Rosier, Camille. *Les Institutions judiciaires de la Basse-Marche.* Limoges, Ducourtieux, 1921. [Thesis for the doctorate in law. Comprehensive and thoughtful study of the rival courts at Bellac and Le Dorat.]

(h) General, post-1789

Garaud, Marcel, *Histoire générale du droit privé français (de 1789 à 1804).* I. *La Révolution et l'égalité civile.* II. *La Révolution et la propriété foncière.* 2 vols. Paris, Recueil Sirey, 1953–1958.

Godechot, Jacques. *Les Institutions de la France sous la Révolution et l'Empire.* 2nd edition. Paris, Presses Universitaires de France, 1968.

(i) Lawcourts after 1790

Bourdon, Jean. *La Réforme judiciaire de l'an VIII.* I. *Les Institutions.* II. *Formation de la magistrature sous le Consulat décennal.* [1800–1802.] 2 vols. Rodez, Imprimerie Carrère, 1942. [A major achievement, comparable in importance and quality to those of Mousnier on venality of office, Egret on the Parlement of Dauphiné, and Bluche on the Parlement of Paris, listed above.]

————— "Magistrats du premier Empire. L'épuration de 1807–1808 en Bourgogne," *Annales de Bourgogne*, 18 (1946), 16–36.

Rousselet, Marcel. *La Magistrature sous la monarchie de juillet*. Paris, Recueil Sirey, 1937.

Sauvel, Tony. "Le Tribunal de cassation de 1791 à 1795," *Etudes et Documents du Conseil d'Etat*, 12 (1958), 179–217.

6. Discussions of concepts: careers, politics, and social change

Barton, Allen H., and Lazarsfeld, Paul F. "Some Functions of Qualitative Analysis in Social Research," *Frankfurter Beiträge zur Soziologie*, 1 (1955), 321–361.

Eulau, Heinz, and Sprague, John D. *Lawyers in Politics. A Study in Professional Convergence*. Indianapolis, Bobbs-Merrill Co., 1964.

Hughes, Everett C. "Institutional Office and the Person," *American Journal of Sociology*, 43 (1937), 404–413.

Ryder, Norman B. "The Cohort as a Concept in the Study of Social Change," *American Sociological Review*, 30 (1965), 843–861.

Weber, Max. "Politics as a Vocation," in *From Max Weber: Essays in Sociology*, translated and edited by H. H. Gerth and C. Wright Mills. (New York, Oxford University Press, 1946). pp. 77–128.

Wilensky, Harold L. "Work, Careers, and Social Integration," *International Social Science Journal*, 12 (1960), 543–560.

7. Intellectual antecedents of the French Revolution

There can be no question of attempting even a select bibliography for this topic. What I found especially throught-provoking was the intersection between three works, listed here in chronological order of publication:

Groethuysen, Bernard. *Origines de l'esprit bourgeois en France. L'Eglise et la bourgeoisie*. Paris, Gallimard, 1927.

Mornet, Daniel, *Les Origines intellectuelles de la Révolution française (1715–1787)*. Paris, Librairie Armand Colin, 1933.

Furet, François; Erhard, Jean; Roger, Jacques; Bollème, Geneviève; Roche, Daniel; Dupront, Alphonse. *Livre et société dans la France du XVIIIᵉ siècle*, I. Paris and the Hague, Mouton & Co., 1965.

8. CAHIERS DE DOLÉANCES

Dupront, Alphonse. "La Société des lumières dans les cahiers de doléances de 1789," a lecture published in his *Les lettres, les sciences, la religion et les arts dans la société française de la deuxième moitié du XVIIIᵉ siècle*. (Paris, Centre de Documentation Universitaire, 1963), pp. 42–62.

Hyslop, Beatrice F. *A Guide to the General Cahiers of 1789, with the Texts of Unedited Cahiers*. New York, Columbia University Press, 1936.

———— "French Gild Opinion in 1789," *American Historical Review*, 44 (1939), 252–271.

———— *Répertoire critique des cahiers de doléances pour les Etats Généraux de 1789*. Paris, Leroux, 1933.

———— *Supplément au Répertoire critique des cahiers de doléances pour les Etats Généraux de 1789*. Paris, Presses Universitaires de France, 1952.

Richard, Jean. *L'Elaboration d'un cahier de doléances. Pierre-Claude Perrot, curé de Brazey-en-Plaine*. Dijon, 1961, as *Révolution en Côte-d'Or*, n.s., 11. [A pamphlet based on unusual sources, the preparatory documents for a village cahier by the local priest.]

Shapiro, Gilbert, and Markoff, John. *A Concrete Analytic Code for the Cahiers de Doleances of 1789*. Revised version, 1970, mimeographed. [The instrument by which Shapiro and his coworkers translate cahiers into an artificial language to be read by a computer, this code is in effect an analysis and ordering of the contents of the cahiers thus far coded for Shapiro's forthcoming Quantitative Studies of the French Revolution.]

Taylor, George V., with the assistance of Knight, Paul G. "Revolutionary and Non-Revolutionary Content in the Third-

Estate Cahiers of 1789," presented at the annual conference of the Society for French Historical Studies in Washington, D.C., on 20 March 1970.

9. PROVINCIAL POLITICS

(a) General

Brinton, Crane. *The Jacobins. An Essay in the New History.* New York, Macmillan, 1930.

Cobb, Richard. *Les Armées révolutionnaires. Instrument de la Terreur dans les départements, avril 1793–floréal an II.* 2 vols. Paris and The Hague, Mouton & Co., 1961–1963.

Troux, Albert. *La Vie politique dans le département de la Meurthe d'août 1792 à octobre 1795.* 2 vols. Nancy, Imprimerie Georges Thomas, 1936. [An extremely detailed narrative, which serves as a model.]

(b) Burgundy

Barbuat, Pierre de. "Le Comité de surveillance révolutionnaire de Beaune," *Mémoires de la Société d'Archéologie de Beaune,* 35 (1911), 155–366.

Bazin, Nelly. "Les Suspects dans le district de Dijon," *Annales de Bourgogne,* 41 (1969), 63–74.

Brelot, Jean. *La Vie politique en Côte-d'Or sous le Directoire.* Dijon, 1932, as *Révolution en Côte-d'Or,* n.s., 8.

Cochin, Augustin, and Charpentier, Charles. "La Campagne électorale de 1789 en Bourgogne," *Action Française,* 1902–1903, reprinted separately and in Cochin's *Les Sociétés de pensée et la démocratie moderne* (Paris, Plon, 1921), pp. 235–282.

Henriot, Marcel. *Le Club des Jacobins de Semur, 1790–1795.* Dijon, 1933, as *Révolution en Côte-d'Or,* n.s., 9.

Hugueney, Louis. *Les Clubs dijonnais sous la Révolution.* Dijon, J. Nourry, 1905.

———— "Une nouvelle contribution à l'histoire des clubs dijonnais," *Enquêtes sur la Révolution en Côte-d'Or,* 2 (1911), 49–63.

Mathiez, Albert. "Dijon en 1789 d'après les lettres inédites de François-Nicolas-Félix Bertheley, commis aux Etats de Bourgogne," *Révolution en Côte-d'Or,* n.s., 2 (1926), 1–20.

Millot, Henri. *Le Comité permanent de Dijon (juillet 1789–février 1790)*. Dijon, 1925, as *Révolution en Côte-d'Or*, n.s., 1.

Quarré, Pierre; Richard, Jean; et al. *Dijon, capitale provinciale au XVIIIᵉ siècle* [catalogue d'exposition]. Dijon, Musée de Dijon, 1959.

Schnerb, Robert. "La Première Mission en Côte-d'Or du Conventionnel Bernard de Saintes," *Annales de Bourgogne*, 5 (1933), 45–61.

———— "Les Administrateurs de la Côte-d'Or et le salut de la République en 1793," *Annales Historiques de la Révolution Française*, 36 (1964), 22–37.

Tartat, Pierre. *Avallon au XVIIIᵉ siècle. I. La Société et la vie avallonnaises avant 1789. II. La Révolution, 1789–1799*. 2 vols. Avallon, Imprimerie l'Universelle, 1951–1953.

Voillery, Philibert. "Vente des biens nationaux dans le district de Beaune, au point de vue économique et social," *Mémoires de la Société d'Archéologie de Beaune*, 32 (1908), 83–283; 34 (1909), i–ix.

    (c) Poitou

Carré, Henri. "Recherches sur la Révolution en Poitou," *Mémoires de la Société des Antiquaires de l'Ouest*, 3rd ser., 12 (1935), 131–293.

Doucet, Roger. *L'Esprit public dans le département de la Vienne pendant la Révolution*. Poitiers, 1908, as *Mémoires de la Société des Antiquaires de l'Ouest*, 3rd ser., 2. [Mediocre.]

Roux, Marie de. *La Révolution à Poitiers et dans la Vienne*. Poitiers, 1910, as *Mémoirés de la Société des Antiquaires de l'Ouest*, 3rd ser., 4. [Extends to 1792.]

———— *Histoire religieuse de la Révolution à Poitiers et dans la Vienne*. Lyon, Lardanchet, 1952. [Despite the title, this posthumously published work is essentially a sequel to the preceding.]

10. EMIGRÉS

The essential guide for the subect:

Bouloiseau, Marc. *Etude de l'émigration et de la vente des biens des émigrés (1792–1830). Instruction, sources, bibliographie, législation, tableaux.* Paris, Imprimerie Nationale, 1963.

An approximate enumeration and analysis of geographic and chronological variation:

Greer, Donald. *The Incidence of the Emigration during the French Revolution.* Cambridge, Mass., Harvard University Press, 1951.

Lists of émigrés:

Bouloiseau, Marc. *Liste des émigrés, déportés et condamnés pour cause révolutionnaire dans le district de Rouen (1792–an X).* Paris, Novathèse, 1937.

Dubois, Jean. "Liste des émigrés, des prêtres déportés et des condamnés pour cause révolutionnaire du département de la Meuse," *Mémoires de la Société des Lettres, Sciences et Arts de Bar-le-Duc,* 4th ser., 8 (1910), 1–193; also published separately, Bar-le-Duc, 1911.

Gain, André. *Liste des émigrés, déportés et condamnés pour cause révolutionnaire du département de la Moselle.* 2 vols. Metz, Les Arts Graphiques, 1925–1932.

Montarlot, Paul. "Les Emigrés de Saône-et-Loire," *Mémoires de la Société Eduenne,* 41 (1913), 75–139; 42 (1914), 149–242; 43 (1919), 17–132; 44 (1920– 1923), 9–100, 129–198, 314–327, 343–370; 45 (1924–1927), 5–64, 113–158, 231–296, 347–398; 46 (1928–1931), 7–46, 105–158, 217–268.

Saint-Marc, Camille de. "L'Emigration et les listes d'émigrés," *Mémoires de la Société Historique et Scientifique des Deux-Sèvres,* 1 (1905), 165–375.

Sangnier, Georges. *Les Emigrés du Pas-de-Calais pendant la Révolution.* Blangermont, chez l'auteur, 1959.

11. Executions

An approximate enumeration and analysis of geographic and chronological variation:

Greer, Donald. *The Incidence of the Terror during the French Revolution. A Statistical Interpretation.* Cambridge, Mass., Harvard University Press, 1935. [Criticized on statistical grounds by Richard Louie, "The Incidence of the Terror: A Critique of a Statistical Interpretation," *French Historical Studies,* 3 (1964), 379–389, and defended persuasively by

Gilbert Shapiro, "The Incidence of the Terror: Some Lessons for Quantitative History," at the meeting of the American Historical Association in New York on 29 December 1968.]
Lists of accused and condemned persons:

Montarlot, Paul. *Les Accusés de Saône-et-Loire aux tribunaux révolutionnaires.* Autun, 1901, first published in *Mémoires de la Société Eduenne,* n.s., 26 (1898); 27 (1899); 28 (1900); and 29 (1901).

Proust, Antonin. *La Justice revolutionnaire à Niort.* 2nd edition. Niort, 1874.

Salliard, Etienne. *La Terreur à Poitiers, d'après des documents inédits ou peu connus.* Paris, Oudin, 1912.

Wallon, Henri. *Histoire du tribunal révolutionnaire de Paris avec le journal de ses actes.* 6 vols. Paris, 1880–1882. [VI, 253–431: "Liste de toutes les personnes traduites au tribunal extraordinaire du 17 août 1792 et au tribunal révolutionnaire de Paris."]

12. Biographies and family histories

(a) Dictionaries

Beauchet-Filleau, Henri; Beauchet-Filleau, Paul; and Beauchet-Filleau, Joseph. *Dictionnaire historique et généalogique des familles du Poitou.* 2nd ed. Poitiers, Oudin & Cie, 1891–1915 (vols. I–III and four of the five fascicules of vol. IV), and Fontenay-le-Comte, Lussaud frères, 1963– , in progress. [The dictionary extended to the Laurencie family when research for this book was completed. The first four volumes are not free from errors and nineteenth-century reticence. But no work comparably detailed and accurate exists for any other province. It was begun by the grandson of Henri Filleau, king's proctor in the sénéchaussée of Poitiers, 1785–1790, and is apparently based in large part on documents and notes accumulated by him and his ancestors, magistrates in Poitiers since the sixteenth century.]

Dictionnaire de biographie française, ed. Michel Prévost, Jean-Charles Roman d'Amat, et al. Paris, Letouzey & Ané, 1933– , in progress. [Vol. XII ends with Espigat.]

Kuscinski, Auguste. *Dictionnaire des Conventionnels.* Paris,

Société de l'Histoire de la Révolution Française, 1916–1919 (in fascicules finally constituting 1 vol.). [Detailed and usually reliable.]

Montarlot, Paul. "Les Députés de Saône-et-Loire aux assemblées de la Révolution (1789–1799)," *Mémoires de la Société Eduenne* n.s., 30 (1902), 281–365; 31 (1903), 141–245; 32 (1904), 133–257; 33 (1905), 181–273; 34 (1906), 33–137; 35 (1907), 43–116, 404–405; 36 (1908), 121–221; 37 (1909), 161–276, 401; 38 (1910), 95–151; 39 (1911), 23–107, and separately, 3 vols., Autun, 1905–1911.

(b) Individual studies

Four exemplary books about revolutionary personages, a major figure, Barère, and three lesser ones, were especially suggestive.

Bouchard, Georges. *La Famille du Conventionnel Basire et quelques aperçus profitables sur le XVIII*e *siècle.* Paris, Librairie Raymond Clavreuil, 1953.

Gershoy, Leo. *Bertrand Barère. A Reluctant Terrorist.* Princeton, Princeton University Press, 1962.

Massé, Pierre. *Pierre-François Piorry, Conventionnel et magistrat (1758–1847).* Poitiers, 1968, as *Mémoires de la Société des Antiquaires de l'Ouest,* 4th ser., 9 (1965).

Nicolle, Paul. *Valazé, député de l'Orne à la Convention Nationale.* Paris, Librairie Félix Alcan, 1933.

Glossary

Institutional and occupational terms unexplained in the preceding text and unlikely to be familiar to some readers of this book are given minimal definitions here.

Armateur. A businessman engaged in maritime commerce, undertaking risks and obtaining profits of voyages.

Avocat. A lawyer whose principal duty was to present oral and written argument as to the law that ought to control decisions on substantive issues in litigation.

Ban et arrière ban. A military levy by which a feudal superior called out his vassals and subvassals.

Bureau des finances. An administrative and, secondarily, judicial agency exercising surveillance over the collection of certain royal revenues.

Cas royaux. Cases at law reserved for decision by royal rather than seigneurial judges, and by ordinary rather than special administrative tribunals.

Chambre des comptes. A court which conducted post-audits of the accounts of many financial officials and of men who had leased franchise rights to collect royal taxes, and which performed a variety of related duties.

Cour des aides. A court of appeals in tax cases such as those decided by an élection.

Election. An administrative and, secondarily, judicial agency assessing and collecting the taille and other direct taxes.

Grenier à sel. An administrative and, secondarily, judicial agency engaged in management of the royal salt monopoly and salt tax.

Lit de justice. A special session of a parlement, with the king or an intendant present to signify, in the face of some challenge to a legislative purpose, the majesty and determination of the royal will.

Maîtrise des eaux et forêts. An administrative and, secondarily, judicial agency engaged in enforcement of laws concerning rivers, lakes, and wooded lands.

Marchand. Any person engaged in buying and selling, from a peddler to a wholesale trader. A *maître-marchand* was a master of a craft engaged in selling products.

Maréchaussée. A tribunal conducting criminal trials of military personnel and of civilians accused of certain kinds of offenses, e.g., brigandage, riot, and others.

Negociant. A businessman. This term was usually applied to men engaged in commerce over long distances involving delayed payments, discounted commercial paper and other operations verging upon banking. The term implied wealth and social elevation. It could, however, be usurped by individuals having none of these characteristics.

Notaire. A notary. He drew up contracts and other documents, advised clients as to the rights involved, and certified the signatures.

Officier. In administrative and legal usage, an incumbent of a public office in which private property rights, notably the right to sell and the right to bequeath, were possessed either by the incumbent or by some other person.

Prévôté. A royal tribunal with jurisdiction over misdemeanors and small claims but not over cas royaux (q.v.).

Procureur. An attorney whose principal duty was to present written statements of facts, claims, and assertions of procedural rights in litigation.

Rente. A fixed income defined in money or in kind and paid as a consequence of a legal obligation in exchange for possession of land or a capital sum, or for some other consideration.

Rentier. A person receiving income mainly or entirely from rentes.

Trésorier de France. An officeholder in a bureau des finances.

Index

In the index, where a magistrate's office is indicated, one of the following abbreviations is used: *lt.* = *lieutenant;* *gén.* = *général;* *prtclr.* = *particulier;* *civ.* = *civil;* *crim.* = *criminel;* *c.* = *conseiller;* *a.r.* = *avocat du roi;* *p.r.* = *procureur du roi.*

Index

Index

HARVARD HISTORICAL MONOGRAPHS

*Out of Print

1. Athenian Tribal Cycles in the Hellenistic Age. By W. S. Ferguson. 1932.
2. The Private Record of an Indian Governor-Generalship: The Correspondence of Sir John Shore, Governor-General, with Henry Dundas, President of the Board of Control, 1793–1798. Edited by Holden Furber. 1933.
3. The Federal Railway Land Subsidy Policy of Canada. By J. B. Hedges. 1934.
4. Russian Diplomacy and the Opening of the Eastern Question in 1838 and 1839. By P. E. Mosely. 1934.*
5. The First Social Experiments in America: A Study in the Development of Spanish Indian Policy in the Sixteenth Century. By Lewis Hanke. 1935*
6. British Propaganda at Home and in the United States from 1914 to 1917. By J. D. Squires. 1935.*
7. Bernadotte and the Fall of Napoleon. By F. D. Scott. 1935.*
8. The Incidence of the Terror during the French Revolution: A Statistical Interpretation. By Donald Greer. 1935.*
9. French Revolutionary Legislation on Illegitimacy, 1789–1804. By Crane Brinton. 1936.
10. An Ecclesiastical Barony of the Middle Ages: The Bishopric of Bayeux, 1066–1204. By S. E. Gleason. 1936.*
11. Chinese Traditional Historiography. By C. S. Gardner, 1938. Rev. ed., 1961.
12. Studies in Early French Taxation. By J. R. Strayer and C. H. Taylor. 1939.*
13. Muster and Review: A Problem of English Military Administration, 1420–1440. By R. A. Newhall. 1940.*
14. Portuguese Voyages to America in the Fifteenth Century. By S. E. Morison, 1940.*
15. Argument from Roman Law in Political Thought, 1200–1600. By M. P. Gilmore. 1941.*
16. The Huancavelica Mercury Mine: A Contribution to the History of the Bourbon Renaissance in the Spanish Empire. By A. P. Whitaker, 1941.*
17. The Palace School of Muhammad the Conqueror. By Barnette Miller. 1941.*
18. A Cistercian Nunnery in Mediaeval Italy: The Story of Rifreddo in Saluzzo, 1220–1300. By Catherine E. Boyd. 1943.*
19. Vassi and Fideles in the Carolingian Empire. By C. E. Odegaard. 1945.*
20. Judgment by Peers. By Barnaby C. Keeney. 1949.
21. The Election to the Russian Constituent Assembly of 1917. By O. H. Radkey. 1950.

47. Chōshū in the Meiji Restoration. By Albert M. Craig. 1961.
48. John Fiske: The Evolution of a Popularizer. By Milton Berman. 1961.
49. John Jewel and the Problem of Doctrinal Authority. By W. M. Southgate. 1962.
50. Germany and the Diplomacy of the Financial Crisis, 1931. By Edward W. Bennett. 1962.
51. Public Opinion, Propaganda, and Politics in Eighteenth-Century England: A Study of the Jew Bill of 1753. By Thomas W. Perry. 1962.
52. Soldier and Civilian in the Later Roman Empire. By Ramsay MacMullen. 1963.
53. Copyhold, Equity, and the Common Law. By Charles Montgomery Gray. 1963.
54. The Association: British Extraparliamentary Political Association, 1769–1793. By Eugene Charlton Black. 1963.
55. Tocqueville and England. By Seymour Drescher. 1964.
56. Germany and the Emigration, 1816–1885. By Mack Walker. 1964.
57. Ivan Aksakov (1823–1886): A Study in Russian Thought and Politics. By Stephen Lukashevich. 1965.
58. The Fall of Stein. By R. C. Raack. 1965.
59. The French Apanages and the Capetian Monarchy, 1224–1328. By Charles T. Wood. 1966.
60. Congressional Insurgents and the Party System, 1909–1916. By James Holt. 1967.
61. The Rumanian National Movement in Transylvania, 1780–1849. By Keith Hitchins. 1969.
62. Sisters of Liberty: Marseille, Lyon, Paris and the Reaction to a Centralized State, 1868–1871. By Louis M. Greenberg. 1971.
63. Old Hatreds and Young Hopes: The French Carbonari against the Bourbon Restoration. By Alan B. Spitzer. 1971.
64. To the Maginot Line: The Politics of French Military Preparation in the 1920's. By Judith M. Hughes. 1971.
65. Florentine Public Finances in the Early Renaissance, 1400–1433. By Anthony Molho. 1971.
66. Provincial Magistrates and Revolutionary Politics in France, 1789–1795. By Philip Dawson. 1972.
67. The East India Company and Army Reform, 1783–1798. By Raymond Callahan. 1972.